REALIST ECSTASY

PERFORMANCE AND
AMERICAN CULTURES

General Editors: Stephanie Batiste, Robin Bernstein, and Brian Herrera

This book series harnesses American studies and performance series and directs them toward each other, publishing books that use performance to think historically.

The Art of Confession: The Performance of Self from Robert Lowell to Reality TV
Christopher Grobe

Realist Ecstasy: Religion, Race, and Performance in American Literature
Lindsay V. Reckson

Realist Ecstasy

Religion, Race, and Performance in American Literature

Lindsay V. Reckson

NEW YORK UNIVERSITY PRESS
New York

NEW YORK UNIVERSITY PRESS
New York
www.nyupress.org

© 2020 by New York University
All rights reserved

References to internet websites (URLs) were accurate at the time of writing. Neither the author nor New York University Press is responsible for URLs that may have expired or changed since the manuscript was prepared.

Library of Congress Cataloging-in-Publication Data

Names: Reckson, Lindsay Vail, 1982– author.
Title: Realist ecstasy : religion, race, and performance in American literature / Lindsay V. Reckson.
Description: New York : New York University Press, [2019] | Series: Performance and American cultures | Includes bibliographical references and index. | Summary: "'Realist Ecstasy' explores religion, race, and performance in American literature"—Provided by publisher.
Identifiers: LCCN 2019015753 | ISBN 9781479803323 (cloth) | ISBN 9781479850365 (paperback)
Subjects: LCSH: American literature—History and criticism. | Realism in literature. | Religion in literature. | Race in literature. | Performance in literature.
Classification: LCC PS169.R43 R43 2019 | DDC 810.9/12—dc23
LC record available at https://lccn.loc.gov/2019015753

New York University Press books are printed on acid-free paper, and their binding materials are chosen for strength and durability. We strive to use environmentally responsible suppliers and materials to the greatest extent possible in publishing our books.

Manufactured in the United States of America

10 9 8 7 6 5 4 3 2 1

Also available as an ebook

for Ben, Ada, and Maxine

CONTENTS

Introduction: Being Beside   1

1. Reconstructing Secularisms   26

2. Archival Enthusiasm   68

3. The Ghost Dance and Realism's Techno-Spiritual Frontier   103

4. Touching a Button   157

5. Born, Again   198

    Coda: Behind, Before, Beside   234

    Acknowledgments   237

    Notes   243

    Bibliography   285

    Index   305

    About the Author   319

Introduction

Being Beside

What does Jim Crow secularism feel like?[1] Consider two moments. In the first, a crowd gathers to witness the performance of a monster, its face covered with a "heavy crêpe veil." The monster is Henry Johnson, the black stable-hand whose disfiguration in a house fire forms the narrative crux of Stephen Crane's 1898 novella *The Monster*. The question of what to do with Henry—driven mad by both the trauma of the fire and the radical dehumanization it precipitates—structures the affective logic of the story. And like the story itself, the white residents of fictional Whilomville approach Henry Johnson with a mixture of fear and fascination. In this scene, that approach is literalized as a group of small boys goad one another to get close enough to touch the monster, doubly veiled in black: "The monster on the box had turned its black crepe countenance towards the sky, and was waving its arms in time to a religious chant. 'Look at him now,' cried a little boy. They turned, and were transfixed by the solemnity and mystery of the indefinable gestures. The wail of the melody was mournful and slow. They drew back. It seemed to spellbind them with the power of a funeral."[2] What might it mean to approach this body? Surrounded by (the progeny of) white men, who study his movements "on the box," the "monster" is surely in some sense a figure for the enslaved, as the kinesthetic details of this scene offer a callback to the auction block as a site of compelled performance. But if this is a scene of postbellum objectification linked to the cultural memory of buying and selling racialized bodies, it is also, and perhaps more explicitly, a scene of ritualized religious experience. A countenance turned toward the sky, arms raised, solemn gestures—a bodily citation that signals the invocation or influx of spirit, the rhythm of (or rhythm as) religious experience. Henry's movements are transfixing, traveling across the space between bodies to (spell)bind others;

even as they "draw back," the boys who witness this performance are incorporated into it, unwilling yet complicit participants in its funereal unfolding. This is a haunted and haunting performance, one in which the vectors of racial violence, compulsion, and the "religious" are, to say the least, difficult to unravel.[3]

If Crane's novella gestures in this scene to some occluded or "indefinable" link between racial violence and spiritualized performance, the second moment I offer—from Charles W. Chesnutt's 1901 novel *The Marrow of Tradition*, a fictionalized account of the Wilmington race riot of 1898—is more direct in its depiction of white supremacy as a haunted affair. Describing the efforts of the prominent newspaper owner Major Carteret and his compatriots to manifest white fears of a miscegenated voting bloc (embodied in the "Fusion party"), *The Marrow of Tradition* invokes the popular racist imaginary of African American men as figures of supernatural rapaciousness: "It remained for Carteret and his friends to discover, with inspiration from whatever supernatural source the discriminating reader may elect, that the darker race, docile by instinct, humble by training, patiently waiting upon its as yet uncertain destiny, was an incubus, a corpse chained to the body politic, and that the negro vote was a source of danger to the state, no matter how cast or by whom directed."[4] Here *The Marrow of Tradition* offers what *The Monster* only glancingly approaches: something like a hauntology of white supremacy. In its dehumanizing construction of blackness as an "incubus" (a mythological creature that preyed on women in their sleep) or corpse, the white imaginary figures the black voting population as a (socially) dead but still threatening demographic, a grotesquely embodied and sexualized threat to whiteness's corpus as well as its political dominance.[5] As the "discriminating reader" of Chesnutt's realism is meant to understand, and as the novel attests with deep irony, the response to such a perceived threat is to produce more and more corpses—Carteret and his friends quickly spread their supernatural "inspiration," inaugurating a devastating outbreak of white supremacist violence in its name.

While strikingly different in their idioms, each of these moments belongs to the affective life of Jim Crow secularism, and to its bodily dramas of ritual (dis)possession, compulsion, inspiration, and contagious enthusiasm. Collectively, I call such dramas *realist ecstasy*, a deliberate contradiction in terms that this book aims not to resolve, but to hold in suspension as it explores how realist representational practices at the turn of the twentieth century mobilize the gestural and performative idioms of religious ecstasy to confront lingering histories of violence and to imagine new modes of social affiliation. Demonstrating how the realist fascination with ecstatic embodiment helped produce and naturalize racial and cultural difference, I argue that realism gives us a sense of how deeply encoded the secular is with structures of white supremacy. At the same time, I excavate the complex, shifting, and dynamic possibilities embedded within realist performance—its production of an immanent, ecstatic "otherwise."[6] In the turn-of-the-century texts and performances I encounter here, the body in ecstasy—literally out of or beside the self, always already problematizing where and how one locates "embodied" experience—offers a challenge and a provocation both for Jim Crow regimes of racial legibility and for realism's fantasies of intelligibility, its drive to make experience legible as such.[7] As in the case of Henry Johnson's transfixing movements, ecstasy operates in literary realism as a source of racialized desire, fascination, projection, and disturbance. In this sense, the boys' small drama of approaching Henry on the box in *The Monster* epitomizes much of realism's approach to race and personhood in the post-Reconstruction era: as inscrutable "problems" simultaneously registered and effaced. Yet in its very resistance to legibility, Henry's performance (much like his hauntingly obliterated face) marks the persistent presence of the unintelligible, that which resists regimes of knowing and thus touches the limits of realism's sweeping effort to parse, manage, and contain the complexities of social experience and social change.[8] This unsettling, transfixing, spellbinding persistence of the unintelligible—circulating in dynamic ways through realism's taxonomic enthusiasms, its broadscale effort to forge sense out of a turbulent social scene—is at least part, I want to suggest, of what Jim Crow secularism feels like.

In ecstasy, the body-in-motion's capacity to function as a stable referent is utterly at stake, and it is the contest over the meaning of such restless bodies to which *Realist Ecstasy* most often attends. Such bodies are by no means always a disruptive force; indeed, I argue that it is in part through its ecstatic sequences that realism habitually constructs and naturalizes a secular order that understands religious and racial difference in tandem, evincing a hegemonic regime of white liberal Protestantism that governs the sensible contours of the real and inscribes alterity onto bodies accordingly.[9] Or as Hortense Spillers has described it, "Christianity, in its ability to stand in for 'civilization,' 'patriarchy,' 'hierarchy,' 'enlightenment,' 'progress,' 'culture'—a series of lexical items that inaugurate the grammar of 'otherness'—renders a text for the dominant culture."[10] Invoking the "incubus" of the white supremacist imaginary, *The Marrow of Tradition* recognizes this grammar—which gives race a supernatural explanatory power and deems religion rational or irrational depending on its proximity to Christianity and to whiteness—as central to a regime predicated on the economic and political disenfranchisement of African Americans. But it also reverses that foundational script, insisting that whiteness constructs and reinforces itself through a fanatical investment in the supernatural (and material) reality of race. This violent form of "inspiration" is what W. E. B. Du Bois would later call a "new religion of whiteness"; as we will see, Du Bois pointedly aligns whiteness and fanaticism at a moment when what constituted "religion" as such became utterly central to the global and imperial formations of secular modernity—formations that, Chesnutt and Du Bois recognize, were themselves deeply haunted.

Drawing a different kind of inspiration from such texts, this book describes post-Reconstruction realism as a set of performances that insist on the presence of the past and its ongoing if occluded impact within the social field that realism purports to describe. Focusing on realism as it emerges specifically in the context of the Reconstruction's abandonment and the consolidation of Jim Crow regimes of racial personhood allows us to understand "post-Reconstruction" as itself a haunted structure, less a periodizing description than an analytic for realism's complex historicity. In approaching realism as a form of hauntology, I draw from Avery Gordon's account of haunting as a way of knowing—and, indeed, feeling—the persistence of violent structures that, within the regime of secular-linear time, might appear as largely overcome.[11] As Gordon describes it, haunting is "one way in which abusive systems of power make themselves known and their impacts felt in everyday life, especially when they are over and done with (slavery, for instance) or when their oppressive nature is denied."[12] Less a return of the repressed than a sense of the way past and present touch and infuse one another, *haunting* suggests a material world structured by largely invisible but nevertheless pervasive systems of racial capital, imperialism, and genocide. Haunting, in this sense, might be the dominant affect of secularism; it is, in any case, "integral to what it means to be modern."[13] Ecstasy, I argue, is one of the ways in which such haunting emerges from within the affective life of Jim Crow.

With its dramas of possession—of bodies "caught," "seized," or compelled by the Spirit—ecstasy bespeaks the lingering question of black freedom in the aftermath of Reconstruction. It thus belongs to what Saidiya Hartman has described as the intimate proximity between "liberty and bondage" under Jim Crow, a regime of subjection that "made it impossible to envision freedom independent of constraint or personhood and autonomy separate from the sanctity of property."[14] Realist ecstasy, as we will see, brings into relief what Hartman describes as the "nonevent of emancipation," with possessed and fitful bodies bodying forth the ongoing terror of white supremacy at the heart of realism's liberal imaginary.[15] But because its "indefinable gestures" are often opaque in the face of realist regimes of sensemaking, and because such gestures challenge forms of autonomy rooted in racial capitalism, ecstasy also evinces alternative arrangements of self and community, always already here.[16] The fact that these possibilities exist alongside one another is fundamental to ecstasy's undecidability—and thus to its realism.

Secular Affects, Realist Repertoires

Realist Ecstasy argues that the post-Reconstruction consolidation of racial apartheid must be understood as part of—indeed, central to—a more diffuse but no less powerfully regulatory regime of secularism. In gleaning the affective life of Jim Crow secularism, I draw on the work of scholars from a range of disciplines who have asked (with Ann Pellegrini), "What does secularism feel like?"[17] Rather than approaching secularism as the absence of religion or as a structure in which belief operates as one choice among many, scholars have articulated the secular and the religious as co-constituting formations, and have explored the historical contexts in which particular formations of the secular have emerged.[18] As Pellegrini argues, "Although narrated as a universal project—as, indeed, the project of universalism—secularism, in its dominant (and dominating) form, remains tied to a particular religion,

Christianity, and a particular history of origins in Enlightenment Europe."[19] In part by demonstrating the hegemony of this particular version of secularism in the US and its historical ties to white liberal Protestantism (what Pellegrini and Janet Jakobsen usefully shorthand as "Christian secularism"), scholars have given the lie to secularization as modernity's most persuasive progress narrative, examining how that narrative has served an important role in naturalizing "religion" as well as race, gender, and sexuality as stable sites of inquiry.[20] What has emerged from this now long-standing critique of secularization-as-progress is a more robust sense of the ways in which secularism(s) operate as affective, discursive, and indeed disciplinary environments, a robust set of behaviors and circulations that are deeply infused with (even as they help manage and identify) affects and practices understood as "religious." This has been crucial work and has—particularly in recent years—helped make visible the secularist assumptions governing much of historiography.[21] As Molly McGarry argues in her study of nineteenth-century spiritualism, "Excavating a narrative in which secularism does not simply or inevitably triumph over an antimodern, atavistic religion not only provides a more nuanced understanding of the past but also reveals a more complicated politics of the present."[22] Similarly, such an ongoing excavation unsettles our capacity as scholars to confidently stand apart from such formations, or to securely narrate their histories via the supposedly linear unfolding of secular time.

In his expansive study of secularism in antebellum America, John Lardas Modern describes the "secular imaginary" as at once epistemic and atmospheric, "occur[ing] at the levels of mood and emotion, underneath the skin."[23] Departing from what philosopher Charles Taylor has influentially termed the "nova effect"—or modernity's proliferation of "moral/spiritual options" that exceed the belief/unbelief divide to produce "a kind of galloping pluralism on the spiritual plane"—Modern offers a version of secularism less tied to the choices of liberal, agentive subjects and more attuned to the "circuitous," even circulatory, mechanisms and techniques that help construct the felt reality of such subjects in the first place.[24] In other words, Modern attends to the affective and disciplinary life of secularism in America, a "metaphysics" that structures relations as much as individuals and that governs and infuses the ordinary and always unfinished articulations of the secular, what Modern calls its "local effects."²⁵ The accretive force of such effects, Modern suggests, was (and is) a powerful delineation of "true religion" (white Protestant Christianity) from its various perversions, seen as deviating from the order, coherency, and clarity of the real. If secularism in America was (and is) very much a "structure of feeling" in Raymond Williams's sense—an unruly set of "social experiences *in solution*," "inalienably physical" and not yet concretized into fixed forms—the sedimented effect of this structure has been to imagine, delineate, and circumscribe subjects understood as "religious" or "secular."²⁶ Secularism, in other words, is both an epistemological comportment and social formation, haunted at every turn by what it regulates and excludes.

Drawing from this account, I trace the local effects and performative enactments of Jim Crow secularism while exploring its historical iterations in the specific context of post-Reconstruction America, with its ever-expanding, complex symbologies and choreographies of racial, religious, class, and sexual difference. I argue that in the post-Reconstruction context, we must understand secularism not solely as an affair taking place "underneath the skin" but also as a drama *at* or *of* the skin, helping produce what Frantz Fanon famously called the "epidermal racial schema"—itself a form of bodily displacement, multiplicity, and projection—as a site of charged contact and zealous categorization.²⁷ Part of what such dramas of contact and categorization suggest, I argue, is the ways in which the production of race has been utterly bound up in narratives of secularization, as well as how a "metaphysics of the secular" has silently governed the cultural (not to mention legal and political) adjudication of personhood in Jim Crow America and beyond. In making such claims, I am indebted to a chorus of scholars who have lately explored secularization and racialization as inextricably conjoined processes, wherein US narratives of (religious) freedom and pluralism have coincided with (and reinforced) techniques of racial management.²⁸ As Vincent W. Lloyd describes it, "Together with the rhetoric of freedom [comes] the reality of management, the subtle technologies of control that create the horizons of possibility for both religious and racialized lives."²⁹ In their important volume *Race and Secularism in America*, Lloyd and Jonathon S. Kahn ask, respectively, "whether it is ever possible to talk about secularism without talking about whiteness," and whether it is time that we call the secularization thesis "for what it is: a version of whiteness, if not white supremacy, that served to question the right of political place of African American citizens" (as well as immigrants, Native Americans, Catholics, and others exceeding the normative bounds of white liberal Protestantism).[30] Or as M. Jacqui Alexander has argued, "It is not that (post)modernity's avowed secularism has no room for the Sacred . . . , it is rather that it profits from a hierarchy that conflates Christianity with good tradition while consigning 'others' to the realm of bad tradition and thus to serve as evidence of the need for good Christian tradition."[31] Secularism, in other words, sets the very ground for the delineation of "religion" as such in its culturally tolerable and intolerable forms, a delineation indelibly linked to the production and maintenance of racial, sexual, and class difference.

Within the vibrant body of scholarship on US secularism, the post-Reconstruction period constitutes a striking lacuna. While it has garnered relatively scarce attention in the critical turn to secularism, the post-Reconstruction era saw intensified links between secularization and racialization, not least because the success of African Americans and the specter of their increased freedom and economic mobility (Major Carteret's "incubus") spurred a reactionary regime of racial violence meant to restore the sanctity of white masculinity and its fictions of secular progress.[32] During this era, as Jacqueline Goldsby points out, "the personal liberties claimed by New Negroes and New Women were no less important to the secularization of American life than the increased authority accorded to science and technology, economics and the market, politics and the art of governance. . . . Unsettling the traditional prerogatives of white men's social authority so thoroughly, these changes helped spur the revival of the 'ancient' rite of lynching."[33] Indeed, reading lynching as a rite—or as ritual performance (as I do in chapter 4)—helps concretize the way fictions of secular progress were (and are) utterly bound up in the repetitive and violent reproduction of whiteness.

In less spectacular if no less insidious ways, the Progressive era's emphasis on "separate but equal" realms of cultural praxis helped reinforce the hegemony of white Christian secularism in defining "religion" as such, as the ostensibly pluralistic logic of Jim Crow—concretized in 1896 by *Plessy v. Ferguson*—aligned seamlessly with an emergent (and ostensibly pluralistic) science of religions.[34] Highlighted at Chicago's 1893 Parliament of World Religions, this comparative discipline aimed to identify "religion" as an observable phenomenon across cultures, understood via their proximity to (or distance from) Anglo-Protestantism. Just as Jim Crow aimed to stabilize and materialize race—to make it legible through a visual regime of racial indexicality, or what Elizabeth Abel succinctly terms "a science of racial signs"—a concurrent discourse of world religions both materialized "religion" and (as Tomoko Masuzawa argues) effectively narrated its disappearance. Masuzawa describes the complex conditions under which "the subject of religion and religions" took on visibility within this turn-of-the-century discourse:

> When religion came to be identified as such . . . it came to be recognized above all as something that, in the opinions of many self-consciously modern Europeans, was in the process of disappearing from their midst, or if not altogether disappearing, becoming circumscribed in such a way that it was finally discernible as a distinct, and limited, phenomenon. Meanwhile, the two new sciences pertaining to non-European worlds, anthropology and Orientalism, promoted and bolstered the presumption that this thing called "religion" still held sway over all those who were unlike them: non-Europeans, Europeans of the pre-modern past, and among their own contemporary neighbors, the uncivilized and uneducated bucolic populace as well as the superstitious urban poor, all of whom were something of "savages within."[35]

In this sense, as Masuzawa observes, the understanding of religion forged in this period was inherently both a narrative of secularization and a "discourse of othering," as "religion" (particularly in its public and purportedly irrational or excessively fleshly forms) became the provenance of colonial "others" as well as ethnic and class-based "savages within."[36] Jonathan Z. Smith similarly asserts that "religion" is fundamentally a colonial category, offering the proliferation of "natural" religions in nineteenth-century anthropological discourse as an exemplary effort to freeze and classify "each ethnic unit at a particular 'stage of development' of the totality of human religious thought and activity."[37] While scholars like Tisa Wenger have helpfully problematized any static link between "religion" as a discourse and colonialism as such by pointing to the dynamic ways in which "religion" has been claimed by indigenous peoples and other non-Europeans as an important category of identity and analysis, I nevertheless take Masuzawa and Smith's points to be instructive insofar as they outline the emergent (though by no means all-encompassing) force of "religion" as a discursive regime in the post-Reconstruction era.[38] In a phrase resonant with Chesnutt's account of white supremacy as a "supernatural inspiration," Masuzawa in particular points to the way the modern discourse on religions was ultimately critical in "forging an enormous apparition: the essential identity of the West."[39]

If this apparition was not a particularly new one at the turn of the twentieth century, it nevertheless took on newly capacious, performative, and media-rich forms in the context of Jim Crow and in the broad set of practices that this study treats under the category of realism. Long a degraded or problematic term (and contested in its own moment as much as in our own), American realism has been read as a representational mode that, notwithstanding its early claims to democratize the space of the literary and to expose previously unexamined corners of American life, served largely to reinforce the late nineteenth century's intensified regimes of economic and cultural stratification. Fredric Jameson sums up this familiar approach, noting that attacks on realism take for granted its ideological itinerary, a project of "adapting its readers to bourgeois society as it currently exists, with its premium on comfort and inwardness, on individualism, on the acceptance of money as an ultimate reality."[40] Yet as a range of readers (including Jameson himself) have shown, that process of "adaptation"—of managing rapid social change and proliferating registers of cultural production—was a complex and variable one, such that to describe realism as a totalizing discourse or a technique of social power does not fully account for the way it both "constructs" and interrogates the field of turn-of-the-century social experience.[41] Furthermore, as Nancy Glazener has emphasized, realism itself has never been a fully "coherent entity, but was rather a term that acquired a *repertory* of uses as a result of its competing appropriations."[42] Largely released by contemporary critics from its associations with a positivist epistemology, "realism" now names less a strict sense of aesthetic commitments than a loose set of historical practices aimed at producing an affectively rich and complexly embodied sense of the real. Circulating through diverse sites of cultural production, borrowing from and contributing to the epistemological and sensorial assaults of modernity and technological change, and constantly buttressing its own unstable authority in relation to an ever-expanding field of popular culture, realism might best be understood as a performative enactment of the real, one rich (as we'll see) with all the unruly liveliness of performance.

Realist Ecstasy explores realism's iterative and embodied production of the real as it animates the secular affects of the post-Reconstruction era, those intensities of feeling that move through, exceed, shape, constrain, activate, and (perhaps ultimately) problematize bodies in relation to one another. The sense of the affective I draw on here is first and foremost dynamic: the sense of moving and being moved, the sense (to borrow from William James) that "*something is transacting*."[43] Realism's effort to give language to affect—and thus to bodily states, as Fredric Jameson, Jane Thrailkill, and others have pointed out—marks the historical emergence of the phenomenological body as an object of concern and description across a range of discourses. Thrailkill, for example, points to James's account of spiritual experience in this period as "a feeling of bodily activity"—the very corporeal activation through which realism (in Thrailkill's account) produces a vivid "moving picture."[44] Similarly, in tracking nineteenth-century realism's crucial shift to the scenic and the present tense, Jameson links this "new affective style" with the historical emergence of the bourgeois body and its onslaught of perceptual data, while insisting (crucially) on affect's autonomization or disembodiment—its belonging properly neither to the body nor to subjective experience.[45] Realism, as Jameson suggests, evinces a fundamental tension or dialectic between the temporality of narrative (or "things done") and the temporality of affect, between the telling of the past and the sense of an eternal present, between "iteration and Event." Such a dialectic helps bring into relief what Jameson describes in Anglo-European realism as "the gap between the lavish, indeed libidinous and garish *jouissance* in daily life and in routine, in the great lists and catalogues of objects, the body's swoons . . . its exhilarations and ecstatic glimpses; and on the other hand the gratuitous explosions, the fires, the bankruptcies, the monstrosities and gratuitous (yet 'fatal') catastrophes, which are the prices we have to pay for the novel's closure"; it also anticipates the breakdown of narrative as the form in which "reality" might best be represented.[46] This foundational—indeed haunting—tension between things over and done with and the present tense, or between ecstatic glimpses and gratuitous catastrophes, is a version of realism's secular affects, wherein the past is distinctly present and ecstasy abuts catastrophe at every turn. At the same time, unfolding these tensions in American and African American realisms means grappling in more direct ways with the post-Reconstruction era's violent regulation of bodily movement, and with the intensities of Jim Crow as a field of affective activation and routinized comportment.[47]

For this reason, *Realist Ecstasy* tracks secular affects through what we might think of as a realist repertoire: a set of complex bodily practices in and beyond the literary that worked to order, disorder, and reify racial and religious difference. I argue that scenes of realist ecstasy—of bodies beyond or *beside* themselves, from local color accounts of black Southern camp meetings to ethnographic photographs of the Ghost Dance—both animate and unsettle realism's drive to order bodily and affective experience at a moment when the body's capacity to reliably signify (or not) was everywhere at stake. Ecstasy, as I unfold in the chapters to come, is not so much a "disembodied" affect as one that takes the imagined, projected, and assumed body as both medium and problematic. Even as it names and makes legible bodily experiences often deemed excessive, fleshy, or primitive in realist discourse—and in the secular delineation of "good" and "bad" religion—ecstasy also challenges any straightforward relationship between "body" and "experience," manifesting and in some cases unsettling the frenzied bodily semiotics and (ill)ogics of Jim Crow. The ecstatic "body," in this sense, marks an originary displacement; it is, importantly, an object of realist description that is never simply or easily an object. Scenes of ecstasy, I contend, demonstrate realism's fantasy that the body might function as a legible sign or even (at its most extreme) exceed the realm of representation altogether, bodying forth reality (including the phantasmatic reality of race) in all its fleshy thereness. Yet ecstasy's very communicability—the uncertainty of its belonging securely to any singular body, its dynamic *happening* or contagious transmission across bodies—also suggests the eclipsed but nevertheless felt recognition, within realism, of a more fundamental (even surreal) communicability at the heart of the "real."[48]

In demonstrating how an affectively rich sense of the real is repetitively enacted and reenacted at the level of bodily practice, *Realist Ecstasy* takes inspiration (or maybe "enthusiasm," the historically pejorative and distinctly contagious sense of inspiration) from performance studies, particularly from its sustained grappling with questions of absence and presence, liveness and reproduction, the "live" and the long dead. My description of realism as a "repertoire," for example, owes much to Diana Taylor's insistence on bodily practice as a dynamic site of knowledge transmission, one that has the capacity to radically expand and transform the archives on which literary studies (among other disciplines) has historically relied.[49] This emphasis on the historical "transmission" of performance is crucial. By analyzing what I term *ecstatic performance*, my effort is not to figure ecstasy as merely performative (though historical efforts to disqualify ecstasy as mere mimicry, or even as minstrelsy, form part of my examination). Instead, I draw on the language and methods of performance studies to emphasize ecstasy's historicity, its belonging to what Joseph Roach has called the "kinesthetic imagination": a cultural mnemonics rooted in and transmitted through bodily movement, and a form of memory-work interdependent with but also strikingly different from the work of textual archives.[50] As Roach points out, if performance is a mode of remembering, it is also—just as crucially—the mark of forgetting. Performance, in Roach's resonant and unforgettable phrase, points to what is "forgotten but not gone."[51] Or in Taylor's slightly different formulation, "Performance makes visible that which is always already there: the ghosts, the tropes, the scenarios that structure our individual and collective life. . . . It provokes emotions it claims only to represent, evokes memories and grief that belong to some other body. It conjures up and makes visible not just the live but the powerful army of the always already living."[52] Tracking what she calls the "hauntology of performance," Taylor (much like Gordon) invites us to examine performance not just for its "liveness" but for its liveliness in reproduction, the way it "continues to act politically even as it exceeds the live."[53]

Approaching realism as both an unruly archive of performance and a wide-ranging repertoire of media practices—including literature, photography, audio recording, and early film—*Realist Ecstasy* attends not to the "live" so much as the still living, or to representational practices that continue to enact worlds in the present (and in realism's "scenic" present tense) while testifying to a haunting past. My effort is in no way meant to eclipse the important differences between literary fiction, archival texts, and live performance, nor is to minimize the ideological work of realism as a discourse that imagines, prescribes, and regulates "the body" and bodily practice at every turn. If realism is a repertoire of turn-of-the-century practices, as I argue throughout, it is also a textual, visual, and auditory archive that stills bodies as much as it enlivens them and forgets as much as it remembers. My readings aim to sustain these contradictions rather than resolve them, in the belief that such contradictions offer important testimony to the hauntology of the realist archive and its embeddedness in the affective life of Jim Crow. I draw on performance studies because as a discipline it has long been attuned to just this hauntology of the archive, and to the repetitions, elisions, and absences that have shaped it. In this regard, I am particularly indebted to black feminist scholars for their accounts of the gaps that mark the archives of nineteenth-century literature and performance. My readings would not be possible, for example, without Saidiya Hartman and Daphne Brooks's crucial accounts of the "mechanisms of power . . . at the site of the archive" and of the racialized and gendered lacunae that emerge there.[54] Drawing from these accounts, and seeking to understand realism's capacious construction of the real as a performative—which is to say haunted—act, I explore not only what new kinds of practices we are able to recover in realist archives but also what kinds of dominant scripts come into relief. Reading realism as a repertoire, in turn, bodies forth the broader stakes of bringing performance theory to bear on literary history: rather than facilitating a confidently linear—which is to say secular—narrative of literary historical development, performance provides a language for the wayward, reiterative, and often occluded relationship between literary enactments and the historical moments in which they emerge.

If turn-of-the-century secularism is a structure of feeling deeply linked to the affective life of Jim Crow, realism might best be understood as the repertoire that sustains and circulates that structure. In this sense, I want to insist that "secularism" and "realism" are not only hegemonic forces but also lived, reiterative, "restored" behaviors.[55] As historical concepts in motion, they are choreo-graphic in the sense that Kélina Gotman describes: "taking place between language and archive, where the archive is embodied as well as written or notated."[56] They are, in a word, haunted transmissions. And the shape of that haunting is complex. As Ann Pellegrini reminds us, "Structures of feeling can serve to transmit and codify relations of dominance; they can also serve as spaces—points of 'virtual fracture'—in which we might become other than who we thought we were."[57] If realist ecstasy often transmits and codifies a sacred/profane binary that operates as a regulatory discourse—ordering the very shape of the possible—it also recognizes, and occasionally invites, ways of being beside or becoming "otherwise."[58] In this sense, realism testifies to the way the "real" is and always has been contested territory. To encounter realism as a haunting repertoire of post-Reconstruction affects is to confront it as just such contested territory: a set of practices that transmit cultural memory, that construct and naturalize an embodied sense of the "real," and that interrogate what it means to move through the world in relation to others—or to be beside oneself.

Being Beside; or, Ecstasy as Method

The desire to find a language for this constitutive *besideness* is at the heart of *Realist Ecstasy* and of much of the work to which it is indebted. In her 2014 study of forms of care among Inuit communities in the northern Canadian Arctic, anthropologist Lisa Stevenson argues for a methodology that might unfix many of the "discursive certainties" that continue to animate contemporary ethnographic fieldwork. "Such fixity," she argues, "works to prevent any transfiguring encounter from taking place—we already know who we are and what we came to find out."[59] Against ethnographic study as a practice of managing uncertainty, Stevenson proposes a method of attentiveness to "uncertainty, hesitation, and undecideability," particularly with regard to the boundaries between the living and the dead. She asks, "Can we so easily identify the ways the dead continue to have a life, to have a hold on us? How do we talk about the ways that life is constitutively beside itself?"[60] Chasing a similar structure of *besideness*, Judith Butler has noted in a very different context that while a straightforward history of feminist and LGBTQ movements might locate ecstasy (as political affect and as experimental drug) in the 1960s and '70s, ecstasy is perhaps "more persistent than that; maybe it has been with us all along." She notes,

"To be ec-static means, literally, to be outside oneself, and thus can have several meanings: to be transported beyond oneself by a passion, but also to be *beside oneself* with rage or grief. I think that if I can still address a 'we,' or include myself within its terms, I am speaking to those of us who are living in certain ways *beside ourselves*, whether in sexual passion, or emotional grief, or political rage."[61] The boundaries of Butler's "we" are both specific and undelimited here; ecstasy as a form of *being beside* marks itself as fundamentally about encounters that shape and reshape the boundaries of self and community. The recognition of besideness is the recognition of an originary collectivity, or as the philosopher Jean-Luc Nancy has articulated it, "Being-with is constitutive of being."[62] Alongside his emphasis on the ontological priority of togetherness—what he calls "the togetherness of Being [*l'ensemble de l'être*]" as well as the "general co-appearance of beings"—Nancy insists "being-with" is also fundamentally "a *praxis* and an *ethos*."[63] For Nancy, the "we" is not simply a question of representation but also (strikingly) of performance: "The staging of co-appearance, the staging which is co-appearing. We are always already there at each instant. This is not an innovation—but the stage must be reinvented; *we* must reinvent it each time, each time making our entrance anew."[64] Togetherness may be ontologically prior to the singular self, in other words, but it is also constantly *acted* and reenacted in every instance of the "we." This emphasis on being-with as praxis emerges as well in the etymological form of "ecstasy," from the Greek *ekstasis*, standing out of place or outside of oneself—a movement out of stillness.

It is this sense of movement and practice that I aim to underline when I refer to ecstasy as *ex-stasis*: an act of transfer, an encounter, and a form of collectivity-in-motion. Realist ecstasy is often, as we'll see, a discourse of othering: a means of imagining and thereby containing religious, racial, gender, class, and sexual others by way of setting the very terms for their intelligibility (in this sense, the ecstasy of Butler's "we" is by no means ensured in the texts I examine). But it is also an occluded recognition of the availability of other epistemologies—what Ashon Crawley names "otherwise epistemologies"—forgotten but not gone in the secular imaginary, with its reiterative performances of a sacred/profane divide.[65] Black feminist and queer studies have long since articulated such epistemologies as they challenge the white supremacist inheritance of a secular Enlightenment, from Hortense Spillers's description of the "Church Insurgent," to M. Jacqui Alexander's account of the sacred as a praxis of "collectivized self-possession," to José Esteban Muñoz's offering of ecstasy as an invitation to a "then and there" against the violence of the here and now.[66] My emphasis on ecstasy as praxis and performance emerges in crucial ways from these works. It also owes much to the articulation in black studies of a revolutionary or insurgent tradition of black Christianity that has constituted itself in fundamental opposition to the violent choreographies of white liberal Protestantism. Cornel West traces such insurgency—or what he calls "subversive joy"—to the traumatic spiritual dislocation of the Middle Passage and the subsequent creative appropriation by enslaved people of Methodist and Baptist revivalism, with its emphasis on emotional conversion, "ecstatic bodily behavior," and spiritual equality under God. Through such practice, "the full-fledged acceptance of the body deems human existence a source of joy and gaiety," and the body possessed by spiritual joy in turn performs a critical relation to the traumatic dispossessions of secular modernity.[67] Realism's ecstatic possessions, I argue, are haunted by just such ongoing dispossessions, but this haunting, importantly, is not the limit of their work.

As a form of standing outside of oneself or out of stillness, *ex-stasis* telegraphs an originary displacement that is also, importantly, an originary (if always provisional) relationality, a relation in and through movement: what I'll call *being beside*. When it emerges in the texts that I treat here, *being beside* signals a crucial displacement of the self as the primary locus of realist concern and fascination—an unsettling that realism courts, regulates, and problematizes. (We see this unsettling in the subtle but significant shift in Butler's articulation of ecstasy, from "transported *beyond* oneself" to being "*beside oneself*"; this shift from beyond to beside may be rhetorical, but is also utterly essential.) Rather than a narrative of transcendence—of moving "beyond" the self or the disciplinary logic of the subject—*being beside* marks the self as fundamentally (not incidentally) social, necessarily constituted by what lies outside or beside it. With its emphasis on the increasingly expansive *data* of social experience, literary realism has long been recognized as attentive to the socially embedded nature of the subject (its constitutive *beside*ness). By examining how realism's investigations of sociality often abut and even depend on ecstatic forms of collectivity, I demonstrate that the realist production of social data is itself *ex-static* and performative, reliant on the very forms of collective practice that it would seem to describe from a secure (and secular) epistemological distance. If realism often aims to colonize and defuse such collective forms, it nevertheless remains indebted to them for its construction of an affectively rich sense of the "real." Like life (or in its likeness), I want to suggest, realism is beside itself—infused with longing and with violence, heterogeneous in its temporalities, and messier (perhaps) than we have yet been able to recognize.

Ecstasy, in other words, is both this study's critical object and its methodology. Eve Kosofsky Sedgwick offers what is perhaps our most resonant articulation of besideness and what it might mean to inhabit it as a critical comportment. In place of seeking to get beneath, behind, or beyond the guises of power, Sedgwick proposes "beside" as a spatial relation that resists dualistic (and ultimately formulaic) diagnoses of repression and liberation, hegemony and subversion. Though I have not fully avoided such dualisms, I take methodological inspiration from Sedgwick's emphasis on the "middle ranges of agency": modes of ambivalence, uncertainty, and indeterminate action that nevertheless open up space for "effectual creativity and change."[68] Insofar as being beside oneself (transported, seized, or possessed) presents an unresolvable drama of agency, ecstasy is a radically unstable site for any clear project of political resistance. As I argue in chapter 1, turn-of-the-century thinkers like W. E. B. Du Bois recognized in ecstatic "frenzy" both racist projections of black religious emotionality *and* the potential resistance that being beside oneself might offer to the historical entanglements of white supremacy with Enlightenment rationality. The undecidability of such moments offers a frustrating but nevertheless powerful hermeneutic. Here I take a cue from Sedgwick in arguing that the very instability of *being beside* might help us produce more robust accounts of the dynamic, always-unstable relations of power we call "religion" and "race" at the turn of the century. For Sedgwick, "beside" importantly resists the fantasy of moving "beyond" power, even as it presents a fuller range of possibilities for describing the way power inflects such dynamic relations: "*Beside* permits a spacious agnosticism about several of the linear logics that enforce dualistic thinking: noncontradiction or the law of the excluded middle, cause versus effect, subject versus object. Its interest does not, however, depend on a fantasy of metonymically egalitarian or even pacific relations, as any child knows who's shared a bed with siblings. *Beside* comprises a wide range of desiring, identifying, representing, repelling, paralleling, differentiating, rivaling, leaning, twisting, mimicking, withdrawing, attracting, aggressing, warping, and other relations."[69] As in Lisa Stevenson's resistance to the discursive certainties of anthropological fieldwork, Sedgwick's "spacious agnosticism" subverts questions of belief to questions of practice; her cumulating gerunds mark a fundamental interest in the turns and twists of relationality, its fundamentally *ex-static* movements. Once again, rather than a fantasy of transcendence—of ascending beyond the immanence and intimacy of power—Sedgwick's list (words beside themselves) situates us in the very middle of things, in the fundamentally transfiguring mode of encounter.

Beside is both a spatial and an affective formation for Sedgwick, linked to her project of nonhierarchical thinking and pedagogy. While I draw heavily throughout *Realist Ecstasy* from this spatial sense of being *beside*—which depends on a sense of intimacy and of bodily proximity—I also use ecstasy to describe an intimate sense of historicity, of being beside in time as well as in space. To do so, I draw from performance studies scholars like Rebecca Schneider and Tavia Nyong'o, who have each explored what Nyong'o terms the "dispossessive force" of reenactment, which refuses (in both radical and reactionary forms) a strict divide between past and present.[70] I also engage queer theory's account of ecstatic temporality as a mode of imagining new relations to the past—of standing or "stepping out" of straight time as a regime of sexual (and indeed secular) regulation. In chapter 5, for example, I explore secularism's stranglehold on queerness, and the challenge that ecstasy in Nella Larsen's *Quicksand* (1929) offers to the gendered and racialized terms of secular progress. In many ways, *Quicksand* demonstrates Jose Esteban Muñoz's claim: "Queerness's time is the time of ecstasy. Ecstasy is queerness's way."[71] While Muñoz's invitation to a utopian horizon that exceeds and challenges the present tense might seem utterly opposed to the realist project, I nevertheless take up this invitation as a crucial methodological provocation: a means of reading with and against the grain of realist ecstasy. Analyzing The Magnetic Fields's 1994 song "Take

Ecstasy with Me" alongside Gian Lorenzo Bernini's seventeenth-century sculpture *The Ecstasy of Saint Teresa*, Jacques Lacan's account of "jouissance," and Martin Heidegger's articulation of timeliness and *ekstatisch*, Muñoz enacts an unlikely interpretive besideness that refuses any strict or linear logic of historical relation and that implicitly speaks to the ways in which straight (secular) intellectual history has long erased queer and ecstatic relationality as a critical method. It is just such an interpretive method that *Realist Ecstasy* aims to (re)enact, insisting on the *besideness* of interdisciplinary method—and on performance's fundamentally *ex-static* transmission across ostensibly discrete fields of study—as a way of learning- and thinking-with, a constitutive togetherness that has itself been effaced by the institutionalization of academic disciplines.

As we will see, part of the force of the secularization thesis has been to render ecstasy as belonging properly to the realm of the historical, safely ensconced in the distant past, while providing a clear vision of what constitutes "good" religion for the present. Realist accounts of the ecstatic can and often do serve this vision, as they consolidate normative, present tense, and white Protestant idioms of religious feeling and expression. But such accounts also recognize alternative ways of imagining a relationship to the past, ways that refuse any straight or linear sense of "bad" religion's overcoming. Often linked to the possibility of cross-temporal connections—intimate relations to the past and to the future, sites of traumatic return or unsettling continuity—ecstasy haunts linear formations like "post-Reconstruction" and "Progressive era," linked as they are to a secular imaginary of social progress. Lodged in the sticky intimacies of history's enactment and reenactment, ecstasy, importantly, is not separate from the rich affective life of secularism. On the contrary, it forms a robust part of it, giving the lie to narratives of secularization and, at the same time, bringing into relief the normative work of such narratives, their naturalization of the secular order (and disorder) of things. If, in other words, secularization is a process that is always "doubling back on itself" (to borrow from Vincent Pecora), it is also one that demands we dwell in the turns and folds, in the constitutive besideness that "secular modernity" doesn't begin to name.[72] *Realist Ecstasy* inhabits such moments of doubling back, a doubled or doubling movement—being beside—which realism evinces as the very rhythm of the real.

Realist Ecstasy is, importantly, neither a religious history nor a straightforward account of racialization under Jim Crow; it is by no means a comprehensive look at the relationship between religion and race at the turn of the century, which is much more variable and expansive than I can possibly account for here and which religious historians have explored in much more specific and deliberate ways.[73] In focusing on the hegemonic force of secularism, I necessarily leave out a wide range of practices through which one might examine the racialization of embodied religion (I do not, to name just one example, mention any Catholics in this study of ecstasy). Similarly, in focusing on the affective life of Jim Crow, I largely ignore those interrelated forms of racialization that do not map in any easy way onto the black-and-white matrix shaped by the legacy of racial slavery in the US; this includes the ways in which religious and racial difference were global formations, invariably and extensively projected onto both colonized peoples and immigrants to the US from Latin America, Asia, and Eastern Europe over the course of the nineteenth and twentieth centuries. My project, in this sense, is haunted by what it excludes. But it is also deliberately partial and deliberately part of a chorus of voices inviting us to explore secularism in ever more capacious ways, not least as a haunting that has shaped the very structure of our inquiry. Like Jordan Stein, I am interested in the history of secularism as "the history of a story we told, not of a thing that happened," though I think the telling and the happening might be closer than we have imagined.[74] Like Avery Gordon, I want to ask about how this story has been assembled and joined, written and embodied—and about the institutional discourses that have helped perpetuate it.[75] *Realist Ecstasy* lies beside these works and others; its work is, fundamentally, a project of being beside.

* * *

Across *Realist Ecstasy*'s five chapters, I describe a palimpsest of secular affects and haunting performances: an intensively labored, reiterative, and temporally heterogeneous mode of representation. Chapter 1, "Reconstructing Secularisms," describes how turn-of-the-century arguments over the boundaries of literary realism were inextricably linked to the politics of secularism. I follow tropes of religious excess as they circulate throughout realist fiction, from William Dean Howells's interlocking diagnoses of racial and religious hysteria in *An Imperative Duty* (1891) to W. E. B. Du Bois's more ambivalent description of the "frenzy" of the black church in "Of the Coming of John," his early experiment with realist narrative and the only fictional chapter of *The Souls of Black Folk* (1903). Resonating through such descriptions, I argue, is a question about the aesthetic, political, and performative function of ecstasy in the aftermath of Reconstruction. While Howells depicts the black church as a site of emotional and bodily excess, situated at the very limits of realist narration, a series of black feminist texts—including Anna Julia Cooper's *A Voice from the South* (1892) and Frances Harper's *Iola Leroy* (1892)—radically challenge this formation, offering an important take on the uses of ecstatic collectivity. They also gesture to the immanent secularism of literary history, which has largely omitted these texts from the boundaries of realism, perhaps in part because they articulate a critical relationship to secularism as a silent but hegemonic force in the post-Reconstruction era's hysterical regulation of racial difference.

While chapter 1 reconstructs secularism as a crucial regulatory discourse in the post-Reconstruction era, the chapters that follow work collectively to trouble the very "post" of post-Reconstruction. In chapter 2, "Archival Enthusiasm," I read the ecstatic performances haunting Stephen Crane's 1895 narrative of the Civil War, *The Red Badge of Courage*. While much has been made of the way the novel strategically "forgets" the political history of the war, I recover a history of performance that allows us to understand *Red Badge* as fully haunted by what remains un-Reconstructed in the US racial imaginary. Through a reading of Jim Conklin, a minor yet crucial figure in the novel, I examine the novel's complex overlay of religious enthusiasm and minstrel performance, exploring how *Red Badge* deploys these forms in order to grapple with the embodied semiotics of the Jim Crow era. Recovering traces of the midcentury minstrel figure "Dandy Jim of Caroline" in Jim's exuberant death scene, I argue that the narrative afterlife of such traces reveals the novel's own archival impulse, its tendency to simultaneously erase and embed the excesses of war and postwar racial violence. Marking the historical overlays between minstrelsy and religious enthusiasm in their complex objectification of the moving body, *Red Badge*'s performances treat bodies as kinetic archives whose stylized gestures offer stunning testimony to history's traumatic returns. In this sense, the novel treats the ambivalence of performance as precisely the arena in which literature might grapple with history's unaccountable remainders.

Consolidated as objects of knowledge across a range of disciplinary practices at the turn of the century, "race" and "religion" came to look at once like material facts of modern experience and like primitive holdovers from the past. In chapter 3, "The Ghost Dance and Realism's Techno-Spiritual Frontier," I examine the mediated life of what realist observers called the Ghost Dance, a pan-tribal prophetic movement that emerged in the 1880s in the context of US colonial expansion, genocide, and dispossession. Spectacularly suppressed at the Wounded Knee massacre of 1890, the Ghost Dance proliferated in turn-of-the-century ethnographic realism, a project that included literary, photographic, filmic, and sonic texts. Focusing on efforts to record and, more distinctly, to reenact the dance, I argue that such reenactments signal the reiterative life of colonial violence in the supposed afterlife of the frontier. Yet they also point to realist media as a temporally and affectively dense terrain of performance. In the aftermath of Wounded Knee, realist ethnography drew its authority from the very visionary practices it aimed to reproduce, insisting on realism's capacity to adequately record spiritual performance while channeling the power of media to resurrect and reanimate the dead. I argue that such performances signal a tight fit between the cultural logic of Indian vanishing and modernity's dreams of high-fidelity preservation. At the same time, I offer reenactment's contingencies of performance and reperformance as a way to rethink the historical nexus between recording and vanishing.

Extending this attention to realist technologies as modes of performance, chapter 4, "Touching a Button," examines turn-of-the-century electrification as a site of both ecstatic possibility and violent materialization. Beginning with little-known photographs by William Van der Weyde of the electric chair at Sing Sing prison, I describe how the electric chair mobilized electricity's spiritual potential for the mass reproduction of death. Exploring how William Dean Howells and other opponents of the chair linked its technological effects to the mass popularity of the push-button photograph, I examine photography's collusion with the electric chair's production of stillness as a form of racial terror while analyzing Van der Weyde's photographs as realist reenactments of an electrified touch. I then turn to James Weldon Johnson's

The Autobiography of an Ex-Colored Man (1912), a text largely left out of the realist canon yet explicitly in conversation with the realist project as Howells and others articulated it. Johnson mobilizes what I call "electric affects" to theorize the circulations of religious feeling and racial terror at the nadir of American race relations, even as the novel itself becomes an electrifying performance, circulating in and through the shock of spectacular violence. Yoking the "electrifying climax" of the camp meeting to the "electric current" of the lynch mob, Johnson channels the language of circuitry to suggest the centrality of both practices in defining and disfiguring the "real" of secular modernity.

Finally, in chapter 5, "Born, Again," I take up Nella Larsen's 1928 novel *Quicksand*, pushing the bounds of realism well into the twentieth century and reading the novel as part of a vibrant debate within the Harlem Renaissance over the aesthetic and political uses of realism. As scholars have long noted, *Quicksand* depicts the reproduction of racial and sexual difference as a distinctly unbearable demand on the queerly embodied subject. In such readings, *Quicksand* rejects both the racial marriage plot and the spiritual logic of rebirth, offering in their place a portrait of the queer creative impulse held hostage by the procreative imperative. Yet this attention to the novel's secular critique of essentialisms has overlooked its insistence on the intersection of queerness and ecstatically embodied religion, a convergence that forces us to reexamine the potential that *Quicksand* invests in both spiritual and sexual forms of conversion. For the novel repeatedly links queer sexuality not to birth (as in contemporary "born this way" discourse) but instead, ambivalently, to rebirth. Even as it attends carefully to more repressive forms of sexual and spiritual administration, *Quicksand* traces a "queer sort of satisfaction"—a fugitive collectivity emerging from moments of ecstatic abandon. In turn, the novel treats ecstasy (and particularly Pentecostalism's kinetically embodied forms of spiritual practice) as a suggestively queer nexus of sexual and religious modes of performance. Offering a timely reconsideration of *Quicksand*'s ostensible secularism, I argue that to read its ecstatic episodes is to discover a more complex account of the ways in which the demands of race, class, sexuality, and religion might indeed be borne out by, or born out of, being performatively born-again.

In the picture that *Realist Ecstasy* offers, the far-reaching project of realist representation emerges as a temporally layered, complex reenactment of intersecting religious and racial histories. As these chapters collectively bear out, such histories are not so much told as rehearsed, lived in the unsettling movements of and between bodies and in the secular affects that structure and police their relations. Through the ecstatic, I argue, realism confronts unfinished histories of enslavement, war, colonialism, and racial terror; it gives us an image of the present that lives with and beside the past rather than simply after it. In this sense, realism's ecstatic visions also serve as radical revisions: a means of calling into question a turn-of-the-century faith in secular progress that left so many "untimely" or (dis)possessed bodies behind. Yet if realist ecstasy is a discourse of othering, it is also a discourse of being other: to ourselves and to one another, but also *with* each other, in *ex-stasis*.[76] In its approach to ecstasy, then, realism recognizes and enacts this immanent being beside: its violence as well as its possibility.

1

Reconstructing Secularisms

In the dramatic revelation that structures William Dean Howells's 1891 novella *An Imperative Duty*, Rhoda Aldgate learns that her grandmother was an enslaved woman. Rhoda experiences the attendant loss of her legal whiteness like a phantom limb: "She emerged from it at moments with a refusal to accept the loss of her former self, like that of the mutilated man who looks where his arm was, and cannot believe it gone. Like him, she had a full sense of what was lost, the unbroken consciousness of what was lopped away."[1] If whiteness secures Rhoda's bodily sense of being continuous with herself (and, in the logic of Jim Crow, with a history of "undiluted" whiteness), the disclosure of her ancestry enacts what the late nineteenth century understood as a more or less hysterical dis-integration of self. In *The Principles of Psychology* (1890), an important source text for *An Imperative Duty*, William James observed that an "incessant and fine-grained form" of discontinuity marked nearly all consciousness; at the same time, he drew on the work of French psychologist Pierre Janet to signal hysteria as an extreme instance of such discontinuity: "How far this splitting up of the mind into separate consciousnesses may exist in each one of us is a problem. M. Janet holds that it is only possible where there is abnormal weakness, and consequently a defect of unifying or co-ordinating power. An hysterical woman abandons part of her consciousness because she is too weak nervously to hold it together. The abandoned part meanwhile may solidify into a secondary or sub-conscious self."[2] In *An Imperative Duty*, the split self of the hysteric operates as a crucial hermeneutic—and in some sense, substitution—for Jim Crow regimes of personhood, with their apportioning of the racialized subject into (in Rhoda's case) "one-sixteenth" blackness. In keeping with what the novel pathologizes and feminizes as a broader hysteria of racial difference under such regimes, the sense of disintegration that marks Rhoda's "loss of her former self" aligns closely with the hysteric's sense of an imposing "secondary personage" (as James noted, "The anaesthesias, paralyses, contractions, and other irregularities from which hysterics suffer seem then to be due to the fact that their secondary personage has enriched itself by robbing the primary one of a function which the latter ought to have retained").[3] Similarly, the attachment to whiteness as a kind of *phantom* limb—that which she ought to have retained—accords with Rhoda's sense that she must face her blackness like the specter of a secondary self: "It's like a ghost: if I keep going towards it, it won't hurt me; I mustn't be afraid of it."[4]

The force of this move, and of *An Imperative Duty* more broadly, is to diagnose the US body politic with a kind of racial hysteria, curable only through a hearty skepticism toward the specters of essential or biological difference. Indeed, as many readers have noted, the novella is structured less as a struggle between black and white (embodied in the trope of the tragic mulatta) than as a struggle between belief and disbelief in the reality of racial difference. This struggle is born out early in the novella in an extended dialogue between Rhoda's aunt, Mrs. Meredith, long the keeper of her ancestral secret, and Dr. Edward Olney, "a specialist in nervous diseases" who treats Mrs. Meredith and who eventually woos and marries her niece. Confiding Rhoda's secret to Olney, Mrs. Meredith frames her identity in decidedly occult terms:

> Mrs. Meredith added, with hysterical haste: "It might come out in a hundred ways. I can hear it in her voice at times—it's a *black* voice! I can see it in her looks! I can feel it in her character—so easy, so irresponsible, so fond of what is soft and pleasant! . . . She cannot forecast consequences; she's a creature of the present hour; she's like them *all*! I think that in some occult, dreadful way she feels her affinity with them, and that's the reason why she's so attracted by them, so fond of them. It's her *race* calling her! . . ."[5]

In response to Mrs. Meredith's insistence on her ability to perceive the signs of racial difference—an insistence that characterized many turn-of-the-century white observers, and that African American writers like Frances Ellen Watkins Harper would treat with rightful derision—Dr. Olney prescribes only a course of very limited intervention: "I think you ought to leave it to her."[6] In such moments, Olney administers a seemingly sagacious corrective; against Mrs. Meredith's hysterical attachment to race, Olney offers a privatized solution to the "problem" of Rhoda's ancestry.[7] Yet Howells figures Olney's romantic interest in Rhoda in terms that reproduce Mrs. Meredith's vision of an occult affinity; for Olney, "the remote taint of her servile and savage origin gave her a kind of fascination which refuses to let itself be put in words: it was like the grace of a limp, the occult, indefinable loveableness of a deformity, but transcending these by its allurement in infinite degree, and going for the reason of its effect deep into the mysterious place of being where the spirit and animal meet and part in us."[8] As in the trope of the phantom limb—a crucial idiom in the postbellum imagining of sectional and psychic repair—here Howells aligns Rhoda's "servile origin" with the de-formation of an ostensibly integrated self, a distinctly sexual allurement that likewise dis-integrates Dr. Olney *himself* into the Enlightenment's higher and lower orders of "spirit" and "animal."

While racial difference is pitched throughout *An Imperative Duty* in the key of the feminized occult, the novella on the whole seems to slouch toward disenchantment, as emotional leveling becomes the fix for the cultural fetish of absolute difference. Olney treats with "tender mockery" Rhoda's outsized sense of duty toward her "mother's race," and in the novella's final chapter, which secures Rhoda's marriage to Olney, her "meditated melodrama" meets with his determination to treat the affair "in no lurid twilight gloom, but in plain, simply, matter-of-fact noonday."[9] In this sense, the debunking of an occult or hysterical perception of racial difference is linked to the realist idiom of a clear-eyed, holistic, and masculinist moral vision (Olney realizes early on that as Mrs. Meredith's physician, he will need to "combine the functions of the priest and the leech").[10] Similarly, the novella treats racial types themselves with a kind of tender mockery, transforming the sentimental type of the tragic mulatta into the realist type of the neurasthenic.[11] By the end of the novella, Olney signals his regret that Rhoda tends less toward the "sunny-natured antetypes of her mother's race" and more toward "that hypochondria of the soul into which the Puritanism of her father's race had sickened her."[12] Here Howells amalgamates racial and psychological types to insist that whiteness, too, is a hysterical formation—a distinctly American pathology in need of realist treatment.

This was a powerful intervention, and one that W. E. B. Du Bois praised in a 1913 essay in *The Crisis* on "Howells and Black Folk." Du Bois noted that in *An Imperative Duty*, Howells had "faced our national foolishness and shuffling and evasion" on matters of race, depicting a woman who "peers beyond the Veil and shudders and then—tells her story frankly, marries her man, and goes her way as thousands of others have done and are doing."[13] Yet if *An Imperative Duty* aims at some level to exorcise an occult vision of racial difference—by priest or by leech—it nevertheless does so under the terms of a secular ideology that is radically commingled with white supremacy. As many scholars have worked to elaborate, secularism's purported absence or diminution of religion as such belies a disciplinary formation linked to the management of what counts as good or "proper" religion, and to the concomitant regulation of race, gender, and sexuality.[14] Vincent Lloyd notes that secularism "create[s] the horizons of possibility for both religious and racialized lives," and it is the management of such horizons of possibility to which *An Imperative Duty* often testifies.[15] It is no mistake, for example, that Howells's novella (as Michele Birnbaum has pointed out) traffics in a distinctly pathologized vision of racial womanhood in its effort to demystify race, or that the physic it applies for hysterical women is ultimately linked to the reproduction of whiteness (Olney believes that through intermarriage his race will "absorb" the inferior qualities of other races, a progress narrative that closely parallels the shift from "occult" racial types to "modern" psychological ones).[16] As in the idiom of the phantom limb or loveable limp, *An Imperative Duty* treats Rhoda's "hypochondria of the soul" as a narrative of racial disease and secular rehabilitation, one in which race and religious difference operate as conjoined "handicaps" that will eventually be overcome.[17]

Historical accounts of secularism in the US context have largely leapfrogged the post-Reconstruction period, focusing either on the antebellum consolidation of what John Lardas Modern describes as a "metaphysics of secularism"—a normative and "invisible consensus . . . that both habituated and secured versions of true religion emanating from the precincts of Anglo-Protestantism"—or on the relationship between twentieth-century American religious pluralism and the regulatory function of secular progress narratives.[18] And while scholars such as Tracy Fessenden, Molly McGarry, and Josef Sorett have explored the hegemonic force of the secular in structuring the imaginative and cultural work of both Anglo- and Afro-Protestantism in the years following the Civil War, few have directly examined links between the affective life of secularism and the protracted violence of post-Reconstruction period.[19] That violence, as Du Bois and others recognized, was as much spiritual as it was material; indeed, it governed the limits of each. In this chapter, I ask how might we approach turn-of-the-century secularism—itself never a stable or uncontested formation—as constituted in part through the backlash against black freedom and self-determination, as well as (in less direct ways) through this period's racialized imagining of the very bounds of immanence and transcendence. If realism could reinforce such boundaries—as, we'll see, in the case of *An Imperative Duty*—it could also, as I'll argue later in this chapter, serve as a performative redrawing of them. Recognizing, with George Schulman, that secularism is part of a structure that "designates who and what is counted as real," then realism—the dominant if strongly contested mode of literary production in this period—offers a crucial terrain through which the normative energies of the secular *and* various challenges to it might be understood.[20]

This approach demands we understand realism and secularism as interlocking but not coextensive, a set of conjoined practices or comportments that reinforce one another without being exactly the same. In this opening section, I'll detail the ways in which realism's secular comportment aligns with the post-Reconstruction consolidation of Jim Crow racial hierarchies, in particular the violence of co-constituting forms of religious and racial otherness.[21] In *An Imperative Duty*, as we'll see, that consolidation takes shape through imagining the black church as a site of emotional and bodily excess, utterly alien to the psychological complexity of its heroine and thus situated at the very limits of realist narration. In the sections that follow, I explore a series of texts that radically challenge this formation, from Anna Julia Cooper's explicit critique of Howells in *A Voice from the South* (1892), to Frances Ellen Watkins Harper's (re)visionary novel *Iola Leroy* (1892), to Du Bois's own early experiment with realist narrative in "Of the Coming of John," the only fictional chapter of *The Souls of Black Folk* (1903). I bring this particular constellation of texts into dialogue in order to demonstrate that turn-of-the-century arguments over the boundaries of literary realism were inextricably linked to the politics of secularism, while highlighting texts that are rarely if ever included within those boundaries. Their exclusion, I would argue, says something important not just about realist discourse and practice in the post-Reconstruction era but also about the immanent secularism of literary history, which has largely omitted texts like "Of the Coming of John" and *Iola Leroy* from the boundaries of realism perhaps in part because they articulate a critical relationship to secularism as a silent but hegemonic force in the post-Reconstruction era's hysterical regulation of racial difference.[22] As we'll see, Cooper, Harper, and Du Bois each attest to secularism's deep reliance on—and fundamental ties with—constructions of whiteness.

Nowhere is the link between secularism and white supremacy more distinct in *An Imperative Duty* than in Rhoda's visit to a black church, soon after learning from Mrs. Meredith that her ancestors were enslaved. Reeling from the revelation, Rhoda drifts toward the "colored" section of segregated Boston with a markedly divided self: "There seemed two selves of her, one that lived before that awful knowledge, and one that had lived as long since, and again a third that knew and pitied them both." This description has been much noted; in describing Rhoda's "double consciousness of trouble," Howells (like Du Bois after him) likely drew from James's *Principles* as well as from a broader and long-circulating discourse on psychic division.[23] In this sense, as Henry Wonham argues, "Howells's speculation on the psychology of racial difference set a crucial precedent for Du Bois by introducing the medical discourse of 'double consciousness' into the context of racial and cultural identity."[24] Yet if Howells's and Du Bois's sense of divided selves owed much to late nineteenth-century psychopathology, it was also indebted to the concomitant emergence of "religion" as a category of ethnographic and sociological description.[25] James would notably return to the notion of double consciousness in his 1901–1902 Gifford Lectures, *The Varieties of Religious Experience*, in which he described the "twice born character" of the religious melancholic as the quality of an "incompletely unified moral and intellectual constitution," a kind of spiritual and psychic "heterogeneity."[26] While James left the cause of such heterogeneity unexplored (he noted that while "heterogeneous personality has been explained as the result of inheritance," such explanation "needs corroboration"), Howells and Du Bois concertedly mapped discourses of spiritual heterogeneity—of being *beside* the self, at once *in* and *out*—onto the "problem" of being black in America.

But whereas Du Bois would insist on the historicity of double consciousness, recasting it as "second sight" or a form of black prophetic vision, Rhoda's sense of multiple selves—of being beside herself as a force of her social and legal otherness—leads less to the collective work of spiritual striving than to an image of grotesque religious expressivity. Indeed, as a remedy for her dis-integrated self, Rhoda attempts—quite ironically, from the narrator's perspective—to integrate herself into an African American religious community that the novella as a whole insists is utterly foreign. Stepping into an evening meeting at a church on Charles Street (possibly modeled after the Charles Street African Methodist Episcopal Church, which Howells would have known as the largest black church in Boston), Rhoda aims "to surround herself with the blackness from which she had sprung, and to reconcile herself to it, by realizing and owning it with every sense." In the scene that follows, Rhoda's desire to *own* her blackness marks the coloniality of "realizing" black religion only as a site of radical alterity:

> The prevailing blackness gave back the light here and there in the glint of a bald head, or from a patch of white wool, or the cast of a rolling eye. Inside the bonnets of the elder women, and under the gay hats of the young girls, it was mostly lost in a characterless dark; but nearer by, Rhoda distinguished faces, sad, repulsive visages of a frog-like ugliness added to the repulsive black in all its shades, from the unalloyed brilliancy of the pure negro type to the pallid yellow of the quadroon, and these mixed bloods were more odious to her than the others, because she felt herself more akin to them; but they were all abhorrent. Some of the elder people made fervent responses to thoughts and sentiments in the lecture as if it had been a sermon. "That is so!" they said. "Bless the Lord, that's the truth!" and, "Glory to God!" One old woman, who sat in the same line of pews with Rhoda, opened her mouth like a catfish, to emit these pious ejaculations.[27]

This notorious passage first collapses, then proliferates difference. Like the preacher himself (described as a "thick, soft shadow" with "no discernible features"), the congregation for Rhoda has no character beyond its exteriorized, "prevailing" blackness. The darkness of the church is, at the level of narrative description, indistinguishable from the darkness of its congregates; Rhoda cannot tell blackness from blackness, shadow from background. And while she soon begins to distinguish various racial "types" amid the crowd, they remain collectively "abhorrent," a collectivity whose challenge to Rhoda's sense of a bounded self is the central source of her repulsion. While Rhoda "distinguishes," in other words, the congregants do not. Confusing the lecture with a sermon, the congregation's emotional response exceeds the bounds of white Protestant interiority; this excess of spirit is coded as a distinctly physical exhalation, a spilling over the threshold of an open mouth, the threshold of body and spirit, the threshold of human and (racialized) animal.

Without depicting ecstasy as such, this scene nevertheless teases at the ecstatic dissolution of singular subjects, marking that dissolution as radically, racially other. Such otherness emerges in part through the merging of putatively separate sense registers, a synesthetic interpenetration that replays interracial sociality at the level of taste, smell, and touch: "The night was warm, and as the church filled, the musky exhalations of their bodies thickened the air, and made the girl faint; it seemed to her that she began to taste the odor; and these poor people, whom their Creator had made so hideous by the standards of all his other creatures, roused a cruel loathing in her, which expressed itself in a frantic refusal of their claim upon her."[28] Like the threshold Rhoda crosses by moving into the church, this passage associates the crossing of taste and smell with religious excess and exhalation—a sense of spiritual and corporeal plurality that Rhoda (as the dis-integrated hysteric) frantically refuses. Erica Fretwell argues that the synesthetic force of this passage is one of violent differentiation: "By way of paradox," Fretwell notes, "sensory assimilation affirms the unassimilable bodily difference that black religious life inculcates."[29] Similarly, the breakdown of social, sensory, and generic boundaries depicted in this scene inculcates a sense of black religion as something essentially other to the unmarked life of white Protestant secularism. With its amalgamation of taste and smell, lecture and sermon, Rhoda's experience in the church offers a challenge to the social and aesthetic boundaries of Anglo-Protestant secularism even as it reinforces the epistemological priority of those boundaries at every turn. In response to the overwhelming "sensory assimilation," Rhoda shuts her eyes, disaggregating sight from sound so that she might return to her properly segregated senses, and thus to a self untroubled by what it ought to have retained (at the end of the service, "she started with a shiver, as if from a hypnotic trance"). Through Rhoda's refusal, this scene constructs the unbounded excess of black religious practice against whiteness's capacity to go untouched—to preserve the ostensible boundaries of self against the "choreosonic" happening of ecstatic communion.[30]

In such moments, "realizing" blackness can only mean a kind of break from the real. Here we see quite clearly what Kenneth Warren has described as a foundational tension in Howells's efforts to square his political commitment to black equality with his commitment to maintaining realism's generic boundaries—and, I would add, with the novella's commitment to secularism as a largely silent but normative frame. As Warren suggests, realism's effort to differentiate itself from competing literary modes like sentimentalism, on the one hand, and from straightforward philanthropy, on the other, largely constricted its radical imaginary.[31] The failure to distinguish that marks this scene, in other words, is presented as both an aesthetic *and* a political problem, one that signals the breakdown that might come from what *An Imperative Duty* depicts as an outsized, excessive, or imperious commitment to the demands of community. Thus if *An Imperative Duty* "properly explodes the fiction of race identity and the 'one drop' belief," it does so by insisting (via Olney) that Rhoda understand her emergent commitment to the project of black uplift in its proper proportions.[32] "You won't find me unreasonable," Olney assures Rhoda, by way of convincing her to marry him instead of traveling to the South as part of a vaguely conceived plan to educate her people. "All that I shall ask of you are the fifteen-sixteenths or so of you that belong to my race by heredity; and I will cheerfully consent to your giving our colored connections their one-sixteenth." Several years later, in an interview with Stephen Crane, Howells would argue, "The novel, in its *real* meaning, adjusts the proportions. It preserves the balances."[33] As Warren and a number of other critics point out, this commitment to "proportions" may have helped realism secure itself from the specter of sentimental (and radical) excess, but it also significantly limited the horizon of possibility for black political mobilization and affiliation within the world of Howellsian realism.[34]

It is perhaps not at all surprising, then, that the secular imaginary of *An Imperative Duty* links what realism identifies as a failure of proportions—aesthetic, affective, and otherwise—to the putative excess and physicality of black religious expression. Given the emergence of "religion" in this period as a descriptive and comparative apparatus that governed "good" and "bad" practices in proportion to their approximation of Anglo-Protestant interiority, it makes sense that the idiom of black religious expressivity would stand in for Rhoda's excessive and outsized sense of duty to an occult, unhealthy, or simply backward understanding of "race." Yet the very metonymic slippage between religious and racial feeling—as co-constituting modes of affective excess that *An Imperative Duty* seeks to regulate in the name of progress—signals the stakes of understanding the novel as part of a larger scene of post-Reconstruction secularism in which it is embedded. Those stakes are significant, and not least because the scene of enthusiastic or embodied religion as a grotesque, archaic, and manifestly racialized performance is one that realism will play out over and over, to widely varying ends. By understanding both essentialist accounts of race and "bad" performances of religion through the hermeneutics of hysteria, *An Imperative Duty* suggests that both might be effectively leeched from the body politic, producing an essentially healthy, modern, or "realist" relation to a rapidly changing American scene.

Rhoda's visit to the black church surely could have been imagined otherwise; indeed, less than a year later, Frances Harper would imagine it otherwise in *Iola Leroy; or, Shadows Uplifted* (1892), in which the church meeting serves a crucial role in reuniting families forcibly separated under slavery. While in Harper's novel (as we'll see), the church meeting enables the re-membering of familial ties, *An Imperative Duty* depicts the church as a deeply unwholesome environs, a scene of "characterless dark" and "thickened air." Despite Howells's effort to distinguish literary realism from competing literary modes, such descriptions mark the continuity between *An Imperative Duty* and the work of urban reform tracts like Jacob Riis's *How the Other Lives* (1890), which connected religious difference to the biological specter of contagious air (as, for example, in Riis's depiction of the cramped and disease-ridden tenements of "Jewtown").[35] In other words, Howells's scene helps underline the reification of racial difference in and through the imagining of religious difference while testifying to what Saidiya Hartman terms the ongoing "paramount importance of the 'biological' . . . in the (con)scripting of blackness," where "the 'biological' stands in for needs and desires, judgments about the health, morality, and prosperity of the population, and the designated duties of the state—protection, withholding, interference."[36] In *An Imperative Duty*, Olney figures the protection and interference of a good-intentioned white male patriarchy, with its claims to ultimate reason ("you won't find me unreasonable") pitched against the exuberant and feminized irrationality of black religion. Yet even as it underscores the church as the site of excess or unwholesome feeling—the height of amalgamated sense and entangled subjects that the novella will work homeopathically to disentangle—*An Imperative Duty* treats it as a critically important narrative pivot, the scene of Rhoda's potential racial conversion. If the novella ultimately rejects this conversion in the name of a less occult form of accounting for racial difference, it nevertheless depends on the church's potential dissolution of boundaries—its (unrealized) possibility for radical sensory and social *communion*, its racialized positioning beyond the bounds of disembodied reason—to secure realism's own position of epistemological authority. The church scene, in other words, marks the height of the novella's secular comportment.

It also echoes in profound ways popular depictions of "primitive" or "innate" black religiosity circulating in newspapers, bourgeois magazines like *Putnam's* and *Harper's*, an emergent sociology of religion, and realist narratives of urban vice. As Curtis Evans details, the post-Reconstruction era saw a transformation from romantic conceptions of black religious feeling (often voiced by abolitionists) to largely negative, often grotesque accounts of black religious difference: "Feelings became unruly emotions, and innate religiosity now meant the possession of a primitive or culturally inferior form of bodily religious expression."[37] Even as this period saw the rapid growth of independent black denominations and religious organizations, Christian and otherwise—among them, the African Methodist Episcopal Church, with a sophisticated missionary apparatus and, by 1884, a membership of nearly four hundred thousand—popular tracts like James W. Buel's *Mysteries and Miseries of*

America's Great Cities (1882) peddled intimate views of black "religious fanaticism," offering readers a glimpse into the religious life of "that race that has so much kinship with the primeval sons of man."[38] Buel's description of his visit to a revival meeting in New Orleans, for example, deploys many of the same tropes on which *An Imperative Duty* relies, depicting a congregation in "hysterics," brought to "paroxysmal exaltation" and "seized" by a "spiritual afflatus" that radically dissolves the thresholds of age, sex, and (at least potentially) race: "Men and women threw themselves recklessly into the arms of each other without regard for age or sex, while others dropped upon their knees and set up the wildest harangues for divine mercy, screaming out such exclamations as: 'I see de Lawd.' . . . Such confusion I never before saw, and for a time there was some doubt in my mind concerning the propriety of longer remaining and taking chances of being smothered in the embrace of one or more female corporations, or drowned in the profuseness of perspiration that streamed from excited bodies."[39] As in *An Imperative Duty*, here the specter of amalgamation haunts the scene of ecstatic communion, a scene that threatens to smother or drown the white observer (and, presumably, reader), throwing his own bodily integrity into temporary doubt. Like Howells's novella, *Mysteries and Miseries* travels in a fundamentally secular circuit, mapping a moral matrix of the United States and juxtaposing "negro life and its superstitions" in New Orleans with the "multitude of gods" among Chinese immigrants in San Francisco and practices of polygamy and "blood-atonement" among Mormon sects in Salt Lake City. Tracts such as Buel's conceived religious and racial difference in strikingly scenic terms while offering titillated readers a "wholesome revelation" of sin.[40]

By reifying the "colored church" as a site of radical alterity, *An Imperative Duty* similarly exemplifies the alignment of secularism with racialization, in spite (or because) of the novel's effort to attend to the moral complexities of color as a lived reality under Jim Crow. (The contempt the novella reserves for Mrs. Meredith's moral absolutism is instructive here; Howells's narrator notes, "That right affected her as a positive body of color, sharply distinguished from wrong, and not shading into and out of it by gradations of tint, as we find it doing in reality.") Black feminist critiques of *An Imperative Duty*—from Anna Julia Cooper's *A Voice from the South* (1892) to Harper's *Iola Leroy*—have demonstrated the failure of vision at work in Howells's own moral chiaroscuro, and I turn next to those critiques to help characterize realism as contested ground for the racialized aesthetics of proportion. In very different modes, Cooper and Harper silently but forcefully push back against the racializing force of the novella's secularism. Cooper's biting rejection, as we'll see, calls out the distortions at work in Howells's image of the black church, reinvesting it with the class distinctions that Howells obscures while insisting on a critical role for religious "enthusiasm" in the reverberating work of reform. Offering a fictional revision of Howells's secular imaginary, *Iola Leroy* replaces an occult version of racial difference (located "in the blood") not with the symptomology of the modern neurasthenic but with a spiritual epistemology that privileges a collective performance of rejoicing.

As both Cooper's and Harper's writings attest, the intimacy between secularism and white supremacy was one to which African American writers in the post-Reconstruction era were closely attuned and against which they enacted what we might call (after Hortense Spillers) an insurgent relation to the normative work of Anglo-Protestant secularism.[41] Perhaps nowhere is this insurgent relation more legible than in Du Bois's account of double consciousness as a "peculiar wrenching of the soul," a spiritual condition that simultaneously brings the normative work of secularism into relief and refuses the terms of its dominance. While scholars have long grappled with the role of religion in *The Souls of Black Folk*—and with what Eddie Glaude accurately describes as a profound "structure of ambivalence" toward religion in Du Bois's body of writing—my effort will be to read *Souls* as an emergent theory of secularism.[42] For example, in "Of the Coming of John" (Du Bois's first published piece of fiction and his most strikingly realist narrative), Du Bois grapples with the affective force of the black church even as he marks the limits of its political imaginary; at the same time, he transforms the lynching of the (secular) black intellectual into a multilayered resurrection, drawing on the power of theological precedent and the spiritual meaning of crucified flesh to transform the historical meaning of antiblack violence. In this sense, I read *Souls* as both strikingly aware of the ongoing violence of Anglo-Protestantism as it names and circumscribes religious and racial otherness, and simultaneously attentive to the power of religious idioms—and especially biblical antetypes—to reconfigure that violence into spiritual power.

Finally, by way of closing, I turn to Du Bois's 1920 essay "The Souls of White Folk," perhaps the post-Reconstruction era's most strident critique of the relation between white Christianity, white supremacy, and global imperialism. Describing a "new religion of whiteness" as central to the West's various forms of conquest, Du Bois depicts race not as a secular category of modernity but as its theological underpinning. By repeatedly framing white supremacist imperial projects through scriptural language, Du Bois refuses the alignment of modernity and secularization while theorizing Anglo-Protestantism's governing of "true religion" as it has been enmeshed in imperialism and racialization. In both *The Souls of Black Folk* and "The Souls of White Folk," Du Bois performs Scripture as a radical profaning of "modernity," the regime of Anglo-Protestant secularism, and enacts a creative reuse of the materials of white supremacist theology. Such performances aim to unmask the coloniality of the West's secular progress narratives, while shifting the terms by which the "real" is understood through an immanent white supremacist frame.

How to Do Things with Fanatics

Recovered by scholars as a landmark text of post-Reconstruction black feminism, Anna Julia Cooper's *A Voice from the South* (1892) offers a surprisingly sustained meditation on the uses of religious exuberance. Originally delivered as a lecture to a convocation of Episcopal clergy in 1886, the volume's first chapter, "Womanhood: A Vital Element in the Regeneration and Progress of a Race," reads in part as a scathing commentary on the relevance of the Church for black souls and solidarity. Noting that Methodist, Baptist, and Congregationalist home missions had enjoyed significant success and surging numbers in the South following the war, Cooper decries the lagging Episcopalian effort: "Thinking colored men almost uniformly admit that the Protestant Episcopal Church with its quiet, chaste dignity and decorous solemnity, its instructive and elevating ritual, its bright chanting and joyous hymning, is eminently fitted to correct the peculiar faults of worship—the rank exuberance and often ludicrous demonstrativeness of their people.

Yet, strange to say, the Church, claiming to be missionary and Catholic, urging that schism is sin and denominationalism inexcusable, has made in all these years almost no inroads upon this semi-civilized regionalism."[43] Cooper's indictment of the Episcopal Church has proved less interesting to scholars than her broader feminist project, perhaps in part because its terms seem to reinforce what some readers have identified as Cooper's class-specific framing of black progress.[44] Indeed, Cooper's emphasis on the "chaste dignity" and "decorous solemnity" of Episcopal ritual—held up against the "rank exuberance" and "semi-civilized regionalism" of Southern revivalism—seems to reproduce a class hierarchy within worship styles even as it charges the Church with its own particular blend of racial and regional bias. Yet the vectors of Cooper's critique are not always immediately self-evident; as Vivian May has pointed out, *A Voice from the South* is itself catholic, full of fragments of other voices that Cooper inhabits ironically to point up their logical insufficiency, "strategically voicing her *readers'* beliefs in complementary gender and racial roles [for example] only to show them wanting."[45] To recognize such virtuosic ventriloquisms, with May, is to read Cooper's voice as continually on the move, inhabiting (as in the above passage) the anthropological accents of the missionary charged with making "inroads," only to mobilize the very same "semi-civilized" religion a few paragraphs later:

> However, Macaulay somewhere criticizes the Church of England as not knowing how to use fanatics, and declares that had Ignatius Loyola been in the Anglican instead of the Roman communion, the Jesuits would have been schismatics instead of Catholics; and if the religious awakenings of the Wesleys had been in Rome, she would have shaven their heads, tied ropes around their waists, and sent them out under her own banner and blessing. Whether this be true or not, there is certainly a vast amount of force potential for Negro evangelization rendered latent, or worse, antagonistic by the halting, uncertain, I had almost said, *trimming* policy of the Church in the South. . . . It is mortifying, I know, to benevolent wisdom, after having spent itself in the execution of well conned theories for the ideal development of a particular work, to hear perhaps the weakest and humblest element of that work asking "what doest thou?"[46]

Here Cooper turns the "mortifying" labor of the Church (the disciplining of bodies through restrained modes of worship) against itself, using the cultural weight of Macaulay's *History of England* to upend the hierarchical logic of religious and racial schism in the American present. Cooper's critique both suggests and employs a pragmatic approach to fanaticism. Invoking the practice of mortification, and thus subtly effacing the major historical and theological rifts that separated Loyola's Jesuits from her own Episcopalians, Cooper's "what doest thou?" voices an ecstatic break (or, in keeping with her lacerative language, enacts a cut) in the "well conned" idealities of white patriarchal Church authority.[47] Cooper's pun on "conned," connecting rote, learned behaviors to broader structures of hegemony, if not outright deceit, makes clear the theoretical thrust of her argument. It is not by "ludicrous demonstrativeness" but by insidious "*trimming*," Cooper seems to suggest, that religious (and indeed secular) ideology works. Thus what reads initially as a dismissal of "rank exuberance" quickly shades into a battle cry for more pluralistic forms of religious practice and evangelization.

Throughout *A Voice from the South*, Cooper returns to and reshapes the utility of "fanatics" for black feminist praxis, often inhabiting the discourses of fanaticism and enthusiasm ironically to mark the limits of the white liberal imaginary. In so doing, she reverses the racializing terms through which writers like Howells—far from exceptional in this period—attached "rank exuberance" and contagious feeling to the forms of black worship. In a chapter titled "Woman versus the Indian" (after Anna Shaw's February 1891 address to the National Women's Council), Cooper condemns the exclusionary racial politics of figures like Shaw and Susan B. Anthony, in part by describing the centrifugal force of their feminism as itself a variety of enthusiasm:

> The American woman of to-day not only gives tone directly to her immediate world, but her tiniest pulsation ripples out and out, down and down, till the outermost circles and deepest layers of society feel the vibrations. It is pre-eminently an age of organizations. The "leading woman," the preacher, the reformer, the organizer "enthuses" her lieutenants and captains, the literary women, the thinking women, the strong, earnest, irresistible women; these in turn touch their myriads of church clubs, social

clubs, pleasure clubs, and charitable clubs. . . . And so woman's lightest whisper is heard as in Dionysius's ear, by quick relays and endless reproductions, through every recess and cavern as well as on every hilltop and mountain in her vast domain.[48]

Several years in advance of French sociologists Gustave Le Bon and Émile Durkheim, who by 1892 were just beginning to describe the dynamics of collectively amplified feeling, Cooper offered an account of enthusiasm as the material of social reproduction in the age of organizations. Relaying across every layer of society, here was (at least potentially) a different "cult of true womanhood": one based not in rigidly delineated gender roles and class-specific codes of respectability but rather in the "irresistible" force of collective feeling and enthusiastic relation.[49] Yet Cooper underscores the failure of this reverberating, emancipatory force to recognize the claims of black women, and indicts white feminist organizations for their wholesale capitulation to Southern white women in their desire to preserve the "talisman" of caste. In taking up the language of enthusiasm here, Cooper decries white feminism as a hollow performance of radical democracy that relied on the ongoing disenfranchisement of African Americans and Native Americans. Insisting that the "woman's mission" was to "plead with her country to cease to do evil and pay its honest debts," Cooper mobilizes the power of her own voice to sound out a reverberative ethics of antiracist praxis. In the final chapter of *A Voice from the South*, "A Gain from a Belief," Cooper outlines the religious underpinnings of such (potentially) good vibrations: "It is the enthusiasms, the faiths of the world that have heated the crucibles in which were formed its reformations and its impulses toward higher growth."[50] Articulating a form of religious pragmatism a decade before James's Gifford Lectures, Cooper continues, "And I do not mean by faith the holding of correct views and unimpeachable opinions on mooted questions, merely; . . . truth must be infinite, and incapable as infinite space, of being encompassed and confined by one age or nation, sect or country—much less by one little creature's finite brain."[51] Reclaiming the effervescent force of enthusiasm while resisting white feminism's monopoly on moral truth, Cooper gives voice to a radically inclusive version of feminist agitation.

Forging an alliance of the dispossessed—including women, African Americans, Native Americans, and the poor—Cooper's feminism found its ostensible literary complement in realism's rhetorical elevations of the everyday. In "The Negro as Presented in American Literature," Cooper articulates the adhesive force of realist aesthetics, insisting, "It is only through the unclouded perception of our tiny 'part' that we can come to harmonize with the 'stupendous whole,' and in order to [do] this our sympathies must be finely attuned and quick to vibrate under the touch of the commonplace and the vulgar no less than at the hand of the elegant and refined. Nothing natural can be wholly unworthy."[52] Rejecting the "preachers" of American literature, Cooper casts her lot with "those who simply paint what they see," and thus tentatively with the realism championed by William Dean Howells.[53] Valorizing the "commonplace and the vulgar," Cooper's aesthetic vision resonates both with George Eliot's account of realism as the "faithful representing of commonplace things" and Howells's frequent call, in his "Editor's Study" columns, for a turn in American literature toward "the simple, the natural, and the honest."[54] It is this shared commitment to the aesthetic value of the commonplace, as well as a challenge to the parameters of the "common," that underlies Cooper's forceful critique of *An Imperative Duty*:

> Among our artists for art's sweet sake, Mr. Howells has recently tried his hand also at painting the Negro, attempting merely a side light in half tones, on his life and manners; and I think the unanimous verdict of the subject is that, in this single department at least, Mr. Howells does not know what he is talking about. And yet I do not think we should quarrel with *An Imperative Duty* because it lacks the earnestness and bias of a special pleader. Mr. Howells merely meant to press the button and give one picture from American life involving racial complications. The kodak does no more; it cannot preach sermons or solve problems.[55]

Reconfiguring late nineteenth-century discourses that linked realism to photography—and that anxiously debated what kind of labor was required to press a button (a question I return to in chapter 4)—Cooper takes aim at Howells and other white realists for their apparent ease in reproducing the Negro from a secure social distance. Opposing the "side light in half tones" to the ostensibly passive work of the "kodak,"

Cooper gives the lie to realism as a process of passive recording even as she insists on a more accurate portrait of the gradations of black life and black experience. "We meet it at every turn," she continues, "this obtrusive and offensive vulgarity, this gratuitous sizing up of the Negro and conclusively writing down his equation, sometimes even among his ardent friends and bravest defenders."[56] Cooper similarly rejects the ideology of proportions that underlies Howells's account of his heroine's "occult" attraction to her race, "so that in some occult and dreadful way one, only one-sixteenth related and totally foreign by education and environment, [she] can still feel that one-sixteenth race calling her more loudly than the fifteen-sixteenths."[57] Resisting this account of race located mysteriously and alluringly in the blood, Cooper demands at the end of the essay a kind of radical disenchantment from racist theologies, so that "we can with clear eye weigh what is written and estimate what is done and ourselves paint what is true."[58]

Here we see realism's aesthetics of proportion as radically contested ground. As with her critique of the Episcopal Church—which doubles down on the history of Anglo-Protestantism in order to condemn its failures of vision—Cooper does not so much oppose the terms of realism's clear-eyed monopoly on the truth as much as she one-ups them, relocating the authority of proportionate representation among the artistically and socially marginalized. As Warren points out, there were limits to Cooper's inclusiveness, and Cooper and Howells were to a certain extent "in agreement" in insisting on Victorian codes of gentility against the upheavals of social unrest and class conflict in the 1880s and '90s.[59] But as we've seen, the class politics of *A Voice from the South* are changeable, and Cooper's pragmatic discourse on enthusiasm embeds—if it does not distinctly champion—a call for collective organization across the lines of race, class, gender, and denomination. It perhaps makes more sense, then, to think of Cooper and Howells as yoked in their parallel but opposing approaches to fanaticism. Directly taking up Howells's depiction of black religious expression in *An Imperative Duty*, Cooper famously takes issue with its closed-eyed verisimilitude:

> I respectfully submit that there is hardly a colored church in any considerable city in this country, which could be said in any sense to represent *the best colored society*, in which Rhoda Aldgate could not have seen,

when she opened her eyes, persons as quietly and as becomingly dressed, as cultivated in tone and as refined in manner, as herself; persons, too, as sensitive to rough contact and as horribly alive as she could be . . . to the galling distinctions in this country which insist on *levelling down* all individuals more or less related to the Africans.[60]

Working from within the terms of Howellsian realism and its call for "an absolute and clear sense of proportion," Cooper diagnoses a crucial distortion at work in the novel: its depiction of black religion as a monolith, and its lack of attention to (or even awareness of) the full spectrum of religious experience and affiliation. Though Cooper's resistance to racial leveling seems to necessarily insist on other, class-based forms of social hierarchy, it also rejects the logic of representation governing black religion as a singularly exotic form of alterity. "In not a few such colored churches," Cooper continues, "would [Rhoda] have found young women of aspiration and intellectual activity with whom she could affiliate without nausea, and from whom she could learn a good many lessons . . . she would have found no trouble in reaching a heart which could enter into all the agony of her own trial and bitter grief."[61] Importantly, Cooper focuses her critique not on Howells's "morbidly sensitive" heroine—she praises his psychological sketch—but on the novel's depiction of the black church as unkempt and unrefined. Upping the ante of racial sensitivity, Cooper's corrective insists that an even more sensitive realism—a more perceptive literary mechanism—is required for true understanding.

From within Howells's own discourse of realism, then, Cooper stages an immanent critique of secularism's casting of black religion in monolithic terms. She also refuses Howells's logic of proportionate feeling, insisting on "high strung" sensitivity as the very mode of political insurgency:

> Everything to this race is new and strange and inspiring. There is a quickening of its pulses and a glowing of its self-consciousness. . . . Something like this, it strikes me, is the enthusiasm which stirs the genius of young Africa in America; and the memory of past oppression and the fact of present attempted repression only serve to gather momentum for its irrepressible powers. Then again, a race in such a stage of growth is peculiarly

sensitive to impressions. Not the photographer's sensitized plate is more delicately impressionable to outer influences than is this high strung people here on the threshold of a career.[62]

Invoking a more sensitive material of reproduction—and thus a more accurate realism—*A Voice from the South* asserts the genius of enthusiasm in the context of repressive historical and material conditions. Here again Cooper's ventriloquisms are demanding: her "peculiarly sensitive" prose turns racist constructions of black emotionalism against themselves in the service of gathering collective political momentum. Reclaiming photographic realism—the ability to give American society back to itself, in all its detail—for her "developing" race, Cooper seizes on both the authority and the ambiguity of the photograph's impression, its play of light and shadow, to "unfix" the racist terms of black representation. To be sensitive, in other words, as Cooper suggests, is to be on the threshold.

Whereas Cooper offers an explicit critique of *An Imperative Duty*, Frances Harper's novel *Iola Leroy; or, Shadows Uplifted* (published the same year as *A Voice from the South*) delivers a more subtle but no less forceful fictional rejoinder. While in no way merely a response to Howells's novella, *Iola Leroy* (as readers have noted) strikingly revisits some of the contours of its narrative, as both novels return to and revise the popular imagining of the tragic mulatta.[63] Iola discovers belatedly that her light-skinned mother was enslaved by her father, and (much like Rhoda Aldgate) is courted by a liberal-minded white doctor who tries to temper her commitment to black solidarity and uplift. Like Olney, Harper's Dr. Gresham challenges the one-drop rule even as he fails to acknowledge the possibilities of cross-generational and cross-class kinship, instead relying on phenotypical sameness as the measure of social equity: "Iola, I see no use in your persisting that you are colored when your eyes are as blue and complexion as white as mine."[64] While Gresham insists that "the color line is slowly fading out in our public institutions," Iola coaxes his admission that (among other institutions) the white church and women's reform movements operate as crucial sites of its enforcement:

> The Church is naturally conservative. It preserves old truths, even if it is somewhat slow in embracing new ideas. It has its social as well as its spiritual side. Society is woman's realm. The majority of church members are women, who are said to be the aristocratic element of our country. I fear that one of the last strongholds of this racial prejudice will be found beneath the shadow of some of our churches. I think, on account of this social question, that large bodies of Christian temperance women and other reformers, in trying to reach the colored people even for their own good, will be quicker to form separate associations than our National Grand Army, whose ranks are open to black and white, liberals and conservatives, saints and agnostics.[65]

As did Cooper, Harper's novel here offers a forceful critique of white Christianity and its women-led reform movements, calling attention to their exclusionary and patronizing racial politics. By placing this critique in the mouth of Dr. Gresham, the novel's central figure for white progressive politics, Harper endows it with significant authority for white readers; at the same time, this passage (and the novel more broadly) makes clear the failure of white progressives insofar as they sought to segregate the "social question" from the political work of achieving black equality.[66] Like Olney, Dr. Gresham's solution to Jim Crow social interdictions is a naïvely privatized one: "No one has a right to interfere with our marriage if we do not infringe on the rights of others."[67] Having gleaned the history of Iola's parents and others like them, careful readers of *Iola Leroy* quickly recognize the fallacy in Gresham's class-based construction of inviolable rights. Iola responds simply: "I feel that our paths must diverge. My life-work is planned. I intend spending my future among the colored people of the South."[68]

Unlike Howells's Rhoda Aldgate, Iola fulfills her promise, refusing both Gresham and the post-Reconstruction sectional (re)marriage plot that structures novels like *An Imperative Duty*. While critics have cited this as Harper's signal revision of Howells, *Iola Leroy* also importantly refuses the secularist terms through which *An Imperative Duty* imagines black religious alterity, and (like many in the black radical tradition) challenges white Christianity's monopoly on "true religion." That challenge emerges in various forms across the novel—and often through dialogue, such as that between Iola's uncle Robert Johnson, who escapes a North Carolina plantation to enlist in the Union army, and Captain Sybil, his white officer:

> "I never did take much stock in white folks' religion."
> "Why, Robert, I'm afraid you are something of an infidel."
> "No, Captain, I believe in the real, genuine religion. I ain't got much myself, but I respect them that have."[69]

Sybil's use of "infidel" to describe Johnson's mode of religious dissent is instructive; though its primary meaning in this passage is disbeliever, it also names a historically racialized form of religious and political subversion.[70] By rejecting this term, Johnson refuses the legacy of religious coercion it signifies, calling attention to the gap between "white folks' religion" and "the real, genuine religion." More than simply a critique of white Christianity, this move contests the hegemonic delineation of "genuine" and "false" religion (or enthusiasm) as it has historically attached to—and helped imagine—bodies deemed subversive to the prevailing order of the Anglo-Protestant establishment.[71]

Perhaps Harper's most forceful revision of the secular imaginary of *An Imperative Duty* comes when Iola and Robert, reunited after the war, travel to a prayer meeting. While Rhoda's dis-integrating experience in the church gives rise to disgust and refused kinship—affirming an "unassimilable" difference imagined in and through black religious expression—the scene of the church meeting in *Iola Leroy* offers a striking contrast, reunifying the "remnants of broken families" separated by the slave trade.[72] In this context, "testifying" becomes a way to narrate the trauma of forced separation, and the physicality and aurality of religious expression articulate the shared material and spiritual experience of being "torn" away: "Some of [the] hearers moaned, others rocked to and fro, as thought of similar scenes in their own lives arose before them."[73] Unlike the "musky exhalations" of Howells's church, here the performance of moaning is what Cornel West describes as the "ur-text" of black cultural expression, what Fred Moten deems an "augmentation of mourning," or what Ashon Crawley recognizes as "*black pneuma*"—a wordless capacity (in Crawley's words) "to enunciate life, life that is exorbitant, capacious, and fundamentally, social, though it is also life that is structured through and engulfed by brutal violence."[74]

That fundamentally social enunciation emerges in *Iola Leroy* as a collective knowledge of rejoicing, a literal and figurative re-sounding of joy in the face of violence, where performative repetition figures the general stake in an antenormative practice of besideness: "It was a happy time. Mothers whose children had been torn from them in the days of slavery knew how to rejoice in her joy. The young people caught the infection of the general happiness and rejoiced with them that rejoiced. There were songs of rejoicing and shouts of praise. The undertone of sadness which had so often mingled with their songs gave place to strains of exultation; and tears of tender sympathy flowed from eyes which had often been blurred with anguish. The child of many prayers and tears was restored to his mother."[75] For Harper, rejoicing is both a knowledge practice and a performance practice, a site of aural and physical transfer rooted in the dynamic repetition across time and across bodies "caught" and (con)scripted by that repetition: a rejoicing *with* rejoicing.[76] The "infection of the general happiness" is a radical one, a contagion that disrupts both the legacy of pathologizing black religious expression and the racialized governance of public expression that is an attendant—perhaps central—part of that legacy. Exultation insists on the knowledge of what has been prohibited, sundered, torn away. And against the clear-eyed emotional accounting that Howells prescribed for the ecstasy of sensory and social communion, we find the double blur of anguish and sympathy: a blur that insists we count as "real" the infectious knowledge of rejoicing, even as it refuses to make the church meeting a subject of positivist inquiry, surveillance, and treatment.

In very different idioms, Cooper and Harper both speak back to what *An Imperative Duty* evinces as secularism's entanglements with whiteness and white supremacy: its regulation of what would count, in the post-Reconstruction era, as true religion (and, indeed, a "genuine" relationship to racial identity and identification). *An Imperative Duty* figures the answer to the social "problem" of race as one of private conscience (and consciousness); for Howells, sectional and psychic reintegration is a matter of emotional modulation, an affective comportment against which he frames the excess physicality of the black church. In their criticism and fiction, Cooper and Harper each testify not only to the radical insufficiency of this approach to Jim Crow segregation but to its complicity with a racist imaginary of black religion as touching the very limits of a realist aesthetic. Evincing a keen awareness of the primitivist construction of black religious feeling as "rank exuberance"—and the distinctly gendered rendering of its public expression—Cooper and Harper work not to dampen but to rewrite the terms of such exuberance, to demonstrate its performative reverberations in a culture devoted to the normative affects of secularism. Nominally committed to the politics of respectability, their texts enact the insurgency of enthusiasm and rejoicing from within the contested terrain of realist prose.[77] If Du Bois, as we'll see, evinces a much more ambivalent and strikingly gendered approach to what he described as the "frenzy of [the] Negro revival," his writings on religion—from *The Souls of Black Folk* to "The Souls of White Folk"—nevertheless align with Cooper and Harper in their immanent critique of Jim Crow secularism and its fanatical forms of racial violence.

Realism's Religious Typologies

A profound sense of the way in which modernity frames the complicity of rationality with the practice of white supremacist terror is the initial vehicle for writing this history of ambivalence.
—Paul Gilroy, *The Black Atlantic: Modernity and Double-Consciousness.*

As scholars have increasingly noted, Du Bois's approach to religious thought, practice, and expression was complex. Signaled by volumes like *W. E. B. Du Bois: American Prophet*, *The Souls of W. E. B. Du Bois*, and *Divine Discontent: The Religious Imagination of W. E. B. Du Bois*, critical interest in Du Bois as a religious thinker—or, at the very least, as someone who thinks "with" religion, strongly invested in what Josef Sorett terms a "spiritual grammar"—is resurgent across a range of disciplines.[78] Many critics point to the deep contradictions adhering in Du Bois's sense of religious affiliation and alienation. As Manning Marable recognizes in an important essay on "Du Bois's Black Faith," Du Bois was "simultaneously an agnostic and an Anglican, a staunch critic of religious dogma and a passionate convert to the black version of Christianity."[79]

Such contradictions have perplexed and challenged critics with good reason. Du Bois's descriptions of black religious expression in the South, for example, often seem "to reproduce the same exoticism that led the white middle-class reading public at the turn of the century to seek out works that revealed how 'the other half lived'" (in Shamoon Zamir's terms), even as his writings evince a career-long effort to probe the aesthetic and political possibilities of the Afro-Protestant imaginary, and to develop a set of "analytic tools" (per Eddie Glaude) for grappling with the historical conditions and multiform enactments of black Christianity.[80]

In this section and the one that follows, I ask whether we might productively shift the terms of this critical preoccupation with Du Bois's relation to religion, in part by exploring his writings as multifaceted theorizations of secularism in the long afterlife of slavery. "It is difficult to explain clearly the present critical stage of Negro religion," Du Bois noted in *The Souls of Black Folk*, laying out a "peculiar wrenching of the soul" that characterized the post-Reconstruction reaction against black equality and political enfranchisement.[81] Such an "Age of Reaction" was, for Du Bois, a kind of post-post-millenialism, a radical declension from emancipation's "literal Coming of the Lord," and one in which the social and political (if not spiritual) function of religion for black Americans was very much unclear. In the era of Jim Crow, Du Bois contended, religious life was itself a form of double consciousness: "Such a double life, with double thoughts, double duties, and double social classes, must give rise to double words and double ideals, and tempt the mind to pretense or to revolt, to hypocrisy or to radicalism."[82] Hypocrisy and radicalism became, for Du Bois, two equally problematic strains or "types" of religious thought, a classificatory schema that bears out the text's predominantly sociological approach to religion. Yet this classificatory enthusiasm in *Souls*—itself a secular comportment, a delineation of the horizons of religious possibility—lives alongside a performance of spiritual typology that refuses the conflation of secularism with historical progress. As we'll see, Du Bois's typological realism (with its play of sociological types and biblical antetypes) underlines the historical return of ritualistic antiblack violence—its status as a function of secular modernity and not its anti- or premodern holdover—even as it signals the ongoing work of spiritual and material liberation.

While Du Bois's writings on religion stretch from his earliest publications in 1883 to his 1962 introduction to a photographic series on storefront churches, much of the critical energy surrounding Du Bois as a religious observer has focused on *Souls*.[83] From the bars of the spiritual "Nobody Knows the Trouble I've Seen"—resonating through the volume's opening chapter "Of Our Spiritual Strivings" and its famous articulation of double consciousness—to Du Bois's infamous account of the "frenzy" of the black Southern revival in "Of the Faith of the Fathers," *Souls* at once resounds the lyric power of black religious expression and (at times) seems to reproduce the popular image of a regionally specific "primitive" religiosity out of sync with the times. It is this latter tendency that has understandably troubled readers like Cornel West, who indicts the Du Bois of *Souls* for his commitment to an Enlightenment worldview that admits no place for the purported "irrationalism" of the revival. Resonating with Howells's description of the black church in *An Imperative Duty*, Du Bois's account of his first experience with "the frenzy of the Negro revival" during his 1886–1887 tenure teaching in eastern Tennessee draws a similar (if less extreme) portrait of black religion as a scene of excessive emotional fervor:

> I was a country school-teacher then, fresh from the East, and had never seen a Southern Negro revival. To be sure, we in Berkshire were not perhaps as stiff and formal as they in Suffolk of olden time; yet we were very quiet and subdued, and I know not what would have happened those clear Sabbath mornings had some one punctuated the sermon with a wild scream, or interrupted the long prayer with a loud Amen! And so most striking to me, as I approached the village and the little plain church perched aloft, was the air of intense excitement that possessed that mass of black folk. A sort of suppressed terror hung in the air and seemed to seize us,—a pythian madness, a demoniac possession, that lent terrible reality to song and word. The black and massive form of the preacher swayed and quivered as the words crowded to his lips and flew at us in singular eloquence. The people moaned and fluttered, and then the gaunt-cheeked brown woman beside me suddenly leapt straight into the air and shrieked like a lost soul, while round about came wail and groan and outcry, and a scene of human passion such as I had never conceived before.[84]

Du Bois later reproduced this scene in his autobiography, with a striking revision; whereas in the 1903 version, the "suppressed terror ... seemed to seize *us*," many decades later, Du Bois would excise himself from this "mass" possession, replacing "us" with "them."[85] For many readers, this replacement perhaps only redoubles the sense of ethnographic detachment that infused Du Bois's original account. West contends, for example, that this "intriguing description reminds one of an anthropologist visiting some strange and exotic people whose rituals suggest not only the sublime but also the satanic," emphasizing the threat that overpowering possession may have posed to Du Bois's liberal sense of self-mastery.[86] Victor Wolfenstein similarly notes that such moments contain "more than a hint of exoticism," while Zamir underscores the sense of "Victorian unease" that permeates this scene.[87] While Du Bois marks the preacher's "singular eloquence," the scene of collective passion is arguably inaugurated by the feminine "shriek," in what is perhaps a latent gendered threat to Du Bois's project of splicing and curating sound across *Souls*; read otherwise, the shriek is an essential part of that project. In either case, there is almost certainly an echo of the Northern press's tendency to treat Southern revivals—and especially black church revivals—as highly consumable scenes of local color (a tendency I treat in more detail in chapter 2). Indeed, when William James sent his brother Henry a copy of *The Souls of Black Folk* with the instruction to "read Chapters VII to XI for local color, etc.," he may well have been describing this scene.[88]

Yet we can certainly read this moment differently. In *The Black Atlantic*, Paul Gilroy notably marks the "suppressed terror" of this scene as belonging not to Du Bois's Victorian anthropological comportment or even to the collective body of the congregation, but instead to a set of citational practices that underscore the centrality of slavery and racial terror in the movements and formations of modernity, part of the structure of what he calls the "slave sublime." As Gilroy argues, "It was in religious practices that the buried social memory of that original terror had been preserved."[89] This description of religious performance as cultural memory is compelling not least because it aligns with the temporal slippage in Du Bois's own account between the witnessed postbellum revival and the retrospective conjuring of slave religion: "Those who have not thus witnessed the frenzy of a Negro revival in the untouched backwoods of the South can but dimly realize the religious feelings of the slave," Du Bois contends in a collapse of historical time that signals the revival as literally reviving (and exorcising) chattel slavery as a residual structure of feeling. "Through frenzy," as religion scholar Anthony Pinn notes, "black bodies were transported beyond the confinements of the Veil and placed in communion with that which affirmed their humanity."⁹⁰ As Du Bois helps us recognize, to be "seized," "possessed," and "transported" in this context is to revisit the object status of kidnapped souls while radically remaking that status, transfiguring it into the manifestation of one's access to God.

Thus while for many readers Du Bois has seemed to consign the frenzy of ecstatic religion to the "backwoods" as a kind of antimodern holdover—echoing if not reproducing a white supremacist imaginary of black religious expression—I argue instead that Du Bois recognizes a crucially irruptive or *antemodern* capacity at stake in the frenzy, what Fred Moten has called an "incantatory . . . tumultuous derangement."⁹¹ I follow Moten, Gilroy, and Pinn in suggesting that Du Bois approaches possession as a site of deranging aesthetic practice: a form of collective resistance to what Gilroy marks as a profound complicity between modernity's constructions of rationality and white supremacist terror. If ambivalence, in other words, structures Du Bois's relationship to what he called the "supernatural joy . . . of Negro religion," such ambivalence offered (and continues to offer) significant aesthetic, critical, and political resources.⁹² Indeed, the very fact that critics have read the revival scene in such widely varying terms signals not simply Du Bois's spiritual ambivalence but also his insistence on an ambiguity or doubleness at the very heart of *ex-static* practice: a movement in and "out" of self, as well as between past and present, subject and object (secular colonial categories that preceded the color line but were increasingly mapped, in the post-Reconstruction era, via its violent configurations). Though Du Bois fully recognized "the political instability of the black church as a political instrument," he nevertheless figured the ecstatic as a crucial form of remembering the bodily and affective life of slavery through performance—remembering the "terrible reality" it reenacts and interrupts.⁹³ In so doing, he identified the dominant post-Reconstruction imaginary of a rational, singular, self-continuous white subject as a fantasy predicated on the psychic (and often physical) dis-membering of black communities while insisting on alternative arrangements of being and being beside.

In "Of the Faith of the Fathers," Du Bois marks out "two extreme types of ethical attitude" (submission or bitterness) between which "wavers the mass of the millions of Negroes, North and South."[94] Such wavering characterizes the affective life of secularism under Jim Crow—a seemingly insurmountable impasse.[95] The closing lines of the chapter, however, enact a kind of prophetic or speculative deliverance from that impasse: "Some day the Awakening will come, when the pent-up vigor of ten million souls shall sweep irresistibly toward the Goal, out of the Valley of the Shadow of Death, where all that makes life worth living—Liberty, Justice, and Right—is marked 'For White People Only.'"[96] Recasting the codified regime of segregation as a spiritual paradigm, Du Bois effectively refuses its terroristic logic, in part through the silent echo of Psalms ("I will fear no evil").[97] This structure of impasse and prophetic deliverance (a deliverance that is also, importantly, an echo and return) is also at the heart of Du Bois's first published piece of realist fiction, "Of the Coming of John." In the story, protagonist John Jones kills his white counterpart in an effort to protect his sister from rape and faces an angry lynch mob in the closing moments of the narrative. Educated far from his Georgia home, Du Bois depicts John as facing the double alienation of a black intellectual barred from cultural equality in the North (where he is evicted from a performance of Wagner's *Lohengrin*) and estranged by experience and education from his previous life in the South. In this sense, John embodies Du Bois's "type" of the bitter soul: "Feeling deeply and keenly the tendencies and opportunities of the age in which they live, their souls are bitter at the fate which drops the Veil between; and the very fact that this bitterness is natural and justifiable only serves to intensify it and make it more maddening."[98] As in his theorization of double consciousness, Du Bois's account of religious types significantly revises and deepens William James's notion of the "sick soul": "those persons who cannot so swiftly throw off the burden of the consciousness of evil, but are congenitally fated to suffer from its presence."[99]

John indeed suffers from a consciousness of evil that he cannot swiftly throw off—an evil congenital (as the narrative's double structure suggests) to the radically conjoined but unequal fates of white and black America. On his return to Georgia, a welcome meeting at the Baptist church signals the extent of John's affective estrangement from the community that enabled his education. His "cold" manner and "air of restraint" radically dampen the spirit of "enthusiasm," even as he calls on the denominationally diverse congregation to unify around shared projects of education and reform.[100] In response to John's unconscious belittling of the particularities of belief—in which he notably dismisses denominational rifts over baptism rites—a lay preacher ascends the pulpit to reunite the congregation:

> He seized the Bible with his rough, huge hands; twice he raised it inarticulate, and then fairly burst into words, with rude and awful eloquence. He quivered, swayed, and bent; then rose aloft in perfect majesty, till the people moaned and wept, wailed and shouted, and a wild shrieking arose from the corners where all the pent-up feeling of the hour gathered itself and rushed into the air. John never knew clearly what the old man said; he only felt himself held up to scorn and scathing denunciation for trampling on the true Religion, and he realized with amazement that all unknowingly he had put rough, rude hands on something this little world held sacred.[101]

Here John's apostasy manifests as an inability to recognize the meeting as first and foremost a gathering of feeling—the concentration of a "little world" around the force of collective catharsis. To the extent that we might read John Jones as something of a stand-in for Du Bois in his decades-earlier approach to the revival in east Tennessee, this scene both repeats and significantly transforms its predecessor. If it marks John (in Houston Baker's terms) as "too elevated to communicate with his own people—the 'ignorant and turbulent' black proletariat," it also effectively turns the narrative focus away from the exoticism of black religious expressivity and toward John himself, highlighting the failure of his critically detached speech (an "unknown tongue" for his listeners) to enact the social and political mobilization for which he calls.[102] This is a crucial revision of Du Bois's own earlier account of the "frenzy" of slave religion. As Eric Sundquist observes, John's "rebuke by a church elder is a powerful sketch of the quality of faith that Du Bois located in the slave generation," even as it "dramatizes the yawning cultural gap between two worlds" that Du Bois repeatedly attempted to bridge through his own commanding (if always provisional) performance of "secular prophecy."[103] Reading backward from "Of the Coming of John," the stakes of that prophecy become even more striking; there is nothing less on the line in Du Bois's spiritual rhetoric than the power or the failure of *Souls* itself to inspire an audience across multiple vectors of division.

If the lay preacher models the kind of powerful convocation of feeling to which *Souls* itself may have aspired, "Of the Coming of John" nevertheless insists on the political limits of such feeling; perceived as having an "almighty air and uppish ways," John is subject to the violent whims of the white judge and the ruling class for which he stands.[104] Once again, the affective life of secularism under Jim Crow looks strikingly like an impasse, and perhaps unlike "Of the Faith of the Fathers," "Of the Coming of John" insists on the uncertainty and irresolution that such an impasse entails. At least at first, John's impending death by lynch mob at the end the story looks less like a movement out of "the Valley of the Shadow of Death" and more like an apocalypse:

> He leaned back and smiled toward the sea, whence rose the strange melody, away from the dark shadows where lay the noise of horses galloping, galloping on. . . . Amid the trees in the dim morning twilight he watched their shadows dancing and heard their horses thundering toward him, until at last they came sweeping like a storm, and he saw in front that haggard white-haired man, whose eyes flashed with fury. Oh, how he pitied him,—pitied him,—and wondered if he had the coiling twisted rope. Then, as the storm burst round him, he rose slowly to his feet and turned his closed eyes toward the Sea.
>
> And the world whistled in his ears.[105]

To read this passage is to register the many revisions it enacts. John's pity for the haggard judge who seeks to avenge his son, for example, offers a stunning reversal of Du Bois's account of white indifference to his own son's funeral in "Of the Passing of the First Born": "They did not say much, those pale-faced hurrying men and women; they did not say much—they only glanced and said, 'N——rs!'"[106] As John's pity seems to suggest, mourning is not a zero-sum game, despite the radically different valorization of white and black lives under Jim Crow. Through such scenes, repetition and revision emerge as central to the very form of *Souls*, often enacting a rhythm of typological fulfillment and transformation. Observing the parallel between Du Bois's description of his son Burghardt's funeral and the scene of John Jones's lynching, for example, Susan Mizruchi argues that such a repetition stages Old and New Testament iterations of violent sacrifice: passover and crucifixion, each of which Du Bois linked to lynching as the post-Reconstruction period's most spectacular sacrificial rite.[107] With Christlike compassion for those that would annihilate him, John Jones is effectively born again in the scene of his death: a "sick soul" transformed into a martyr and thereby transforming the spiritual meaning of black death.

With its turn to the sea—a kind of nondenominational baptism—John's imminent lynching also importantly echoes the closing lines of the previous chapter in *Souls*, "Of Alexander Crummell," which memorializes the prominent Episcopalian priest, scholar, and missionary.[108] "Of Alexander Crummell" repeatedly invokes the ocean as both material presence and powerful trope, from Crummell's childhood (in which "the slave ship still groaned across the Atlantic"), to his migration to Liberia ("he turned at last home across the waters"), to his death.[109] In keeping with Crummell's legacy, Du Bois figures his death as an imaginative flight "across the Seas," a striking reversal of the Middle Passage's inaugurating deathliness: "He sat one morning gazing toward the sea. He smiled and said, 'The gate is rusty on the hinges.' That night at starrise a wind came moaning out of the west to blow the gate ajar, and then the soul I loved fled like a flame across the Seas, and in its seat sat Death."[110] Strikingly, this depiction of Crummell's death mobilizes an immensely popular postbellum religious idiom ("the gate ajar") in the service of both individual and collective black salvation, however ambivalently coded.[111] Adding the creak of the rusty gate and the moaning wind to the groaning of the slave ship, Du Bois marks the sea as generating—in its very sonic and semiotic turbulence—the spiritual significance of the post-Reconstruction black freedom struggle. If Death comes to replace Crummell in his flight—marking, for Du Bois, both the very real loss of an intellectual forebear and the broader sense of a spiritual nadir for black America—the meaning of that flight nevertheless remains resonant.

By reiterating the terms, if not the tone, of Crummell's flight, the ending of John's narrative fulfills Du Bois's promise (in "Of Our Spiritual Strivings") to "tell again in many ways" the spiritual comportment of black America. "Of the Coming of John" notably resurrects Crummell's narrative at the level of form *and* consolidates his status as the type of a tragic spiritual hero. In this sense, the text itself is typological, repeatedly returning to and reconfiguring spiritual types as well as biblical antetypes (including, as many have noted, John the Baptist, Queen Esther, and Christ). Throughout *Souls*, this performance of typological reenactment effectively roots the virulence of post-Reconstruction racism in deep time—signaling the ongoing historical returns of enslavement and liberation—while marking the future as a deliverance that must be actively and repeatedly achieved (not least in the grammatical rhythm and movement of the gerund, or that which is still "coming"). In "Of the Coming of John," the layering of reference (including, notably, to the apocalyptic vision of the Book of Revelation) works to transform the material and spiritual apocalypse of the post-Reconstruction era into a hermeneutics of deliverance and resurrection. And if the lynch mob's galloping horsemen signal the coming of a messianic Last Judgment, Du Bois's depiction of that mob as a rising and bursting storm anticipates the version of history that Walter Benjamin would later articulate: "This storm is what we call [secular] progress."[112]

A New Religion of Whiteness

Wave on wave, each with increasing virulence, is dashing this new religion of whiteness on the shores of our time.
—W. E. B. Du Bois, "The Souls of White Folk"

To feel one's "two-ness": this too is the affective life of Jim Crow secularism, itself a "peculiar sensation" or another form of being beside oneself, with others.[113] While *The Souls of Black Folk* often articulates secularism as a kind of impasse, many readers (past and present) have embraced it as a sacred text—one with the power to performatively enact the very speculative deliverance it describes.[114] By way of contrast, "The Souls of White Folk"—first published in the *Independent* in 1910 and revised for the 1920 publication of *Darkwater*—has been treated with decidedly less reverence, despite its extension and elaboration of the critique of secular modernity that emerges in *Souls*. When it has been read, "The Souls of White Folk" has been celebrated as a sophisticated account of the political economy of white supremacism and, as such, a crucial (if often overlooked) contribution to studies of antiblackness. But in this final section, I suggest that "The Souls of White Folk" is also and perhaps more fundamentally a theory of secularism, aiming as it does to unmask and desacralize a hegemonic secular Christianity underwriting imperial conquest in the age of world war. By 1920, Du Bois would position white supremacy as both the theological underpinning of Western imperialism and a heresy of global proportions, or what he describes as "conquest" in the guise of Christianity—"sugared with religion."[115]

In the essay, Du Bois outlines a "new religion of whiteness" as the foundation of colonial exploitation and global geopolitical conflict. Whiteness, in Du Bois's account, is a powerful and world-shaping set of beliefs and practices, but it is also a form of idolatry: a spectacularly false if massively influential faith in the reality of whiteness as a sign of godliness. Insisting on the modernity and ingenuity of whiteness as a tool of subjugation, Du Bois constructs Western modernity itself as an affective (and indeed spiritual) attachment to the theology of phenotype: "The discovery of personal whiteness among the world's peoples is a very modern thing,—a nineteenth and twentieth century matter, indeed.... The Middle Age regarded skin color with mild curiosity; and even up into the eighteenth century we were hammering our national manikins into one, great, Universal Man, with fine frenzy which ignored color and race even more than birth. Today we have changed all that, and the world in a sudden, emotional conversion has discovered that it is white and by that token, wonderful!"[116] Notably, Du Bois's critique of white supremacy emerges here as a part of a broader discourse of worship *style*. From nearly the opening lines of "The Souls of White Folk," white supremacism is positioned within an evangelical Protestant framework of conversion, with "personal whiteness" operating much like the fervent discovery of a personal salvation in Christ. Yet Du Bois turns such experience inside out, demonstrating the public (and indeed global) dimensions of an ostensibly salvific whiteness. Applied to what

Jared Hickman calls the "sociocultural orthodoxy of white supremacy," this emotional conversion to whiteness marks whiteness itself as a bad religion, an outsized and heretical display of false belief.[117] In this sense, Du Bois ironically inhabits the very same anthropological discourse of religion that marked black spiritual practice as radically other, offering an immanent critique of the logic of white (supremacist) secularism. Similarly, Du Bois's return to the language of frenzy in this passage is crucial. Read alongside "Of the Faith of the Fathers," this passage serves as something of a mirror to Du Bois's ambivalent articulation of the "frenzy" of slave religion, casting the enlightenment's version of "Universal Man"—its violent production of sameness and difference—as itself a frenzied affair.[118]

The metonymic slippage between whiteness and salvation is, Du Bois insists, a "very modern thing"; without saying as much, Du Bois theorizes a secular cosmology in which enthusiastic whiteness operates as a dogma perfectly adapted to colonial conquest. At the same time, the passage refuses a narrative of secularization in which racial schemas come to supplement or supersede religious difference under the sign of modernity.[119] On the contrary, by deploying the language of conversion to account for the global ascendency of white supremacism in the nineteenth century, Du Bois demonstrates the centrality and persistence of a white Protestant theological vision in the construction of Western modernity and its various dogmas of racial difference. I follow Hickman in this sense, who argues that "racial discourse has fundamentally constituted itself in the asking and answering of theological questions arising in the course of global modernity."[120] Or as Hortense Spillers phrased it earlier in an important reading of the post-Reconstruction-era black sermon, "Christianity, in its ability to stand in for 'civilization,' 'patriarchy,' 'hierarchy,' 'enlightenment,' 'progress,' 'culture'—a series of lexical items that inaugurate the grammar of 'otherness'—renders a text for the dominant culture."[121] "The Souls of White Folk" both names this text (a "new religion of whiteness") and refuses its theological priority; whiteness, Du Bois argues, might be (has been) violently inscribed through a reading of Scripture, but one might also "read between the lines" of white Christianity's collusion with Western imperialism.[122]

What Spillers offers, and what Hickman also develops, is an account of the ongoing and concomitant rendering of race and religion not as reified identities but as interarticulated scripts whose reading operates as "process, encounter, and potential transformation."[123] And it is finally, I would argue, a potentially transformative encounter with the violently self-authorizing grammars of white Christianity that Du Bois's writings on religion everywhere enact—calling attention both to the historical (and typological) return of enslavement and to the ordained (and always to-be-achieved) work of liberation. While, until recently, scholars have largely characterized Du Bois's use of religious rhetoric as merely pragmatic (pointing to his personal agnosticism and, later, his Marxist critique of religion), Spillers in particular helps us understand such rhetorical performances as precisely the arena in which the writing/sounding of an insurgent relation to Christianity is made possible.[124] In "The Souls of White Folk," Du Bois offers both a scathing critique of white Christianity and a hermeneutics that centers blackness within (and *as*) the biblical promise of deliverance. In this sense, Du Bois's writings signify "an act of religious defiance and theological creation at the very same moment."[125]

Du Bois accomplishes such a double move—outlining the theological dimensions of white supremacism while calling attention to its heresy—in part through careful, repetitive reference to biblical precedent. Consider Du Bois's account of the "extraordinary self-deception of white religion," with its unmitigated association of whiteness with godlike power. Not deceived by this ruse, colonized peoples everywhere, as Du Bois suggests, recognize the human weakness and cruelty at work in such theological maneuverings. Du Bois notes, "These super-men and world-mastering demi-gods listened, however, to no low tongues of ours, even when we pointed silently to their feet of clay," invoking Daniel 2:41–42: "And whereas thou sawest the feet and toes, partly of potter's clay and partly of iron, the kingdom shall be divided. . . . And as the toes of the feet were part of iron and part of clay, so the kingdom shall be partly strong, and partly broken."[126] Gesturing to "feet of clay"—or to the structural inconsistency, and ultimate weakness, of whiteness as a cultural fantasy—Du Bois underlines the blasphemy of world conquest while defiantly amplifying the "low tongues" of insurgent critique; he also signals the spiritual brokenness of a world divided into demigods and colonized subjects. And in case such low tongues remain unheard for Du Bois's reader, he points repeatedly in the same paragraph to the "utter failure of white religion" to guarantee America's spiritual well-being; "a nation's religion is its life," he signals, "and as such white Christianity is a miserable failure."[127]

Throughout "The Souls of White Folk," Du Bois repeatedly deploys and revises Scripture in an effort to mark the close fit between white Christianity, white supremacist violence, and global imperialism. Scripture, in this sense, becomes a racialized script against which Du Bois enacts an insurgent, improvisational reuse; what Spillers might call a "reading between the lines" of white supremacy's long investment in biblical justification. A key example of this revisionary use of Scripture comes in the essay's twofold use of 1 Kings 12:16 ("To your tents, O Israel!," itself a revision of 2 Samuel 20:1). Transforming the Israelites' war cry into a striking refrain, Du Bois enfolds twentieth-century global imperial conquest within a deep time of white supremacist mobilization: "Do we sense somnolent writhings in black Africa or angry groans in India or triumphant banzais in Japan? 'To your tents, O Israel!' These nations are not white!"[128] Later in the essay, Du Bois doubles down on the cleavage of the tribes of Israel as an idiom for racialized entrenchment:

> It is curious to see America, the United States, looking on herself, first, as a sort of natural peacemaker, then as a moral protagonist in this terrible time. No nation is less fitted for this role. For two or more centuries America has marched proudly in the van of human hatred,—making bonfires of human flesh and laughing at them hideously, and making the insulting of millions more than a matter of dislike,—rather a great religion, a world war-cry: Up white, down black; to your tents, O white folk, and world war with black and parti-colored mongrel beasts![129]

Figured as a "great religion" and bolstered with the authority of biblical precedent, white supremacy here is nothing new; on the contrary, it is rooted in an ongoing history of colonial and racial violence, which persists with wavelike frequency in Du Bois's present. Ventriloquizing Scripture in such moments, Du Bois points to its long-standing use as a self-authorizing discourse for white supremacy. At the same time, in its deeply ironic rewriting ("to your tents, O *white folk*"), this passage identifies white supremacy as a radical misreading—even desecration—of Scripture. Returning again and again to white supremacy as a heretical formulation throughout the essay, Du Bois signals the exhausting historical iterations of such virulent whiteness, wearying the blues of Anglo-Protestant hegemony. Or as Frederick Douglass intoned a generation earlier, "My spirit wearies of such blasphemy."[130]

Like Douglass and many others before him, Du Bois performatively deploys Scripture to call attention to the extraordinary (and ordinary) hypocrisy of white Christianity in its complicity with antiblackness. In the face of a growing imperial world order, "The Souls of White Folk" challenges white Christianity's monopoly on the meaning and performance of a sacred text, its invocation as the justification for white supremacy. In this sense, Du Bois practices a version of what Tavia Nyong'o has described as a critical "profanation" of the US social order. Profanation, as Nyong'o argues, draws attention to the performative consecration of existing social orders—their ongoing and repetitive iteration—even as it improvises on the scripts through which such orders are reinforced. Rather than reinforcing a sacred/secular divide, profanation operates as a "passionate unworking of the codes" by which that divide is regulated; in Du Bois's case, this meant drawing out modernity's emotional conversion to whiteness as a "religion," refusing both the sacralization of white supremacy *and* the hegemonic force of white secularism.[131] Against what even sympathetic observers often took to be the ordained triumph of whiteness (recall here Olney's belief, in *An Imperative Duty*, that "superior" races would absorb the "inferior"), Du Bois insists, in the final lines of "The Souls of White Folk" that such a triumph—and the wavelike return of white supremacist violence—was not inevitable. In so doing, he refuses to treat history itself as a sacred text: "I will not believe that all that was must be, that all the shameful drama of the past must be done again today before the sunlight sweeps the silver seas."[132]

In its acute recognition of the relationship between white supremacy, white (secular) Christianity, and modernity, "The Souls of White Folk" anticipates contemporary efforts to account for religion and race as complementary and interarticulated regimes of governmentality. As an early theorist of race and secularism, Du Bois prompts us to ask, with Vincent

Lloyd, "whether it is ever possible to talk about secularism without talking about whiteness" and to contend, with Jonathan Kahn, that "the long arc of the twentieth century's secularization thesis, with its claims that religion is irrational, on the wane, and inappropriate for political work in the public sphere, should be called for what it is: a version of whiteness, if not white supremacy, that served to question the right of political place of African American citizens."[133] In "The Souls of White Folk," Du Bois effectively does just that, demonstrating how performances of secular Christianity work to disenfranchise not just African Americans but a global community of those of African descent, on whose bodies the secular colonial project has been enacted and reenacted.

The Modern American Mood

Even recognizing the political and philosophical shifts that took place across Du Bois's career, his early praise for Howells and *An Imperative Duty* appears difficult to square with what "The Souls of White Folk" (along with *The Souls of Black Folk*, *A Voice from the South*, and *Iola Leroy*) identifies as a violent alignment between secularism's governing of "true religion" and modernity's twin projects of imperialism and racialization. Yet reading across these texts helps demonstrate the extent to which post-Reconstruction secularism was always a contested formation, notwithstanding its cultural hegemony. Together, these texts point to the affective life of secularism as fundamentally bound to the political order of Jim Crow, and to the rising tide of US imperialism; what they variously construct and contest as "modernity" has everything to do with the regulatory force of Anglo-Protestantism. In this vein, Howells's writings remain particularly instructive. In a July 1897 essay for *Harper's* on "The Modern American Mood," for example, Howells noted that the turn-of-the-century American disposition was one of calm self-assurance: "Nothing in our modern mood, I think, is more notable than the quiet of our patriotism. In this we are like people whose religion has become their life, it is no longer an enthusiasm, and it is certainly not ceremonial. They do not seek for a sign; the light is in them. I cannot answer for the new generation which is soon to inherit America, but I believe we who are about bequeathing it to them desire nothing so little as a miracle."[134] Delivered less than four years after the overthrow of the Hawaiian monarchy and less than a year before the beginning of the Spanish-American War, Howells's insistence on patriotic "quiet" in 1897 constitutes a remarkable disavowal. But perhaps even more remarkable is the way that Howells's account of American confidence slides into the characterization of a particular mode of American religious sentiment. Self-contained and self-assured, Howells's patriotism corresponds to (and implicitly demands) a restrained style of Protestant worship: "no longer an enthusiasm" nor simply empty ceremony, American patriotism, like moderate religious belief, is practiced with easy conviction in the afterlife of miracles that is Howells's 1897.[135] Neither seeking for signs nor directly laying claim to an immanent "light," Howells articulates the prevailing mood with litotic restraint: "We . . . desire nothing so little as a miracle."

That Howells linked religious feeling in its "proper proportions" to national belonging helps signal the extent to which racialized citizenship was silently governed in the post-Reconstruction era (and beyond) by a commitment to the norms of white Protestantism. And while Howells's model of sober patriotism eschews outward sign in favor of quiet inward conviction, his description of the modern mood simultaneously recalls a historical discourse of religious "enthusiasm" long obsessed with disfiguring excesses of feeling. As in *An Imperative Duty*, Howells's effort is to mark the passing of just this mode of excess, to articulate modernity as constituted in part through its temporal distance from enthusiasm, as it were: if the nation that Howells inherited had its share of ecstatic subjects, the one he will bequeath has apparently moved beyond them. The logic of this passage inculcates a familiar flow of progress in which enthusiasm, if not religion itself, has been willfully overcome.

This articulation of the modern mood could easily be read as a generically "realist" version of nationalism: a sobered vision of American society that neatly corresponds to Howells's oft-articulated emphasis on aesthetic and emotional proportion.[136] Yet amid Howells's profession of a secular nationalist faith, enthusiasm reemerges as precisely the unquiet element in American patriotism: the specter of a disproportionate, disordered version of national feeling that brings nationalist excess—and the "modern mood" that helped authorize it—into relief (as if one could, in the cathexis of patriotism, be anything other than beside oneself). Thus within the very disavowal of enthusiasm lurks its diffuse return:

Howells's ambiguous claim—"the light is in *them*"—instantiates an internal difference within the singularly secular "American mood" as distinctly as it draws on the language of "inward" religion that was (during the Great Awakenings and in the broader history of Protestant sectarianism) the cause of so much "outward" controversy. As Ann Taves has argued, enthusiasm's disruptive force lay precisely in its tendency to breach the boundaries between private experience and public spectacle, focused as it was on the outer, skin-level manifestations of a supposedly "inner" light.[137] Secularism, in this sense, is indeed a modern mood: an affective comportment that regulates the subject not just "underneath the skin" but also through Jim Crow's very production of skin as a highly symbolic and overdetermined surface.[138]

As we've seen, secularism in the post-Reconstruction era was (and is) inextricably tied to projects of racial knowledge and management. As I'll detail in chapter 2, the links between enthusiasm and racial minstrelsy in a novel like *The Red Badge of Courage* (1894) point to Jim Crow secularism's deeply interarticulated (and strikingly antic) imaginary of religious and racial difference. Minstrelsy and enthusiasm point to intersecting histories of enfleshment—modes of possession and dispossession—that the novel's obsession with fitful corpses suggests cannot be fully laid to rest. To read the performances of those corpses, as we'll see, is to glean just how haunted the secular imaginary of realism is with the specters of racial violence past and present. In the chapters that follow, I'll tell again in many ways the story of realism's complex reliance on the very ecstatic subjects it often violently forgets, marginalizes, or disavows. Part of the secular imaginary of realism is to render such subjects minor or eccentric: consigned to the status of the detail, the ephemeral, the dead, or the soon-to-be-dead. Yet as we'll see, realism's repetitive returns to "enthusiastic" religion, its attention to the haunting liveliness of the dead, and its fascination with racialized boundaries—between spiritual and material, past and present, performance and script—signal the extent to which "realism" was always already a discourse of ecstasy, of life beside itself.

2

Archival Enthusiasm

Roughly midway through Stephen Crane's *The Red Badge of Courage* (1895), we witness the unfolding of a peculiar postmortem:

> The tattered man stood musing.
> "Well, he was reg'lar jim-dandy fer nerve, wa'n't he," said he finally in a little awestruck voice. "A reg'lar jim-dandy." He thoughtfully poked one of the docile hands with his foot. "I wonner where he got 'is stren'th from? I never seen a man do like that before. It was a funny thing. Well, he was a reg'lar jim-dandy."[1]

The anonymous tattered man stands poking at the corpse of Jim Conklin, whose death he has just witnessed alongside the novel's protagonist, Henry Fleming. The scene is disquieting, but also not particularly unique in the novel; as critics have long noted, *The Red Badge of Courage* is steeped in the thematic and formal visibility of death, in the stakes of death's imaginative visualizations, and in its halting, repetitive appearances in the narrative.[2] Fleeting examinations of corpses—casual touches or "long looks"—punctuate the novel, itself a postmortem of the Civil War that it obliquely reproduces. So like death more generally, and like the particular deaths in *Red Badge*, this scene archives what we know to be a "regular," repetitive event as much as it calls attention to the singular strangeness of death's arrival at any particular moment, its status as a "funny thing." Repeatedly translating "Jim" as a character into a "reg'lar jim-dandy"—collapsing "regular" as an army ranking with the degraded ontological status it signifies—these lines enact the transition from the ostensibly singular to the essentially repetitive, from man to sign, that the novel's title (the *badge* of courage) announces in advance.[3] The work of memorializing Jim Conklin drives home what the novel's episodic, nonlinear unfolding demonstrates on a larger scale: that signification is a repetitive and often violent affair.

Alongside their striking, iterative appearances in the novel, Crane's corpses have enjoyed a long critical afterlife. In the decades since Michael Fried's influential reading of Crane's reflexive realism in *Realism, Writing, Disfiguration* (1987), in which the obsessive attention paid to corpses in *Red Badge* and other texts makes visible the process of writing itself, critics have engaged a wide variety of approaches to account for what Bill Brown fittingly describes as the novel's "corporeal archive": its collection of bodily remains offered up as deeply uncanny objects of fascination and cathexis. Brown, for example, argues that *Red Badge*'s photographic casualties register the "reproduction and circulation of the body as image, site of mass identification and mass affection," while Jacqueline Goldsby (in a reading of the 1898 novella *The Monster*, an important complement to *Red Badge*) demonstrates the representational economy of lynching central to Crane's realism.[4] Though they reach quite different conclusions, together these readings and others point to the material and political unconscious that surfaces in Crane's deathly tableaus; they collectively poke, in other words, at the funny "things" that Crane's dead bodies so frequently seem to be, pointing to the way they index the various modes of reification that characterized post-Reconstruction modernity.

This chapter extends that long-standing process of historical recovery, but it does so by turning to a very different set of corporeal archives haunting *Red Badge*'s decontextualized image of the war. At the risk of reproducing the novel's disproportionate musing over the corpse, I perform my own postmortem of sorts on the body of Jim Conklin and on the "jim-dandy" that haunts his fall into signification. To this end, I return repeatedly to the extended sequence of Jim Conklin's death to poke at its details, to meditate on the possibilities encoded in the visceral, and to unfold the novel's fascination with what bodies might and might not transmit. Drawing from an archive of performances of "Dandy Jim"—an inverted minstrel resonance haunting Jim Conklin's "jim-dandy"—as well as a history of racialized religious feeling, I argue that by tracking the returns of this seemingly ephemeral character, we glean a very different take on the reification of violence that critics have often read in Crane's realism. While Jim's descent into a "reg'lar jim-dandy" might seem to typify that process—repeatedly translating the once-suffering subject into a racialized object of curiosity—I'll demonstrate that within that rhythmic transition lurks a much more complex approach to the narrative's imbrication with historical memory. Reanimating interwoven histories of racial minstrelsy and religious enthusiasm—varieties of antic embodiment that capitalize on the semantic uncertainty of the body—the novel's "reg'lar jim-dandy" invokes an archive of lingering losses and incomplete returns, inspired subjects and bodies compelled to move.[5]

To refocus the critical gaze on Jim Conklin, and on the "jim-dandy" that he becomes, is to write in tension both with the novel's own narrative mode—which closely follows Henry's consciousness—and with an immense body of criticism that has predominantly worked to unpack the literary, psychological, and historical implications of Henry's exhaustive navel-gazing.[6] Yet Jim's marginalization in this critical history belies his outsized role in *Red Badge*'s narrative of violent self-making. By devoting extended, even excessive, attention to this ostensibly minor character, we glean the various ways in which *Red Badge* routes the problem of embodied subjectivity through the very grammar of Jim Crow racialization, with its obsessive attention to the semiotics of the flesh and to what bodies might or might not signify.[7] Throughout the novel, bodies are understood only via their approximation to the funny "things" they are or will become, a proximity that makes violent racialization a violent metaphor for life itself.[8] At the same time, *Red Badge* imagines bodies as kinetic archives: the accreted *effects* or remainders of history, less encoded in Crane's realism than they are enacted and reenacted, lodged in vernaculars of performance that refuse, in some sense, to die.

In the first part of this chapter, I track one such vernacular, offering a deep dive into the archive of black dandy performances as they resonate in the death of Jim Conklin. Reanimating a history of racial fantasy, appropriation, and bodily citation, Jim's "jim-dandy" suggests that the modernity of *Red Badge*—its ability, as contemporary critics registered, to capture "real motion"—depends (at least in part) on its uncanny reproduction of minstrel gestures.[9] Minstrelsy, in this sense, becomes a crucial idiom, one in which the historicity of the novel's strained embodiments emerges through a legacy of performance. Reading Jim's death as both echoing and exceeding the minstrel idiom, the second half of this chapter tracks the novel's attention to communicable religious feeling and the striking consonance between possessed and dispossessed flesh. An unlikely couple, racial minstrelsy and religious enthusiasm each pivot on the fantasy of the body's communicability, its ability to function as an imminently reproducible sign. Standing in for and complicating the historical trauma that demands representation, these performances dwell on the impractical desire that the body itself might become legible as an imprint or badge of experience, a desire that *Red Badge* both entertains and problematizes. As we'll see, such performances present the realist body as a kind of archive—the site of history's remains or repetitions—even as such remains resist easy consolidation into historical narrative.

For all its poking at corpses, *Red Badge* offers less a dispassionate musing over history's remains than a meditation on the (sur)real materiality of its repetitions. Tracking a series of haunting repetitions, I argue that *Red Badge* deploys repetition as a figure for what turn-of-the-century narratives of secular-Protestant progress necessarily occlude: the ongoingness of the war in realism's dramas of personhood and the powerful centrality of both religion and race in shaping those dramas.[10] In this sense, *Red Badge* testifies in narrative form to the ability of performance to (in Diana Taylor's terms) "[make] visible not just the live but the powerful army of the always already living. The power of seeing through performance is the recognition that we've seen it all before—the fantasies that shape our sense of self, of community, that organize our scenarios of interaction, conflict, and resolution."[11] Like the archive to which they are uneasily consigned, Jim's remains register both a disappearance and its historical trace: an uncanny "before" whose erasure signals a destruction at the heart of realism's social constructions, and whose returns allow us to track realism's investment in history's sardonic repetitions. Through the figure of Jim Conklin, then, I read *Red Badge* as haunted by performance—by the "powerful army of the always already living"—while attending to the historical amnesia that subtends realism's vivid impressions.[12] By marking this double movement of remembering and forgetting, I aim to revivify an archive of practice without reifying the archive itself as an indexical site of authority. Instead, I work toward what Tavia Nyong'o describes as "performative historiography," a method that draws from textual archives while emphasizing the "performative effects of history"—its repetitions, stumbles, lapses, and wounds.[13]

Reading the details of *Red Badge*'s "jim-dandy," I insist on a history of performance that informs and exceeds the literary archive of Crane's text. The work of recovery enacted here thus depends on textual archives, but it gestures toward a set of practices and affects—a set of gestures—that is "taken up in writing but always enacted in excess of it," to use Shane Vogel's articulation.[14] In this, I aim to inhabit the method of Crane's novel, which at once drives home the repetitively violent work of signification—the rote reproduction of jim-dandies—and exuberantly reanimates what we might think of as realism's intimate other: the ecstatic body, spectacularly beside itself. If such a body—imagined and projected—is in many senses an effect of secular realism's effort to diagnose communicable feeling as an excess proper to some bodies, it also helps us account for realism itself as a discourse of excess, fully haunted by what it forgets, excludes, and brings back to life.

A "Reg'lar Jim-Dandy"

But what kind of "jim-dandy" does Jim, in death, become? And what does realism archive as a means to forget? The *Oxford English Dictionary* lists *jim-dandy* as a colloquialism meaning "an excellent person or thing"; the term seems to have been popularized in the late 1880s through its use as an encomium for particularly agile baseball players.[15] Baseball loomed large in Crane's imaginary and, as Bill Brown has demonstrated, Crane's investment in play continually materializes in the representational economies of his fiction.[16] But Crane's "jim-dandy" was also distinctly a Jim Crow formation. As Gerald Cohen notes in *Studies in Slang*, it most likely derives from the popular antebellum minstrel song, "Dandy Jim from Caroline," written either in 1843 or 1844 and attributed variously to Dan Emmett, J. T. Norton, and others.[17] William Mahar indicates that the song may have first emerged as a caricature of South Carolina governor James ("Dandy Jim") Hammond, who defended racial slavery and the class system it maintained.[18] Reprinted widely and frequently arranged for piano forte, "Dandy Jim of Caroline" moved fluidly, as Mahar notes, "from the streets and theaters into the American home" (Emily Dickinson's family library, for example, included an 1844 version of "Dandy Jim" arranged by Joseph W. Turner).[19]

Like minstrelsy's racial masquerade more broadly, "Dandy Jim of Caroline" was a family drama. Across many variations in the song's lyrics, Dandy Jim narrates his comeliness ("For my ole Massa tole me so / I was de best looking N——r in de County O / I look in de glass an I found it so / Just what massa told me O"), his courtship of Dinah ("Oh, beauty is but skin deep / But wid Miss Dinah none compete"), and their growing family ("De preacher christen'd eight or nine, / Young Dandy Jims of Caroline"). Monica Miller contends that like other midcentury blackface dandies, "Dandy Jim" staged the hypothetical of black freedom for white audiences, at once imagining and containing the economic/sexual threat embodied in the dandy's fancy dress and explicit pleasure. Foregrounding complex choreographies of cross-racial mimicry and desire, Dandy Jim and other black dandies "menace even as they amuse, revealing the affinity between effeminacy associated with extreme attention to dress and appearance, and hypermasculinity linked to a sexual rapacity that exceeds racial boundaries."[20] Miller argues compellingly that the song's emphasis on Jim's proliferating offspring links the spectacle of black freedom to the threat of that freedom's rampant reproduction. Yet it also attests to the very popularity of the "Dandy Jim" type—its replication in performance after performance, as newly christened Dandy Jims and their kin appeared regularly in theaters. Such performances were at once ephemeral and utterly repeatable, a duality emanating from their archival remains (see figure 2.1). As in the image shown here, the performer's body—itself continually reproduced and circulated—offers a rhythmic reproduction of minstrelsy's racial imaginary, a vernacular lodged in choreographed (and reprinted, or literally stereotyped) gesticulation.

While the text of "Dandy Jim" locates it within the discursive and geographic parameters of Southern slavery, midcentury blackface dandy performances more often addressed themselves to the virtuosic self-fashioning of free black men in the urban North, condensing antebellum racial and class animosities in regionally specific terms.[21] As Mahar describes, "Topical references to fiddlers, dancers or dancing, courtship practices, and public rituals in some of the 'Dandy Jim' songs were tied to the promenade scenes on New York streets, that is, the typical ... display activities that took place on Sundays and holidays on lower Broadway and the Bowery."[22] A careful student of the Bowery

Figure 2.1. D. D. Emmit [Daniel Decatur Emmett], *Dandy Jim from Caroline*, ca. 1844. American Minstrel Show Collection, Harvard Theater Collection, Houghton Library, Harvard University.

public and its immanent theatricality, Crane might well have recognized the mirrorlike returns of that display in "Dandy Jim," which at once celebrates and ridicules the black dandy's performance, mocking desire coded in respectability while winking at the layers of artifice embedded in blackface itself (where "beauty is but skin deep"). Thus while "Dandy Jim" consolidates stereotypes of racial mimicry and class aspiration, it also depicts race as a function and outcome of coded desire, literally refracting white fantasy and anxiety back onto itself via an assumed and alluring blackness (like a mirror, Jim merely repeats what the white enslaver reports of his beauty: "I look in de glass an I found it so, / Just what massa told me O"). Slyly juxtaposing Jim Dandy's masterful performance with the slavish admiration it induces, and foregrounding the commodification that blackface both signaled and represented—a commodification rooted in but extending far beyond chattel slavery—the dandy makes visible and audible the complicated cathexis involved in such performances, the desire they at once display and prohibit.[23]

Reading *Red Badge* through this archive of minstrelsy allows us to understand its formal investment in repetition as wedded to the history of racist reproduction. In these terms, the transformation of Jim Conklin into a "jim-dandy" (a transformation that marks the violence of language, its reduction of persons into things) points to the repetitive reproduction of racial violence in the post-Reconstruction era: its embeddedness in the very semantics of realism, its "there-ness" as part and parcel of realism's perlocutionary or performative real. Yet it also points to the novel's immanent or uncanny sense of repetition as the very site of historicity. Here I follow Saidiya Hartman's account of repetition as deeply linked to what history has not and cannot redeem and to the "subterranean history of rupture" to which performance gestures.[24] "Gesture" as in *gerere*, to carry or to bear: as Hartman suggests, repetition bears witness both to what the body has been made to bear (as the site of race's violent enactment or enunciation) and to practices of knowledge and transmission through which the body is made the site not of continuous memory but of repetitive counterinsistence, "catalyzed by the inadequacy of redress and the regularity of domination and terror."[25] In this sense, *Red Badge*'s "jim-dandy" may indeed be a figure of remembrance, but one whose very existence signals an ongoing history of forgetting. To approach the novel's "jim-dandy" as fully haunted by performances of Dandy Jim is to reckon with what remains fully alive, albeit occluded, in that repetition—with what it archives and reproduces.

Importantly, while performances and printed reproductions of Dandy Jim served to reify racial parody, the form also yielded a range of improvisational variations. The song was frequently co-opted and revised for explicitly political ends: during the 1844 and 1848 election seasons, campaign versions of the song proliferated in the press, alternately glorifying or lampooning candidates as iterations of the virtuosic (if not dandified) Dandy Jim. In 1844, "Jimmy Polk of Tennessee" went up against "A Whig Melody" in support of Henry Clay (both to the tune of "Dandy Jim"), while the 1848 cycle saw Dandy Jim songs in support of Zachary Taylor, Lewis Cass, and Free Soil candidate Martin Van Buren.[26] But the most extraordinary repetition of the song came in the form of an abolitionist earworm penned by the self-emancipated dramatist and lecturer William Wells Brown. Set to the tune of "Dandy Jim," "A Song for Freedom" appeared in Brown's 1848 *Anti-Slavery Harp* and was reprinted the same year in Frederick Douglass's *North Star*. It begins with the lines "Come all ye bondmen far and near, / let's put a song in massa's ear, / It is a song for our poor race, / Who're whipped and trampled with disgrace."[27] Written for use at abolitionist meetings, "A Song for Freedom" rejects a solo display of class-specific virtuosity for a collective performance "for our poor race." Preserving the popular tune of minstrel performance while changing the lyrics opens up space for ironic critique: Brown transposes "for my ole massa tole me so" into "let's put a song in massa's ear," and finally into wry commentary on the perversities of American exceptionalism: "My old massa tells me O, this is a land of freedom, O."

Brown deployed the song repeatedly, most notably in his 1858 play *The Escape; or, A Leap of Freedom: A Drama in Five Acts*. Here, as Daphne Brooks argues, Brown used minstrelsy's racial masquerade to destabilize the line between mastery and slavishness, wielding blackface as a fugitive form of self-emancipation. Through the figure of Cato—a sartorially minded "house servant" reminiscent of Adolph in *Uncle Tom's Cabin*—Brown stages what Brooks calls the play's "most spectacular escape."[28] Clothing himself so well in the drag of freedom that he actualizes it, Cato transforms his enslavement into a masterful deception under the guise of minstrel buffoonery. Importantly, this transformation echoes *The Anti-Slavery Harp*'s transposition of "Dandy Jim" into "A Song for Freedom." Left alone in the third act of *The Escape*, Cato peels back the minstrel mask, revealing his plan to flee to Canada and singing an "original hymn": "A Song for Freedom." Reappropriating the popular tune of "Dandy Jim" for an "original" composition, and repeatedly pressing it into the service of abolitionist activism, Brown retook the terms of the song's ridicule and redirected its popularity toward the production of contagious enthusiasm for abolition. Staging dramatic readings at antislavery meetings and keeping "A Song for Freedom" in the ears of his listeners, Brown turned the trope of Dandy Jim's reproductive prowess into sheer power in numbers, begetting one right-minded audience after another.[29]

Transforming the minstrel song into an abolitionist hymn meant more than simply mobilizing the song's familiar tune; on the contrary, Brown seamlessly knit the minstrel song's reproductive energies to the popular work of religious feeling. In his reading of *The Anti-Slavery Harp*, Aaron McClendon argues that Brown's appeal to audiences owed as much to the affective and spiritual power of the hymn as it did to the antic reversals of minstrelsy. Drawing out the antebellum links between music, affect, and abolition, McClendon roots the transformative affects of Brown's antislavery music in the broader religious climate of the Second Great Awakening, where the emphasis on ecstatic conversion experience strengthened the felt possibility of social change. McClendon notes: "If ecstatic music could reform an individual's soul, it could, reasoned many, help reform the nation's moral and social soul as well, an idea that Garrison's abolitionists in particular embraced, as moral suasion was thought by them to be the best approach to abolition."[30] Brown certainly directed the strains of popular religious conversion toward explicitly abolitionist ends, even in the midst of his deeply sardonic critique of white Christianity, which (especially, though not exclusively, in its Calvinist forms) pitted the interpretive authority of preachers against the Second Great Awakening's emphasis on the individual experience of sanctification: "Our preachers, too, with ship and cord, / Command obedience in the Lord; / They say they learn it from the book, / But for ourselves we dare not look." Yet as we'll see, Brown's masterful retooling of "Dandy Jim"—his transposition of minstrel song into religious hymn—also recognized and reversed an emergent association of African

American religious practice with minstrelsy. In this sense, Brown's version of "Dandy Jim" was antiphonal, a sonic callback to minstrelsy's antic popularity in the service of emancipatory *ex-stasis*.

Set to the tune of "Dandy Jim," Crane's "jim-dandy" sounds remarkably different. Onto the death of Jim Conklin, *Red Badge* superimposes a fraught performance of racial mimicry, an archive of productions, reproductions, and revisions that become apparent only belatedly, in the aftermath of Jim's fall. Minstrelsy offers one way to read Jim's body, a discursive frame for a performance-in-death that remains only partially legible within the space of the novel. To be clear, hearing the strains of Dandy Jim's multiple incarnations in Jim's discursive declension into a "jim-dandy" does not require a direct correspondence. There is no evidence that Crane witnessed performances of Dandy Jim, though his predilection for Bowery entertainment makes it plausible that he saw at least one of its postbellum incarnations, and "Dandy Jim" almost certainly remained in wide circulation at the turn of the century. Paul Laurence Dunbar, for example, mobilized minstrel semiotics in his 1903 collection, *In Old Plantation Days*; "Dandy Jim's Conjure Scare" depicts Jim as an enslaved man who claims he's been conjured in terms that strategically deploy the slippage between religious affect and infectious performance (Jim's enslaver exclaims, "Why, you look like you'd been getting religion," and Jim replies, "No, I ain't quite as bad as dat, Mas' Henry. Religion 'fects de soul, but hits my body dats 'fected.").[31] Still the provenance of Crane's "reg'lar jim-dandy" may or may not have been audible to contemporary readers.[32] What it suggests, however, is the ghostly presence of minstrelsy more broadly—the way its encoded appearance operates as the very sign of historical return. Thus while critics have characterized *Red Badge*'s representational effect as that of a historical blind spot, citing its emphasis on Henry's singular perceptual experience over the political context of the war, turning our attention to Jim Conklin helps uncover the novel's representational investment not in historical knowledge per se but in history's sardonic repetitions.

Red Badge deploys minstrelsy less as a direct historical reference than as an uncanny gesture toward the ongoingness of that history in the post-Reconstruction era in which Crane wrote, with its own theatrics of black objectification. Bill Brown has described this uncanny effect as the "residual ontology" of slavery's reduction of humans to objects (always incomplete, always ongoing under colonialism and capitalism).[33] Analyzing the post-Reconstruction circulation of minstrel objects—dolls, games, cookie jars, piggy banks—Brown argues that they register the repressed history of slavery's "ontological scandal," its reduction of humans into things.[34] Yet as Robin Bernstein and Uri McMillan remind us, such histories are not merely repressed or routed through the material unconscious; they are also carried through and reenacted at the level of bodily performance (compelled or otherwise), and perhaps especially where the body's fleshy materiality has been violently enforced and reinforced.[35] Bernstein describes the uncanny return that performance itself constitutes, arguing that while "performance can appear to leave no trace (a gesture does not mark the air in the way that ink marks a page)," its repetitions nevertheless "habituate and thus deeply inscribe the body; for this reason performance usefully appears ephemeral when in fact it lingers and haunts."[36] In *Red Badge*, the "funny thing" that Jim's "jim-dandy" is—the mordant thing-ness it reanimates—emerges not simply as historical detail but as bodily and textual repetition, one that attaches itself to "Jim" across a series of Crane's texts.

Read through Jim's very iterability (as anonymous "tall soldier," as "jim-dandy"), *Red Badge*'s impression of the war looks less like a narrative of individual development and more like embodied testimony to the eventfulness of the past: "'Yeh know,' said the tall soldier, 'I was out there.' He made a careful gesture. 'An', Lord, what a circus! An', b-jiminey, I got shot—I got shot. Yes, b'jiminey, I got shot.' He reiterated this fact in a bewildered way, as if he did not know how it came about."[37] *As if he did not know*—a phrase that buckles under the weight of a history it references but cannot hold. The realist fact here is reiterative and bewildering; it is, furthermore, linked to the fundamental violence that produced the war itself, the conflation of humans and objects (evidenced here again in the repetitive exclamation, "b-jiminey," another becoming-word or becoming-object for Jim, another resurrection). Circular and circus-like, Jim's performance in battle, like Crane's novel more broadly, is indeed a performance: a rhythmic, gestural retelling or reenactment of the violent event.[38] Into the space of historical knowledge, then, *Red Badge* inserts reiteration, replacing narratives of national reunification and suture with the circularity of traumatic repetition and the wound's belated impact. Bound up in the novel's effort to make the flesh communicative—to press meaning from wounded and fallen bodies—history emerges here not exactly as the text's unconscious but as the fitful disappearance and reappearance of gestures that realism at once depends on and yet cannot fully process.

Creeping Strangeness

Still, this outlay of historical detail, this archival enthusiasm, may seem excessive, particularly given Jim Conklin's apparent status in *Red Badge* as little more than a foil for Henry Fleming—the sacrificial hero to Henry's morose, self-conscious survivor, almost nowhere to be found in readings of the novel. This critical elision of Jim parallels and reproduces an explicit diegetic elision, both in *Red Badge*, where Henry must turn his back on Jim's corpse for the narrative to proceed, and in its brief 1896 sequel "The Veteran." In the later text—one of a series of Civil War sketches commissioned on the basis of *Red Badge*'s popular success—an elderly Henry Fleming recalls his wartime experience in the very terms of Jim's nonrecollection: "Now, there was young Jim Conklin, old Si Conklin's son—that used to keep the tannery—you none of you recollect him—well, he went into it from the start just as if he was born to it. But with me it was different, I had to get used to it."[39] Henry narrates a history for Jim (a father and a trade) even as he marks its utter erasure in the local memory of the town, an absence registered rhetorically in his halting, dash-heavy speech. Producing a narrative through-line for Jim in place of the broken genealogical line, "The Veteran" gestures to the memory loss that makes such testimony necessary.

And yet Jim does not simply stand in for this loss. One of Henry's auditors is his grandson "Jim," a detail that underscores "Jim's" repetitive returns and hints at a level of intimacy that the narrative both reveals and obscures. Indeed, this move—the conversion of Jim into a familial relation in the subsequent sketch—recalls the peculiar intimacy born of his noncharacterization in *Red Badge*, his status as a strictly relational yet somehow crucial figure. This strange status emerges near the opening of the novel, as Henry works to retain Jim's formal function as foil, revealing a personal history in the very act of its repression: "The tall soldier, for one, gave him some assurance. This man's [Jim's] serene unconcern dealt him a measure of confidence, for he had known him since childhood, and from his intimate knowledge he did not see how he could be capable of anything that was beyond him, the youth. Still, he thought that his comrade might be mistaken about himself."[40] Here the claim to knowledge cuts in both directions, assuming a knowable subject—and an intimate one, at that—even as it effaces the reliability of any such knowledge, maintaining a blankness to Jim-as-character that secures his marginal status in the narrative. Underscored by the proximity between "childhood" and "youth," the narrator renders Henry's self-knowledge deeply ironic but also acutely intimate, routed and rerouted through the imagined, projected, and racialized double.

The passage simultaneously introduces and undermines a narrative logic whereby Jim (here, significantly, the "tall soldier") can only be the mimetic sacrificial "other," whose death in battle allows the reconciliation of self-difference on Henry's path to manhood, self-knowledge, self-sameness, and whiteness—a violent psycho-socialization.[41] As Susan Mizruchi notes, Crane's novel depicts "society itself [as] a blood-swollen god that feeds on human armies," and indeed the text might be said to quite literally devour Jim as testimony to the logic of whiteness *as* consumption and expenditure.[42] One of the few details offered by way of characterization is Jim's love for food: "During his meals, he always wore an air of blissful contemplation of the food he had swallowed. His spirit seemed then to be communing with the viands."[43] This trope of minstrel corporeality finds its grotesque reversal later in the novel, as in death Jim's body itself resembles something partially eaten: "As the flap of the blue jacket fell away from the body, he could see that the side looked as if it had been chewed by wolves."[44]

Jim's death becomes, in this formula, the ritual expenditure enabling Henry's socialization: the sacrificial violence that produces and reinforces his whiteness, a microcosm of Jim Crow racialization more broadly. To read Jim's body as implicitly racialized is to insist, with Jacqueline Goldsby, on a historical, cultural, and narrative "logic" of sacrificial death, where racial violence is encoded in the very grammar and economy of realist fiction.[45] In these terms, the violence done to Jim's body functions as the excess detail, the "reality effect" that locates Crane's text concretely in its post-Reconstruction moment of racial terror. If the half-eaten thing-ness of Jim's corpse epitomizes the silent speech-act that Roland Barthes famously attributed to realism's superfluous details (which testify only *"we are the real"*), it also suggests that the excess securing Crane's realism aligns, in some sense, with the very expendability of black lives at the nadir.

But turning now to Jim's deeply strange, extended death scene, we might also ask what it means to read his extinction not only as a violent purging of novel's expendable surplus but also as a scene haunted by—and indeed archiving—performance. As his conversion into a "jim-dandy" suggests, Jim's body functions as the site of an archive, repeatedly marked and marking historically specific bodies-in-motion while reminding us of that forgetfulness, that death drive at the very heart of archive fever. To borrow a phrase from Joseph Roach, Jim is "forgotten but not gone": he is invoked and erased, singular subject and repetitive sign, a "funny thing" and a "regular jim-dandy."[46] His body is (like the archive) a palimpsest, and never more so than in death:

> The tall soldier turned and, lurching dangerously, went on. The youth and the tattered soldier followed, sneaking as if whipped, feeling unable to face the stricken man if he should again confront them. They began to have thoughts of a solemn ceremony. There was something rite-like in these movements of the doomed soldier.
>
> And there was a resemblance in him to a devotee of a mad religion, blood-sucking, muscle-wrenching, bone-crushing. They were awed and afraid....
>
> At last, they saw him stop and stand motionless. Hastening up, they perceived that his face wore an expression telling that he had at last found the place for which he had struggled. His spare figure was erect; his bloody hands were quietly at his sides.... He was at the rendezvous. They paused and stood, expectant....
>
> Finally, the chest of the doomed soldier began to heave with a strained motion. It increased in violence until it was as if an animal was within and was kicking and tumbling furiously to be free.
>
> This spectacle of gradual strangulation made the youth writhe and once as his friend rolled his eyes, he saw something in them that made him sink wailing to the ground. He raised his voice in a last, supreme call.
>
> "Jim—Jim—Jim—"...
>
> Suddenly his form stiffened and straightened. Then it was shaken by a prolonged ague....

He was invaded by a creeping strangeness that slowly enveloped him. For a moment, the tremor of his legs caused him to dance a sort of hideous hornpipe. His arms bent wildly about his head in expression of imp-like enthusiasm.

His tall figure stretched itself to its full height. There was a slight rending sound. Then it began to swing forward, slow and straight, in the manner of a falling tree. . . .

The body seemed to bounce a little way from the earth. . . .

The youth had watched, spell-bound, this ceremony at the place of meeting.

His face had been twisted into an expression of every agony he had imagined for his friend.[47]

It is worth lingering at this rendezvous, as the text does—Jim's death stretches over the length of an entire chapter, culminating in the (here much-abbreviated) climax. Like the corpses it will soon resemble, Jim's body is unsettling in its wounded endurance, its extended and mostly mute teetering on the brink of extinction, its bewildering mobility in death itself. Part of the intense strangeness of this scene is the difficulty of locating where in the text Jim actually dies: described as a "spectral soldier" from the beginning of the chapter, his death seems both to have already occurred and to occur repeatedly, as the passage's rhetorical transitions point to a larger transition ("At last," "Finally") repetitively and painfully postponed. Death is descriptively dispersed, a "creeping strangeness" that resists any effort to situate it within the flow of the narrative. The prolonged death ague—a fever that the text cannot shake—simultaneously stokes and frustrates Henry's expectancy (as well as our own), cultivating spectatorial desire while refusing the dividend, as Jim's "hideous hornpipe" both compels and resists the interpretive gaze. The stakes of witnessing here are manifold. Henry's attention to Jim at the moment of his death is an act of protective supervision, as Jim is threatened both by his wound and by the possibility of being trampled on the road by an approaching battery (Henry promises, "I'll take care of you, Jim! I'll take care of you!").[48] But as the above passage demonstrates, it is also a self-interested, quasi-scientific investigation, a study in the physiology and performance of death. Eager to make the death scene instructive, Henry questions Jim repeatedly, desperate for clues to the knowledge that he has gained or ostensibly will gain by dying: "Where you going, Jim? What you thinking about? Where you going? Tell me, won't you, Jim?"; "Why, Jim . . . what's the matter with you?"[49] Insisting on the proper name here—against the depersonalizing effect of the narrative, which more consistently refers to Jim as the "tall" or "spectral" soldier—Henry is soon left with only the proper name in his effort to arrest, and thereby understand, the transition from person to thing that the passage describes ("Jim—Jim—Jim—").

Against Henry's arresting impulse, the entire sequence seems to occupy a transition, tarrying with Jim in suspended motion: "He seemed to be awaiting the moment when he should pitch headlong. He stalked like the specter of a soldier, his eyes burning with the power of a stare into the unknown."[50] If Henry's spellbound observation is complicit with the narrative's scene of subjection—a complicity that extends to the reader—it also exceeds an uncomplicated consumption of violence insofar as it enters into a succession of nonreciprocal looks; Henry watches Jim watching, looks to penetrate the repeated fastening of Jim's gaze on the "unknown," his search for "the mystic place of his intentions."[51] Jim is looking for a place to die in this passage, but he is also "going" somewhere that Henry cannot—a pairing that imparts to Jim's abjection a monstrous form of privilege. When Jim reaches the appropriate spot, he is "at the rendezvous," the "place of meeting" where the dance ensues and where Henry cannot hope to look away. As the subject who gazes and the object of Henry's gaze, the abject and the privileged, "Jim" or Jim's remains become the place of meeting, a dynamic rendezvous for competing signifiers.

The specifics of the scene support the minstrelsy reference that directly follows it: historical evidence suggests, for example, that "Dandy Jim" was often performed with castanets made of animal bone, a detail that helps us read Jim's "bone-crushing" movement as a suggestive overlapping of minstrelsy and ritual sacrifice.[52] Sacrificial resonances abound: the "solemn ceremony" that Henry anticipates and the "rite-like" quality to Jim's procession suggest that Jim's death *is* a rite—of sacrifice or passage.[53] This framing of the death as a ritual—an exorcism of social tension that consolidates the sociopolitical order, much like minstrelsy in these terms—heightens the strangeness adhering to Jim's body, a strangeness that might rationalize, in nineteenth-century racial politics, his violent removal from the narrative for the sake of Henry's development. But while Jim's body is no doubt a problem that the text simultaneously purges and archives, his performance exceeds the formal bounds of ritual, gesturing toward alternative resonances that complicate the logic of Jim's sacrifice and Henry's salvation. It is the hornpipe, perhaps, that best signals the ambivalence attached to Jim's restless body: a folk dance derived from the wind instrument that shares its name (and associated with the stage since the sixteenth century), the hornpipe is an up-tempo, rhythmic variation on the jig that was popularized in the US during the nineteenth century and generally performed solo, a vehicle for virtuosic display and popular recognition.[54] Thus while the passage is propelled by the expectation of stillness—the suspense dependent on where and when Jim will finally stop moving—the hornpipe reinvests the body with an uncanny liveliness, drawing our attention to its ongoing movement as the death scene is momentarily transfigured into the site of exuberant performance.

Neither willed nor obviously compelled, neither fully naturalized nor clearly supernatural, the hornpipe serves as a kind of floating signifier, with Jim's body dangling hideously in the uncharted space between life and death, past and present. In reanimating Jim's body through performance, *Red Badge* might be said to historicize the affective structure that Sianne Ngai has termed "animatedness," wherein "the seemingly neutral state of 'being moved' becomes twisted into the image of the overemotional racialized subject, abetting his or her construction as unusually receptive to external control."[55] Ngai points out that within such a structure—made particularly visible by moving image technologies and their emphasis on "liveness"—the racialized subject-in-motion resembles both person and thing, automaton and virtuoso. As scholars have noted, *Red Badge* is deeply indebted for its representational effects to the technologies of late nineteenth-century visual culture, and particularly to the halting movement sequences of early film.[56] Contemporary responses focused almost obsessively on the animating force of the narrative: describing the "appalling realism" of Jim's death, George Wyndham wrote, "The book is full of sensuous impressions that leap out from the picture: of gestures, attitudes, grimaces, that flash into portentous definition," while Harold Frederic famously compared the novel to Muybridge's motion studies. Similarly, Frank Norris gestured toward emerging film techniques in likening Crane's fiction to "scores and scores of tiny flashlight photographs, instantaneous, caught, as it were, on the run."[57] As such responses registered, the novel fully partakes of early film's hypnotic sequences, projecting the image of Jim's body in faltering, flickering motion and—at the same time—demonstrating the strangely objectifying force of these animating sequences.

This is, indeed, a creeping strangeness. If such "strained," strange animation is precisely the work of historical narrative—literally bringing the past back to life, as it were—*Red Badge* insists on the performative bodies that haunt any such project, and on the impact of their bewildering repetitions. And if the lurching movements of Jim's body archive a singular trauma ("An', b-jiminey, I got shot—I got shot. Yes, b'jiminey, I got shot"), they also signal the instability of the novel's larger archive of fallen bodies, its refusal to remain a still collection. Jim's final collapse resembles a fall into history as linear progress; in contrast to the grotesque levity of the "hideous hornpipe," the treelike manner of the body's fall—"forward, slow, and straight"—conveys the linearity achievable only in the aftermath of a death that resists any such naturalized account. Here we might be tempted to envision Jim's death through the progressive account of history that secularism assumes and reifies: what is unaccountable within that history is soon rendered an object for inspection. Yet even this apparent linearity circles back on itself: before the fall, Jim's enthusiasm is described as "implike," a word onto which is grafted not only the idea of a mischievous (minstrel) spirit but also the very notion of grafting. In its archaic sense, "imp" indicates the "young shoot of a plant or tree," an outgrowth or offspring.[58] Thus if Jim's body swings swiftly into stillness, "in the manner of a falling tree," it nevertheless carries the trace of live performance with all its reproductive unruliness.[59] In death, Jim's body remains a living archive: the novel's root system or family tree.

Enthusiasm and the (Il)logic of the Flesh

In the immediate aftermath of this strange scene, recovering the resonances of minstrelsy offers one way to historicize the novel's dance of death. Once the uncanny conjunction of mobility and constraint mapped onto Jim's body becomes legible as minstrel performance, we are able to read the very ontological uncertainty of that body—dead or alive, person or thing—as central to the novel's antic imagining of racial difference. Furthermore, Jim's "jim-dandy" gives historical weight to the conjunction of performance and violence that the text everywhere demonstrates: Henry's dilemma around the wound is itself a sort of performance anxiety, a repetitive tendency to falter at the prospect of a violent self-making and unmaking. In these terms, the novel confronts Jim's death as a limit point, a site of intense curiosity and desire, and one where the ontological slippage between life and death—emerging in the metonymic slide between Jim, "jim-dandy," and Dandy Jim—stands in for a variety of other differences made and unmade. Read as minstrelsy, Jim's "jim-dandy" become richly citational, at once archiving and revivifying unwieldy histories of performance and racialization.

But alongside and irrevocably tangled up in this theatrical scene is another figure that haunts the hornpipe, and one that critical attention to minstrelsy alone threatens to obscure. This is the figure of the imp-like enthusiast: that spectacularly embodied subject of ecstatic inspiration or virtuosic pantomime. An idiom at least since the Great Awakening (when debates over religious sectarianism shaped a broader transnational discourse on experience, deception, and communicable feeling), the enthusiast—inspired or imitative, ecstatic or excessive, and always potentially in error—offered an unruly and ongoing challenge to liberal subject formation.[60] As religious studies scholar Ann Taves argues, the deployment of "enthusiasm" among both revivalists and skeptics operated as a form of epistemological discernment: a means of separating authentic experience from spiritual affectation. Yet this was a form of classification that always threatened to break down, as enthusiasm's contagious popular feeling haunted and helped produce the explanatory and disciplinary mechanisms of religious and secular philosophy. The ambiguous source of animation, echoed here in the tattered man's postmortem inquiry ("I wonner where he got 'is stren'th from?") condenses both the promise and the threat of enthusiasm: its emphasis on direct communion with the divine, its pre- or post- or intersubjective transmissions of feeling, its fundamental threat to (and indeed dialectic production of) the timely, autonomous, and disembodied subject.

As Nancy Ruttenburg, Alberto Toscano, and others have argued, debates over enthusiasm and fanaticism were at the very heart of liberalism's dramas of agency, authority, and individuation.[61] Detailing a crucial prehistory of the "self-possessed" liberal-democratic subject, Ruttenburg describes enthusiasm in the Great Awakening as a spectacle of decentered authority, where anybody might in theory give voice to the divine directive. As Ruttenburg argues, "One might say that the modern era of possessive individualism was anticipated or accompanied by that of possessed individualism, where the invisible world came to signify not the domain of God's determinations but the hidden realm of individual imagination and desire, simultaneously elicited and rejected in the performance of spectral possession."[62] Spectral possession was, in turn, subject to close scrutiny—what Ruttenburg calls a "semiotics of authenticity"—as spiritual authorities, lay preachers, and critics each attempted to codify the external expression of internal grace.[63] With its obsessive attention to bodily inscriptions—to wounds, badges, and other corporeal signifiers of experience—*Red Badge* attests to the ongoing life of this semiotics of authenticity. Yet it also courts the very ambiguity that motivated such intensive efforts to authenticate the bodily "fruits" of religious inspiration. Hence the strangeness of Jim's death seems enmeshed with the possibility entertained throughout the scene of an otherworldly agency literally invading Jim's body, animating its fits and starts and signaling the communion that Henry so ardently desires. Likewise, Jim's wild gesticulations and "imp-like enthusiasm"—which rehearse the movements of minstrelsy without fully collapsing into it—trouble the categories of performance and experience that might otherwise contain them.

In the antebellum era, "enthusiasm" helped name a variety of religious experience whose validity *as* experience was always in question. It also helped name the insurgent threat of "possessed individualism" when enacted by women, African Americans, Native Americans, and others excluded from liberalism's universalist vision—enthusiasm was in this sense a technique of management, or a version of what Tracy Fessenden describes as the "secularist-gendering-racializing knot," in which the feminization and racialization of "religion" as a knowable category works historically and in tandem to discipline subjects deemed irrational by the secular liberal state.[64] Antirevivalists, for example, depicted the enthusiasm of the Great Awakening as "an affair of the passions particularly attractive to emotionally and intellectually weak women whose public display of emotion in uncontrolled screams and groans infected 'the Credulous' around them"—essentially a drama of politico-erotic possibility, where enthusiasm might bind gendered (and thus grotesquely public) subjects in a form of uncontrolled, infectious, fleshy communion.[65] While, as Fessenden notes, the feminization and privatization of religion often works to reinforce the secular state's reproduction of whiteness and masculinity, the discourse of enthusiasm during the Great Awakening also helped produce distinctly raced and gendered subjects as the irrational, fleshy exceptions to possessive individualism. At the same time, the specter of subjection to divine grace fully haunted the discourse of individualism, as the potential for African Americans and, even more crucially, enslaved persons to embody divine inspiration threatened to illuminate the foundational irrationality of white liberalism with its conception of personhood (and indeed whiteness) as property.[66] In this sense, the enthusiast's status as "possessed"—an object or mechanism of external agency—provides a foundational echolalia with the enslaved person's status as the object of external possession. Hence what Ruttenburg describes as the enslaved person's "involuntary and unanticipated revelation of the nation's invisible content," or democracy's constitutional irrationality, contained and violently externalized (in distinctly gendered forms) as the erotic symbology of racial difference.[67] In this sense, enthusiasm was less a challenge to normative modes of political subject formation than it was an impetus to them, an antenormative and relational disturbance.

While Ruttenburg traces the trajectory of democracy's irrational utterance toward the production of an American authorship rooted in the aesthetics of de-centered selfhood (deployed by Walt Whitman and Herman Melville, among others), one might also point to the potency of enthusiasm for antebellum figures like Nat Turner, who mobilized the prophetic strain in the service of self-emancipation. As John Mac Kilgore suggests, the history of enthusiasm itself was always already haunted by the "historical specter of black rebellion," as "the language of enthusiasm was used pejoratively with respect to black politics, not so much because it represented an instance of inadmissible terror to white audiences but because it represented an instance of familiar democratic revolt inadmissibly applied by black people."[68] In the antebellum era, as Kilgore suggests, enthusiasm was used alternately to signal a democratic love of liberty and to contain and marginalize minoritarian radicalisms; in its pejorative form, it helped name a discourse of American freedom that was (and is) entirely apiece with white supremacy. Thus Emerson could claim in his 1841 essay "Circles" that "nothing great was ever achieved without enthusiasm"—without throwing off the bounds of reason—while Turner's 1831 rebellion and John Brown's 1859 raid on Harper's Ferry were prime examples of what many onlookers deemed a dangerously politicized enthusiasm, by way of defusing their radicalisms. Yet as Kilgore argues, enthusiasm's *ex-stasis* was also a politically potent form of affective transmission, as Turner, Brown, and others figured themselves as prophetic vessels for radical emancipation's otherworldly force.[69]

The history of enthusiasm is deeply interwoven with Crane's family history. Here we might consider the prominence of his father and grandfather in the Methodist ministry and their postwar familial rift over Holiness revivals, which emphasized a return to dramatic spectacles of intense religious experience.[70] As Christopher Benfey points out, Crane's maternal forebears referred to 1870s revival campsites as "battlegrounds," extending and literally "reviving" the war as a mass metaphysical reckoning and pointing toward the unfolding of the Holiness movement in immanently repeatable (and deeply theatrical) scenes of individual battle with the Holy Ghost.[71] Crane's father, in contrast, rejected the "second blessing" at the heart of Holiness theology and preached against contagious outbreaks of religious and political sentiment. Of itinerant preaching and revivals, Rev. Jonathan Townley Crane noted, "In the minds of a certain class it fosters a love of excitement which wars directly with true devotion."[72] In the wake of Brown's raid, Reverend Crane preached caution against precisely this excitement. In a December 11, 1859, sermon titled "Christian Duty in Regard to American Slavery," Reverend Crane noted, "I am aware that every strong tide of popular conviction and emotion creates what men call enthusiasts, just as every mountain stream creates foam. Still, he is not a prudent helmsman who makes a bubble his pilot through a tortuous, rocky channel."[73] Registering both the effervescence and the political force of enthusiasm in fomenting popular antislavery feeling, Jonathan Townley Crane worked to naturalize it, charting a course away from its unpredictable currents.

It is also worth noting that this critique of enthusiasm easily comports with the tract for which the elder Crane is best known: his 1849 "Essay on Dancing," which denounced the practice in nearly all its forms. Aligning religious dancing alternately with Bacchanalian excess and with "savagery," for example, Crane both universalized and condemned (in racist and colonial terms) the impetus to dance:

> Dancing formed, and yet forms, a part of the religious ceremonies of the savage and the semi-civilized, the bond and the free. In the East, the devotees of Brama and Vishnoo perform dances in honour of their vile superstitions. Troops of dancing girls belong to every temple there, who bring great revenues to the establishment, though not by dancing alone. The degraded inhabitant of Western Africa puts a few gravel stones into a calabash, and sings and dances around some thick bush, in which his superstitious fears tell him that an evil spirit resides. Thus it is seen that no great degree of intelligence, or refinement, or virtue is necessary to an appreciation of the dance, but that the barbarous, the sensual, and the degraded of all nations admire it, and practise it, to at least an equal extent with others.[74]

Crane's account of religious dances anticipates what a late nineteenth-century discourse of comparative religions would offer in less explicitly denunciatory terms: an effort to track and analyze transhistorical modes of ecstatic religious practice (an effort I'll explore further in chapter 3). As we'll see, such efforts—part of secularism's wide-scale production of normative religious feeling and religious embodiment under the sign of rationalist investigation—helped produce religion as a knowable category *across* cultural difference while, at the same time, cementing that difference as a naturalized fact.[75] In its conjuring of "savage" and "semi-civilized" dancing across time and place, Crane's tract also articulates what Kélina Gotman has described as "choreomania": "a hyperbolic, feminine, and queer sort of expansive gesturality spilling beyond the individual body into public space," closely linked to discourses of enthusiasm in their shared focus on the insurgent threat of contagious affect and comportment.[76]

As the Reverend Crane's response to Harper's Ferry highlights, enthusiasm was at its heart a colonial discourse. The invocation of enthusiastic religion was also thoroughly racialized, both in the antebellum era and during Reconstruction, when white reformers scrutinized black worship practices as a moral gauge of the freedman's readiness for citizenship. In *The Burden of Black Religion*, Curtis Evans describes the transition from antebellum "romantic racialism"—which attributed to blackness an innate and emotional religiosity, in terms ranging from benign to celebratory—to the post-Reconstruction era's more insidious alignment of African American religion with pathological feeling and grotesque physicality. As Evans argues, white Northern observers mobilized racial difference to account for difference in worship styles, developing an emergent psychopathology of black religion while treating ecstatic worship as a particularly intoxicating form of local color. Evans points to the example of Elizabeth Kilham, who traveled south after the war to serve as a schoolteacher for newly freed children, and whose 1870 "Sketches in Color" for *Putnam's Monthly* details a worship service in Richmond, Virginia, following a visit by General Oliver Otis Howard, founder of the Freedman's Bureau. Kilham begins her sketch with an imperative to honor the Civil War wounded (including Howard, who lost his right arm in battle), then describes the church service in terms that ascribe to blackness itself a form of fanaticism: "So wild is the torrent of excitement, that, sweeping away reason and sense, tosses men and women upon its waves, mingling the words of religion with the howling of wild beasts and the ravings of madmen."[77] Standard in its anxiety about the "wild" unreason of black religion, Kilham's description emphasizes the transmission of feeling in terms that resonate with the enthusiastic (in)sensibility at the heart of Jim's death sequence:

> A fog seemed to fill the church; the lights burned dimly, the air was close, almost to suffocation; an invisible power seemed to hold us in its iron grasp; the excitement was working upon us also, and sent the blood surging in wild torrents to the brain, that reeled in darkened terror under the shock. A few moments more, and I think we should have shrieked in unison with the crowd.
>
> We worked our way through the struggling mass, sometimes pushed and beaten back, by those who, with set eyeballs and rigid faces,—dead, for the time, to things external,—were not conscious what they did. With the first breath of cool night air upon our faces, the excitement vanished;

but the strain upon the nervous system has been too great, for it to recover at once its usual tone. More than one of the party leaned against the wall, and burst into hysterical tears; even strong men were shaken, and stood trembling and exhausted.[78]

"Dead, for the time, to things external": this may very well be a version of the "documentary anaesthetics" that Mary Esteve attributes to Crane's many rigid-faced bodies. But a version in which the excess of feeling—not least among white observers—amounts to a kind of insensibility (which, in its queer illegibility, in its challenge to normative constructions of religious feeling, in its sonic virtuosity, in all the layers of violence *and* possibility attached to black worship under and after slavery, may very well have served as a radical refuge from "things external"—what is "beaten back" in this passage, consciously or not, is the denial of that possibility, as well as the very possibility of feeling in "unison").[79]

While Kilham's sketch registers the anxiety of being "swept away"—a persistent trope in the description of enthusiasm since at least the eighteenth century—local color depictions of postbellum black or interracial camp meetings almost invariably reified the racialized distance between religious and secular forms of witness, often by attributing a mix of emotional excess and mimetic (or minstrel) skill to African American worshipers. In August 1872, for example, *Harper's Monthly* profiled "A Negro Camp Meeting in the South," where "under the shadow of the mighty forest trees, singing sweet, weird melodies, and in the wild exaltation of religious devotion, the poor creature finds some compensation for the bitter, thankless toil of daily life."[80] Posing as the "calm observer," the author notes the "true devotion" of the camp meeting while reproducing a series of minstrel types, depicting the "pickanniny, solemnly munching her bit of corn-bread," as "evidently 'taking notes' for future use. She watches with a knowing air the coquettish damsel who is 'posing' with natural grace, and doing her religion most becomingly. The small pupil will be able to do the same thing when she gets big enough, for the negroes are apt scholars." Here "religion" is imminently consumable as a feminized form of racial minstrelsy, an "apt" outward performance linked both to the suspect emotionalism of ecstatic worship and to the seductions of the "coquettish damsel" (close cousin to the black dandy's hypermasculinized courtship).[81] As "A Negro Camp Meeting in the South" makes clear, at stake in "enthusiasm" was the believer's mimetic potential: her realist performance of "true devotion," as well as the capacity for that performance to reproduce such feeling in others (the illustration that accompanied "A Negro Camp Meeting in the South" placed women and children in the foreground as observers and in some cases as fallen bodies, dead for a time to the scene around them; see figure 2.2).

By the early twentieth century, a nascent psychology of religion would categorize African American religion as "emotional and hypnotic to the core," authorizing popular ideologies of race with the imprimatur of academic discourse.[82] Psychologist G. Stanley Hall, for example, coalesced racial and religious typologies in his account of "The Negro in Africa and America": "To the negro of the lower type religion is a kind of Pythian frenzy and the devotee becomes mad with supernal joy. He communicates with God in abandon, in vision and trance. Depravity, damnation, ecstasy, goodness, heaven and hell, are a simple and forcible creed."[83] As

Figure 2.2. Sol Eytinge Jr., *A Negro Camp Meeting in the South*, illustration in *Harper's Weekly*, 16 (August 10, 1872), 620. Library of Congress Prints and Photographs Division.

Evans details, Hall and his followers produced a moralized spectrum of religious expression ranging from simple primitive emotionalism to the "true" and "proper" religion of disciplined citizens. While religious revivals provided the highly sought material of sociological inquiry, Hall and others worked to corral the threat of outsized religious feeling by approaching it as racialized pathology. Or as Evans argues, "Self-restraint was crucial for a free people: Emotional excess meant a loss of rational control. Thus the emotional Negro embodied all that was threatening to the nation."[84] That threat, I would emphasize, carried with it the persistent, if transmuted, logic of possessed flesh: the excess of irrationality embodied by slavery's hyperrationalized forms of control projected outward onto bodies deemed decidedly too "free."

The sociological treatment of religious affect as a primitive atavism (which I explore in detail in the following chapter) was, at its core, a project of racial knowledge and management, a project made even more explicit in works by Hall's students and inheritors. In his 1905 tract *Primitive Traits in Religious Revivals*, sociologist Frederick Morgan Davenport (a student of Hall's) offered an evolutionary narrative of religious development that explained black and indigenous religious expressions as "reflex phenomena" rooted in gestures belonging to "primitive passion" and to "child races" (Davenport noted of the black enthusiast, "Here is a primitive man with primitive traits in a modern environment").[85] Davenport linked religious feeling to the rhythms of the flesh, and thereby to racial difference, figured as a kind of arrested development: "The group of motor manifestations, the rhythm, the shout, the 'falling out,' are exceedingly characteristic. High feeling, discharging itself in muscular action, and discharging itself rhythmically, is everywhere a spontaneous manifestation of children and of child races."[86] Describing a "simple 'experience meetin'" in much the same terms as Kilham's local color, Davenport narrates one speaker's lyric success as the production of contagious affect:

> He spoke in rhythm, and the audience rhythmically responded. He was speedily in full movement, head, arms, feet, eyes, face, and soon he was lost in ecstasy. And the contagion swept everything before it. Even the sound sleepers on the fringe of the crowd were caught and carried into the movement as if by a tide of the sea. At the very climax of the

meeting, a woman rose to her feet, moved forward to the open space in front of the pulpit, evidently under the compulsion of the lyric wave. Having reached the front, in one wild burst of pent-up emotion, she fell rigid to the floor and lay there motionless during the rest of the service. She was not disturbed. Like the devotees of the ghost-dance, she, too, was believed to be enjoying visions of the unseen world.[87]

As I'll explore in chapter 3, Davenport's analogy—between the camp meeting and the Ghost Dance—exemplifies a broader effort to consign religious difference to an evolutionary time scale, with the ecstatic figured as a primitive holdover, the infectious residue of the past in a secular present. Learned and spontaneous, muscular and hereditary, the camp meeting's "irrational rhythmic ecstasy" was read as an atavism at odds with modern society, as debates over worship style (entrenched in racial and regional stereotypes) were interwoven with the status of African American social progress at large. From local color to sociological treatise, black "enthusiasm" proved ripe material in the post-Reconstruction era, which layered the investigative energies of newly professionalized disciplines with the production of cultural difference as an eminently consumable "variety."[88] At the same time, the attention paid to black enthusiasm served as the negative image of white supremacy's own enthusiastic production of bodies: its wildly contagious sentiments, its enforcement—through lynching and other forms of violence—of the (il)logic of the flesh.

What is archived or let loose, then, in Jim's gesticulations but these multiple and intersecting histories of enfleshment, performed in and at the moment of death as the very limit point of realist articulation? Certainly *Red Badge* participates in the religious and secular management of enthusiasm, superimposing Dandy Jim's iterative inscription of race as outsized embodiment with a Protestant semiotics (and erotics) of enthusiastic religion, and containing both within the realist desire for an expressive body—one that might transmit experience (including the experience of the past) in all its perceptual immediacy. Yet if enthusiasm operates in this sense as a mode of subjection in *Red Badge*, it also circulates as a fantasy of communicability, of reproducing experience across bodies in time. Indeed, as the novel suggests almost from its opening pages, enthusiasm operates not simply as a transmitted affect but indeed as *the* affect of transmission, as Henry's decision to enlist emerges as the effect not of individual resolve but of popular feeling: "One night, as he lay in bed, the winds had carried to him the clangoring of the church bell as some enthusiast jerked the rope frantically to tell the twisted news of a great battle. This voice of the people rejoicing in the night had made him shiver in a prolonged ecstasy of excitement."[89] Ecstasy here is a model of self-as-communion; inaugurating its narrative of violent subject formation through the shivering, visceral reverberations of the vox populi, *Red Badge* treats enthusiasm both as a powerful mode of attachment and as a resounding echo—an affect that will, by the end of this cacophonous novel, sound like a question mark about how far and how long history lingers.

Unaccountable Remainders

If Jim Conklin is soon forgotten in the space of the narrative, he invariably reappears elsewhere in altered form. Indeed, Crane returned time and again to scenes that seem to echo and redouble the creeping strangeness of Jim Conklin, his teetering on the brink of multiple figurations. Perhaps the most striking of these appears in Crane's 1898 novella *The Monster*, a narrative in which the disfiguration of a black stable-hand brings into a relief a deeper, anterior dehumanization that expresses itself through layers of mesmerizing performance. Like Jim Conklin, the "monster"—formerly Henry Johnson—is an object of extreme curiosity and ambivalence, figured through the inscrutability of ritual performance: "The monster on the box had turned its black crêpe countenance toward the sky, and was waving its arms in time to a religious chant. 'Look at him now,' cried a little boy. They turned, and were transfixed by the solemnity and mystery of the indefinable gestures. The wail of the melody was mournful and slow. They drew back. It seemed to spellbind them with the power of a funeral."[90] The monster (no longer "Henry" or "he," only "it" and the object pronoun "him") oscillates on the box between subject and object, saint and spectacle; subject to whiteness's consuming gaze, the unsettling ambiguity of Henry's "indefinable gestures" and mournful wail recalls the auction block as much as the camp meeting. It also recalls and revises Henry's earlier figuration as a black dandy; before the grisly fire that defaces Henry, "profane groups" of onlookers taunt him with the kinesics of minstrelsy: "Hello, Henry! Going to walk for a cake to-night?"[91] As the narrative unfolds, *The Monster* substitutes violent trauma for minstrel performance, highlighting their proximity; it also treats Henry's monstrosity as a form of mysticism, rendering Henry at once an inscrutable subject and a spectacular object of white observation (we see the same dynamic at work in Henry's black crepe veil, which evokes a grotesque description of Henry's burned flesh through the very idiom of its concealment). If, in this sense, *The Monster* reproduces the popular idiom of black religious feeling for white consumption, it also recognizes the violence that adheres to such spellbound looking.

Throughout *The Monster*, Henry is an object of amusement and of horror; in Jacqueline Goldsby's crucial reading (which links Crane's story to the 1892 lynching of Robert Lewis in Port Jervis, New Jersey), the violence done to Henry's body operates as the disavowed but no less spectacular sign of lynching's cultural logic, its status as endemic to the imbrications of capitalism and white supremacy. In this sense, Henry's "accidental" defacement literalizes the historical effacement of lynching as a function of its violence; as Goldsby argues, Crane's story "archives how easily it was then, has been, and continues to be for white Americans to remember to forget the violence done to black people in the name of progress and achievement."[92] For Goldsby, this remembering to forget constitutes the "realism" of *The Monster*: its simultaneous participation in and depiction of a post-Reconstruction economy that depended on the repetitive, mundane, and violent disavowal of black personhood. Much as in *Red Badge*, the realism of *The Monster* operates not through historical reference but through a repetitive enactment of the very forgetting that constitutes its historicity. Lynching may be forgotten, but it is not gone. On the contrary, it emerges everywhere in Crane's depersonalizing repetitions.

Such depersonalizing repetitions, as we've seen, are fundamentally rooted in the traumas of the post-Reconstruction era, even as they attest to a longer and co-imbricated history of religion and racialization. Enacted as a ritual of compulsion and producing bodies as objects of external force, the ecstatic, too, is a site where history emerges not as reference but as spellbinding performance. Here we witness history's "indefinable gesture": arms waved, ropes jerked, feeling dislodged and made communicable (not least through the literary text). Indeed for Crane—deeply versed in Methodist debates over the "proper" expression of religious feeling—the very uncertainty of gesture made it a potent corporeal idiom, a site from which to interrogate the limits of communicability. Consider the commerce in religious forms evinced in *The Black Riders and Other Lines* (1895), where Crane's "bitter rejection of religious texts"[93] is nevertheless haunted by religion's nearly constant and performative reanimation as a form of bodily citation:

> I stood upon a highway,
> And, behold, there came
> Many strange peddlers.
> To me each one made gestures,
> Holding forth little images, saying,
> "This is my pattern of God.
> Now this is the God I prefer."[94]

Moving away from patterns of metrical regularity yet testifying to a kind of motor memory—an insistence on evangelism's afterlife in gesture—the poem holds forth a tantalizing but ultimately suspect image of divine inspiration, even as it points to a larger pattern in Crane's oeuvre. Rehearsing the dynamics of performance embedded in *Red Badge* and *The Monster*, where a reader/spectator confronts a figure whose agency is multiple, constrained, and ambiguous (here, the work of "strange peddlers"), such moments offer a sense of occluded but no less potent possibility embedded in gesture itself—in its capacity both to recall something and to produce something as yet unarticulated.

Potent with the threat of self-delusion or theatrical deception, it was ultimately enthusiasm's communicability—its tendency to spread from body to body in patterned expressions of grace—that most unsettled critics of religious exuberance. Fittingly, Jim Conklin's death scene, like Henry himself, is entirely preoccupied with the possibilities of enthusiastic transmission. Returning once more to that scene, we might note how enthusiasm appears to graft onto Henry via mimetic sympathy, with his face "twisted into an expression" of Jim's imagined agony. Henry's self-interested spectatorship—his desire to glean some knowledge of death without having to experience it—transitions here into a fascinated, agonized mimicry of enthusiasm's disfigurations, as Henry himself grows desperately corpse-like in his effort to understand. And while the tattered soldier later interprets Jim as a "jim-dandy," fitting him (as we've seen) into a recognizable idiom of racialized personhood, Henry performs an alternative critical praxis: "The youth desired to screech out his grief. He was stabbed. But his tongue lay dead in the tomb of his mouth. He threw himself again upon the ground and began to brood."[95] Henry's writhing, wounded response is to circumvent his own linguistic arrest by throwing himself "again" upon the ground, performing his com-passion with the corpse—a practice less of identification than of being-with.[96] Here observation and participation are irrevocably blurred, and if he is not literally wounded by Jim's death, Henry does not emerge unscathed from the experience of witnessing it. The "intimate knowledge" that Henry claims of Jim is both exploded and extended, as Jim's enthusiasm suggests the possibility of intimacy without knowledge, a grafting of experience across bodies drawn—and drawn together—by its strange, performative force.

With practiced gesture, Crane's texts habitually return to scenes that seem both to register and to exceed the terms of racial trauma, groping for what Cathy Caruth terms "an *ethical* relation to the real" even as they hold in suspense whether obsessive return might constitute such a relation.[97] Crane's repetitions do little to diminish the ambiguity of the scene of suffering/performance, nor do they dampen the aesthetic and political stakes of reproducing them in realist description. Rather, in repeatedly archiving the ecstatic body, Crane's texts offer ecstasy as a figure for history's own erratic movements: if history *is* anything, it is beside itself (*exstasis*, out of place or body, quite literally animating the present). This is the "real" that *Red Badge* makes palpable, without redeeming the violence—and specifically the racial violence—that reinforces it. Jim's "jim-dandy" reanimates a violent history without claiming to comprehend it and gestures toward the ambivalence of performance as precisely the arena in which literature might grapple with history's unaccountable remainders. Dramatizing the proximity between ecstasy and abjection that Julia Kristeva has theorized, *Red Badge* suggests that both linger within the very process of signification; that is, literature's "making sense" of the body and of the war invariably archives the rhythmic return of their spectacular senselessness.[98] At the site of Jim's transition into a regular "jim-dandy," we find the return of that repressed enthusiasm at the very heart of realist aesthetics.

Mirrorlike Reversals

In his introduction to a 1960 reprint of *Red Badge*, Ralph Ellison described Crane as the most "war haunted" of nineteenth-century American novelists, despite his having been born six years after the end of the war.[99] Always attuned to the uses of haunting, Ellison reads the novel less as a postmortem on the Civil War than as a sustained grappling with its aftershocks, less a historical fiction than a fictional testimony to history's ghostly—but no less effectual—returns. Republished in *Shadow and Act* (1964) as "Stephen Crane and the Mainstream of American Fiction," the essay subtly testifies to the reverberations between Crane's 1890s and Ellison's 1960s, continually evoking the war's twentieth-century afterlife:

> To put it drastically, if war, as Clausewitz insisted, is the continuation of politics by other means, it requires little imagination to see American life since the abandonment of the Reconstruction as an abrupt reversal of that formula: the continuation of the Civil War by means other than arms. In this sense the conflict has not only gone unresolved but the line between civil war and civil peace has become so blurred as to require of the sensitive man a questioning attitude toward every aspect of the nation's self-image. Stephen Crane, in his time, was such a man.[100]

Ellison's vision of history (much like Crane's) is chiastic, rhetorically registering the injurious reversals and continuations—the proliferation of Dandy Jims and jim-dandies—that marked Crane's moment as well as his own.[101]

Like Ellison after him, Crane wrote from within the blur of post-Reconstruction America, performing radical stylistic breaks while insisting on a yet unexorcised or underexorcised historical excess within modernity's streamlined aesthetics.[102] Part of Crane's work was to keep that excess spectacularly visible, to register the lingering ambiguity of the wounded national body, itself a figure of constant, strange reanimation, always threatening to fall or fall flat. And like Ellison after him, he had an ear for sardonic rhythms in the background or underground; he knew well that writing realist fiction in the aftermath of the war meant representing the "mirrorlike reversals" that were everywhere on display.[103] Crane had his own army of invisible or less visible men (and women), ostensibly minor characters whose performances are nevertheless central to how we read his fiction. If such figures invariably disappear in fictional and literary-historical memory, their disappearance itself is significant; moreover, it is never complete.[104] We might look, for example, to what Jim's performance itself represses or archives: that of an earlier, even more obscure figure in *Red Badge*, whose fleeting presence has repeatedly perplexed critics (Ellison and others). In the early pages of the novel, we are briefly introduced to "a negro teamster who had been dancing upon a cracker-box with the hilarious encouragement of twoscore soldiers," who is "deserted" as soon as Jim begins to prophesize about the movement of the army.[105] In the absence of an audience, the teamster sits "mournfully down," anticipating the scene with which we began, the dance that it both mourns and archives.

It is possible to read the teamster's dance—and others have—as a self-conscious gesture toward the novel's omission of historical and political context, a figure for what must be forgotten in order to represent the experience of a single soldier.[106] But such a reading would need to avoid reinscribing the teamster and Jim as Henry's sacrificial others, for in their very repetition, they are not simply visualized and discarded, nor do they submit fully to the stillness that the realist text would seem to impose. Read together, it is easier to see how Jim's dance repeats and transforms the teamster's, testifying in gesture to its reverberative force. Without collapsing these two performances or losing sight of the compulsion and violence that they also register, we might note that each complements the interpretive impulse—Henry's and our own—with embodied (performed) relation. If *Red Badge* remains obsessed with badges, wounds, and other signs of codified experience, these dances—their very status as undetermined play, as fitfully embodied performances—resist the realist effort to order experience through language. Instead, they archive—bury, mourn, and revivify—enthusiasm, that invariably suspect, indeterminable force that welds bodies together in the fantasy of shared experience, which is also what we call history.

3

The Ghost Dance and Realism's Techno-Spiritual Frontier

A shadow becomes his signature.[1] In image after image, we see the ethnographer's outline. In early photographs, he is standing next to a tripod; we see hands positioned to manipulate the wet-plate glass negative (see figures 3.1 and 3.2). Later, the tripod has been replaced by a Kodak handcamera.[2] In the Kodak's rounded images, the shadow is almost always the same, lingering at the bottom of the visual field, recognizable by its narrow-brimmed bowler hat (see figures 3.3–3.5). In the deracinated logic of the archive, the Kodak images are labeled simply "Ceremony—Ghost Dance."[3] While the dancers appear in blurred motion, the shadow is still, the clearest focus of the image. At least, it figures stillness (we know shadows move with the sun—a way of telling time—just as photography choreographs stillness only through the coordinated motion of bodies and light). Occasionally, the shadow overlaps the subject; in such cases, the image literalizes ethnography's institution as the production of self-portraits, the portrait of self through other. Or we might say the shadow haunts the production of the ethnographic subject as a racialized, photographic object of knowledge. Here the shadow functions as a material and temporal trace of a viewing process that colonized Native Americans by transforming them into the fleshy material of empirical investigation—and that concurrently fixed "Indianness" as an index of religious, racial, and temporal difference. We might also say the shadow anticipates the death of this process and the inauguration of something new. These possibilities are not mutually exclusive.[4]

In its most literal sense, the shadow on the image belongs to James Mooney, an early member of the Bureau of American Ethnology. Mooney is best known for his 1896 report on what he called "the Ghost Dance religion," a pan-tribal movement centered on the Paiute prophet Wovoka.[5] This chapter examines Mooney's effort, beginning in the immediate aftermath of the 1890 massacre at Wounded Knee, to archive the Ghost Dance through photographic and phonographic recordings.

Figure 3.1. James Mooney, "Chief of Tribe Holding Pipe near Wood Frame Building 1892." Gelatin Glass Negative. National Anthropological Archives, Smithsonian Institution. [NAA INV 06257300]

Figure 3.2. James Mooney, "Mother and Maiden Daughter Both in Native Dress, n.d." Gelatin Glass Negative. National Anthropological Archives, Smithsonian Institution. [NAA INV 06320900]

Figure 3.3. James Mooney, "Ceremony—Ghost Dance [1891]" (view from outside the circle). National Anthropological Archives, Smithsonian Institution.

Intent on reproducing a ritual practice he believed to be disappearing, Mooney sought to capture and save the dance as an index of Native authenticity. Yet as we will see, Mooney's technological reproductions demanded the dance's repeat performance, giving the lie to its purported "death" and brokering a complex relationship between realist practices and the Ghost Dance's own promise of revivification. Reading Mooney's recordings alongside a broader set of late nineteenth and early twentieth century popular reenactments of the dance, I argue that ethnographic realism borrowed its epistemological authority from the very visionary practices it aimed to reproduce, insisting on its own capacity to record spiritual practices while channeling the power of media to preserve, resurrect, and reanimate the dead. In the texts that I treat here, the Ghost Dance was at once an object of ethnographic knowledge and an aesthetic production requiring constant reiteration; its purported

Figure 3.4. James Mooney, "Ceremony—Ghost Dance [1891]" (showing two standing figures). National Anthropological Archives, Smithsonian Institution.

disappearance as a cultural practice was both the effect and the engine of an immense cultural output. As I suggest, realism's drive to constantly reenact the Ghost Dance as a lost ritual rehearses the relentless vanishing of time and of people that seamlessly sutured Native American genocide to modernity, but it also points to the performative labor that such suturing required, with its accompanying fantasies of time regained or recovered. Despite their investment in the progress narratives that consigned Native Americans to the sphere of historical conclusion, realist reenactments of the Ghost Dance nevertheless offer a fundamental challenge to the temporality of vanishing, raising the specter of the supposedly vanished in ways that echo, if not redouble, the Ghost Dance's own insistence on the very real presence of the dead.

In this chapter, I track these reenactments across a wide range of visual, sonic, and literary texts, stretching from James Mooney's

Figure 3.5. James Mooney, "Ceremony—Ghost Dance [1891]" (showing single figure with others in background). National Anthropological Archives, Smithsonian Institution.

ethnographic photography and phonographic performances, to Sioux dancers filmed by Thomas Edison and William Cody, to Hamlin Garland's ethnographic realism in *The Book of the American Indian* (1923). In describing this body of texts as "ethnographic realism," my aim is not to eclipse the spaces between ethnographic reportage and recording, filmed performance, and literary realism; it is instead to articulate a similarity in how these texts produce racial and religious difference as intertwined and knowable categories, functions of a performed "thick description" that would come to characterize the emergent disciplines of ethnography and anthropology. As Nancy Bentley and Michael Elliott have each argued, narrative realism is rooted in the production, observation, and preservation of cultural difference, a project it shared with anthropology and ethnography at the turn of the twentieth century.[6] As Bentley points out, ethnographic realism neither fully consolidates nor necessarily subverts the colonial mechanisms that underwrite it. On the contrary, it revels in the pleasures and anxieties of difference while securing its own observational expertise. Following Bentley, I argue that we do well to insist on the proximity between reveling and expertise, or between the ecstatic dance—borrowed, rehearsed, and endlessly replayed as the sign of racial and cultural otherness—and the theatricalized production of the "real."

At stake in reading these texts as cross-medial reenactments—rather than simply as efforts to document or record the "real Indian" presumed to be vanished or vanishing—is the complex temporality of realist practice that emerges.[7] The archive of ethnographic realism at times confirms the long-standing critical narrative of realism: that in reproducing the dominant order of the present, its temporality is wedded to the ideological contours of progress.[8] But it is worth asking what happens to that temporality if we expand our account of realism to include the temporally and affectively saturated "real" produced through ethnographic performance. As we'll see, part of what emerges are even clearer links between colonial violence, the linear progress narratives of liberal reform, and "imperialist nostalgia" for Native spirituality, wherein the fantasy of reenactment makes and remakes the vast spiritual frontier as a space to be colonized over and over again as part of an inevitable (and indeed technological) march forward.[9] In this sense, realist ethnographies of the Ghost Dance exemplify what Fredric Jameson describes as realism's "insatiable colonization of the as yet unexplored and inexpressed," a telos it shares (as Jameson notes) with modernism.[10]

Much like *The Red Badge of Courage*—which both rehearses and revivifies the violence of racial personhood—various reenactments of the Ghost Dance in the aftermath of Wounded Knee raise crucial questions about what Rebecca Schneider calls the "queasiness" of time turning back on itself. In reenactment, the unfinishedness of the historical event "pulses with a kind of living afterlife in an ecstasy of variables," troubling the "when" of historical origins as much as the possibility of exact replication.[11] Read in these terms, realism's mimetic excess begins to look less confidently tethered to the present and more thickly weighted or "sticky" both with the violence of the past and with the prophesied future.[12] Reading realism as reenactment, or as tarrying with a past it believes distinctly past enough to reenact, we encounter the capacity of its repeat performances to produce an unsettling, ecstatic "liveness" in the face of death.

The ethnographer's shadow, as we will see, lives in excess of the kind of realism that his images were meant to secure. As Mooney narrated in his 1896 report to the Bureau of Ethnology, entitled *The Ghost-Dance Religion and the Sioux Outbreak of 1890*, the prophecy that gave rise to the Ghost Dance was received by delegates from the northern Arapaho, Cheyenne, and Sioux, among others, and carried by railroad and telegraph from the prophet Wovoka's home on the Walker River Reservation in Nevada to the northern plains in 1889 and 1890. It called for a series of ritual deaths that might inaugurate the larger death of white colonialism, as well as a collective return of grieved relatives, decimated buffalo herds, and habitable spaces.[13] Ghost dancers would "die" into another world: "When the time comes there will be no more sickness and everyone will be young again."[14] Mooney would later recount of Wovoka that he received his revelation of the other world "when the sun died" (what Mooney describes as a solar eclipse) and he was taken up to heaven in a feverish fit.[15] There he received the message he would continue to preach until his death in 1932: that, performed correctly and in the spirit of peace, the dance would "hasten the event" of the new world.[16] Less messianic than syncretic in its cosmology, the dance enfolded Christian redemption while making the return of the Native dead and the restoration of a rotten earth its telos.[17] Ghost dancers formed a circle in the late afternoon or evening, when the shadows were long. They moved from right to left, to the rhythm of songs composed specifically for the ritual. One by one they cast their bodies down, reenacting past, present, and future deaths. Punctuated by individual falls—what Mooney would call, in the language of nineteenth-century positivism, cataleptic "fits"—the

Ghost Dance demanded its performers cross into the other world in order to usher in a new one. In Wovoka's vision, the dance would hasten the time when the project of empire itself would become spectral, buried, a shadow at the margins.

Mooney's images of the Ghost Dance are at once the event and the trace of colonial surveillance. First and foremost, they telegraph the continued expression of a forcefully prohibited practice; many were taken in the months and years following Wounded Knee, the December 29, 1890, massacre of nearly three hundred Lakota men, women, and children who attempted to flee the US military's suppression of the Ghost Dance at Pine Ridge, South Dakota. At the same time, signaling the photograph's collusion with both the colonial logic of vanishing and the ethnographic urgency of preservation, they register the future anterior, or "will have been," of the dancers themselves. In this sense, what Roland Barthes described as every photograph's anticipation of death, its future anterior, is built into the reiterative was-ness that attaches to Indianness as the very operation of empire.[18] Jodi Byrd has argued that "even in the present of their removal," Indians are "always already past perfect," always receding in the temporal imaginary that underwrites colonial conquest.[19] "Indians are spectral," Byrd notes, "implied and felt, but remain as lamentable casualties of national progress who haunt the United States on the cusp of empire and are destined to disappear with the frontier itself."[20] In turn, the genocidal violence that produces the Indian as a "spectral" or "felt" presence mirrors the ethnographic photograph's incessant reproduction of the death of "Indianness" to come.

Like many of his contemporaries, Mooney believed that indigenous cultures were destined to disappear (effacing and naturalizing a violent history of removal), though he did not subscribe to the mission famously articulated by Richard H. Pratt, founder of Carlisle School—"kill the Indian" to "save the man," a policy of assimilation wherein "Indianness" might be leeched, amputated, or disciplined out of the potentially civilized, self-sufficient, individualized body. Nevertheless, both Mooney's fieldwork and his photographic practice—early versions of "salvage ethnography"—were motivated at least in part by the temporality of vanishing that structured both the Bureau of American Ethnology's efforts to document Native cultures and the assimilationist policies of the US government. Assimilation, the narrative went, would not only transform Indians into proper liberal, landowning, capitalist subjects; it would also bring them up to speed with modernity, in part by forcefully disappearing any trace of Indianness, a quality consigned to the haunting stillness of the photograph as ethnographic evidence. Importantly, the documentation of the Ghost Dance as a disappearing "religion" closely intersected with the racializing logic of ethnographic salvage, in which religious difference was imagined, projected, and preserved in the moment of its apparent vanishing. In this vein, Tomoko Masuzawa points out that "religion" comes to be a category of modern thought at precisely the moment when it is presumed by white Europeans and Americans to be disappearing, "becoming circumscribed in such a way that it was finally discernible as a distinct, and limited, phenomenon." Thus, according to Masuzawa, "the modern discourse on religion and religions was from the very beginning—inherently, if also ironically—a discourse of secularization; it was clearly a discourse of othering."[21] Disappearance was the idiom that linked religion as a discrete and observable phenomenon to Indianness as a category of both racial and temporal otherness. In the secularism of ethnographic preservation, the Ghost Dance signaled a double obsolescence, as both "religion" and "Indians" became objects of historical knowledge, legible only via their imminent death.

The Ghost Dance teases and transforms this logic of death.[22] Despite the US government's violent effort to suppress the practice at Pine Ridge, revivals and reenactments of the Ghost Dance proliferated in the aftermath of Wounded Knee, both among the Kiowa, Pawnee, and Canadian Dakota and in the efforts of white ethnographers, writers, and entertainers. For this latter group, the spiritual frontier of the dance—its invocation of another (uncolonized) world—intersected with and surrogated for the mytho-geographical frontier, whose discursive closure necessitated its constant and performative return.[23] Focusing on realist efforts to record and, more distinctly, to reenact the dance, I argue that such reenactments signal the ongoing and reiterative life of settler-colonial violence in the supposed afterlife of the frontier, while manifesting realist practice as a temporally and affectively dense terrain of performance and representation. To read these texts as realism is to understand their role in a capacious Progressive-era knowledge-machine, the apparent "fidelity" of realism's photographic gaze or phonographic ear mobilized in the service of producing and codifying "Indianness" as a form of racial and religious difference. To read them as realist performance is to understand ethnographic preservation as itself a deeply theatrical production of high fidelity, where the "realness" produced is as much an apparition of whiteness as it is a projection of disappearing Indianness. In so doing, we encounter realism's own colonization project—its effort to annex both the sensible and the spectral world—as contingent, antiphonal, and durational: a project in which the stakes of fidelity and preservation are anything but given, and in which the violence done to indigenous subjects is both seen and unseen.

This approach means holding fast to the multiform ghostliness of both the Ghost Dance and its colonialist archive while refusing to fix the dance securely in space or time. To do otherwise—or to treat Mooney's texts as archives of indigenous performance, as a way of definitively knowing the Ghost Dance—threatens to reproduce the very colonialist logic of preserved "presence"; performance, after all, has been linked to the irreproducible "live-ness" of the event, the happening that necessarily disappears. Thus while attending to how colonialist performances produced "Indians" as specters, I follow Diana Taylor in arguing that performance's ontology is in many ways a hauntology: a process of "ghosting" in which the event reverberates far beyond the present tense of its unfolding and proliferates across a set of mediated remainders that continue to participate in a hoped-for resurrection. Mooney's photographs purportedly document indigenous performance, but they also constitute a performance, if we understand performance, with Taylor, as "that visualization that continues to act politically even as it exceeds the live." In this sense, realist performance functions as a form of "(quasi-magical) invocational practice": one that lives on in its photographic, auditory, and textual remains.[24]

Choreographing Realism

The earth is getting old, and I will make it new for
my chosen people, the Indians, who are to inhabit it,
and among them will be those of their ancestors who
have died, their fathers, mothers, brothers, cousins,
and wives—all those who hear my voice and my words

through the tongue of my children. I will cover the earth with new soil to a depth of five times the height of man, and under this new soil will be buried the whites, and all the holes and the rotten places will be filled up.
   —Kicking Bear's speech (October 8, 1890)

There is nothing new under the sun.
   —James Mooney, *The Ghost-Dance Religion and the Sioux Outbreak of 1890*

The interpretive shadow cast by ethnographer James Mooney on the Ghost Dance was a long one. Leaving off his years-long work on Cheyenne linguistics as news of a "messiah craze" among the Lakota Sioux began to appear in the press in the final days of 1890, Mooney asked and received permission from the Bureau of American Ethnology to travel through Indian Territory and the Northern Plains to document the Ghost Dance as it was practiced among the Arapaho, Cheyenne, Kiowa, Sioux, Paiute, and others.[25] While many bureau agents and reporters characterized the Sioux version of the dance as a dangerous preamble to violent uprising, Mooney depicted the Ghost Dance as a variety of enthusiasm, part of a universally recognizable taxonomy of religious practice. In *The Ghost-Dance Religion and the Sioux Outbreak of 1890* (1896), Mooney acknowledged: "With its scenes of intense excitement, spasmodic action, and physical exhaustion even to unconsciousness, such manifestations have always accompanied religious upheavals among primitive peoples, and are not entirely unknown among ourselves. In a country which produces magnetic healers, shakers, trance mediums, and the like, all these things may very easily be paralleled without going far from home."[26] The slippage between religious, national, and temporal difference is instructive here. In his effort to domesticate the dance's bodily intensity by annexing it to familiar spiritual and ideological territory, Mooney's text treats embodied religion as an evolutionary phenomenon, available to expert observation and diagnosis. As Mooney notes, "The Indian messiah religion is the inspiration of a dream. Its ritual is the dance, the ecstasy, and the trance. Its priests are hypnotics and cataleptics. All these have formed a part of every great religious development of which we have knowledge from the beginning of history."[27] In an extended appendix devoted to continuities in prophetic and revival movements across history, Mooney compared ghost dancers to Quakers, Shakers, Jumpers, Joan of Arc, Adventists, Beekmanites, Heavenly Recruits, and Methodists, among others, producing a series of susceptible, spasmodic bodies that link past and present, foreign and domestic, positioning religion itself as the ur-form of "primitive" life. Similarly, in a 1910 speech to the Nebraska Historical Society, Mooney would draw parallels to "earlier periods of our own history in the shape of religious revivals or spiritual ecstasies which spread over great areas or among several nations at once."[28] Recognizing and authorizing the Ghost Dance as ecstatic "religion," Mooney underscored cultural similarities in religion as such while insisting on a temporal distance separating the dance from the ostensibly secular present to which it nevertheless belonged.

Mooney's approach hewed closely to the evolutionary model of human history that dominated at the Bureau of Ethnology during his tenure there. Articulated by anthropologist Lewis Henry Morgan in his 1877 *Ancient Society: Researches in the Lines of Human Progress from Savagery to Barbarism to Civilization*, the evolutionary model positioned Indians as belonging to—and indeed visualizing for the present—an earlier moment of human development (as Freud would later note of "those we describe as savages or half-savages," "Their mental life must have a peculiar interest for us if we are right in seeing in it a well-preserved picture of an early stage of our own development").[29] In her study of the Pueblo Indian Dance Controversy of 1921, Tisa Wenger describes Morgan's model as progressive in spirit: "By arguing for the shared origins and equal potential of all people, Morgan and other evolutionists hoped to conquer the persistent idea that the human races were permanently unequal."[30] Yet the sense of shared origins that underwrote the evolutionary approach assumed and reinforced a temporal distance between Native Americans and secular modernity. As Mooney noted, "The human race is one in thought and action. The systems of our highest modern civilizations have their counterparts among all the nations, and their chain of parallels stretches backward link by link until we find their origin and interpretation in the customs and rites of our own barbarian ancestors, or of our still existing aboriginal tribes."³¹ The Ghost Dance, Mooney contended, was an evolutionary holdover—a throwback to the very origins of the "human race"—and a potential source of knowledge about those origins.³² As an argument for religious pluralism, Mooney's study neutralized a practice deemed threatening both to white Protestant modernity and to the colonial gaze that structured it, even as he consolidated a Protestant-secularist narrative of religious belief and its overcoming.³³ Situating the dance within a universalizing framework that treats all embodied religion as the disappearing material of ethnographic reproduction, Mooney naturalized "religion" and "history" as categories to which Indians belonged only in retrospect, in the very moment of their erasure.

Not unlike the choreography of Mooney's shadow—to which we will soon return—realist ethnology required a robust drama of representation, one that granted the ethnographer himself the status of "buffered," un-buffeted observer.³⁴ Writing of Morgan's evolutionary approach, John Lardas Modern describes the ethnographic performance of secularism as "a placement and, to some degree, enforcement of specific definitional boundaries—religion as a solitary epistemic endeavor; religion as an interior assessment of external forces; religion as a means of 'spiritual independence.'"³⁵ As readers of Mooney have argued in various ways, "realism" (in its colloquial and epistemological senses) functioned as a kind of inoculation against the ecstatic vulnerability or "porousness" demanded by the Ghost Dance.³⁶ Michael Elliott, for example, has argued that Mooney's sympathetic rendering of the dance was at once in keeping with the "realist" approach to Indian life at the turn of the century—which took for granted the inevitable disappearance of indigenous peoples and cultures—and, in its comparative methodology, at least occasionally at odds with Morgan's evolutionary model. Positioning Indians as a living memorial to the past and an interpretive key to the present, Mooney's study at times rehearses Morgan's figuring of racial and cultural difference as temporal difference. Still, by emphasizing the Ghost Dance's connections to multiple religious traditions, Elliott argues, Mooney's synchronic account of embodied religion emphasizes cultural similarity, "suggest[ing] that all religious movements are equally deluding," as "religion itself becomes part of the romance that the scientific monograph dispels." Developing a "cross-cultural homology" between forms of religious ecstasy, Mooney materialized religion as a function of the observable "real" and secured his own status as detached observer.[37]

Mooney's identification of religion as an observable phenomenon positioned the ethnographer as radically immune to the physical and spiritual susceptibility that the dance both referenced and enacted. However sympathetic in posture, Matthew Taylor argues Mooney's approach was rooted in a positivist epistemology that diagnosed and pathologized religious belief as a version of physiological—and indeed, communicable—disease, amounting to "a naturalistic collapse of metaphysics and biology."[38] In contrast to the "radically non-humanist ontology" of the Ghost Dance, Mooney's normalization of the discrete, well-bounded, and self-regulating subject—inoculated against the threat of contagious feeling—aligns closely with the biopolitics of assimilation, which produced both subject and nation as strictly impermeable structures, confidently immunized from foreign invasion (including invasion from within).[39] In Taylor's reading, Mooney's text everywhere effaces the vulnerability that structures both the cosmology of the Ghost Dance and the fact of interconnected personhood, at once assimilating Indians to and quarantining them from the category of the human. It is clear that Mooney's text consistently treats religious ecstasy as the "real" and communicable material of ethnographic observation, with *The Ghost-Dance* functioning as a contained, if expansive, specimen. Yet while Taylor's account of contagious emotion and the biopower that governs it is a powerful one, it's worth pressing on the inoculatory mechanisms that he describes, particularly the mode of prophylactic exposure or contact that Mooney's ethnographic practice demonstrates.

This exposure looks decidedly different when set against the photographic exposures that punctuated his fieldwork. Mooney's images of the Ghost Dance function at a basic level as an arrest of movement, making static what is a fundamentally dynamic and timely practice. Similarly, their status as evidentiary texts—meant to illustrate and support the truth claims of Mooney's text—highlights the extent to which Mooney's camera functioned as a racializing technology, able (in Leigh Raiford's terms) "to fix and to archive . . . the so-called fact of race" through the imaging of religious ecstasy.[40] Yet the work of these images cuts in multiple directions, in part because of field photography's technologically and ideologically shaky mechanisms, its necessarily improvisatory use. These images can be said to colonize a spiritual frontier made visible at the level of observable bodily practice, whereby the photograph annexes ghost dancers into the service of realist knowledge production. But they also insist on the photographer's implication in that process, as Mooney's shadow allows us to visualize the choreographies of observation and participation that produce the evidentiary and aesthetic force of the image, its currency as an index of the "real." Indeed, almost by necessity, Mooney's images seem to court the very kind of exposure or contact that his text works to contain.

As scholars and archivists have observed, Mooney's field photographs are casual productions. Most point out that while he carried a Kodak during two extended trips to document the dance between 1890 and 1892, he had neither technical skill nor the time to learn it. As Paula Richardson Fleming and Judith Luskey note, Mooney wrote to the Bureau of American Ethnology from Indian Territory on January 19, 1891—four days after the Sioux leader Kicking Bear surrendered to US Army forces—requesting materials and support from bureau photographer John K. Hillers: "Please have sent at once several dozen 5 x 8 plates. The Indians are dancing the ghost dance day and night and as a part of the doctrine, they must discard as far as possible everything white man [sic]. They are bringing out costumes not worn in years. . . . I have written Mr. Hillers in regard to work on Kodak before starting and a box of plates sent on from here, but have not heard from him."[41] Mooney's urgency in obtaining the proper equipment signals his robust faith in the camera's ability to capture race, visible here in the reverberation between discarding whiteness and photographing "authentic" Indianness. In his introduction to *The Ghost-Dance*, Mooney notes, "To obtain exact knowledge of the ceremony, the author took part in the dance among the Arapaho and Cheyenne. He also carried a kodak and a tripod camera, with which he made photographs of the dance and the trance both without and within the circle."[42] Quickly abandoning the unwieldy tripod-and-flash setup, within a week Mooney wrote again to the bureau requesting a Kodak manual so that he might determine proper exposure times. As Ira Jacknis notes, Mooney's capacity to photograph ceremonies like the Ghost Dance was both a technical and an ethnographic feat; the Kodak flexible film made possible a "real-time record" of the dance, while "Mooney's warm rapport with his native subjects" enabled his (apparent) access to the circle.[43]

While Mooney's close access to the Arapaho and Cheyenne enabled him to photograph (and participate in) the Ghost Dance, photography also enabled access. When Mooney traveled to the Walker River Reservation in January 1892 to meet with Wovoka, he reported knowing many of the delegates that had received Wovoka's prophesy the previous summer: "Nearly all of the members of this party were personally known to me, and the leader, Black Coyote, whose picture I had with me and showed to him, had been my principal instructor in the Ghost dance among the Arapaho."[44] Mooney was in turn "anxious to get Wovoka's picture," promising him "my regular price per day for his services as informant and to send him a copy of the picture when finished" (see figure 3.6).[45] In Mooney's account of the process, we see the photograph operate simultaneously as currency, evidence, and (at least potentially) the medium of long-distance revelation:

> When the subject was mentioned, he replied that his picture had never been made; that a white man had offered him five dollars for permission to take his photograph, but that he had refused. However, as I had been sent from Washington especially to learn and tell the whites all about him and his doctrine, and as he was satisfied from my acquaintance with his friends in the other tribes that I must be a good man, he would allow me to take his picture.... After some demure he consented and got ready for the operation by knotting a handkerchief about his neck, fastening an eagle feather at his right elbow, and taking a wide brim sombrero upon his knee. I afterward learned that the feather and sombrero were important parts of his spiritual stock in trade.[46]

While Jacknis characterizes Mooney's portrait photography as "an act of friendship, or at least an attempt at data gathering," here the mobilization of photography's evidentiary potential emerges as a distinctly collaborative effort, with Wovoka (at least in Mooney's analysis) using the visual image to manifest and distribute the material signs of spiritual power. Initially dressed in what Mooney describes as "a good suit of white man's clothing," Wovoka's getting ready—adding the handkerchief, feather, and hat—signals close attention on both men's parts to

Figure 3.6. James Mooney, "Wovoka [the Cutter] or Kwohitsaug [Big Rumbling Belly] Called Jack Wilson, with Another Man, n.d." National Anthropological Archives, Smithsonian Institution. [NAA INV 06285500]

the aesthetic and symbolic registers of clothing, to portrait-taking as a formalized performance (a series of stylized movements and poses, of exchanged looks), and to the contested work of the image in spreading Wovoka's prophecy. While Elliott argues Mooney included the portrait of Wovoka in his study to highlight the image of "an Indian man who refuses to accept that indigenous cultures were incapable of both material and spiritual adaptation," it seems possible that the photograph itself does much more than this, broadcasting a double message of adaptation and survivance.[47] *Survivance*, as Gerald Vizenor has articulated it, is a set of practices deeply rooted in the symbolic; it is a performance of presence as "an active resistance and repudiation of dominance."[48] In these terms, Wovoka's act of dressing himself is a figurative practice; rather than being simply subjected to the camera, Wovoka mobilizes the changeability of clothing—its ability to function simultaneously as ethnographic detail and spiritual iconography—as part of a strategic act of self-determination.[49] Even granting Mooney's potential misreading of Wovoka's "spiritual stock in trade," his narrative suggests the prophet recognized the visual image as a critical site of exchange and circulation, a site through which his spiritual message might be translated across various Native communities and (at the same time) assimilated to the surveillance state in Washington.

The shadow of that surveillance falls everywhere in these images, even when Mooney's shadow (as in the portrait of Wovoka) is not clearly visible. Where the shadow is visible—as in nearly every image that Mooney took of the Ghost Dance, many of them among the northern Arapaho—it complicates even further the dynamics of performance, preservation, and ethnographic encounter. Mooney's shadow has been read as a function of his amateurism, a haunting but likely unintentional half presence, equivalent to a finger on the lens.[50] The few scholars who comment on Mooney's images point out that, unlike those of Edward Curtis, Gertrude Käsebier, and other professional photographers who sought out Native subjects, Mooney's were taken primarily in the service of ethnographic evidence, without too much care for composition and focus. That the shadow appears more often in photographs of ritual performance might help corroborate this reading; faced with the difficulty of capturing bodies in motion "both [from] without and within the circle," Mooney may have simply positioned his back to the sun and shot. The shadow of colonial viewing practices preserved in the image as a result is, in this sense, not much more than a useful technical glitch.

Yet read as a group, in which the shadow registers the persistent presence of the photographer, these images can be seen to blur the boundary between ethnographic vision and the visionary or prophetic perception that structured the dance.[51] Mooney's proliferating self-portraits—the shadow that overlaps and at times eclipses the subject as the center of focus—work to produce the ghost as a material possibility in multiple directions: the shadow registers white surveillance, but it also (at least potentially) stands in for the ghosts of ancestors accessed through and revived by the dance. Perhaps most compellingly, the shadow anticipates the ghosting of white colonialism that the dance aimed to initiate. There is, at the very least, an excess of ghostly matter in these images.[52] Recalling Wovoka's vision as an event (apparently) timed to the solar eclipse—a shadow crossing the sun—the photographic shadow stands in dynamic conversation with the cosmology and performance of the dance, and its vision of a new world engendered by and through performance. In this sense, it is also difficult not to see the stillness of Mooney's shadow as a distinct reversal of the broader cultural logic that isolated Indians in a static past, out of sync with the relentless forward movement of progress. The dancers themselves are often out of focus and blurred, a function of movement that tends to abstract individual performers rather than rendering them the knowable objects of ethnographic description, while the shadow (occasionally doubled or tripled, as Mooney found himself in company with other observers) remains distinctive and distinctively available to our gaze (see figure 3.7). At the same time, the shadow figures whiteness—rather than Indianness—as the apparitional past-ness of a presence, the photograph's (as much as the dance's) "will have been."

Performances of Encounter

What is exposed in these images is not, then, the Ghost Dance as a well-preserved, racialized image of the religious past in the present but rather the complex practice through which the dynamics of ethnographic preservation created both race and religion as apparently knowable and overlapping categories of the "real." Despite their collusion with this process, Mooney's images also work to expose it. Even more strikingly, these

Figure 3.7. James Mooney, "Ceremony—Ghost Dance [1891]" (showing multiple shadows). National Anthropological Archives, Smithsonian Institution.

images suggest that the very idiom of exposure through which Mooney understood and diagnosed ecstatic religion as a form of feverish contagion might double back on the work of photography itself. Reading Mooney's images alongside his text opens up crucial moments where the photographic mechanism aligns with the spiritual mechanism of the Ghost Dance as Mooney describes it.

Consider, for example, Mooney's account of the process by which dancers achieve a state of trance and, through it, access to the spirit world. Relying on a firsthand account of the dance from his interpreter Paul Boynton, a former Carlisle student who described his experience of the trance and (with the help of Sitting Bull) his ability to see his recently deceased brother, Mooney noted, "From his account it seemed almost certain that the secret was hypnotism," a form of "practical knowledge" that helped explain the many accounts of "how people died, went to heaven and came back again, and how they talked with dead friends and brought back messages from the other world."[53] Insisting on his own practical knowledge, and his vantage from "within the circle," Mooney's description superimposes the bodily manifestation of the Ghost Dance's spiritual vision onto the visual choreography of the photographic process:

> We shall assume the subject is a woman.[54] The first indication that she is becoming affected is a slight muscular tremor, distinctly felt by her two partners who hold her hands on either side. The medicine-man is on watch, and as soon as he notices the woman's condition he comes over and stands immediately in front of her, looking intently into her face and whirling the feather or the handkerchief, or both, rapidly in front of her eyes, moving slowly around with the dancers at the same time, but constantly facing the woman. . . .
>
> For a few minutes she continues to repeat the words of the song and keep time with the step, but in a staggering, drunken fashion. Then the words become unintelligible sounds, and her movements violently spasmodic, until at last she becomes rigid, with her eyes shut or fixed and staring, and stands thus uttering low pitiful moans (plate CXVII). If this is in the daytime, the operator tries to stand with his back to the sun, so that the full sunlight shines in the woman's face (plate CXVI).[55]

Linking what he diagnoses as hypnosis to illustrations based on his own photographs (figure 3.8), Mooney's place within the circle—as both participant and observer—begins to look strikingly like the position of the medicine man or skilled hypnotist himself. Standing with his back to the sun, Mooney would have photographed in place of the "operator," his image producing its own form of hypnotic stillness, its own access to another world (figure 3.9).

Constantly facing his subjects, Mooney's photographic choreography is also a hypnotic practice, squaring the difference between surveillance and spiritual vision: "From the outside hardly anything can be seen of what goes on within the circle, but being a part of the circle myself I was able to see all that occurred inside, and by fixing attention on one subject at a time I was able to note all the stages of the phenomenon from the time the subject first attracted the notice of the medicine-man, through the staggering, the rigidity, the unconsciousness, and back again to wakefulness."[56] Mooney's circular Kodak images visually insert him

Figure 3.8. James Mooney, "Ceremony—Ghost Dance [1891]" (showing figure with arms outstretched). National Anthropological Archives, Smithsonian Institution.

into the circle, in a complex brokering of the space between witnessing and participation, ghost and shadow. By "fixing attention," Mooney performs the very act he describes (the dancer's hypnotic "death" into the other world), producing a kind of charged stillness. The photograph, in this sense, is an ethnographic record—diagnosing the bodily signs of religious and racial otherness, enmeshed in the colonial and genocidal

Figure 3.9. James Mooney, "Ceremony—Ghost Dance [1891]" (showing "operator"). National Anthropological Archives, Smithsonian Institution.

violence that sutured Native subjects to the past tense—but it is also a performative work of imitation or reenactment, a means of conjuring ghosts through the idiom of exposure.

Alongside the Ghost Dance then—itself an encounter between the (still) living and the (not fully) dead—the ethnographic photograph produces its own series of visionary encounters, embedded in but not fully explained by realism's capacious surveillance mechanisms, its will to visualize a material world increasingly understood to include the influence of the unseen.[57] In these terms, we might mark the relationship between Mooney's ethnographic images and the spirit photograph, which "played on photography's capacity to capture worlds beyond natural human sight, proposing that the camera might also record a *supernatural* realm beyond the range of ordinary vision."[58] What William James proposed as the "margin" of the empirical self was by spiritualists understood as a permeable boundary, one to which they ascribed Native subjects privileged access.[59] As Molly McGarry has argued convincingly, the white spiritualist conjuring of Indian ghosts could work in multiple directions, consolidating a romantic attachment to vaguely understood Native cosmologies while materializing the presence of Native subjects over and against the mythos of vanishing. McGarry notes that in the spiritualist encounter with Native Americans, the uncanny "liveness" of the Indian ghosts "suggest[s] an urgency and specificity of presence that belies broader cultural narratives of Indians as vanished and vanquished."[60]

Still, Native Americans appearing in spirit photographs often served colonial and/or appropriative purposes, functioning (as Shawn Michelle Smith observes) to "suture the natural and supernatural worlds" for white spiritualists while reinforcing the spectrality of Indian subjects via the photograph's long-standing association with death.[61] Indeed, Smith argues that such images press the logic of colonialism to its extreme, appropriating figures of Native resistance like Sitting Bull for the purposes of white spiritual succor, as in one circa 1880s cabinet card, where a figure resembling Sitting Bull facilitates the reunion of father and son on the visual and spiritual plane of the image (see figure 3.10).

By materializing the Ghost Dance's vision in the name of empirical investigation, Mooney's photographs perform a similar function. Not unlike Mooney, white spiritualists used ostensibly objective mechanisms such as the camera to investigate the spiritual world, extending the reach of the US empire into the cross-temporal geographies of the afterlife.[62] Yet juxtaposed with the spirit photograph, Mooney's shadow-laden images look less like high-fidelity ethnographic records than like complex, appropriative, and occasionally collaborative performances—a mode of "playing Indian" that borrows from the Ghost Dance's own reiterative performance of encounter.[63] In their desire to see themselves seeing (or to materialize the shadow's always-vanishing presence), Mooney's images perform the ethnographic encounter as a fully haunted and haunting one, possibly not so different in its drive to self-preservation from the Ghost Dance itself, albeit from within a radically different system of power. Indeed, what each of these photographic practices shared with the Ghost Dance was the dream of self-preservation—both the spirit photograph and the ethnographic

Figure 3.10. "Spirit Photograph," cabinet card, ca. 1880. Courtesy of Greg French Early Photography.

photograph sought to provide access to the dead for the living. Such an account of time as recoverable mingles, in Mooney's broader project, with a distinct sense of irrevocable loss. During the years that he studied the Ghost Dance, Mooney collected Native objects to be displayed at the Smithsonian as a function of salvation; as Arapaho artist and former Carlisle student Carl Sweezy reported in his memoir *The Arapaho Way*, Mooney "had everything, from a full-sized tipi to small rattles and charms, from cooking vessels to sacred bundles. He explained that he was now getting ready to pack all these things and ship them to the Smithsonian Institution in Washington, where they would never be lost or destroyed and where everyone that came to visit would see what we had accomplished and how we had lived."[64] Mooney's salvage practice enacts a violent substitution of objects for people, a metonymic effort to protect a way of life from destruction by scavenging its materials. In this sense, we can understand Mooney's fieldwork as a version of what anthropologist Lisa Stevenson has described as "colonial care," an act of purported preservation that is nevertheless an extension of colonial power.[65] Actively archiving subjects-as-objects understood to be vanishing to time, the bulk of Mooney's ethnographic project testifies only to the fact that the Indians "had lived," not that they would again, free from the shadows of colonial history. Mooney's photographs operate both in and beyond this logic, visually testifying to the fact that the Ghost Dance was neither dispelled nor fully assimilated in this project, but instead enacted and reenacted through ethnographic realism.

It is crucial to distinguish between Mooney's version of archive fever—the ethnographic drive to (self-)preservation—and the spiritual fever that he attributed to Wovoka, whose vision was not simply about preserving a pristine precolonial past but an active effort to make the world new again. This form of vision demanded the dancer's iterative "death" (a practice that cited and rewrote the violence of removal at the level of bodily practice) and extended beyond human losses to include the environmental and ecological decimation wrought by colonial expansion. Or as Kicking Bear described it in the voice of the Great Spirit, "The earth is getting old, and I will make it new for my chosen people, the Indians, who are to inhabit it . . . all those who hear my voice and my words through the tongue of my children."[66] Lee Irwin argues that prophetic movements like the Ghost Dance "were not simply a 'revitalization' but an ongoing vitality . . . whose expression was creative and syncretic."⁶⁷ Kélina Gotman argues that the choreopolitical force of the dance enabled participants to resist the biopolitical management of Native life and to "imagine new forms of collective desire, grounded in a memory of the old."⁶⁸ Whereas the cross-temporal imaginary of the Ghost Dance meant repeatedly dying to resurrect the dead, Mooney's images strove to materialize and record a practice he believed to be unrecoverable. But by framing the Ghost Dance as a form of an iterative, performative encounter, these images also make visible realism's investment in the very idioms of belief that Mooney and others assigned to the past.

In other words, what vanishes and what persists in these images is thus difficult to discern, and this fundamental uncertainty is crucial to their work—in Mooney's moment and in our own. The photographs register the "will have been" of their subjects, but they also preface another world to come in which white people will be ghosted, buried under

Figure 3.11. James Mooney, "Ceremony—Ghost Dance [1891]" (showing child looking at camera). National Anthropological Archives, Smithsonian Institution.

new soil, or (in some accounts of Wovoka's prophecy) "push[ed] ... to their own proper country across the ocean."[69] White colonialism, these images suggest, is both seen and unseen, a material-and-spectral vision that lingers at the margins. By way of contrast, Mooney's subjects often seem to face head-on the political and technological mechanisms that would make them into artifacts. In more than a few images, Mooney's subject looks back at him and at us, squinting into the sun, insisting on a world that exceeds the colonial frame.

Sonic Specimens

In the spring of 1894, after twenty-two months of observing, performing, and photographing the Ghost Dance across the West, Mooney returned to Washington, DC, where he prepared his findings for publication in the Bureau of American Ethnology's annual report. In illustrations accompanying the text—many of them based directly on Mooney's photographs—the shadow disappears. Yet Mooney apparently continued performing, enlisting Emile Berliner (inventor of the gramophone) and composers John Philip Sousa and Frederick William Gaisberg to help record and arrange Ghost Dance songs that Mooney had collected and transcribed during his travels among the Arapaho, Caddo, Cheyenne, Comanche, Kiowa, Paiute, and Sioux.[70] In Mooney's report, the transcribed songs (161 total, of which 15 are rendered in Sousa's notations) serve a paratextual function, detached from the main text's "narrative" of the Ghost Dance and (as Michael Elliott argues) "catalogued as a kind of cultural property, neatly divided and ordered within the arrangement of the volume." Collected alongside Native glossaries, symbologies, and other explanatory texts, Elliott notes that Mooney used the songs to provide a version of Clifford Geertz's "thick description," or what we might also call a proliferation of realist detail.[71]

In the months after his return from Washington, Mooney would record a selection of the Ghost Dance songs he transcribed onto twelve zinc Berliner discs. Like his photographs, which used the camera both to preserve and to perform the dance's spiritual mechanisms, Mooney's Berliner recordings extend realism's expansionist tendencies beyond the textual and photographic proliferation of detail and into the technological (and imaginary) frontier of recorded sound. The effort to record the

Ghost Dance, stretching as it did across textual, photographic, sonic, and filmic media, signals the intersection between recording faith and faith *in* recording, or in the modern technologies that might freeze, conserve, and replay religions and cultures believed to be discordant or out of sync with modernity itself. As Jonathan Sterne observes, "The very choice of the term fidelity (first applied to sound in 1878) indicates both a faith in media and a belief that media can hold faith, a belief that media and sounds themselves could hold *faithfully* to the agreement that two sounds are the same sounds."[72] Mooney's recordings certainly partake of what Sterne describes as an "ethos of preservation" in turn-of-the-century ethnography's use of audio technologies, which mobilized the phonograph's much-touted capacity to save the voices of the dead in the service of preserving ostensibly dying races.[73] The project of recording indigenous music—as practiced by Mooney, Jesse Walter Fewkes, Alice Fletcher, and other prominent ethnologists—depended on a fundamental faith in the phonograph or gramophone's capacity to salvage and reproduce Indianness through a specifically "Indian" sound.[74] Music thus functioned as a "sign of race": a method of reifying racial typologies at the level of sound—or (indeed) *as* sound emerging from particularized bodies.[75] This ethnographic fantasy, as Philip Deloria details, was part of a larger popular effort to locate, reproduce, and capitalize on the "sound of the Indian"—a translated, hybridized sound pitched in the minor key of vanishing and contributing to the nationalist demand for a distinctly American music.[76]

The Ghost Dance songs in turn served a nascent recording industry in its efforts to exploit white fascination with racialized voices, a fascination that shored up links between the preservationist fantasies of phonographic modernity and the violent consumption of racial others. In an analysis of lynching phonographs, Gustavus Stadler argues that the convergence of commercial sound recording and racial violence at the end of the nineteenth century meant that (alongside and in addition to indigenous life) black life became a site where the struggle over the meaning of sound technologies played out, as fascination with black voices deemed inhuman or insufficiently human overlapped and replaced cultural perplexity with the machine's own seemingly human voice.[77] At the supposed end of the Indian Wars, and in the aftermath of Wounded Knee, the ability to consume the sound of "the Indian" similarly signaled the "artifactualization" of Indianness at the level of both cultural understanding and technological reproduction, a process that made it possible to draft the Ghost Dance songs into a form of nationalist racial sampling.[78] In this way, listeners would be encouraged to hear and compare a range of racial (and musical) types. Berliner's United States Gramophone Company, for example, listed "Three Melodies from the Ghost Dance" in its January 1895 catalog alongside "Star-Spangled Banner," several of Sousa's marches (such as "Semper Fidelis" and "Washington Post"), minstrel songs like "The Coon That Got the Shake," and a vocal quartet performing "Blind Tom (negro shout)," in mock tribute to the African American pianist and composer Thomas Wiggins, whom Willa Cather referred to as a "human phonograph" (see figure 3.12).[79]

If "savages" for Freud and others offered a "well-preserved picture" of the past, then, such recordings suggest that they also offered an eminently consumable sound bite of a supposedly vanished moment. Corresponding closely to Sousa and Gaisberg's fifteen notations, the very fact of Mooney's recordings suggests an effort to seal the Ghost Dance songs in time, pressing them into metal (and into the time signatures of Western notation) as a means of storing them for future performances. Yet recording the voices of the dead (or the soon dead) was itself a culturally contingent and ephemeral project; the ethnographic faith in modern recording technologies as tools of preservation obscured the fact that "decay" was not the domain of indigenous cultures alone. As Sterne points out, early phonographs testified as much to corrosion and disappearance as to preservation; they were themselves ephemeral, even as they promoted a fantasy of permanence. Far from a straightforward preservation of the past, then, Sterne argues that early ethnographic recordings highlight the complex temporal dynamics of phonographic technology more broadly, which embedded at least "three conflicted senses of time for its early users": a concept of linear time (in which the present disappears and requires preservation); the fragmented, repeatable time of the recorded sound (which might potentially be replayed over and over); and the physical temporality of the record as an ephemeral object that decays over time.[80] Thus "the bourgeois

LIST OF PLATES.
JANUARY 1895.

BAND MUSIC.

118 Dude's March
130 Black and Tan
~~141 Marching Through Georgia~~
    (with cheers)
~~114 The Same—Patrol~~
~~2 La Serenata~~
~~114 Star Spangled Banner~~
8 Coxey's Army
11 Salvation Army
9 Semper Fidelis (with drums.)
~~139 After the Ball~~
~~126 Boccacio March~~
~~144 Liberty Bell March~~
140 Washington Post March
142 Admiral's Favorite March
4 Friedensklange
105 National Fencibles
~~13 Gladiator March~~
19 Schottische, Nancy Hanks
15 Loin du bal
17 Waltz, Aphrodite
20 Mendelsohn's Wedding March

INSTRUMENTAL QUARTETTE.

~~807 Die Kapelle~~
803 Circus Band
~~806 March, King John~~
800 Ein neues Blatt

BARYTONE.

163 When Summer Comes Again
182 Sweetheart Nell, and I
175 Old Kentucky Home
191 Black Knight Templars
~~180 Throw Him Down McCloskey~~
183 Oh, Promise Me
~~176 Irene Me Little Love Me Long~~
~~150 Oh, Fair Art Thou~~
155 Anchored
~~170 Mamie Come Kiss your Honey Boy~~
~~166 Then You'll Remember Me~~
~~160 The Maiden and the Lamb~~
165 Red, White and Blue
169 The Coon That Got the Shake
157 Tramp, Tramp, Tramp
158 Sweet Marie
196 The Whistling Coon
189 Phœbe
~~193 Back among the old folks~~
198 Swim out O'Grady
902 Sword of Bunker Hill

CLARIONET.

300 Allegro (Verdi)

CORNET.

200 Polka, Elegant
205 Call Me Thy Own
206 Emily Polka
202 U. S. Military Signals
203 Welcome, Pretty Primrose

Cornet Continued.
211 Cloverleaf Polka

CORNET DUETTS.

242 Alpine Polka
248 Swiss Boy
243 La Paloma

DRUM AND FIFE.

700 Biddy Oates
706 American Medley
702 St. Patrick's day
705 The Spirit of '76
    (very dramatic)

TROMBONE.

75 In The Deep Cellar

PIANO.

256 Geisterfunken
253 March, Jolly Minstrels

INDIAN SONGS.

51 Three Melodies from the Ghost Dance
52 Three Melodies from the Ghost Dance
50 Three Melodies from the Ghost Dance

ANIMALS.

53 Morning on the farm

Hebrew Melodies.

400 Parshe Zav

SOPRANO.

359 Oh, Promise Me
352 Oh, How Delightful
355 Star Spangled Banner
353 I've something sweet to tell you
363 Tell her I love her so
362 Some Day
350 Past and Future
365 Punchinello
354 In the gloaming
356 Loves Sorrow

CONTRALTO.

550 Beauties Eyes
551 Drink to me only
552 Oh, Promise me

RECITATION.

We have for this important department secured the co-operation of the eminent, versatile elocutionist, **Mr. David C. Bangs.**
602 Mare Anthony's Curse
    A Lesson in Elocution.
600 The Village Blacksmith
    (Many others in preparation.)

VOCAL QUARTETTE.

851 Blind Tom (negro shout)
853 Grandfather's Birthday
855 Negroes' holiday

It is expected that between 25 and 50 New Pieces will be added every month.

THE UNITED STATES GRAMOPHONE CO.,
1410 Pennsylvania Ave., N. W.,
Washington, D. C.

Figure 3.12. United States Gramophone Company, *List of Plates, January 1895*. Emile Berliner collection, Motion Picture, Broadcasting and Recorded Sound Division, Library of Congress. [RPA 00842, box 12]

modernity of sound recording," Sterne notes, "moves between the ephemerality of moments and the possibility of an eternal persistence."[81]

This account of hybrid phonographic temporality turns out to be an apt description of Mooney's take on the Ghost Dance songs, recorded or otherwise. Though Mooney emphasized that the songs were proliferating and ephemeral, specific to the visions of individual dancers and iterations of the dance ("every trance at every dance produces a new one . . . which is sung at the next dance and succeeding performances until superseded"), he nevertheless privileged the possibilities of retention over improvisation: "While songs are thus born and die, certain ones which appeal especially to the Indian heart, on account of their mythology, pathos, or particular sweetness, live and are perpetuated."[82] In his report to the bureau, Mooney emphasized what he figured as the songs' own preservative function, their capacity to store supposedly obsolete customs: "The Ghost Dance songs are of the utmost importance in connection with the study of the messiah religion, as we find embodied in them much of the doctrine itself, with more of the special tribal mythologies, together with such innumerable references to old-time customs, ceremonies, and modes of life long since obsolete as make up a regular symposium of aboriginal thought and practice."[83] Here the fantasy of preservation collapses the technology of sound recording with the very sounds it was meant to preserve: effacing the singers themselves, Mooney figures the Ghost Dance songs both as archives of the dead and as potential messages to the future, iterable fragments shored against (and, at the same time, shoring up) the ruins of US empire.[84]

It is difficult to say what we hear when we actually listen to Mooney's records, or to the static grain of a decayed sound preserved (for now) in a series of digitized audio files. We might argue that recordings of the Ghost Dance redouble the purported ghostliness of the medium itself, producing a tight fit between the logic of vanishing and modernity's dreams of preservation. In this sense, as Sterne notes, "the medium is the metaphysics"; the technological frontier of recorded sound extends the colonial project of extermination by repeatedly resurrecting its ghosts.[85] Here I follow Renée Bergland's important observation that "first and foremost, the ghosting of Indians is a technique of removal."[86] Yet Mooney's recordings importantly challenge any high-fidelity understanding of either realism (here, the correspondence between recorded sound and its referent) or race (as the sonic sign of "Indianness"). While they echo and aspire to the medium's logic of preserved presence—effacing the present tense of Indian removal with the "always already past perfect" of a sonic lament—they also fundamentally disturb the apparent "realness" that audio recording affords to the vanishing Indian as a colonial, racial, and temporal configuration.[87] This is in part because what we almost certainly do not hear on Mooney's Berliner records are the voices of Native performers themselves. Though much of the context surrounding Mooney's production of the records is lost or missing, archivists note that the single voice we hear on the records is most likely Mooney himself, reenacting the songs from memory or from his own transcriptions.[88] The sheer difficulty of recording sound in the field in the 1890s meant that the songs were probably performed in Berliner's studio in Washington, DC, and while ethnographers like Alice Fletcher would later invite Omaha, Otoe, and other Native performers to Washington to make similar recordings, no evidence exists to suggest that Mooney did so.[89]

Though we cannot know for sure, it seems far more likely that Mooney made the recordings himself to amplify his textual and photographic accounts of the Ghost Dance and to collect and study its sound as a form of intelligible, transposable cultural material. By 1910, for example, Mooney likely used the Berliner recordings alongside the photographs to offer multimedia lectures on the dance. In an address to the Nebraska Historical Society on "The Indian Ghost Dance," Mooney argued (as he had in his initial report) that, contrary to popular opinion, the Ghost Dance was not an incitement to rebellion among its practitioners; on the contrary, it had encouraged the end of intertribal warfare. "The dance has gone," Mooney announced, "but the doctrine, or the hope that it held out, has made a lasting impression and has brought about a permanently peaceful feeling among the Indians." To demonstrate this "lasting impression," Mooney offered "a few specimens of the songs" to close the evening, presumably playing the Berliner records to punctuate his accounts: "In all these songs in the various tribes you learn to recognize the ghost songs by the meter. It is intended to fit a certain slow constant dance step as the dancers go round in a circle. At first they sing low, and then, after a while louder, and with a somewhat quicker movement, raising their voices as they go. [Song begins playing.]"[90] In laying out "specimens" of the Ghost Dance for his historically minded white listeners, Mooney prescribed the historical terms through which they might be heard as artifacts of a (mostly) extinct human "species." By figuring such specimens as metrically recognizable, Mooney insisted on their cultural specificity and, at the same time, on their translatability. As Jann Pasler has argued, ethnographic and anthropological efforts to transcribe and preserve non-European musical forms at the end of the nineteenth century were driven by a dual effort to reinforce racial categories and to identify cross-cultural musical "universals."[91] Similarly, Mooney's account of the songs' distinctive meter echoes in Sousa and Gaisberg's musical notations, which press the songs into measurable (reproducible) time, even as they shift time signatures rapidly to account for the changes of pace that Mooney both describes and (re)enacts. Thus it is possible to hear in these various inscriptions of the Ghost Dance—stretching across written reports, photographs, recordings, musical notations, and amplified lectures—less a faithful accounting for racial and temporal difference than a faith *in* that difference and in the capacity of modern technology to materialize, capture, and make sense of it.

If pressing the songs into notation and into Berliner's zinc discs meant pressing them into sonic modernity, Mooney's efforts also help us see that modernity as its own fantasy of "retrievable time."[92] For as in Mooney's photographs—which picture the shadow of colonial surveillance—what is preserved is less the voices of the Native dead than a distinct question about the ways in which white colonialism itself might and might not be heard, and to what extent it lives on in and through media. To reenact the Ghost Dance songs after Wounded Knee was, for Mooney, to participate in a mediated process of white ethnographic salvage (pitched in a mournful tune) that naturalized the genocidal work of US empire as the inevitable work of time; it was also to invest in the power of media technologies to stop, replay, and otherwise transform the temporality of vanishing. Thus even while Mooney declared the death of the dance, he helped signal its reiterative (and indeed, proliferating) returns, sonic and otherwise. As Mooney's repetitive reenactments of the dance suggest, ethnographic preservation was itself a highly theatrical performance of high fidelity, one that resurrected the dead as a *function* of realist representation rather than its unruly, irrational exception.

Reading Mooney's Berliner records as dense sites of realist performance—rather than simply as inscriptions of absence, the past perfect "was" or future anterior "will have been" of the vanishing Indian—presents a fundamental challenge to the absent/present and past/present binaries through which colonialism framed and continues to frame indigenous subjects.[93] This is not to suggest that Mooney's reenactments themselves serve as radical challenges to the Progressive era's temporal order of colonial conquest; it is instead to mark the ways in which Mooney's realist investment in materializing (recording, inscribing, and visualizing) the Ghost Dance belies its temporal and methodological remove from the dance's own project of haunting and resurrection. Which is to say that in its approach to what it identifies as religious enthusiasm, realism's forms of knowing look and sound particularly haunted; as Avery Gordon notes, "Haunting is a very particular way of knowing what has happened or is happening."[94] Similarly, the realist archive of the Ghost Dance—the repetition of the dance across media and the use of media both to still and to reanimate the dance—insists that what has happened *is* still happening. Indeed, the challenge to linear time—or to the time of vanishing—embedded in Mooney's recordings is one inaugurated and paralleled by the Ghost Dance itself, which (across its many variations and repetitions) insists on the material presence of absence, or on the living reality of ghosts—our proximity to them—and the ongoing colonial mechanisms that produce them.

Ghost Dance Reenactments and the Refusal to Stay Dead

In the final section of Mooney's 1896 report, he noted that, for the most part, the Ghost Dance had disappeared: "The movement is already extinct, having died a natural death, excepting in the case of the Sioux."[95] Though Mooney conceded that the dance continued among the Kiowa ("now dancing as religiously as ever . . . although the progressive element in the tribe is strongly opposed to it") as well as several Oklahoma tribes (including the "Arapaho, Cheyenne, Caddo, Wichita, Pawnee, and Oto," for whom the dance "has become a part of tribal life and is still performed at frequent intervals"), he emphasized the Ghost Dance's "natural death" as a function of religious movements more broadly.

Wounded Knee served as a notable exception to Mooney's naturalization of religious and cultural decline; Mooney argued that the Sioux version of the Ghost Dance was a coherent response to the dismantling of collectively held lands, restriction of rations, and evisceration of tribal cultures, all of which reached a peak in the final months of 1890. "There can be no question that the pursuit was simply a massacre," Mooney wrote scathingly of the military suppression of the Ghost Dance at the Pine Ridge agency in South Dakota.[96] Mooney's first visit to the Pine Ridge agency and the site of Wounded Knee came nearly a year after the December 1890 massacre; as he reported, "the troops still camped there served as a reminder of the conflict, while in the little cemetery at the agency were the fresh graves of slain soldiers, and only a few miles away was the Wounded Knee battlefield and the trench where the bodies of nearly three hundred of their people had been thrown."[97] As Mooney's biographer L. G. Moses points out, "The survivors had fenced off the trench and smeared the posts with paint made from the clay of western Nevada given to Sioux delegates by Wovoka . . . the grave had been marked so that those recently dead might be among the first at the Indian resurrection."[98]

The visit to Pine Ridge was brief and, despite Mooney's desire to learn about the Ghost Dance from Sioux participants, largely unyielding. Mooney noted, "To my questions the answer almost invariably was, 'The dance was our religion, but the government sent soldiers to kill us on account of it. We will not talk any more about it.'"[99] Yet as Sam Maddra points out, reluctance among Sioux participants to speak of the dance in the aftermath of Wounded Knee was only one reason why Mooney relied heavily on government documents, Indian police reports, and other sources hostile to the dance. A more likely reason, Maddra argues, is that Kicking Bear, Short Bull, and other surviving leaders of the Ghost Dance movement were not at Pine Ridge when Mooney visited; they were performing in Buffalo Bill's Wild West show as it toured Great Britain. Briefly imprisoned at Fort Sheridan following their January 15, 1891, surrender to General Nelson Miles, twenty-three Lakota Sioux ghost dancers joined William F. Cody's 1891–1892 tour of Wales, Scotland, and England, where they ritually reenacted the stages of American imperial expansion, moving audiences through various "eras" of the frontier.[100] As Maddra suggests, Sioux participation in the Wild West show was strategic. For many, it offered a viable alternative to dependency on the government's unreliable and often hostile stewardship; it was also significantly more remunerative than farming the largely intractable South Dakota landscape.[101] The participation of the ghost dancers was used both to publicize the show and to affirm its "realism"; as Cody's press agent John Burke reportedly affirmed, "The object of the show was not to present a circus performance, but to give a true picture of American frontier life with real characters who had played their part in the history of a portion of the American continent which would soon be a thing of the past."[102] Relying on the spectacle of the "unassimilated" and resistant Indian, Cody's shows both perpetuated the nonthreatening historicity of Native Americans—their belonging strictly to the past—and offered up at least an outward challenge to the US government's programs of forced assimilation.[103]

Despite the Wild West show's frequent restaging of earlier battles (such as the 1876 defeat of General Custer at Little Big Horn) and despite using the ghost dancers' notoriety to drum up ticket sales, Cody's 1891–1892 tour did not feature reenactments of either the Ghost Dance or the battle at Wounded Knee. Cody himself had participated in the suppression of the dance at Pine Ridge and claimed to prohibit the dance in his camps. Furthermore, as Maddra notes, Lakota ghost dancers would likely have been resistant to performing the ritual as a form of entertainment.[104] Still, reenactments of the dance proliferated in the years following Wounded Knee. Maddra points out that a satellite company performed the Ghost Dance in Glasgow at the end of the Wild West show's winter season, and William F. Carver's rivaling Wild America show similarly advertised a specimen of "the Ghost Dance by the Indians who first performed it" in its July 1892 program.[105] Jacqueline Murphy argues compellingly that while Buffalo Bill's hiring of the Fort Sheridan prisoners was partially aimed at containing the spread of the Ghost Dance, this effort was largely a failure. Murphy suggests that Buffalo Bill's Wild West show may in fact have provided a space of improvisational survivance, as Indian performers "[found] within it ways of continuing dance practices and of exploring and transforming their relation to them in a changing world."[106]

While the Ghost Dance circulated as both ethnographic and popular spectacle, it also quickly became fodder for vaudeville billing. An undated broadside for a Millerton, New York, performance of the Kickapoo Indian Medicine Company—one of the most popular traveling medicine shows of the 1890s, run by promoters John Healy and Charles Bigelow—lists "The Indians in the Ghost Dance" alongside comedy acts, sleights of hand, interferences, and a "laughable farce" (see figure 3.13). Hawking the Cody-endorsed cure-all "Kickapoo Indian Sagwa" between the acts—perhaps relying on a metonymic slippage between the Ghost Dance's restorative cosmology and the restorative power of patent medicine—Healy and Bigelow employed up to eight hundred Native Americans to sing songs, reenact frontier scenes, dance, and sell "authentic" indigenous remedies to white audiences. As Ann Anderson notes, shows included "a mixture of soft shoe, chalk talks, Irish and blackface comedy, acrobatics, and afterpieces."[107] Not unlike the popular sampling that characterized Berliner's early records, such performances signaled the collapse of religious ritual and racial minstrelsy as consumable signs of otherness.

Against what Mooney declared a "natural death," the dance remained very much alive after Wounded Knee: among the Kiowa, Arapaho, and Cheyenne, for whom the practice was and is ongoing; in the traveling spectacle of frontier reenactments and medicine shows; and in the ethnographic effort to record and preserve the dance as an artifact of vanishing. It also lived on in early film productions, which capitalized simultaneously on the commercial success of variety entertainment, the popular demand for Native American performers as living artifacts, and the ethnographic drive to preservation. In September 1894, for example, a group of Buffalo Bill's Wild West performers (including members of the Brulé and Oglala Sioux) traveled from Ambrose Park in Brooklyn—where Cody had contracted with the Edison Illuminating Company to light the arena for the show's 1894 season—to Thomas Edison's Black Maria studio in West Orange, New Jersey.[108] There, they appeared in a series of kinetoscope films, including *Buffalo Bill, Sioux Ghost Dance, Buffalo Dance*, and *Indian War Council*.[109] As the Edison catalog described *Sioux Ghost Dance*, "One of the most peculiar customs of the Sioux Tribe is here shown, the dancers being genuine Sioux Indians, in full war paint and war costumes."[110] Pausing in the early seconds of the film as if awaiting Cody's offscreen instruction, children and adults perform the dance (or perhaps simply *a* dance) in "war costume,"

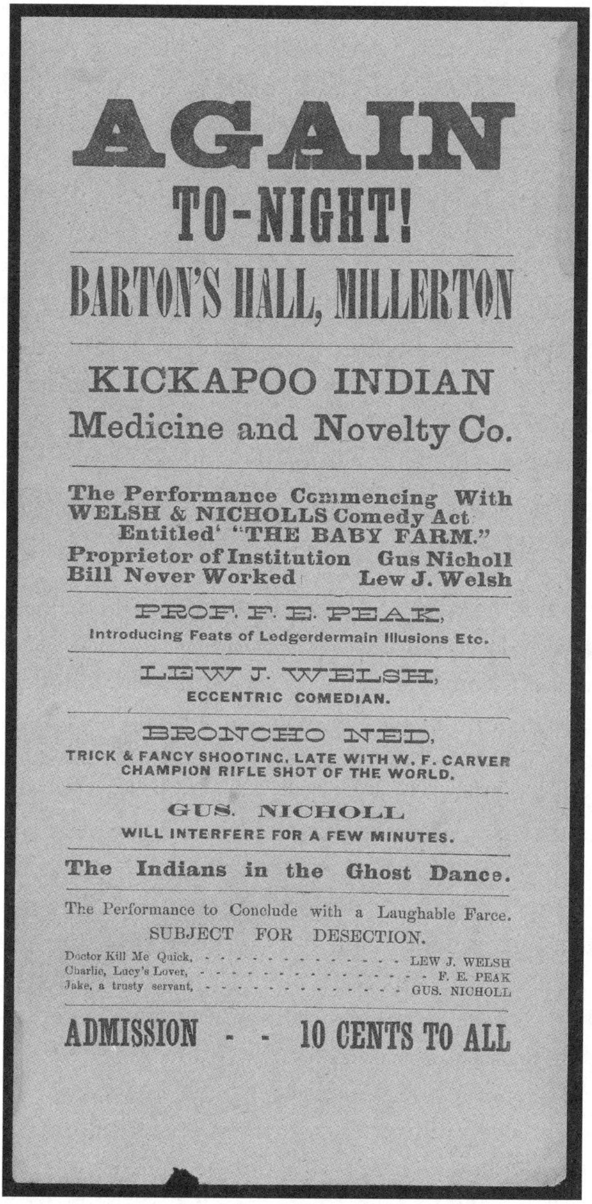

AGAIN
TO-NIGHT!
BARTON'S HALL, MILLERTON

KICKAPOO INDIAN
Medicine and Novelty Co.

The Performance Commencing With
WELSH & NICHOLLS Comedy Act
Entitled "THE BABY FARM."
Proprietor of Institution   Gus Nicholl
Bill Never Worked   Lew J. Welsh

PROF. F. E. PEAK,
Introducing Feats of Ledgerdermain Illusions Etc.

LEW J. WELSH,
ECCENTRIC COMEDIAN.

BRONCHO NED,
TRICK & FANCY SHOOTING. LATE WITH W. F. CARVER
CHAMPION RIFLE SHOT OF THE WORLD.

GUS. NICHOLL
WILL INTERFERE FOR A FEW MINUTES.

The Indians in the Ghost Dance.

The Performance to Conclude with a Laughable Farce.
SUBJECT FOR DESECTION.
Doctor Kill Me Quick, - - - - - - - - - - - - - - LEW J. WELSH
Charlie, Lucy's Lover, - - - - - - - - - - - - - - - F. E. PEAK
Jake, a trusty servant, - - - - - - - - - - - - - - GUS. NICHOLL

ADMISSION - - 10 CENTS TO ALL

Figure 3.13. *Again To-night!*, Barton's Hall, Millerton, Kickapoo Indian Medicine and Novelty Company with "The Indians in the Ghost Dance," ca. 1890. General Collection, Beinecke Rare Book and Manuscript Library. [BrSide40 Zc12 890ag]

moving in an artificially tight circle, in and out of rhythm, occasionally looking directly into the kinetoscope lens.[111] If Edison's catalog recirculated an image of the Ghost Dance as an expression of Indian hostility and resistance, the film itself largely diffuses any such reading; dancers move behind a placard that announces their belonging to Buffalo Bill's Wild West show, marking the Ghost Dance as simultaneously genuine via the logic of the show ("a true picture of American frontier life") and fully contained within the parameters of popular performance.

Edison combined the Wild West show's stereotyped image of the unassimilated Indian with what Joanna Hearne calls "the educational realism of ethnographic spectacle."[112] Filmed in the early days of production at the Black Maria studio, alongside vignettes of ordinary life (a sneeze, a shave), novelty acts (strong men, acrobats, dancers, jugglers, trick dogs, contortionists), and theater acts restaged for film (comic operas, musical burlesques, and minstrel shows), *Sioux Ghost Dance* offers more than anything a spectacle of bodies in motion that paralleled and reinforced the novelty of moving images, both of which became readily consumable as the new material of popular entertainment. As Charles Musser notes, in the first years of film production, motion itself was the mark of cinematic realism: "'Life-like' motion in conjunction with 'life-like' photography and a 'life-size' image provided an unprecedented level of versimilitude."[113] In *Sioux Ghost Dance*, the ethnographic image helps produce and secure the veracity of film as a medium, offering movement as the material sign of "real" racial difference and transposing a "life-size" (and carefully choreographed) image of the Indian onto the moving bodies of indigenous performers.[114] At the same time, and much like Mooney's photographs, the film transforms ecstatic possession into a phenomenon that might be fully and confidently visualized.[115]

In the cramped space of Edison's studio, those performers may or may not have been practicing movements associated with the Ghost Dance itself. As Sandra Sagala suggests, the film may have been so named *after* its production, "when, the next day, the *New York Herald* commented on the 'memorable engagement' and reminded its readers that the 1890 battle of Wounded Knee was no doubt still fresh in the warriors' minds."[116] As with the insistence on "full war paint and war costumes" in the film's promotional materials, the Ghost Dance serves in these texts (and possibly in the film itself) less as a cinematically preserved ritual than as an artifact of defused Indian resistance. Furthermore, white consumption of the Ghost Dance as filmic entertainment signals the widespread desire (evident in Buffalo Bill shows and beyond) on behalf of audiences to repeatedly reenact the Indian Wars from a safe geographical and historical distance; here, we see the popular equivalent of what Jodi Byrd describes as the process by which "U.S. empire orients and replicates itself by transforming those to be colonized into 'Indians' through the continual reiteration of pioneer logics."[117] The reiterative and mediated life of the Ghost Dance, in these terms, works to consolidate US empire by extending, replicating, and reenacting the frontier through the technological pioneering of early film.

Reanimating the Ghost Dance in the filmic present as a way of demonstrating its belonging to the past, *Sioux Ghost Dance* also exemplifies the complex temporality of early cinema. The dance's cinematic reenactment depends at once on a sense of temporal distance—the threat posed by the dance decidedly in the past—while (as the *Herald* proclaimed) it bespeaks the "freshness" of the filmic "event," its sensory immediacy both for survivors of Wounded Knee and for white audiences eager to consume the recent past. Edison's Black Maria studio provided a controlled space through which to reproduce the event of dance—a present tense performance whose spiritual and experiential vectors remain contingent and indeterminable (however clearly staged)—while consolidating the historical image of Wounded Knee as a coherently "memorable engagement." As Mary Ann Doane has argued, this tension between contingency and the production of coherent time was central to the actuality films in which Edison specialized. As Doane describes them, actualities—topical "records" that emphasized an indexical relation to an event purportedly unfolding in real time, though often reenacted—were in fact "technolog[ies] of temporality," working to "produce the image of a coherent and unified 'real time.'"[118] Like the early actualities it approximates, then, *Sioux Ghost Dance* offers an image of the Ghost Dance unfolding in time, even as it evinces a fundamental uncertainty about the time to which the ritual belongs. Similarly, it challenges our ability to distinguish between the "real" or "live" performance and the ethnographic record, as the film "delicately negotiates the contradiction between recording and signification."[119]

This contradiction—between the drive to document and the performative effort to signify, as well as between linear and retrievable time—would be exponentially intensified in William F. Cody's epic sequel to Edison's *Sioux Ghost Dance*. Filmed in the fall of 1913, near the end of his career, Cody's *Indian War Pictures* aimed to replicate the Indian wars on a grand cinematic scale, filming on location at the relevant battle sites and using actual participants (including both Indians and US soldiers) rather than actors.[120] The film included reenactments of battles at Summit Springs (1869) and War Bonnet Creek (1876)—both of which figured regularly in Cody's Wild West shows—as well as Wounded Knee, to which Cody devoted more than double the footage allotted to the previous two battles. As Joy Kasson notes, Cody's commitment to reenactment meant "abandoning cinematic believability in the interests of historical accuracy"; elderly participants (like Buffalo Bill himself) guaranteed the authenticity of the film, if not its verisimilitude.[121] Still, as Kasson details, Cody's effort to restage Wounded Knee on the outskirts of the Pine Ridge reservation produced a deeply unsettling proximity between the event of the massacre and its filmic rehearsal:

> Bringing Indian survivors to the scene of the massacre, representing Ghost Dance ceremonies, re-enacting their terror-stricken flight into a ravine, simulating the fire of the deadly Hotchkiss gun that killed so many—Cody found all this unleashed more passion than he had anticipated. According to one account, Indian women chanted death songs and wept when they returned to the scene of the slaughter, and it was reported that some of the young men vowed to use live ammunition in the battle scene to avenge their fathers. Opting for the greater realism made possible by the film medium, Cody had disrupted the delicate balance between role-playing and memory that his [Wild West] show had managed to maintain for thirty years.[122]

While Sagala notes the possibility that Cody himself circulated this account of a potential "second Wounded Knee" to boost excitement as part of the film's promotion, she points out that the filming of the reenactment over the graves of massacred Sioux would have been justification enough for such a response.[123] Despite Cody's best efforts at translating his showmanship to the cinema, the film never gained a wide audience; existent copies of the film have deteriorated or been lost, and what we know of *Indian War Pictures* today comes from a three-minute fragment, a series of still photographs, and production manager Theodore Wharton's list of filmic sequences used in editing Cody's footage.[124]

In Cody's realist restaging of Wounded Knee, the temporal distance between original event and performed repetition threatens to collapse, as the very possibility of "live" ammunition signals the ongoing, durational life of the massacre for Native participants, if not for Cody and other white reenactors. Shot through with all the uncertainty of the relationship between "live" performance, filmic record, and "real" event, Cody's efforts—and the purported reaction to them—inhabit the temporal and affective "queasiness" of reenactment, "the uncertainty of where and how time *takes place*."[125] Importantly, this temporal uncertainty—the capacity for times to touch, enfold, and inhabit one another and for the past to remain distinctly alive in the performative space of the present—easily coincides with the figuring of the Indian as artifact, a necessarily lost and regained object that sutures national identity in its iterative returns. In this sense, Cody's multiple reenactments of Indian removal depend on a sense of the past as fully past, even as they produce an image of the present riddled by the ongoingness of the historical event. Thus in its various and variously mediated reenactments, the Ghost Dance itself takes on a "freighted, cross-temporal mobility," one that lives on, in, and through bodily practice, and one in which the performance of the "real" belies any fundamental link between realist practice and linear or progressive time.[126]

This is not to suggest that *Indian War Pictures* offers a radical critique of progressive time. In an essay that helpfully illuminates the tension between colonial projects (like Cody's) and the temporal disruptions they produce, Tavia Nyong'o notes that "deeply normative projects . . . possess their own deviations from straight time."[127] Augmenting Schneider's account of reenactment as a form of "temporal drag" (a challenge to confidently linear and secular forms of historical thinking), Nyong'o points to the fact that reenactment—with its emphasis on an embodied relationship to the past and on the past as an affectively forceful construction of the present—can also reinforce a fantasy of purified origins. In this form of reenactment—legible, for example, in the Tea Party's January 2011 reading of the US Constitution on the floor of the House of Representatives—the past is "imagined as something that can be both preserved in perpetuity and be repeated without variation."[128] Against this conservative sacralization of the past (at work in Cody's realist mania for historical details, including the expensive construction of replica buildings to be destroyed in the reenactment), Nyong'o resurrects the work of radical black profanation—performances of critique that both cite and transform the repressive logics of documents like the US Constitution.[129] By using language to performatively denaturalize the logic of progressive history, such acts of radical profanation (as we saw Du Bois offer in chapter 1) give us a window onto the very mechanisms by which white supremacy repeats and consolidates itself as governing force.

In a much more tentative sense, we might point to how Native performers similarly mobilized the theatricality of Cody's reenactments to flip the historical script, at once acting within and challenging the parameters of historical repetition. As Sagala reports, "When cameras ceased rolling on the reenactment of the bloody business, Cody made much of the fact that some Indians had been too excited to remain 'dead' and rolled over to watch the others 'die.' 'Thus,' he remembered, 'comedy is injected into an otherwise very serious affair.'"[130] Such a refusal to realistically "die" on the same grounds as their predecessors may indeed have injected a form of comedy that profaned the high seriousness of Cody's reenactments; it certainly would have called attention to the theatricality that underwrote them, refusing the conservative fantasy of exact historical replication that wrote itself onto Native bodies by demanding (in both cinematic and political terms) that they remain dead. In the space of the filmic reenactment, playing dead is made visible as strategy and as performance, disrupting the showman's feat of high fidelity.

Despite significantly different registers of performance, we might also tentatively align this refusal to remain dead with the Ghost Dance's many iterative resurrections, from Wovoka's initial "death" and return (as Mooney and other ethnographers reported it described), to the deathlike falls of individual ghost dancers in the space of the dance (what Mooney accounted for as trances or "cataleptic attacks"), to the vision of mass resurrection at the heart of nearly all versions of the religion. As the Cheyenne ghost dancer Porcupine reported of his visit with Wovoka, "He told us . . . that all our dead were to be resurrected; that they were all to come back to earth, and that as earth was too small for them and us, he would do away with heaven, and make the earth large enough to contain us all."[131] In *Radical Hope: Ethics in the Face of Cultural Devastation*, Jonathan Lear describes the Ghost Dance's vision of resurrection in the face of genocide as "a case of what Freud called 'turning away from reality'": a refusal on the part of the Sioux to recognize the fundamental destruction of Native frames of meaning, and thus an inability to grapple with the uncertainty of what might come after such destruction.[132] In Lear's account, the messianic aspect of the dance functions as a form of wish fulfillment, "a way of avoiding the real-life demands that confront one in the everyday."[133] But what Lear's reading of the Ghost Dance misses is the extent to which its repeat performances of death and resurrection function as a form of mourning and, at the same time, a refusal to move "forward" in time under the terms dictated by white colonialism. We might understand this refusal in the terms that Audra Simpson offers in her study of the Mohawks of Kahnawà:ke: a refusal "in the teeth of constraint" and (at the same time) a registration of the ongoing violence of settler colonialism.[134] Or as the Oglala Lakota medicine man Black Elk reported of the dancing at Wounded Knee Creek, "Then we began dancing, and most of the people wailed and cried as they danced, holding hands in a circle; but some of them laughed with happiness. Now and then someone would fall down *like dead*, and others would go staggering and panting before they would fall. While they were lying there *like dead* they were having visions, and we kept on dancing and singing, and many were crying for the old way of living and that the old religion might be with them again."[135] Rather than an incapacity to imagine the future, the Ghost Dance here offers a performance of death—a being "like dead"—that challenges the very terms of a genocidal "real" whose consolidation always already demanded the destruction of Native peoples and epistemologies.[136] Kélina Gotman argues that this performance of death also interrupts the ceaseless forward motion of capitalist accumulation, resisting the terms through which Native Americans dancers were deemed excessive and thus expendable within the US body politic.[137] In this sense, being "like dead" becomes a strategy for survivance not within but *beside* colonialism and capitalism, a formation that demands comedy and laughter as well as grief.

Without effacing the complexity and variation across different performances and interpretations of the Ghost Dance, we might argue that in refusing a strict boundary between life and death, past and present, self and other, ghost dancers rejected the politics of recognition[138] through the straight time of secular Progressive and ethnographic nostalgia while keeping alive (at the level of the moving body) the very real and material losses effaced by discourses of vanishing. To be "like dead," in Black Elk's terms, might then be less a performance of verisimilitude than a way of insisting on how the dead linger and inhabit the ghost dancers' bodies in their repetitive falls and resurrections. Transmuted across time and across bodies, the Ghost Dance functions as a performance of mourning that refuses temporal closure; its ecstasy lives in close intimacy with its grief, is the very form of it. As Judith Butler notes, "To be ec-static means, literally, to be outside oneself, and thus can have several meanings: to be transported beyond oneself by passion, but also to be *beside oneself* with rage or grief. I think that if I can still address a 'we,' or include myself within its terms, I am speaking to those of us who are living in certain ways *beside ourselves*, whether in sexual passion, or emotional grief, or political rage."[139] As the Ghost Dance suggests, to be ecstatic is also to be beside oneself in time; this, perhaps, as a strategy for living with and against what Mark Rivkin calls "settler time," or time made meaningful by the logic of events with a clearly delineated end (in this case, the purported end of Native cultures).[140] In its own reiterative returns to the Ghost Dance, realism points to the way that any such ends are invariably haunted by the grief they disavow.

The uncanny liveness produced in realism's rendering of the Ghost Dance thus raises crucial questions about the grievability of indigenous and racialized subjects—about what it might mean to grieve for subjects figured as "always already past perfect" and even about how the recursive temporality of a disavowed grief might structure realist practice.[141] We've seen how this recursive temporality informs a novel like *The Red Badge of Courage*; in the next chapter, we'll see how James Weldon Johnson's novel *The Autobiography of an Ex-Colored Man* grapples with the cyclical, circuit-like returns of racial trauma even as it seeks to mobilize ecstatic communicability as an aesthetic praxis. In realism's approach to the Ghost Dance, though, ecstatic bodies repeatedly become objects of literary and visual fascination in a way that echoes the ethnographic desire to turn racialized subjects into the "material" of positivist science—a biopolitics of racial and temporal difference. Such a move renders Native Americans both present and absent, or suspended in (unlivable) time, even as it renders them "real." Like the shadow on the image, however, the materiality of realism exceeds its ideological contours, registering its entanglements with the very performances of the cross-temporal encounter that it claimed to demystify or assimilate. Communing with the ghosts they would soon become, ghost dancers took what we might describe as a "realist" approach to cultural decimation and the ongoing threat of physical annihilation: an effort to make the invisible visible or to bring into relief the active vanishing of indigenous subjects. Whereas realism repeatedly reenacted such vanishing, ghost dancers made the violence of colonialism materially visible again and again through a collective practice of mourning, making bodies-in-motion the site of spiritual encounter. They danced, to use Joseph Roach's terms, "to possess themselves again in the spirit of their ancestors, to possess again their memories, to possess again their communities."[142] This "collective *re*possession" was not a turning away from the reality of genocide and displacement but a performance that might affirm Native survivance by transforming falling bodies into something other than the static objects of colonial violence and ethnographic representation.[143] Refusing the false choice between resistance and assimilation to liberal subjecthood, ghost dancers assumed an ecstatic practice that would allow them to "tarr[y] with grief"—or to be beside themselves in colonized space and time.[144]

Secular (Dis)possessions

In October 1900, the prominent regionalist writer Hamlin Garland—best known for his collection of autobiographical stories in *Main-Travelled Roads* (1891) and his manifesto of realist or veritist aesthetics in *Crumbling Idols* (1894)—wrote to James Mooney to thank him for his work on the Ghost Dance: "I am re-reading—I may say studying—your Ghost Dance vol. which I find extremely valuable. I have been twice to Standing Rock in search of material concerning the Sitting Bull and the Ghost

Dances there. Your material comes in to corroborate and enrich my narrative, and I want permission to quote you and I want also to thank you for your sane view of the whole matter."[145] Between 1895 and 1900, Garland made multiple trips to Indian territories in the West, including two stays at Standing Rock Reservation in South Dakota, where he consulted agency records, interviewed Sioux leaders, and observed the Ghost Dance.[146] Garland would go on to treat the Ghost Dance in at least two pieces of short fiction: "Rising Wolf—Ghost Dancer" (1899), based on an interview with the Cheyenne ghost dancer Porcupine, and "The Silent Eaters" (1900), a sympathetic rendering of the life and death of Sitting Bull. Both stories were later published in *The Book of the American Indian* (1923), a popular giftbook that juxtaposed Garland's narratives with illustrations by Frederic Remington, many of which had first appeared in *Harper's Weekly* as part of the coverage of the Sioux "outbreak."[147]

Written in the years after his most prominent successes in literary realism, these stories—like many of Garland's writings on Native Americans—combined a critical take on US assimilation policy with a deterministic approach to the decline of indigenous cultures. Like Mooney, Garland was dismayed by what he saw as the inexorable realities of Indian life at the end of the nineteenth century: the breaking up of collectively held territories, imposed subsistence farming on barren plots of land, and forced assimilation, including the violent suppression of ritual practices. Yet also like Mooney, Garland largely took these realities to be inescapable and positioned Indians as belonging to a world whose changes would (for better or worse) outpace them. Steeped in the language and postures of scientific positivism, Garland's writings combine the idioms of Spencerian survivalism with a critique of colonial dispossession. In a 1902 essay on "The Red Man's Present Needs," for example, Garland described Indians as "survivals in our midst of the Stone Age"—archeological remnants of an earlier era of human development—even as he went on to insist to white readers of the *North American Review*, "We are answerable to them, just as we are answerable for the black man's future."[148] Like many white observers, Garland characterized Indians as either "progressive" (able and willing to adapt to white colonial structures of power) or "traditional" (resistant to assimilation, holding to tribal practices), distinctions that largely worked to obscure the range of complex, improvisational responses to a world of eviscerated possibility, and that were themselves a function of white colonialism's inability to imagine an alternative beyond assimilation or death.[149]

Drawing heavily from Mooney's report in his own description of the Ghost Dance, and incorporating several of Mooney's transcribed Ghost Dance songs, Garland's stories largely rationalize and contextualize the dance, situating its "outbreak" as a response to increasingly dire conditions on the reservation. In "Rising Wolf—Ghost Dancer," Rising Wolf (a stand-in for Porcupine) narrates the history of forced removal and poor government stewardship that gave rise to the dance: "Soon we became poor. We had then no buffalo at all. We were fed poor beef, and had to wear white men's clothes which did not fit. We could not go to hunt in the mountains, and the land was waterless and very hot in summer, and we froze in winter."[150] Detailing the flood of white settlers, the impossibility of farming barren land, and the devastating effects of hunger and disease, Iapi, the Washington-educated Sioux narrator of "The Silent Eaters," notes similarly of the Ghost Dance, "So it was that in the prepared soil of my people's minds this seed of mystery fell. It was not a new religion; it was indeed very old. Many other races had believed it; the time was come for the Sioux to take it to themselves. In their despair they greedily seized upon it. In their enforced idleness they welcomed it."[151] Much as Mooney had diffused the radical vision of the Ghost Dance by comparing it to other historical religious outbreaks, Garland here refuses to distinguish between the Ghost Dance and other forms of prophetic belief, treating belief in secularist terms as a function of the (passing) times, and situating the Ghost Dance as a rational (even organic) response to a climate of rapid political and cultural change.

Yet also like Mooney, Garland's ethnographic gaze is not fully immune to the possibility held out by the Ghost Dance of ecstatic, cross-temporal connection.[152] Indeed, it courts this possibility in "The Silent Eaters" through the figure of Iapi, whose education situates him between worlds even as it reinforces an essentialist understanding of both race and religion. As Iapi's tutor Lieutenant Davies (assigned to the War Department) tells him, "A race is the product of conditions, the result of a million years of struggle. I do not expect a red man to become a white man. Those who do, know nothing of the human organism. On the surface I can make some change; but deep down your emotions, your superstitions are red and always will be; that is not a thing to be ashamed of."[153] In moments such as these, Garland's stories articulate a resistance to assimilation that is fully consistent with the logic of white supremacy; here "race" and "superstition" reinforce one another to produce the transtemporal "always" of Indian difference. And indeed "The Silent Eaters" works to bear out this particular temporal configuration, in which the past (aligned with both race and religion) is carried *in* the body. Having returned to the parceled-out Sioux reservation after four years in Washington and witnessed the effects of dispossession and starvation, Iapi watches the Ghost Dance (brought to Standing Rock by Oglala Sioux leader Kicking Bear) and listens to the dancers as they sing:

> As they sang my head was filled with many great but confused thoughts. In that light, with those surroundings, any magic seemed possible. It was thus that the disciples of Christ of Galilee came together and talked of his message. I had listened often to the white man's religion, and yet the hymns of the martyrs could not move me as did these songs. The past and the present fused together strangely in my mind as the ancient shining winds blew and the old rejoicing days came back. . . . Some strange power seemed to go with the motion of The Bear's hands. We all seemed to be looking upon the very scenes of which he sang, and my throat closed with an emotion I could not control. . . .
>
> Suddenly The Bear's head began to rock violently from side to side; it seemed as if it would wrench itself from its place. His eyes set in a dreadful stare, his mouth fixed in a horrible gape. Then shaking himself free, he fell close to the fire, face downward.[154]

Working on behalf of the Indian agent at Standing Rock, Iapi's observation is a form of surveillance that closely echoes Mooney's treatment of the dance as a cross-temporal phenomenon, linking the ecstatic body to its predecessors in earlier moments of religious and political upheaval. Thus while Garland's stories revel in the strangeness of the ecstatic body—its flickering between movement and stillness—they also insist on its familiarity, annexing it to a history of (white) religious belief. Like Mooney, Garland would repeatedly draw parallels between the Ghost

Dance and early Christianity (as Garland wrote to Mooney, "Your fearless relating of the Ghost Dance to various forms of Christianity seemed to me very unusual in breadth and candor of thought"), incorporating the dance into what for white readers would have been a familiar and credible history of messianic deliverance.[155] Observing the Ghost Dance from afar, Iapi notes, "In some such way, perhaps, the white fisher folk of Galilee drew together to greet the coming of their Messiah. Was this Saviour of the west any more incredible than Christ?"[156] Against the image of the Sioux Ghost Dance as a prelude to violent resistance, Garland offers a sympathetic version of the dance that reiterates and secularizes a distinctly "white" Christian narrative of resurrection even as it projects a privileged spiritual capacity onto the songs themselves ("yet the hymns of the martyrs could not move me as did these songs"). At the same time, for Iapi, the Ghost Dance's vision of resurrection seems to mark the death of his "race," consolidating Garland's ethnographic nostalgia even as it holds out the possibility of a rapturous pluralism, of radically different *times* coming together: "As I looked my heart contracted. It seemed as if I was looking upon the actual dissolution—the death pangs—of my race. My learning was for the moment of no avail. I shook like a reed in the gust of this primeval passion. Was it insanity or was it some inexplicable divine force capable in truth of uniting the quick and the dead in one convulsive, rapturous coalition?"[157] In his fictional reenactments of the Ghost Dance, Garland himself united the quick and the dead, producing Indianness as a function and manifestation of the past—even (as here) the primeval past—but one capable of being resurrected and reanimated, at least "for the moment," in the realist present. In these terms, realism both colonizes and borrows from the Ghost Dance's ecstatic temporality, tarrying with the dissolution and nonautonomy of the secular liberal subject even as it consolidates the (dis)posession of Native Americans. Iapi's question—Was it insanity or divine force?—replays the uncertainty lingering at the heart of embodied religion since the second Great Awakenings, while Garland's stories at a broad scale transform the ecstatic, racialized body into a new source of "material" for realist fiction and a new "frontier" of representation.

In his 1903 essay "The Red Man as Material," Garland rejected as false the inherited image of Native Americans (propagated by James Fennimore Cooper, Robert Montgomery Bird, and others) as alternately dangerous and cowering primitives. Garland offered a strident critique of American fiction's history of capitalizing on such images: "While I do not like to malign my own profession," Garland wrote, "I fear that if a real story of a kindly redman would pay better than a false story of a very horrid redman, we would all be doing our best, in every possible way, to furnish our readers that kind of material."[158] Realism, Garland argued, required a break with this history and a literary (if not necessarily political) recognition of common humanity: "We spring from the same good brown earth, and we return thereto with an equal awe of the 'great mystery.'"[159] Similarly, in *Crumbling Idols*, Garland articulated a vision of the realist novel untethered to the past: a prophetic form that delineated the future through unceasing attention to the shape, textures, and outgrowths of the present. For Garland, the novel's prophetic vision was a naturalized one, rooted in Spencerian and Darwinian theories of evolutionary development. The central impact of these theories, for Garland, was that they provided the very possibility of adequately accounting for the passage of time: "Until men came to see system and progression, and endless but definite succession in art and literature as in geologic change; until the law of progress was enunciated, no conception of the future and no reasonable history of the past could be formulated."[160] If change was the natural law of the present, Garland argued, then the realist novel could intuit the future by studying its every detail: "There is small prophecy in it, after all. We have but to examine the ground closely, and we see the green shoots of the coming harvest beneath our feet."[161]

Deeply wedded to what Garland (like many) understood as the law of progress—which naturalized the deaths of indigenous persons as much as it sanitized the ground to which they returned—Garland's fictional reenactments of the Ghost Dance nevertheless offer a fundamental challenge to the idea that realism's time is fully reducible to secular time. This is in part because Garland's realism diagnoses "primeval passion"—a consolidation of religious, racial, and temporal difference as an object of realist knowledge—even as it dreams of a "rapturous coalition." Such dreams, as we've seen, could function as much to disrupt the present tense, secular subject of realism as they could to obscure the violence that secured it. In the following chapter, I'll demonstrate how James Weldon Johnson refused such erasure—and the convergence of technological modernity and racial violence—by channeling ecstatic, electrifying speech into the realist narrative.

Realism's investment in ecstatic religion was never merely ethnographic, even (as we have seen) in the case of realist ethnographies. Treating spiritual experience as the material of thick description, realism rehearses the idioms of ecstatic religion while borrowing its choreographies and affective intensities as an index of the real. In proximity to the Ghost Dance, this meant a deep-seated faith in realist media's ability to conjure indigenous ghosts, a project in which the very terms of verisimilitude—the theatrical production of a likeness—come to look and sound distinctly haunted by histories of colonization and genocide. Realism, in this sense, cannot be divorced from the normative force of secularism, which links religious "excess" to the production of racial difference and marks religion and race as temporal configurations, distinct from the ostensibly unmarked white secular/Protestant progressive time of modernity.

Realism's secularism, in other words, is deeply bound to Jim Crow's expansive work of racial regulation. Yet reading realism's iterative performances also allows us to see white supremacist constructions of religiosity as themselves discourses of excess, rooted in an ecstatic reenactment of difference. Approaching Mooney's efforts at ethnographic preservation as robust performances of high fidelity, for example, we see how raising the dead was a function of realist representation rather than its irrational exception: the photograph a complex choreography of ecstatic exposure, the Berliner record an act of mournful mimicry sealed into wax. As these performances attest, realism's secularism is less a rejection or repression of ecstatic religion than an attachment to it as the material (and, at times, the mechanism) of realist reproduction—a form of being beside that is as full of longing as it is of violence.

4

Touching a Button

Is it I, God, or who, that lifts this arm?
—Herman Melville, *Moby-Dick; or, The Whale*

In the winter of 1887, as New York's state legislature debated a bill introducing the use of the electric chair for capital punishment, William Dean Howells wrote to the editor of *Harper's Weekly* with a wry protest: "One journal has drawn an interesting picture of the simple process, and I have fancied the executions throughout the State taking place from the Governor's office, where his private secretary, or the Governor himself, might touch a little annunciation-button, and dismiss a murderer to the presence of his Maker with the lightest pressure of the finger."[1] Linking lethal electrocution to public taste for spectacular performances of long-distance electrification, Howells decried the abstraction of death enabled by the electric chair, its transformation into entertainment in an increasingly electrified American infrastructure.[2] Conceding "no good reason why this mysterious agent which now unites the whole civilized world by nerves of keen intelligence . . . which has added to life in apparently inexhaustible variety, should not also be employed to take it away," he observed that electricity—while making connective sympathy across the globe a technological reality—could also be used to inflict death at a remove.[3] Drawing on an emergent discourse of the nervous system to figure a newly unified social body, Howells characterized electricity's aesthetics of connectivity as shadowed by the threat of collective loss, a threat lodged in the increasingly mundane gesture of touching a button.[4]

Howells's sardonic invocation of electricity's limitless potential capitalized on its status as a contested aesthetic, religious, and material force, rewriting romantic electricity for the age of techno-industrialization. As David Nye, Paul Gilmore, and others have demonstrated, electricity suffused nineteenth-century conceptions of aesthetic experience as they circulated between transcendent individualism and embodied connectivity, natural occurrence and technological mastery, metaphysical fluidity and physical force.[5] From Walt Whitman's body electric to Frederick Douglass's embrace of electric technologies as potential agents of democratization, electricity was almost unequivocally celebrated as both the medium for and the material of America's "enlightened" trajectory.[6] By the end of the century, as Howells registered, electricity increasingly functioned as a form of bureaucratic power, defining the limits of social and individual bodies even as it retained its capacity to produce terror, awe, and collective excitation. Mediating bodily presence and absence, the "little annunciation button," as Howells figured it, was the site of secularism's violent incarnation: the event of a body at once inaugurated and dismissed by "the lightest pressure of the finger," the smallest flourish of a performative gesture.

Howells's not-so-fanciful imagining of the electric chair, as we'll see, draws on the radical indeterminacy of what it meant to touch a button at the turn of the century.[7] Here we might think of Thomas Edison describing (in laudatory terms) the gestural life of the electric chair: "When the time comes, touch a button, close the circuit, and . . . it is over."[8] Or, a few decades later, of Walter Benjamin's taxonomy of industrial gestures: "Of the countless movements of switching, inserting, pressing, and the like, the 'snapping' of the photographer has had the greatest consequences. A touch of the finger now sufficed to fix an event for an unlimited period of time. The camera gave the moment a posthumous shock, as it were."[9] In both instances, what Giorgio Agamben describes as gesture's transformation from *res* to *res gesta*—from thing to event—happens at the touch of a finger, a literally shocking interface. And yet, in the logic of the camera and the electric chair, this touch also threatens to turn the res gesta back into res; it marks the moment of shock, of some unaccountable thing being "done," finished, or posthumous—of stillness wrought from gesture's movement.[10]

In this chapter, I argue that the gesture of touching a button coalesces a set of kinesthetic, affective, and political concerns specific to the turn of the century, when push-button technologies like the camera and (at least figuratively) the electric chair mediated new choreographies and temporalities of social power. I'll ask, What kind of gesture is touching a button? How might we begin to understand the historical, spiritual, and figurative power of this gesture? And what might it have to teach us about how realism approaches the body as a site of materialization and abstraction? In both mundane and spectacular ways, touching a button signals what Lauren Berlant has described, building on Agamben, as gesture's affective and ethical orientation—its status as "a medial act, neither ends-nor means-oriented, a sign of being in the world, in the middle of the world, a sign of sociality."[11] Yet as we'll also see, this gesture was often (both literally and figuratively) a means to an end—a performance that violently delineated the "realness" of racial difference while managing the parameters of sociality and social contact. Embedded in modernity's dream of instantaneity, the photograph and the electric chair yoked speed to stillness, bridging the gap between res gesta and res, eventfulness and objectification. Read in the context of these closely imbricated technologies, the gesture of touching a button indexes a violent conflation of progress and process, a convergence that (as we'll see) touched some bodies differently than others.

This chapter tracks the gesture of touching a button across a series of photographic and literary texts, mapping the uneven shock and pleasure of electrified contact as it emerges under the body politic of Jim Crow. I'll argue that to place this gesture under the pressure of the visual and the literary is to demonstrate what a deracinated history of button-pressing threatens to obscure: the technological and aesthetic reproduction of racially marked subjects as objects of violence under the sign of modernity.[12] While historians of technology have recovered the push button as a crucial interface—a site of charged contact between humans and machines—they have not yet attended to how push-button technologies functioned equally as racial technologies, mediating almost instantaneously between bodies deemed human or object. Conversely, while scholars of Jim Crow have characterized the objectifying power of the lynch mob, situating lynching as a function of (rather than an exception to) industrial modernization, I recover the ways in which the electric chair's equally systematic transformation of humans into objects circulated as a complementary form of racial terror at the nadir. Exploring texts that attempt to still this terror—to hold its power in reserve—I examine the potential that electrification offered as a means of making and remaking social contact, of managing modernity's distinct but interrelated forms of violence and possibility.

To think of touching a button as a gesture that instigates (pricks or punctures, as in *stigma*) is to remind us of the violent and often unpredictable force of electricity, a force that early twentieth-century push-button technologies worked simultaneously to insulate, abstract, and channel.[13] In the first half of the chapter, I explore images that evince a violent conflation of touch and vision, coalescing what photographer Alvin Langdon Coburn called "fast seeing" with the electric chair's logic of instantaneous death.[14] Analyzing William Van der Weyde's largely forgotten images of the electric chair at Sing Sing prison, I'll argue that such images mark gesture's objectifying force—its transformation of res gesta into res—by producing a racialized and criminalized body as the site of electrical contact. And yet they do not merely recirculate the terror of Edison's closed circuit. Documenting less a singular event than a re-creation, Van der Weyde's images perform a choreographed pause in the spectacular disciplining of racialized flesh, offering the photograph as a site where scripted forms of racial violence might be visualized, rehearsed, and at least potentially rewritten.

In the second half of the chapter, I track the rhetorical force of touching a button through James Weldon Johnson's 1912 novel *The Autobiography of an Ex-Colored Man*, a novel that at once channels the possibilities of electrified collectivity and, at the same time, grapples with the shock of racial terror as part of the very wiring of modern life. Recalling and recirculating a discourse of romantic electricity, *The Autobiography* reminds us with its button-pressing that by 1912, America was already two decades into a "progressive" project of electrocuting bodies: a project disproportionately applied to racially marked bodies in Johnson's time as in our own. Yoking the extralegal terror of the lynch mob to the horror of the electric chair, Johnson's novel points to the fiction of enlightenment-by-electrocution, even as it mobilizes electricity to theorize the unpredictable turns and reversals embedded in black life. *The Autobiography* thus works to convert the *res* back into *res gesta*, in part by rerouting the objectifying force of electricity through the affective and ecstatic power of sound. Addressed to the itinerant motion of electricity, Johnson's button-pressing itself migrates between the technological, the religious, and the affective, as distinct but interrelated modes of touching and being touched.[15] In this sense, Johnson's novel theorizes what Alexander Weheliye describes as the "force field of the flesh": its excluded yet constitutive possibility, its status as both "a tool for dehumanization and a relational vestibule to alternate ways of being."[16] Asking what spiritualized flesh might conduct as an alternative to racial terror, *The Autobiography* treats electro-ecstatic conversion as both an aesthetic and political imperative.

Tracking the material, figurative, and affective work of button-pressing across visual and literary texts helps emphasize electricity's potential to travel or be converted across various mediums. So while attending to the ways in which Van der Weyde's photographs and Johnson's novel offer formally distinct meditations on the reproduction of suffering, I'll read both as intimately engaging the rubrics of performance, of electricity's gestural life as it configures the affective and bodily arrangements of modernity. If we can say that these texts act on us, they do so by pressing our buttons: moving us in historically recognizable yet still unpredictable ways. In this sense, we might read turn-of-the-century push buttons as what Robin Bernstein calls "scriptive things," the materials of cultural life that shape the contours of our bodily interactions as citational performances, prompts for interpellation and improvisation.[17] Reading push buttons in this way allows us to see the gesture of touching a button as a ritualized prompt, a performance of cultural and kinesthetic memory that supplements and subtends language. Focusing on the gesture as performance—a physical and rhetorical action that alternately rehearses and interrupts the organization of life under Jim Crow—I argue that button-pressing figures, disfigures, and rewrites the corporeal as an unstable conductor of meaning, while troubling strict binaries between liveness and death, the live and the reproducible.

As a gesture, touching a button illuminates the early twentieth-century relay between race and personhood, categories that themselves begin to look increasingly gestural—and thus increasingly linked to temporalities of repetition, citation, and reenactment. By calling us to linger on the uncertainty of touching a button, Van der Weyde and Johnson work to disrupt the forward drive of modernity and resist its repertoires of subjectification, though not in any straightforward sense. Lingering, then, becomes a deliberate effort to unsettle the instantaneous temporality that button-pressing both indexes and enacts. So even as I trace electricity's kinetic-kinesthetic logic through Van der Weyde and Johnson, I'll emphasize the breaks or pauses, or what I'll call "fugitive intervals": moments of potential readjustment or reconfiguration, where electricity might be directed elsewhere, used to enliven rather than deaden its material.[18] Lingering in such fugitive intervals allows us to rethink the photograph's strict alignment with what is unrecoverable, lodged in the singular pastness of the singular event, the moment of touching a button. Similarly, reading modernity's gestural life helps contextualize Johnson's career-long effort to theorize the conversion of electrifying performance into text: to mobilize the force of feeling as a means of imagining what power might look and sound like.

Secular Skin

If the preceding chapters have worked to lay out the way ecstasy both animates and unsettles realism's normative technics, this chapter and the one that follows it go in search of a shift from within, a way of figuring ecstatic entanglement that recognizes—but does not reproduce—the ecstatic body as a site for the recirculation of colonial and racial fantasies. This is precarious work, and as I argue in what follows, the realism of texts like James Weldon Johnson's *The Autobiography of an Ex-Colored Man* and Nella Larsen's *Quicksand* manifests in part through their recognition of how ecstatic embodiment attends the violent production and management of racial difference. This proximity, as William Hart suggests, emerges historically as the disordering of religious passion within a racialized economy of feeling. Rooted in an imperial-colonial imaginary, tropes of religious frenzy (closely linked to ecstasy, enthusiasm, and other terms emerging in the context of post-Reformation Protestantism) are "reborn" within secular discourse as apparently neutral or even reclaimed modes of expression. Yet as Hart argues, such tropes are necessarily haunted by their colonial conditions of emergence. Indeed, in its secular iterations, a trope like "frenzy" signals the duration of colonialism's historical and semantic half-life, a toxic form of lingering: "Given the ongoing construction of black people as irrational, where frenzied violence is the flipside of frenzied religious expression within a general economy of disordered passions, there is little reason to believe that the secular incarnation of this trope is less radioactive."[19] As a regulatory trope, the ecstatic similarly helps us name realism's colonialist incarnations—its repetitive inscription of religion and race as modes of excessive, irrational embodiment—even as it registers the fact of entangled life under the affective and political regime of Jim Crow.[20]

This chapter aims to map the contours of one particular way of accounting for (and managing) ecstasy's secular incarnations, in part by paying attention to what John Modern has described as secularism's disciplining of the subject "at the levels of emotion and mood, underneath the skin."[21] In Modern's account of secularism in antebellum America, the embodied self is less a *site* of secularization than an *effect* of secularism's vast capacity to organize subjects in relation to religious possibilities and modes of thought. The secular self, in other words, is a circuit: a feedback loop of social forces, habits, and normative distinctions between (among other things) rational and irrational religion.[22] While Modern locates this organizing energy as it pools and gathers "underneath" the antebellum skin, I argue (building on Hart) that secularism under Jim Crow also produces the skin as a point of contact and a boundary: a racialized and racializing surface. As I'll suggest in what follows, this production of a secular skin is manifested in realist accounts of electrifying contact—contact imagined, channeled, managed, mediated, and choreographed at the turn of the century, as electricity itself shifted from a contested spiritual and material force to a bureaucratized utility.

To unfold this account of realism's secular skin as a management of social contact, I explore the rhetorical, physical, and performative work of touching a button. Touching a button constitutes a distinctly turn-of-the-century gesture, one whose contested status as event—a performance with immediate and ongoing consequences—helps characterize secularism as (in Modern's terms) "a haunted and haunting affair."[23] In this sense, touching a button is also a distinctly secular gesture, bound up in realism's attention to the affective organization of life and the normative production of an impossible, ecstatic body. As a gesture whose undetermined and yet determining motion emerged as a site of rhetorical anxiety and possibility, touching a button figures a social field in which electricity might operate as a metaphor for ecstatic connectivity *and* as the mechanism of literal and social death—electricity's status as a material and social force meant it could go either way. Similarly, through the idiom of touching a button, realism enacts a circuit between power's literal impress and its figurative potential, and channels electricity's aesthetics of *ex-static* transformation, knowing that under Jim Crow, such transformations could work in multiple directions. The images, texts, and performances that I examine in this chapter thus experiment with electricity's dynamic tropism, seizing on its capacity to figure the unseen mechanisms of social power and the unseen flows of collective feeling while registering electricity as a material threat, one increasingly directed toward the reproduction of racial difference through technologically innovative forms of discipline. By tarrying with this gesture in all its performative complexity, we gain a sense of how realism (at least in some of its iterations) recognized that the very form of ecstatic sociality that threatened black life was also the source through which a different organization of life might come.

Touched and Retouched

For me, the Photographer's organ is not his eye (which terrifies me) but his finger.
—Roland Barthes, *Camera Lucida: Reflections on Photography*

By the first decade of the twentieth century, the electric chair had become America's preferred method of capital punishment, as well as an important site for the mediated construction and contestation of the real. Politicians and reformers celebrated the chair as a critical improvement in executions, a boon to modern death that paralleled and reinforced the boon that electric technologies had offered to modern life. Yet the avowed hope of the chair's proponents—that electrocution would be quicker, cleaner, and less painful than hanging, and that, as Howells put it, "killing by electricity was almost the same as not killing at all"—was repeatedly shown to be a false one. Despite a gag order attached to New York's 1888 Electrical Execution Law intended to limit what journalists could write about executions, reports continually surfaced of multiple shocks, bodies singed, and witnesses sickened by the spectacular violence of death by electricity.[24] In 1904, Howells would offer an even more strident critique of electrocution as a form of state-inflicted manslaughter. Responding to the perhaps inevitable failure of the electric chair to kill without killing, Howells wrote of the failure of vision that plagued the chair's early advocates: "They could not foresee that the mystical element whose agency they had invoked . . . could bungle its sacred mission. The culprit would be carefully seated, somewhat as the subject of photography is, and assuming as cheerful or as submissive an expression as possible, would be thrilled into the other world with the touch of a button, or the turn of a key, by the hand of a scientific gentleman, or at least an educated electrician, on the other side of a wall or screen."[25] At least part of what Howells calls his readers to witness here—what the screen looks to conceal and the gag order attempts to silence—is an unsettling proximity between the disciplinary function of the electric chair and the aesthetic function of the photograph. If to be electrocuted is to be thrilled by the touch of a button, then electrocution's attractiveness as a method of capital punishment might echo and redouble the popularity of the hand camera, which, as Alfred Stieglitz observed in 1897, offered photography to the masses as entertainment, or "no work and lots of fun." As Stieglitz put it, Kodak's marketing slogan—"You press the button, we do the rest"—worked to "enlarg[e] . . . the ranks of enthusiastic Button Pressers" to potentially "enormous dimensions."[26] Invented in 1888—as the first chair was being installed in New York's Auburn prison—Kodak's hand camera made button-pressing available to the masses. With the lightest touch of a button, then, Howells linked the cultural shock of electrocution to the work of art in the age of mechanical reproduction: thrilling, but also potentially numbing or deadening, and available to almost anyone.

By imagining the death chamber as a photographic studio, Howells made visible the reifying force of electrocution: its transformation into cheerful routine, with the concurrent transition of death itself from "sacred" event to streamlined manufacture. At the same time, he evinced a distinctly realist anxiety about the location of cultural authority, denouncing the electric chair in terms that emphasized its strikingly ominous proximity to photography as a form of mass culture. Tracking this anxiety, Nancy Bentley argues that literary realism's efforts to picture a unified social world emerged in a "generative rivalry" with the advent of mass culture, whose sensational displays at once informed realist practice and required its analytical expertise.[27] For Howells in particular, the realist novel was a site where social distinctions were both represented and practiced, distinctions that the electric chair and the hand camera threatened—"with the lightest pressure of the finger"—to erode. At the same time, the imaginative labor that Howells devoted to picturing electrocution suggests the extent to which his representational practice was intimately bound to the visualization of a complex social field, with its often invisible (and sometimes electrifying) machinations of power. In terms that mark realism's ambivalent fascination with photographic reproduction as the idiom of mass culture, Bentley notes that "with something like the exhilaration of watching a developing photograph, proponents believed realism was bringing into view a social world usually too changeable and fast-paced to be seen steadily."[28] Hence Howells's account of electrocution invokes its "thrill" in terms recognizable to an increasingly photographed and photographing public sphere while channeling cultural fascination with electricity toward the cultivation of a critical readership.

Meant to mitigate the spectacle of capital punishment by moving executions indoors and largely out of sight, the impact of the electric chair was in fact everywhere (photographically) reproduced. As Tim Armstrong points out, the proliferation of media reports surrounding early electrocutions meant that death itself looked increasingly like a function of technological reproduction, an event at one's fingertips.[29] The proximity between death and technological reproduction is precisely what Howells's critique of state manslaughter calls us to witness. Offering the photographic pose as corollary for the electric chair's terrifying production of stillness, Howells's analogy might be said to literalize photography's mortifying quality—its seemingly fundamental link to what is (or will be) unrecoverable.[30] In these terms, reading about the electrocution might indeed be as exhilarating as watching a photograph develop, insofar it manifests the striking reality of electricity's unseen and nearly instantaneous effects. Yet Howells's analogy also registers a fundamental tension in both technologies: that of stillness shot through with performance, as, more than anything, in Howells's description we glean the careful staging of the image of death, the choreographed production of stillness. Howells's attention to the gestural idiom that sutures photography and the electric chair—his insistence on reproducing the act (res gesta) of taking a photograph or a life, which the push button both enables and effaces—reinvests the projected image with a strange kind of action. In the kinesthetic imaginary of touching a button, Howells calls his readers to witness what the chair makes possible: the mass reproducibility of corpses as both objects and images.

Howells's analogy thus invites us to reconsider what Rebecca Schneider has described as the "inherent gestic hail of the photo itself," or what Roland Barthes characterized as the photograph's gestural mode of signification ("the Photograph is never anything but an antiphon of 'Look,' 'See,' 'Here it is'; it points a finger at certain *vis-à-vis*, and cannot escape this pure deictic language").[31] Without conceding Barthes's notion that the gesture of photography is reducible to the *purely* deictic (as Schneider observes, the gesture of the photograph can also be an invitation, a call toward a future moment of response), examining the gestural life of the image allows us to consider what it is that the photograph fingers—what it sees and enables us to see but also what it touches, how it interfaces with the bodies it represents and circulates between. As Elizabeth Abel has argued, the "haptic" quality of the photograph—its ability to both produce and problematize a shared surface, a common "skin" or texture of experience—demands we attend to the ways in which the image can invite a response that (at least potentially) reaches outward across racial and temporal boundaries.[32]

To think of photography's language as the language of gesture—of touching, pressing, pointing, hailing, beckoning, and other nonverbal communicative acts—is also to recover, with Schneider, the irresolvable "liveness" that infuses the photographic still. Recovering such liveness allows us to unsettle the firm distinction between photography (as the "still" image that records or remains) and performance (as the "live" movement that does not or cannot remain, which necessarily disappears).[33] Situating these forms in opposition to one another, as Schneider indicates, obscures the ways in which they are each embedded in repetition and reenactment, in the promise (realizable or not) of "retrievable" time, and in the cross-medial and cross-temporal reverberations that mark our charged relation to the past. We might think here of the strange temporality of Howells's conditional ("would be thrilled"): looking back on the failed promise of electrocution, Howells reinhabits the hoped-for future in order to mark the gap in its realization, thereby unsettling the logic of technological progress that underwrote the chair. Like the photographic scene it conjures, Howells's language seems haunted by the touch it reenacts—its "live" possibility—as well as by the death it figures or calls (back) to life.

Howells's pointed reenactment of electrocution is at once performative and photographic, and it is in these terms—terms that read the still as haunted not solely or simply by death but also by the "live"—that I want to consider William Van der Weyde's turn-of-the-century images from the death chamber at New York's Sing Sing prison. These are images of which we know very little and that I reproduce here with and against the risks embedded in such decontextualized looking. Almost entirely unknown today, Van der Weyde (1871–1929) was a descendant of the fifteenth-century Dutch painter Roger van der Weyden, the grandson of Peter Henri van der Weyde—a scientist who questioned the safety of Edison's DC current—and the nephew of the photographer Henry van der Weyde, who pioneered the use of the electric flash from his studio in London.[34] William Van der Weyde was what the turn of the century called a new species of "news-photographer," with most of his images commissioned to illustrate investigative reporting in newspapers and weekly magazines. As *Broadway* magazine noted in December 1898 in a brief profile, "One can scarcely pick up two consecutive copies of progressive newspapers like the *World* and *Journal*, *The Illustrated American*, *Harper's Weekly* or *Munsey's* without seeing on one or more of the most absorbing pictures the legend, 'Copyright by Van der Weyde.' These words are never found on a 'slow' picture."[35] Employing faster film and shutter speeds, newly linked to the temporality of the news and the rhythms of mass communication, Van der Weyde's images were clear-eyed, "quick," and apparently ubiquitous.

Van der Weyde's archive covers an immense range of subjects, documenting major events of the 1890s (the Spanish-American War, the assassination of William McKinley) and prominent figures (Thomas Wentworth Higginson, Edward Everett Hale, William Dean Howells) as well as working conditions in factories, train derailments, scientific experiments, wrestlers, baseball players, bowlers, domestic and zoo animals, marble busts, still lives, and the city of Pittsburgh illuminated with electric lights. Situated in this historical and archival catalog, largely stripped of contextual information (including how or when they may have circulated), Van der Weyde's images from Sing Sing prison appear first and foremost as dispassionate entries in an early twentieth-century visual taxonomy of persons and things.

These images body forth Howells's analogy in terms that square the difference between witnessing and button-pressing. As in the camera obscura, light enters a dark chamber (figure 4.1). The event of the button-pressing is both singular and immanently reproducible, a repetition formally embedded in the images themselves, as in the way the lines of the condemned man's uniform echo the straps of the chair (figure 4.3), the uniform itself attesting to a logic of restraint as well as to the punishment that arrives in advance: the reduction of the subject to a uniform and reproducible object, the corpse that can be instantaneously reproduced. That the images appear official (not fugitive or clandestine) suggests their complicity with state power, even as they also raise the possibility that the event has been staged, that the death it archives is a reenactment as well as a reproduction.[36] At the very least, Van der Weyde's images delineate what had, in the early years of the twentieth century, already become the highly ritualized choreography of the death chamber, its series of exact postures and poses: the calm procession from cell to chair (figure 4.2), the careful strapping in (figure 4.3), the guarding or waiting (figure 4.4).[37] Embodying the tension between posing and performing, with looks that variously address the camera or the process itself, the men in these images collaboratively rehearse the death sequence, from the condemned man's entry on the arm of a chaplain (figure 4.2) to the staging of the execution-as-investigation (figure 4.5). If the ritual is strict, the performance is awkward; execution here looks distinctly like a question of where to put one's hands. Even so, these images are strikingly posed and composed: note, for example, a deliberate centering of the passive hands of the condemned man surrounded (and indeed everywhere touched) by the hands of his executioners (figure 4.3). This intimate touch at once anticipates and archives the touch that happens out of frame, "on the other side of a wall or screen"

Figure 4.1. William M. Van der Weyde, *Electric Chair at Sing Sing*, ca. 1900 (showing empty chair). Digital positive from the original gelatin silver negative in the George Eastman Museum's collection. Courtesy of the George Eastman Museum. [1974.0056.0384]

Figure 4.2. William M. Van der Weyde, *Electric Chair at Sing Sing*, ca. 1900 (entering the execution chamber). Digital positive from the original gelatin silver negative in the George Eastman Museum's collection. Courtesy of the George Eastman Museum. [1974.0056.0385]

(figure 4.4), here and elsewhere the negative and sanitized image of an interracial touch that the electric chair, like the lynch mob with and before it, ostensibly sought to police.

Which is to say that in these images, the button has, in multiple senses, already been pressed. Following Schneider, we might describe Van der Weyde's images as "still lives" in order to wrestle with the ways in which they meditate on the production of stillness: on photography's ability to freeze time's movement, with and alongside electricity's capacity to interrupt and end life. We must also recognize the way they manufacture, as part and parcel of this stillness, the racialized subject-as-object. As Robyn Wiegman has argued, "To trace the racial technologies of power that create, address, and proscribe modernity's emergent subject entails returning to the question of vision and visibility" and particularly to the way in which (in Coco Fusco's terms) "photography

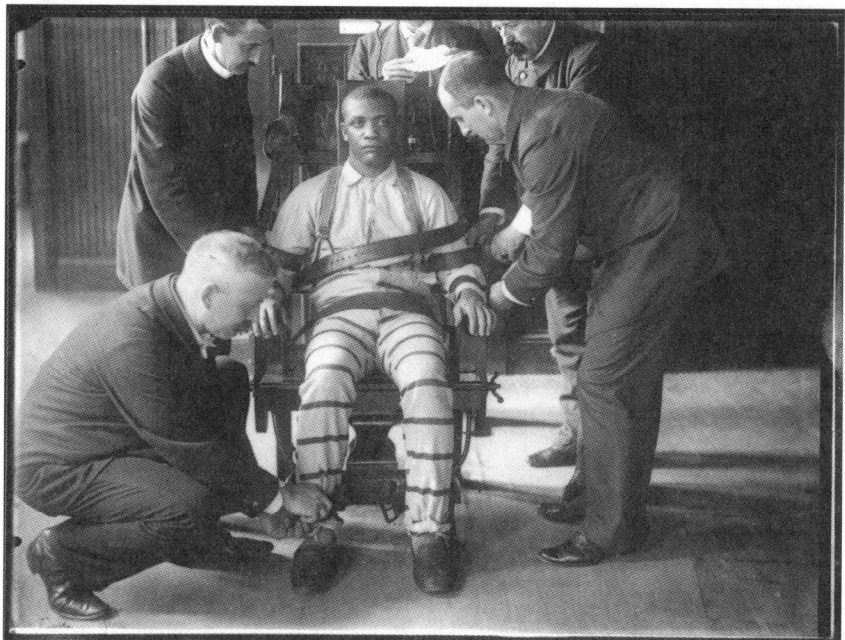

Figure 4.3. William M. Van der Weyde, *Electric Chair at Sing Sing*, ca. 1900 (strapping into the chair). Digital positive from the original gelatin silver negative in the George Eastman Museum's collection. Courtesy of the George Eastman Museum. [1974.0056.0386]

produced race as a visualizable fact."[38] To consider the production of race in this context is to see Barthes's notion of the photograph's deictic gesture ("Look, see") as unmistakably bound to the visual economies of Jim Crow, which linked blackness to criminality in order to underwrite systematic white violence against bodies pointed to or fingered as criminally black. It is also to route Barthes back through Frantz Fanon's crucial description of the "racial epidermal schema" inaugurated by a moment of visual (and implicitly gestural) hailing: "Look, a Negro!"[39] As scholars of lynching have shown, photography served in part to authorize these ways of looking; lynching photographs served to publicize the lethal threat attached to "reckless eyeballing" while sanctioning white spectatorship of mutilated bodies.[40] If such images circulated and extended the work of the mob as a force of social and sexual regulation, Van der Weyde's photographs testify to the corollary intimacies of state

Figure 4.4. William M. Van der Weyde, *Electric Chair at Sing Sing*, n.d. (showing fingerprints on negative). Digital positive from the original gelatin silver negative in the George Eastman Museum's collection. Courtesy of the George Eastman Museum. [1974.0056.0395]

power, responding to lynching's fiction of black male sexual rapacity by picturing the condemned man as a passive object of touch.

While proponents of the chair argued that electricity would leave no mark on its victims—that its corpses would not be disfigured was seen as an index of the method's "humaneness," its distance from the disfiguring work of the lynch mob—nevertheless, here we see the body *as* a mark, transformed by the visual regime of Jim Crow into a limit point for discourses of justice.[41] Such images reinforce Nicole Fleetwood's contention that blackness emerges as a troubling excess in the visual logic of modernity; as Fleetwood notes, "Blackness fills in space between matter, between object and subject, between bodies, between looking and being looked upon."[42] Similarly, Van der Weyde's images call on us to reconfigure Barthes's description of the photographic experience as that of "a subject who feels he is becoming an object."[43] Here the "micro-version of death" that Barthes describes as part of the experience of being photographed materializes a distinctly real and historically urgent threat to black life linked to the "macro" processes of mass cultural production and technological modernization.[44] Electrocutions, like lynchings, emerged not in opposition to but as a function of these developments; despite their differences, each made the specter of becoming-object a terrifying reality for black Americans. Noting that Van der Weyde's images double and in some ways respond to the imagery of ritualized lynching at the turn of the century serves as a reminder that electric technologies functioned to distinguish some bodies from others, complicating the connective circuitry that promised to unify the American body politic. Celebrating the electric chair as a sign of technological and human advancement, the turn of the century figured electricity's power to thrill/kill as distinctly a function of *white* power; as Jurgen Martschukat argues, "Electricity and the sublime were woven tightly into a discourse that constructed a belief in racial and civilized superiority."[45] Displayed among other electric technologies at the 1893 Chicago World Fair's White City, the chair signaled the linear progress of "electrified civilization" in opposition to the darker, "slower" societies displayed at its boundaries.[46]

In an even more direct demonstration of its complicity with white supremacy, the chair was employed as a device of terror that shadowed and at times spurred lynch mobs in the early decades of its use. A May 1918 NAACP report on the murder of Jim McIlherron in Estill Springs, Tennessee, for example, described shouts of "electrocution is too good for the damned n——r" coming from the mob.[47] As James Weldon Johnson noted the same month in an address to the National Conference of Social Work, "This happened on a Sunday between church hours."[48] Following racial violence in Elaine, Arkansas, in 1919, an electric chair at the Helena county jail was used to "shock and frighten" black men and women until they confessed or incriminated others.[49] In such instances, lynch mobs both recognized and refuted the supposed "humaneness" of electrocution. And just as the rise of lynching in the postbellum era attended the rise of mass production—its cultural reproducibility linked to what Gustavus Stadler has described as the "cheapness and tenuousness of black lives as shaped by the white supremacist turn-of-the-century United States"—the history of electricity as a force of racial terror is concurrent with its transformation from the material of religious and aesthetic awe to a rationalized and bureaucratized utility.[50] Just as Bishop Henry McNeal Turner of the African Methodist Episcopal Church warned in 1886 of an apocalypse imminent in "the invention of the white man in controlling electricity," the electric chair's output in the twentieth century would show that warning to be substantially (if not literally) true.[51] In the years between 1908 and 1930, as urban electrification brought America to light, the state of Virginia electrocuted 148 people, "all but 17 of them black."[52]

Thus part of what we see in Van der Weyde's "quick" images is the ability, by the end of the nineteenth century, to channel electricity's spiritual energy into the dream of technological immediacy, a dream intimately bound both to secularism and to white supremacy. Van der Weyde's images yoke the development of photographic technologies to the speed of modern punishment—to the chair as well as the lynch mob (which, despite aiming to inflict "slow" death, often positioned itself as a form of "swift" justice in opposition to the purported slowness of trial by jury).[53] This discourse of speed was at once cultural and physiological; juxtaposing electricity's movement to the comparatively slower work of the nervous system, for example, early experiments in electrocution aimed to prove that an electric current would travel through the body faster than nerve signals, making the process entirely painless. Similarly, the instantaneity of shock and image increasingly paralleled the speed of modern information; the telegraph and the newspaper were each central in communicating (and in some cases enabling) the work of the chair and the lynch mob.[54] This emphasis on instantaneity linked the disciplinary to the informational; as Mark Seltzer notes, turn-of-the-century push buttons figured a form of "violent immediacy," forging "an identity between signal and act and an identity between communication and execution—'execution' in its several senses."[55] If Van der Weyde's images point to anything, then, they point to the turn of the century's specific conjunction of aesthetic, disciplinary, and material fascination with immediacy, which both required and produced/executed blackness as a site of resistance. In the photograph's vis-à-vis, then, we find the facing or surfacing of blackness as a function of this violent stillness, of motion caught or captured.

Yet I want to linger on the possibility that the temporality I've just traced—that of the foregone conclusion, the "usual crime," and instantaneous punishment—is not the only one at work in these images. For while they may "arrest" us in the sense that Barthes describes, they also haunt us in ways that expand beyond the frame, calling us to witness not only the violence of the past but also its belonging to the present, the moment in which we encounter the image.[56] In these terms, we might consider, with Harvey Young, how the "arrested" subject "actively perform[s] stillness" as testimony to modernity's historical enforcement of black stasis, revealing "the touch of the past on the present."[57] Indeed, the pictured subject may or may not have been under arrest, but his performance of stillness insists on something powerful in the photographic reenactment of it—something more than simply a recirculation of necromantic state power.[58] Reading these photographs as realist performances, we might consider how stillness itself enacts what Erin Manning calls a "minor gesture," which "creates sites of dissonance, staging disturbances that open experience to new modes of expression. In making felt the event's limit, the operational interval where the event exceeds the sum of its parts, the minor gesture punctually reorients experience."[59] Stillness read as a gestural performance, in this sense, creates a fugitive interval wherein the reproduction of racial violence might be paused and interrogated.

Furthermore if, as Eduardo Cadava argues, the photograph is "always already touched (or retouched) by death," the status of these images as potential reenactments signals their complex relation to the "live"—and to the gestural performances that (re)constitute it.[60] Evidence suggests that these photographs may indeed have been retouched (see figure 4.5 and 4.6) to illustrate different executions at different moments (including, by 1899, the electrocution of women).[61] While bound up in the commercial demand for news, the gesture of retouching disarticulates the image from the immediacy of the event. Similarly, the presence of fingerprints on the negative (figure 4.4) attests to the photographer's physical trace, while making the surface of the image a site of potential contact: a "kind of skin *with* skin," as Shawn Michelle Smith describes it.[62] Touches thus abound in these images, in ways that trouble the electric chair's irreversible gesture. Read as reenactment, the touched and retouched image functions less as documentary than as effigy: a way of surrogating for what has been lost.[63] Van der Weyde's photographs become sites of contact, citation, and rehearsal, things that "still live," to

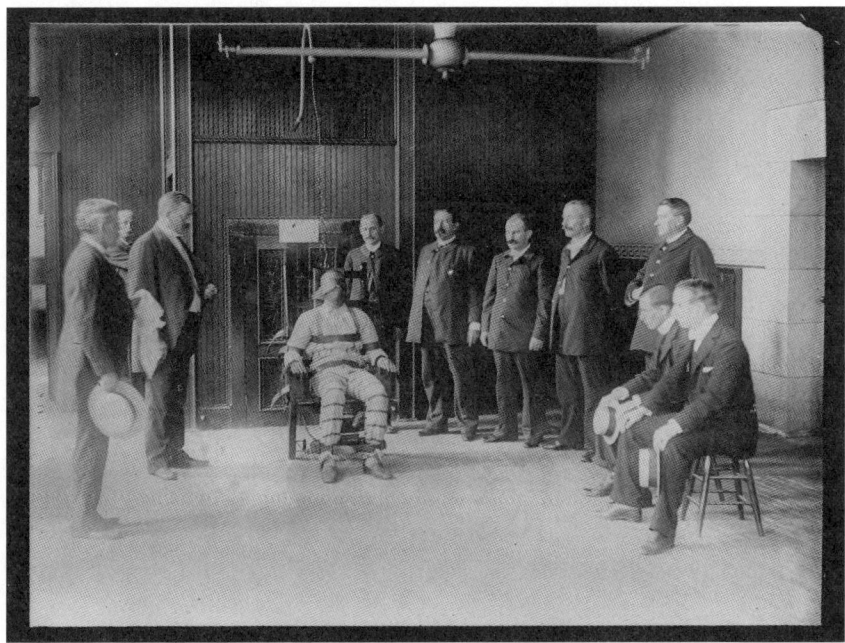

Figure 4.5. William M. Van der Weyde, *Electric Chair at Sing Sing*, ca. 1900 (staged observation of execution). Digital positive from the original gelatin silver negative in the George Eastman Museum's collection. Courtesy of the George Eastman Museum. [1974.0056.0387]

borrow Schneider's formulation, where the still marks less an arrest of time than a switchback, a gestural reenactment that disrupts the pastness of the past and highlights the "temporal drag" of the present.[64] Hence I draw our attention to the repetitive, electrified touches surrounding these images, and to the gestures that mark photography's belonging not to static, irreversible temporalities but at least potentially to the time of performance, to time "touched, crossed, visited, or revisited."[65]

In these terms, Van der Weyde's images allow us to reexamine modernity's fixation on the temporality of the event, to which early twentieth-century photography and film claimed privileged access. Alongside Van der Weyde, for example, we might consider the popularity of early "actuality" films, many of which were in fact electrocution films, such as Edison's 1901 *Execution of Czolgosz*, a reenactment of Leon Czolgosz's death by electric chair in New York's Auburn prison on October 29, 1901,

Figure 4.6. William M. Van der Weyde, *Electric Chair at Sing Sing*, n.d. (retouched image showing figure in dress). Digital positive from the original gelatin silver negative in the George Eastman Museum's collection. Courtesy of the George Eastman Museum. [1974.0056.0388]

for the murder of President William McKinley. As Mary Ann Doane argues, the reenactment film in particular, a genre that remained popular until around 1907, figures the very instability of filmic temporality, the irreversible forward drive of the protonarrative film punctuated by the arresting force of the still image.[66] Reanimating the execution process through a series of stills, Van der Weyde's images anticipate Edison's filmic sequences even as Edison's film is haunted by the threat and the possibility of stillness.[67] Similarly, Van der Weyde's images at once enter into, and place on hold, the relentless forward drive of technomodernization through the visual idiom of photographic execution: the objects it makes, the subjects it makes and unmakes. Van der Weyde's portrait of Czolgosz (figure 4.7) is a case in point. Disheartened by the Gilded Age's vast disparities of fortune, marginalized by the Protestant discourse of secular progress, and inspired by the project of anarchist dissent, Czolgosz—a millworker and son of Polish immigrants—noted that he shot the president "for the sake of the common people."[68] Somewhere between an annunciation and a mug shot, Van der Weyde's image fingers Czolgosz as criminal under the sign of political, ethnic, and religious difference even as it figures him as potential martyr (a status notably not afforded to the subject of Van der Weyde's Sing Sing photographs). Taken in the lead up to Czolgosz's execution, the image marks his becoming-object in advance. Yet it also does more than this. With a haunting stillness, the photograph simultaneously enacts and unsettles the logic of speed and instantaneity that underwrote industrial modernity. Mediating the space between bodies and machines, persons and things, the push button choreographs and consolidates this stillness, organizing the category of the human as a gestural one, wrought in the very automaticity of repeat performance.

To look at Van der Weyde's images in these terms is to face the death that progressive discourse would otherwise occlude, and to see that death as a central feature of technological modernity rather than its grisly exception. Van der Weyde's images index the way that modernity's confluence of making and unmaking, bringing to light and bringing to death, maps itself onto the body of the racialized other. Yet they also *still* this process—if they cannot preserve life, they nevertheless return us, through the logic of reenactment, to the moment before the button is pressed, and invite us to hold that moment distinctly in reserve. As Homi Bhabha has suggested, "To slow down the linear, progressive time of modernity [is] to reveal its 'gesture,' its *tempi*, 'the pauses and stresses of the whole performance.'"[69] In this context, the image risks complicity with the visual logic of instantaneous punishment, but it also highlights its own status as interface, a site of haptic connectivity rather than optical distancing. Viewing Van der Weyde's images at a distance, the witness is not left untouched. To read the still in this way—with an eye toward touch—is to reinvest, tentatively, in the image's capacity to perform a kind of drag or resistance to the logic of (white) modernity. Stilled and interrogated, the gesture of touching a button reveals that modernity *as* performance: as movement predicated on, and producing, the stillness of some bodies.

Figure 4.7. William M. Van der Weyde, *Leon F. Czolgosz*, 1901. Digital positive from the original gelatin silver negative in the George Eastman Museum's collection. Courtesy of the George Eastman Museum. [1974.0056.0098]

A Fugitive Interval

To subsist in the force field of the flesh, then, might just be better than not existing at all.
—Alexander G. Weheliye, *Habeas Viscus: Racializing Assemblages, Biopolitics, and Black Feminist Theories of the Human*

So that mourning turns.
—Fred Moten, *In the Break: The Aesthetics of Black Radical Tradition*

Touching a button can enact something, and it can also bring something (repeatedly) to an end. As Van der Weyde's images from Sing Sing suggest, the proximity of these outcomes comes into sharp focus at the turn of the century, as the combined work of the electric chair and the hand camera made the mass reproduction of corpses more efficient than ever, and cultural workers increasingly recognized electricity as a force that could be seized on and channeled in multiple directions. If that recognition emerges in Van der Weyde's images—despite themselves—it emerges with more clarity and urgency through a series of electrifications in and around James Weldon Johnson's 1912 novel *The Autobiography of an Ex-Colored Man*. Following the circuitous making and unmaking of its anonymous narrator as he moves back and forth across the color line, *The Autobiography* theorizes collective action through the idiom of electrification, drawing on electricity's mutability—its potential to travel or be converted across various mediums, particularly from the visual to the sonic—to name both the terror and the possibility embedded in the reproduction of life under Jim Crow. Reenacting a series of vocal performances that touch, enliven, and propagate mass feeling in order to slip the deictic touch of state power, Johnson recognized the potential for rhythmic speech to convert static scripts into ecstatic communion. Yet he also consistently aligned electricity's movement with the violent enforcement of white supremacy. Through a series of narrative and affective tropes or turns, *The Autobiography* demonstrates electricity's capacity to figure and disfigure life, and brings into relief the repetitive shocks through which modernity is constituted. Recognizing what Van der Weyde's images make strikingly visible—the capacity for romantic electricity to be channeled toward the destruction of black life—Johnson's novel seizes on the tropism of the electric: its metaphoric and material link to ecstatic conversion. Turning from Van der Weyde to Johnson, then, and redirecting the haptic logic of Jim Crow visuality through the sonic impress of the fictional text, we find an effort to still and redirect the terror of electrical execution, to turn it into something other than itself.

In its attention to the spiritual impact of electrifying speech, Johnson's novel in many ways returns to and reconfigures the nineteenth century's "technological enthusiasm"—its quasi-religious worship of electricity's material and spiritual potential, its full-out "electric theology."[70] Moving between the "electrifying climax" of a revival meeting and the "electric current" of a lynch mob, *The Autobiography* limns the possibilities and perils of electrified contact as the medium of mass feeling. Yet while the novel could be said to yoke lynching and religious ecstasy, binding these ostensibly discrete moments of contact via a disturbing repetition, we can also read them as forming a refrain in the novel—building an affective circuit in which ecstasy might indeed turn quickly into terror and mourning, but in which mourning, too, might turn. Such "turns" are crucial, for Johnson himself repeatedly raised the possibility of turning an audience, of turning public feeling by in fact electrifying it. Alongside Van der Weyde's choreographed effort to *still* life in the moment of its erasure, then, we might read Johnson's fictional autobiography as recognizing and performing a glitch in the trajectories of early twentieth-century social power. Situated at the pivot (or turn) of two very different electrical possibilities, *The Autobiography* signals the need for a method that could at once keep up with the accelerated tempos of techno-industrialization and enact an interruption, pause, or drag—a fugitive interval.

Writing life with and alongside the threat of death, *The Autobiography* represents the written self as constituted by, subject to, and conducting a series of shocks, jolts, turns, and detours. That is, a self not unlike electricity *itself*, which, as Jane Bennett notes, "sometimes goes where we send it, and sometimes . . . chooses its path on the spot, in response to the other bodies it encounters and the surprising opportunities for actions and interactions that they afford."⁷¹ *The Autobiography*, in other words, writes the self as a strange loop or circuit, a relay between impression and expression, accident and inspiration, pain and pleasure, aurality and textuality, none of which remain stable poles or binaries. As the novel suggests, this autobiographical self-as-circuit—a circuit forged in the flow of experience as much as in the narrative work of retelling and rehearsing—is also continually reconfigured by larger circulations of force and feeling. Such circulations figure the ecstatic possibilities of electrification, possibilities lodged distinctly in sound and in the mastery of sound's modulation. Traveling in the rural countryside outside of Macon, Georgia, for example, in search of a vernacular sound that he can turn into popular music with mass appeal, the narrator finds a "mine of material" in the Big Meeting, a revival scene anchored by the charismatic preacher John Brown:

> As far as subject matter is concerned, all of the sermons were alike; each began with the fall of man, ran through various trials and tribulations of the Hebrew children, onto the redemption by Christ, and ended with a fervid picture of the judgment day and the fate of the damned. But John Brown possessed magnetism and an imagination so free and daring that he was able to carry through what the other preachers would not attempt. He knew all the arts and tricks of oratory, the modulation of the voice to almost a whisper, the pause for effect, the rise through light, rapid fire sentences to the terrific, thundering outburst of an electrifying climax.⁷²

If the trajectory of John Brown's subject matter here is hardwired—the "heavenly march" his sermon recounts a theologically predetermined route—the climax demands rhythmic variation, an ability to convert the emotional vectors of sound and to carry an audience through, reproducing religious feeling in one charged body after another. The success of John Brown's oratory, then, as much as the success of the ex-colored man's musical project and Johnson's narrative one, depends on the reproduction of electrifying sound, the ability to make both an aural and a textual impression. "I was a more or less sophisticated and nonreligious man of the world," Johnson's narrator notes, "but the torrent of the preacher's words, moving with the rhythm and glowing with the eloquence of primitive poetry swept me along, and I, too, felt like joining in the shouts of 'Amen! Hallelujah!'"[73] Swept up into the electrical, affective current, the ex-colored man becomes a congregant, if not a believer; as Johnson's narrator discovers, it is next to impossible to simply consume an electrifying sound.

In its attention to the conversion of folk religion into aesthetic material, *The Autobiography of an Ex-Colored Man* offers an important example of what Josef Sorett describes as an "ambivalent attachment to Afro-Protestantism" in the New Negro movement.[74] As Sorett details, Johnson (despite his avowed agnosticism) celebrated vernacular religious forms, and especially the rhetorical sophistication of the "old-time Negro preacher," insofar as it provided the source material—indeed sonic material—for a new racial aesthetic. Thus while in many cases "New Negro clergy sought to counter popular images of the 'primitive' religiosity associated with the masses of black folk migrating from the South"—and to thereby resist white supremacist accounts of black religiosity—the relationship between religion and the New Negro movement (a relationship I explore further in chapter 5) was by no means simply one of disavowal.[75] Johnson, in this sense, was part of the New Negro movement's larger reimagining of the social and aesthetic role of religion for a modern, heterogeneous, and increasingly mobile black citizenry. And while debates over the shape and place of religious expression played a significant role in the New Negro movement, the movement's ostensibly secular debates around racial aesthetics were, as Sorett argues, also deeply intertwined with the shifting and always unstable meaning of Afro-Protestantism. Recasting the force of ecstatic worship as electrical—that is, fundamentally dynamic, an oscillation or displacement of energy with "aleatory effects"—Johnson materialized the unstable but powerful work of collectivity, partaking in what Sorett calls a "spiritual grammar" in African American literature. At the same time, he used electricity to theorize instability itself as fundamental to the affective and bodily experience of Jim Crow.[76]

As singular as he is, John Brown signals a striking repetition: not only in the historical sense of his name (associated, as we've seen, with a specifically political version of religious enthusiasm) but also in Johnson's wider body of work, which seems everywhere to test the radical possibilities of electrifying, charismatic speech.[77] John Brown's electrifying climax notably recasts an earlier scene in which the narrator's classmate "Shiny" delivers a familiar oratory, the sound of which creates a kind of aural/haptic/affective circuit: "When, in the famous peroration, his voice, trembling with suppressed emotion, rose higher and higher and then rested on the name 'Toussaint L'Ouverture,' it was like touching an electric button which loosed the pent-up feelings of his listeners. They actually rose to him."[78] If the nickname "Shiny" registers a troubled photographic history of representing blackness, "Toussaint L'Ouverture" touches a different button; a history of radical black resistance emerges in the rhetorical gesture of the pause or rest.[79] Thus Shiny's performance is both scripted and a site of inscription: a gesture that at once resounds and exceeds historically proscribed forms of contact.[80]

For Shiny as for John Brown, touching a button renders spontaneous and spectacular a learned practice—a rigorous attention to form and performance that Johnson's works everywhere exhibit. Johnson repeatedly insisted on the formal ingenuity required in public speaking, noting in his 1933 autobiography, *Along This Way*, that "the inner secret of sheer oratory is not so much in the *what* is said as in the combination of the *how*, *when*, and *where*. The *how* is the most important of these factors, and its chief virtue lies in 'timing': that is, in the ability of the speaker to set up a series of rhythmic emotional vibrations between himself and his hearers."[81] Here Johnson's insistence on the rhythmic *how* anticipates Houston Baker's critical observation that form *moves*, that it has the structure of an electrical event: "motions of hypothetical particles immeasurable."[82] In such moments, *The Autobiography* also offers what Erica Edwards has described as an "intra- and intertextual charismastic contagion," a scenario staged and restaged in post-Reconstruction-era representations of black political power. As Edwards argues, the consolidation of charisma as the sign of black political modernity at the turn of the century produced a set of powerful "performative prescriptions" that at once shaped and foreclosed the possibilities of black political desire and expression.[83] The trope of charisma, Edwards notes, was as much a response to the containment of black political freedoms after Reconstruction as it was an expedient adaptation of antebellum religious expression to the politics of respectability. John Brown and other singular figures of black charismatic authority (including, in *Along This Way*, Johnson himself) were, in these terms, singularly capable of modeling "the proper mix of emotionality and literate, secularist poise."[84] Depicting the modulation of emotion as a performance of rhetorical power, Johnson and others flipped the script on white supremacist constructions of black emotionality.

In this sense, Edwards's dynamic account of charisma provides a useful framework for understanding the electrified flows of feeling that Johnson everywhere theorizes and channels: "More than a static form of authority, charisma names a phenomenon, a dynamic structure, a figural process of authoring and authorizing."[85] But as Edwards notes, and as Johnson recognized, such ritualized fictions of power were also disfiguring, not least in the way they tended to collapse the messy and collective work of historical change into a teleological narrative of progress inaugurated by exceptional men. Booker T. Washington's *Up from Slavery* (1901) famously deploys this idiom, reprinting James Creelman's account of Washington's 1895 Atlanta Exposition Speech for the *New York World*:

> While President Cleveland was waiting at Gray Gables to-day, to send the electric spark that started the machinery of the Atlanta Exposition, a Negro Moses stood before a great audience of white people and delivered an oration that marks a new epoch in the history of the South . . .
>
> It is the first time that a Negro has made a speech in the South on any important occasion before an audience composed of white men and women. It electrified the audience, and the response was as if it had come from the throat of a whirlwind.
>
> . . . His voice rang out clear and true, and he paused impressively as he made each point. Within ten minutes the multitude was in an uproar of enthusiasm—handkerchiefs were waved, canes were flourished, hats were tossed in the air. The fairest women of Georgia stood up and cheered. It was as if the orator had bewitched them.[86]

Helping cement Washington's celebrity as a "Negro Moses," Creelman juxtaposed the spectacular effect of his speech—the "new epoch" it promised to inaugurate—with the exposition's other spectacle of achievement, the feat of technological creativity and kitsch rigging that allowed President Grover Cleveland to press a telegraph button from his summer home in Buzzard's Bay, Massachusetts, and illuminate the exposition grounds at Atlanta (a similar electrical feat, of course, allowed Creelman to telegraph his story to New York and allowed the event of Washington's speech to be circulated, its infamous compromise consumed en masse).[87] Creelman's account insists on electrification as collective progress, drawing a seamless parallel between the new technologically advanced South and the moral advancement signified by the very fact of Washington's presence before a white audience. Like the crescendo of Shiny's speech (though to dramatically different effect), Creelman's careful attention to the temporality of Washington's performance—the setting sun, the pauses for effect, the ten minutes it takes to create an uproar—allows his narrative to build to an uneasy pitch, until Washington is engulfed in "a delirium of applause," nearly consumed by the cheering white women of Georgia.[88]

If Washington cites Creelman's account in order to evade the appearance of self-congratulation, he also uses it to give voice to the potential for mass feeling and disorderly affections that his own text largely forecloses.[89] Indeed, Washington reassures readers in the same chapter of his ability to parse the varieties of emotional excess: "I know that on such occasions there is much that comes to the surface that is superficial and deceptive, but I have had experience enough not to be deceived by mere signs and fleeting enthusiasms. I have taken pains to go to the bottom of things and get facts, in a cold, business-like manner."[90] Against the heat and spark of Creelman's narration—which notably if obliquely raises the specter of bewitched white womanhood and the corollary threat of bodily peril—Washington negotiates a space for his electrified audience while remaining himself distinctly untouched. By way of contrast, if Johnson's texts often reproduce scenes of affective and charismatic contagion—routed through and (indeed) reproducing the singular individual—they do so with an acute emphasis on the unpredictable charge of the collective, a charge Johnson repeatedly registered through the idiom of electricity, with its turns, jolts, and conversions.

In later works, Johnson would repeatedly draw on electrification as a figure for the power of charismatic speech, a power that Johnson located not simply in the text itself but in its conductive logic of feeling, its ability to move through and across singular bodies. In the preface to his 1927 volume *God's Trombones*, for example, Johnson recounts hearing a Kansas City preacher whose off-book performance enacts a stunning transformation: "Suddenly he closed the Bible, stepped out from behind the pulpit and began to preach. He started intoning the old folk-sermon that begins with the creation of the world and ends with Judgment Day. He was at once a changed man, free, at ease and masterful. The change in the congregation was instantaneous. An electric current ran through the crowd. It was in a moment alive and quivering; and all the while the preacher held it in the palm of his hand."[91] Johnson stripped the electrical language from this episode when he reprinted it in *Along This Way*. Yet he also reinforced its electrical effect by depicting, in the very next section, his own January 1919 Carnegie Hall address in similar terms—terms that make the wired brain and body a site of collective innervation:

> As I sat on the platform I felt depressed, almost listless. When I rose, every nerve in my brain and body quickened by the intensity of feeling that came across the footlights from the audience to me. As I talked, I was lifted up and swept along by the sense of demi-omnipotence which comes to a speaker at those moments when he realizes that by an inflection of the voice or a gesture of the hand, he is able to sway a mass of people. . . . Words surged to be uttered; and uttered, they were effective beyond their weight and meaning. One passage of my speech had an electrical effect.[92]

Explicitly borrowing what he calls the "rhythmic emotional vibrations" of the "oldtime Negro preachers" for the secular work of political speech-making, Johnson describes the circuit of sound and feeling that works to produce a critical mass, in the moment of its utterance as well as in its recirculation as autobiographical text.[93] Words surge, as electricity becomes the medium for an ecstatic outing of self, the autobiographical subject positioned less as singular speaker than as amplifier. As Katherine Biers has observed, Johnson's works continually queried sound as (at least potentially) "phonographic" or technologically reproducible, even as they trouble the ability to consume sound at a physical distance or without being moved.[94] Here the phonographic quality of Johnson's writing adheres as much to the autobiographical as to the fictional self: a self born in the oscillatory motion of a sound wave, emerging distinctly in reverberation, and pointing up a long-standing circuit between religious and secular modes of excitation. Referencing without reproducing the passage of his 1919 speech—which decried disenfranchisement, segregation, and (crucially) lynching—Johnson describes his conversion of nervous energy into the very pitch of resistance.

The "electrical effect" here is, importantly, not strictly metaphorical; Johnson links the nervous system's electric circuit between "brain and body" to the communicative feedback loop between audience and speaker, a loop that turn-of-the-century sociology everywhere aimed to delineate. Gustave Le Bon's seminal study *The Crowd: A Study of the Popular Mind*, for example, which appeared in English in 1896, carefully analyzed the space between the "real meanings" of words and their "magical" or even "supernatural" power to evoke mass feeling; as Le Bon notes, "Certain transitory images are attached to certain words; the word is merely as it were the button of an electric bell that calls them up."[95] Later, in 1912 (when Johnson's *Autobiography* first appeared), Émile Durkheim would describe the "demi-omnipotence" of the speaker as an empirical phenomenon:

> He feels filled to overflowing with an overabundance of forces that spill out around him. Sometimes he even feels dominated by a moral power that is larger than he is, for which he is merely the interpreter. This quality marks what is often called the demon of oratorical inspiration. This unusual surplus of forces is quite real; it comes to him from the very group he is addressing. The feelings provoked by his speech return to him inflated and amplified, reinforcing his own. The passionate energies he arouses echo back to him and increase his vitality. He is no longer a simple individual speaking, he is a group incarnate and personified.[96]

Durkheim saw this resounding dynamic as defining religious phenomena, which he described as "real" events available to scientific study; through this construction of religion as a category of and for modernity, the performative production and circulation of religious affect—the mechanism of its force—became the concrete subjects of analysis and debate (by 1920, Du Bois would similarly assert, "The meaning of America is the beginning of the discovery of the Crowd").[97]

Contributing to the production of collectively embodied excitation as a distinctly secular religious phenomenon, Johnson's rhetorical performances also signal the possibility of converting old scripts into new performances and new configurations of power. As Johnson recognized, and as Hortense Spillers notes, the sermon form "locates the primary instrument of moral and political change within the community ... the sermon not only catalyzes movement, but *embodies* it, *is* movement."[98] Similarly, Brent Edwards argues that Johnson's career-long effort to theorize the transcription of oral/aural performance at once shapes his modernity and gives rise to a form of distributed or collective agency. Drawing on Johnson's electrical language to describe the ecstatic "swing" of Johnson's transcribed sermons, Edwards observes a kind of indecision in the bodily logic of swing: "Does it surge through one body, or is there a common current that jumps from one body in the congregation to the next or inhabits the entire group as though it were a single body, all at once?"[99] Though it is precisely the convertibility of electrical feeling that Johnson required to describe the work of transcription, Edwards's observation is an instructive one. Not least because (as Edwards argues) in Johnson's works, collective agency "turns (in the sense of 'trope,' of course; it turns a metaphor) not on the foundation of some intentional physical act, or of some communicated black 'essence,' but on the ground of form *itself*."[100] Disarticulated from the individual body, the act of touching a button here looks less like an individual performance than the spark of collective resistance, one that works by eclipsing the space between literal and metaphorical turning, forging a circuit between mere rhetorical gestures and electrifying speech.

In its emphasis on the "demi-omnipotence" of a singular speaker, Johnson's retrospective account of the Carnegie Hall speech is perhaps haunted as much by the specter of fascist mobilization in Europe as it is by the lynch mob, the topic of that electrifying passage.[101] But before turning to the perils that Johnson insists lie alongside the possibilities of electrification—the very mutability of electricity, as Johnson recognized, meant that it could also switch directions—I want to pause to introduce one more circuit, reaching back even further into the quickening of sound to which Johnson's fictional and autobiographical projects repeatedly return. This is the narrative of Johnson's own early religious experience in *Along This Way*, in which he recounts being "troubled" by the sounds of his Aunt Venie's ring shout, a kinetic performance coded as the ligature to Johnson's Afro-Caribbean genealogy, "the whole pagan rite transplanted and adapted to Christian worship. Round and round the ring would go: one, two, three, four, five hours, the very monotony of sound and motion inducing an ecstatic frenzy."[102] Lodged in the power of repetition, the black Protestant revival in turn resounds the ring: "The air is charged. Overlaid emotions come to the surface. A woman gives a piercing scream and begins to 'shout'; then another, and another."[103] I make a necessary detour here to suggest that if Johnson's life writings seem to privilege a straight lineage of singular male performances, including his own, the textual trace of Aunt Venie's ecstatic shout troubles any accounting for the self that would not be somehow frenzied, circular, circuit-like, and indebted to the maternal signifier. From ring shout to preacher to Johnson's own voice resounding in Carnegie Hall, electrifying speech emerges within the autobiographical circuit of sound and gesture, as the very rhythm of historical return.

Like Johnson himself, like Johnson's voice, and like the narrator of *The Autobiography*, sound travels—and it is this very traveling that enables what Johnson describes as the "intoxicating" force of mass feeling, which "carries within itself all the perils of intoxication."[104] Leaving the Big Meeting "full of enthusiasm," the narrator is swept up into an affective current, joining what Kimberly Benston has described as the "ex-stasis of communitas."[105] But before he can sound out his belonging, he takes a devastating detour and, "instead of going to the nearest and most convenient railroad station," witnesses a lynching.[106] In ways that disturbingly resound the electrifying work of the revival, it is sound that carries the murderous action through: "The men who had at midnight been stern and silent were now emitting that terror instilling sound known as the 'rebel yell.' A space was quickly cleared in the crowd, and a rope placed about his neck; when from somewhere came the suggestion, 'Burn him!' It ran like an electric current. Have you ever witnessed the transformation of human beings into savage beasts? Nothing can be more terrible. A railroad tie was sunk into the ground . . . and a chain brought and securely coiled around the victim and his neck."[107] Writing of this scene, Jacqueline Goldsby has argued that lynching is at once the "structural secret" on which the novel turns and a fundamentally interchangeable event, metonymically reproduced at various points in the narrative. As Goldsby notes, "Lynching *turns* into so many other forms *besides itself*," a formal doubling and tripling that marks its proximity to mass culture's particular blend of uniqueness and ubiquity, as well as to the stamp (or undeveloped negative) of trauma.[108] It is lynching's dangerous reproducibility, in this sense, that helps account for its formal parallel to the Big Meeting. But where Goldsby reads the Big Meeting as disturbingly like a lynching, I would argue that we might also read the lynching as disturbingly like a Big Meeting, in that both scenes turn on the promise or threat of the narrator's electrified embodiment:

> Some of the crowd yelled and cheered, others seemed appalled . . . and there were those who turned away sickened at the sight. I was fixed to the spot where I stood, powerless to take my eyes from what I did not want to see. It was over before I realized that time had elapsed. Before I could make myself believe that what I saw was really happening, I was looking at a scorched post, a smoldering fire, blackened bones, charred fragments sifting down through coils of chain, and the smell of burnt flesh—human flesh—was in my nostrils.[109]

Fixed to the spot, unable to turn from the sight and thus coiled with the victim, Johnson's narrator experiences the lynching as a collapse of time and space, at once agonizingly elongated and distinctly instantaneous. The promise of electrification is turned inside out here, as the narrator's own flesh takes in the smell of flesh, the boundaries between victim and witness crumbling into a mutual form of shocked stillness. Subject to the mob's electric current, Johnson's narrator is psychically, if not literally, electrocuted in the act of witnessing. And insofar as the lynching's traumatic impress becomes the impetus for the narrator's desire to pass—to turn himself into an ex-colored man—we see the pain of electrified contact as that which, in Sara Ahmed's terms, "makes us aware of our bodily surfaces, and points to *the dynamic nature of surfacing itself* (turning in, turning away, moving towards, moving away)."[110] "My heart turned bitter within me," the narrator notes, mapping the autobiographical self as a series of turns or passes, a circuit of feedback that takes the secular skin as an entry point as well as a boundary.[111]

The lynching scene might then be said to mark the limits of electrification, mapping its complicity in the conversion of men into beasts and of free movement into involuntary stillness. Surely it turns the revelatory potential of touching an electrified button into something more literal and more terrifying at the very moment when electrocution reached the status of culturally legitimized death. Johnson recognized that electrocution more accurately approximated what his contemporary Theodore Dreiser described as "lynching sublimated by legality," where the electric current might indeed sublimate or simply redirect the energy of the mob.[112] Writing to Johnson and other prominent officials in 1931 as part of campaign to raise defense funds for the Scottsboro boys—African American teenagers falsely accused of rape and sentenced to die in the electric chair—Dreiser noted that it "took three days in all for a Scottsboro, Alabama court to try, convict and sentence these eight boys to death," identifying the shocking swiftness of the trial as a legalized form of lynching.[113] Here and elsewhere, Johnson's archive attests to his recognition of the electric chair as a specific peril for black Americans. In an undated précis for a play called "Circumstantial Evidence; or, The Ordeals of Adele," for example, Johnson mapped out the story of a chemical inventor named John Hudson who is falsely accused of murder and sentenced to die. Sketched as a tale of competing technologies, Hudson's conspiring accusers communicate via "pocket wireless," while his friends "race against time" to exonerate him as he is being strapped into the chair.[114] Thus Johnson emphasized the cascading speed of technological circulation, which demanded both a pause and an equally expedient reaction: a race against the temporality of modernity, the temporality of the lynch mob as well as the electric chair.

If the promise of the chair was that it left its bodies uniformly unmarked, Johnson's repeated return to the perils of electrical execution was an effort to make visible the ways in which black Americans were, from the outset, already marked; reading lynching and religious enthusiasm together helps us see both as part of the very wiring of modernity, central to its affective infrastructure. Johnson's realism might be said to emerge precisely in this circuit, which is at once a demand for representational accuracy—a call to witness the material realities menacing black freedom—and a troubling of the strict logic of reproduction, a method of converting the commonplace (lynching) into something other than itself. In Johnson's electrifying reproductions, touching a button becomes a means of holding out for this unspoken alternative, of holding an audience in one's hand, of reassembling and redirecting the all-too-real horror of the mob. "I reassembled the picture in my mind," Johnson wrote in *Along This Way* of the lynching of Ell Persons in Memphis in May of 1917. "The mob disperses, many of them complaining, 'They burned him too fast.'"[115] Reenactment, as Johnson knew well, could reproduce and consolidate terror; but it could also reveal the tempos of modernity and the bodies used to measure it. Repetition builds to revelation: "The truth flashed over me that in large measure the race question involves the saving of black America's body and white America's soul."[116]

Johnson's autobiography reroutes the electrical and criminal charges of modernity, forging a new circuit between the haptic and the *hap*—or between prescribed gestures and a sense of fugitive possibility. Ahmed describes the politics of the hap as remaking the very possibilities of subject formation through an openness to what might happen, a "being perhaps."[117] In a forceful example of such "being perhaps" in the very face of terror, *Along This Way* recounts Johnson's experience of being nearly lynched in Jacksonville, Florida, in May of 1900. Walking in the park with a light-skinned woman, Johnson described facing a mob of men that seem to "surge" instantly around him; "quick as a flash of light," he realizes that the woman has been taken for white and that he has been instantaneously charged with her defilement. In the grip of death, Johnson is saved by a kind of momentary circuit of affinity with a white, uniformed soldier: "He breaks through the men who have hold of me. We look at each other; and I feel that a quivering message from intelligence to intelligence has been interchanged. He claps his hand on my shoulder and says, 'You are my prisoner.'"[118] Through the performance of arrest, the soldier manages to get him onto an electric streetcar, where again Johnson feels "waves of mental affinity" passing between him and the man who will convey him to safety.

Facing the possibility of death head-on, Johnson noted the "quick turn" of mental relay that saved him, where another turn might not have: "You know as well as I do, if I had turned my back once . . . or taken a single step in retreat, I'd now be a dead man."[119] What could have been tragedy, Johnson noted in the aftermath of this scene, turns quickly into melodrama; the aesthetics of life under Jim Crow mean that the spectacle of black suffering could (and often did) go either way, not least to serve a rigorous set of generic expectations.[120] Yet here the very mutability of electric and aesthetic forms allowed Johnson to convert the haptic charge into a narrative hap—a sense of possibility emerging in and through touch. In this scene, gesture functions as a kind of passionate arrest: a hand on the shoulder at once supplements and commutes the spoken sentence. Narrating the near-lynching as part of what he called the "horror complex," Johnson's kinesthetic imaginary—the gestural force of the arrest, the unspoken but potentially queer intimacy of looking and touching—registers a fugitive interval wherein feeling itself might be quickened and turned.

As Goldsby notes, W. E. B. Du Bois was the first to publicly reveal Johnson's experience with the Jacksonville lynch mob, in remarks he made to the NAACP on the occasion of Johnson's retirement from the association in 1931. "Addressing the crowd of well-wishers," Goldsby details, "Du Bois delivered a shocking tribute to his colleague's activism when he divulged that 'Mr. Johnson . . . was once nearly lynched in Florida, and quite naturally lynching to him, despite all obvious excuses and explanations and mitigating circumstances, can never be less than a *terrible real*.'"[121] Du Bois's phrasing here is not incidental; just as we have seen Du Bois infuse terror into ecstatic religion, *The Autobiography of an Ex-Colored Man* allows ecstasy and terror to unfold in dangerous proximity. This doubling of ecstasy and terror testifies, for Goldsby, to the cultural logic of lynching itself, which "turns out to be terribly real because it is both reproducible and unique, commonplace and unprecedented in the terms of narration set forth in the novel."[122] As Goldsby notes, the function of electricity in the lynching scene is to underscore the imbrications of technological modernity with archaic forms of violence, but it is also to rewrite (indeed, to resound) the physically and spiritually electrifying force of the Big Meeting in the face of extreme terror. In Johnson's novel, lynching is not merely a mirror image of the Big Meeting's effervescent outbursts; it functions instead as a devastating node in the affective circuit through which the "real" of Johnson's novel emerges.

In this sense, Johnson's autobiographies emerge as the writing and rewriting of life in the face of death, where autobiography becomes a different means of holding life in reserve or in the palm of one's hand. With his own "quivering message," Johnson theorized the turn, the surge, the relaying of trauma's static impress into ecstatic text. To be galvanized, as he repeatedly reminds us, is be electrified by contact; it is to call on bodily and ethical energies mobilized "by sonorous and other linguistic-affective means."[123] If we cannot look away or turn our backs, Johnson insists that we are not therefore powerless. As his narrator announces at the opening of *The Autobiography*, "I know that I am playing with fire, and I feel the thrill which accompanies that most fascinating pastime; and, back of it all, I think I find a sort of savage and diabolical desire to gather up all the little tragedies of my life, and *turn* them into a practical joke on society."[124] Here the fascinating pastime—writing—becomes a gesture of gathering or passing time, a way of queering the past to imagine, for the future, a different turn.

Performances of Contact

Gestures make and unmake sense. Lodged in repetition and citation, they are themselves a kind of itinerant archive, testimony to the body's historical and political conditioning. By recovering the turn of the century's promiscuous forms of button-pressing, we can begin to see the gestural body as a crucial "nodal point" for realism's performances of power, as well as for the kinesthetic variations that exceed and rewrite (or indeed re-choreograph) embedded forms of contact.[125] In *The Autobiography*, touching a button becomes an almost-literal seizing of the terms (and turns, and tropes) of power; the gesture at once articulates and bridges the gap between the literal and the figurative, or material forms of resistance and aesthetic forms of endurance and duration. Through the push button's ecstatic electrification, Johnson enacts a critical circuit between mere gestures and politics as such, a reading that both historicizes and complicates Giorgio Agamben's claim that in gesture "nothing is being produced or acted, but rather something is being endured and supported."[126] For what is produced in at least some forms of turn-of-the-century button-pressing—the violent enfleshment of race—is also distinctly what is endured in Johnson's autobiographical reenactments. Similarly, if Johnson's button-pressing highlights what Lauren Berlant has described as gesture's "performance of contact," it also helps us see and hear that performance as touched, always, by the technologies of race and representation that mediate it.[127]

Early twentieth-century discourses surrounding this gesture recognized its indeterminable politics—a politics bound up as much in the mass reproduction of images as in the rituals of reproducible death. In the face of such rituals, black writers following Johnson would repeatedly flip the switch on electricity's racializing force. Indeed, Johnson's attention to the disfiguring potential of electricity might be said to inaugurate a series of critical counternarratives, from George Schuyler's "Black-No-More"—a whitening technology said to resemble "a cross between a dentist's chair and an electric chair"—to the Invisible Man's "battle with Monopolated Light & Power" in the wake of his own violent electrifications.[128] Across significantly different political and aesthetic projects, Schuyler and Ellison both worked to contain and redirect the shock of racial violence, in part by channeling electricity's affective potential toward a broader gesture of cultural button-pressing. Such texts invite us to recast early twentieth-century black resistance in electrical terms—terms that expose racial violence as a function of technological progress while, at the same time, reclaiming electricity as a form of material and rhetorical contestation. Central to my thinking here is Fred Moten's reminder: "The history of blackness is testament to the fact that objects can and do resist."[129] To think the resistance of the object in electrical terms is to consider modernity's construction of black subjects as black boxes: forcibly embodied records of trauma. Yet it is also to recover the ways in which Johnson and others used electricity as a performance of contact, dramatizing the conflation of persons and things in order to transform hardwired social structures into electrifying alternatives.

In the case of both Van der Weyde's images and Johnson's narratives, the haptic impress of touching a button works to reroute electricity's social and material force at the very threshold of a secular skin that channels and resists it. To read the gesture outside of this context is to miss the way it draws our attention to race and secularism as ongoing, unevenly distributed formations lodged in the movements of social power and in the unpredictability of social contact—of things done and undone. It is also to miss the ways in which these texts continue to touch us long after the historical moment they index. Lingering over such gestures, then, might offer its own performance of arrest: a way of holding out for different configurations of power and of gesturing toward a future that might (still) be otherwise. As we'll see in the next and final chapter, the still or the pause is at once a grammatical and an embodied refusal; reading the pregnant pauses of Nella Larsen's 1928 novel *Quicksand*, we gain a sense of the novel's insistence on ecstatic rebirth, with and against the reproduction of secular modernity.

5

Born, Again

Early in the pages of Nella Larsen's 1928 novel *Quicksand*, we find an account of queer transgression hiding in plain sight of heteronormative privilege. Lamenting her lack of family connections, the novel's heroine Helga Crane notes that in the world of Naxos, the strictly regimented black college where she teaches, "You could be queer, or even attractive, or bad, or brilliant, or even love beauty and such nonsense if you were a Rankin, or a Leslie, or a Scoville; in other words, if you had a family."[1] Family, as Helga figures it, covers for all manner of queerness—sexual, for sure, but also moral, intellectual, aesthetic—all modes of disturbing the dominant order of sensemaking with a non-sense that queerness (in the dominant imaginary) always threatens to unleash. A luxury that Helga cannot afford, queerness is possible at Naxos only within the rigidly policed bounds of the family. In what the novel points to as the deeply mixed-up logic of Naxos, Helga cannot be queer or crooked because her lineage isn't straight enough; it is mixed or crossed and, therefore, according to Helga, the "crux of the whole matter."[2]

In this final chapter, I take up a text that resides uneasily at the boundaries of both realism and ecstasy as I have described them. Published in 1928—the height of the Harlem Renaissance, the year that Alain Locke described as the "floodtide of the present Negrophile movement"—Nella Larsen's *Quicksand* arrived more than three decades after the moment proper to American realism.[3] Its historical vectors are more Great Migration than post-Reconstruction, more Jazz Age than Gilded Age. Furthermore, *Quicksand* is distinctly modernist in technique, with its peripatetic, dislocated narrative hewing closely to the consciousness of its peripatetic, dislocated heroine, Helga Crane. Thus while we've encountered realism in these pages as a mobile term—a dynamic practice more than a fixed literary quality, something (in Nancy Glazener's terms) to be "read for"—still it is a term that does not adhere comfortably to Larsen's text.[4] And neither does ecstasy. As Sianne Ngai has argued, *Quicksand* is a novel of decidedly ugly feelings; its predominant mood is one of irritation, evincing the anxiety and rupture more typical to modernism than to realism and demonstrating in its aesthetic chaffing the psychic lacerations of racial imperatives.[5]

Irritation and ecstasy share some unexpected similarities, as we'll discover. Nevertheless, Larsen and *Quicksand* are still strange candidates for this study, and their presence here signifies my jumping ahead in this final chapter to realist ecstasy's twentieth-century reverberations. I call attention to the queerness of Larsen's position in my study in part because her novels' narrative and psychological displacements thematize the queerness of positionality more broadly. As Judith Butler has argued of Larsen's 1929 novel *Passing*, her fictions articulate "convergent modalities of power" that remain difficult to frame beyond the familiar "list of attributes separated by those proverbial commas (gender, sexuality, race, class)."[6] Part of my effort in this chapter will be to add the question of religion to that list of attributes, and to probe its general absence in a body of criticism that otherwise manages to navigate the complex overlays of subject formation, a palimpsest to which the list form (as Butler reminds us) can bear only inadequate witness.[7] That *Quicksand* requires an even more rigorous (maybe "realistic") mapping of such overlays is signaled from its epigraph: "My old man died in a big fine house. / My ma died in a shack. / I wonder where I'm gonna die, / Being neither white nor black?" Rendering racial, sexual, class, and spiritual location as a lingering question, these lines from Langston Hughes's "Cross" offer a chiasmus that resists definitive identifications—a fit opening for a novel full of familial cruxes, transatlantic crossings, and psychic and social crucifixions.[8]

Adding "religion" (as though it were a singular, identifiable quality) to this list of crossings is more difficult than simply requesting an additional comma. As Ann Taves has argued, what counts as religion or "religious experience" is often what gets "deemed" religious in specific historical and cultural contexts.[9] That is, religion and secularism (like gender, sexuality, race, and class) are lived, situated contexts—historically specific methods of ordering and disordering the self in relation to others.[10] While it seems superfluous to point out that the subjects and objects of religious studies are as heterogeneous as the subjects and objects of our other "studies"—because they are so often the *same* subjects and objects—still the complex role of religion in the formation of our modern, secular "subject(s)" remains a minor consideration, as, for example, in most readings of *Quicksand*.¹¹ Furthermore, as Ann Pellegrini has argued, when "religion does enter into the frame, it tends to do so in highly reduced belief-centered terms in which religion gets figured as the expression of irrational superstition, fear, archaic holdover, modernity's remainder."¹² Religion as a category (much like realism) retains the air of the reactionary, the conservative, the outdated, so much so that its various psychic pressures and releases, its social constrictions and possibilities, its status as an arena for both dramatic and mundane acts of transformation, are largely dismissed.

And yet *Quicksand* is full of ecstasy, or what the novel also calls "a queer feeling of enthusiasm": a pleasurable pain or painful pleasure that is decidedly relational (linked to longing and belonging), coded variously as religious and/or sexual, and restricted by the demands of the racial marriage plot. Such a "queer" feeling, as we'll see, demands attention to what Eve Sedgwick calls the "lapses and excesses of meaning" as well as the "fractal intimacies" that constitute (without delimiting) queerness.¹³ Queerness, as I'll use it in this chapter, might also be another word for what Carla Peterson has described as the double-edged "eccentricity" that has been attached to black female embodiment: "evok[ing] a center not concentric with another, an axis not centrally placed (according to the dominant system)" as well as "the notion of off-centeredness to suggest freedom of movement stemming from the lack of central control and hence new possibilities of difference conceived as empowering oddness."¹⁴ Simultaneously displaced from and displacing dominant centers of power, eccentricity is both an embodiment of and a challenge to the spatially conceived order of things—not the least, as we'll see, to secularism's normative ordering of the body. In ecstasy, Helga Crane is both "in" and "out" of body, and *Quicksand* repeatedly grasps at the speculative possibilities of this dis-placement—an off-centeredness or non-concentricity that operates both thematically and formally in the novel. A narrative that privileges movement and migration, *Quicksand* invokes ecstasy (or being beside oneself) to problematize the location of the queerly racialized and engendered subject, and indeed to problematize the body itself as a site of realist enactment and concern.¹⁵

In addition, and as I'll argue in what follows, within Peterson's double-edged eccentricity lies yet another edge: between the singular oddness of the individual and the oddness of being-together that *Quicksand* also probes. Even as ecstatic moments in the novel signal the individual subject's desire to escape fixed notions of identity and socially sanctioned feeling—they are literally ex-centric or dis-associative, a standing apart from the overdetermined self—they importantly do not transcend the pleasures and demands of the social. Rather, they enable (however fleetingly) something like a collective being beside—or queer relationality, a kind of togetherness unfolding alongside and through "convergent modalities" of individual subjection. Here I am drawing once more on Sedgwick's championing of the "beside" as a spatial logic that disrupts linear and dualistic thinking. As Sedgwick notes, "*Beside* is an interesting preposition also because there's nothing very dualistic about it; a number of elements may lie alongside one another, though not an infinity of them. . . . *Beside* comprises a wide range of desiring, identifying, representing, repelling, paralleling, differentiating, rivaling, leaning, twisting, mimicking, withdrawing, attracting, aggressing, warping, and other relations."[16] Sedgwick's list (as we'll see) provides an important reimagining of that "list of attributes separated by those proverbial commas"; enacting the very besideness it describes, the cumulative work of Sedgwick's gerunds might be to insist on relationality as a dynamic (or *ex-static*) and ongoing movement, rooted in but not reducible to bodily practice. As I'll argue in what follows, this is also the work of *Quicksand*'s ecstatic sequences, scenes of performance that enact a fecundity of relations (and names for relations), straining against any strict or static logic of positionality.

The spatial logic of ecstasy's "being beside" is also, as I've argued throughout this book, a temporal logic—a performative proximity in time as well as space. With *Quicksand*, we'll continue to explore this sense of proximity, as well as the ways in which ecstasy's queerness complicates the persistence of linear narratives of secularization (in which religion is overcome or replaced by secularism) as well as persistently linear narratives of literary history (in which realism is overcome or replaced by modernism).[17] Part of what my reading will suggest is the ways in which these narratives have been interdependent and self-reinforcing, rendering novels like *Quicksand* (and, later, James Baldwin's 1953 novel *Go Tell It on the Mountain*) as racialized exceptions to the "rule" of secularization, rather than complex explorations of its specific pressures and constraints. What such a rendering signals is (in part) the hegemonic force of modern secularism, or what Vincent Lloyd terms its "management of practices and bodies, not just as an elite exercise of power but also as the management of lives of ordinary people."[18] In what Lloyd terms the "secularist-racializing knot," secularization and racialization work in tandem to produce whiteness and secular Protestantism as unmarked universals that "jointly mark their others."[19] As Tracy Fessenden, Saba Mahmood, and others have argued, this process cannot be separated from the management of religion and sexuality, and particularly from modernity's consignment of sexuality to the sphere of the private, interiorized subject. Fessenden argues in this vein that "the category of religion in modernity is not only implicitly racialized but also feminized in being counterpoised to the public sphere as the domain of reason," producing marked subjects "made to bear the fleshly limitations from which white men are ostensibly emancipated, by reason, for the work of secular governance."[20] What Fessenden terms the "secularist-gendering-racializing knot," Mahmood emphasizes as a function of political economy, a technique of management central to the modern biopolitical state. As Mahmood suggests, "It is not so much that regulatory norms produce modern sexuality as that the compulsion to speak in its name shapes its valorized interiority."[21] Just as the biopolitical state en-genders the very possibilities for articulating sexual subjectivity, it also manages the relation between the secular and the religious, "defining, in the process, what the proper meaning, substance, and locus of modern religion should be."[22]

Secularism, in other words, is a quicksand.[23] And it is perhaps precisely because of this quality—what Jordan Stein describes as the historiographic difficulty of making secularism a "positive object"—that it has remained the unspoken term in critical accounts of Larsen's novel.[24] As we'll see, *Quicksand* dramatizes the crux or crossing by which the reproduction of familial and racial ties—and specifically childbearing—comes to define the limit point or horizon of queer possibility, a horizon that Helga Crane arguably spends much of the novel chasing. Indeed, we might read Helga's peripatetic movements—from the deep South of

Naxos to Chicago, then New York, Amsterdam, New York again, and finally back to the deep South—as a series of failed efforts to legitimate her queerness. And yet I also want to suggest that alongside this series of failed efforts emerges an alternative discourse of queer possibility, one that links queerness not to birth but instead, ambivalently and pleasurably, to rebirth. For while queerness looks distinctly like a birthright at the opening of *Quicksand*—if not inborn precisely then a function or privilege of birth—the novel also traces a "queer sort of satisfaction" emerging from moments of ecstatic abandon, moments that themselves queer the space between religious and secular modes of generating a subject. So I'll argue that even as it attends carefully to the repressive matrix of sexual and spiritual administration, the novel treats ecstatic conversion—and particularly Pentecostalism's kinetically embodied forms of spiritual practice—as a suggestively queer nexus of sexual, religious, and racialized modes of performance.

In this sense, *Quicksand*'s ecstasy carries with it the trace of what José Esteban Muñoz has described as the "ecstatic temporality" of queer utopianism. Building on Martin Heidegger's articulation of *ekstatisch*, or ecstasy as a sense of timeliness—a feeling of time's movement and its unity—Muñoz insists on the ways in which ecstasy troubles a normative sense of "straight time" in which the dominant or repressive logic of the present holds sway.[25] And while realism would seem to many critics entirely invested in something like straight time—the claim so frequently lodged against the politics of realist representation being that it naturalizes the order of the present—Larsen's text insists on the queer crossings of realism and utopianism, of constricted "subjects" and the expansive, ecstatic alternatives that open up within, beside, or beyond them. Something like "realist ecstasy," then, would demand that we resist singular understandings of each of these terms and the defiantly hybrid texts they describe. In Muñoz's reading of the contemporary indie band The Magnetic Fields's melodic call to "Take Ecstasy With Me" (1994)—which he places in conversation with Gian Lorenzo Bernini's seventeenth-century sculpture of the ecstasy of St. Theresa and Lacan's articulation of jouissance—ecstasy exceeds "the singular shattering that a version of *jouissance* suggests or the transport of Christian rapture." In this context, ecstasy is not an individual experience (deemed definitively sexual or religious) but a collective disordering of time, "an invitation, a call, to a then-and-there" against the violence of the here and now.²⁶ As Muñoz notes of the song's magnetic proposition: "Take ecstasy with me thus becomes a request to stand out of time together, to resist the stultifying temporality and time that is not ours, that is saturated with violence both visceral and emotional, a time that is not queerness. Queerness's time is the time of ecstasy. Ecstasy is queerness's way."²⁷ Ecstatic moments in *Quicksand* show us Helga Crane behaving badly, but they also count on and produce time's misbehavior: they stop time, launch it backward, project it forward, and mark the pressures and pleasures of the present in ways that are not particularly easy to read. Born in movement, ecstatic moments are indeed "moments," registering the temporality of quick, stolen contact, of being queerly beside, for a while, in ways that point to but do not guarantee alternative (even utopian) forms of collectivity.²⁸ At the same time, such moments point to the self *itself* as a form of standing or stepping out—an extension or *ex-stasis* through which the novel presents a decidedly immanent possibility of transport from the normative bounds of the secular.²⁹

Critics have frequently read ecstasy in *Quicksand* as a manifestation of Helga's repressed sexuality, praising Larsen's text for its insistence on portraying black female sexuality in the face of the historically objectified and commodified image of the black female body.³⁰ In these readings, moments of psychic rupture—of orgasmic release and (implicitly secular) self-shattering—do political work, but largely on behalf of the psychologically complex individual and her need for self-determination in a world of racist interpellation. And while they point to the crucial ways in which Larsen carved out a literary space for the black female (sexual) self, such analyses tend to treat that self as individually determined, and Helga Crane as the agent of her own narrative. Yet as Hazel Carby points out in her influential reading of the novel, *Quicksand* more often critiques this logic of the individual subject, where alienation is a "frame of mind" subject to "purely individual transformation," as opposed to a social condition subject to broadscale change.³¹ Similarly, Barbara Johnson notes that *Quicksand* consistently challenges the boundaries of the self, displacing its location as the textual center of value; the novel, she argues, "does not ask the reader to choose between a psychic and social model [of selfhood], but rather to see the articulations between them."³²

Taking up the emphasis on relational selfhood embedded in these readings—and extending Muñoz's notion of ecstatic temporality—I want to return to *Quicksand*'s scenes of ecstatic self-shattering (which are also, as we'll see, scenes of self-constitution) and to examine the kinds of collectivity they register. From within a novelistic world of ugly feelings, alienation, and disassociation, such moments proffer complexly queer forms of relationality. So while Butler registered the inability of the list and its proverbial commas to fully represent the relational quality of these categories, I'll argue that *Quicksand*'s ecstasy often seems to queer the list form itself, allowing us to revisit the deep strangeness of that (distinctly realist) inventory and (perhaps) to reclaim the outmoded form of the list. As we'll see, this is a form that in its very excess—deploying what we might call the queer work of the comma, which reproduces itself through language's own fecundity—offers something akin to the ecstasy that Larsen's novel repeatedly and ambivalently approaches.[33] I will focus on these proximities and convergences, arguing throughout that "communion remains a muted but obsessive theme" in *Quicksand*.[34] In this way, Muñoz's performative "queer" might also name the strangely imbricated work of the religious and the secular in Larsen's text, repeatedly insisting—as this chapter does—on the "articulations between them." Or in Larsen's words, on the persistent "mixedness of things."[35]

My sense is that by reconsidering the secular terms in which *Quicksand* has largely been read, we might begin to offer an even more complex account of the ways in which the embodied demands of race, sexuality, and religion might indeed be borne or borne out by being (performatively) born again. Not least because being born again—and again—disrupts and unsettles the work of "born this way," a contemporary discourse of queerness that (as Janet Jakobsen and Ann Pellegrini have argued) can easily begin to approximate a naturalized account of race as "immutable difference."[36] The religious logic of *born again* also strains against what Lee Edelman has described as the "secular theology" by which futurity is figured exclusively as reproductive futurity and by which queerness in turn gets coded as "the negativity opposed to every form of social viability."[37] If critics have long read in Helga Crane's queerness a kind of obstinate negativity—an irritable or ironic refusal to play by the self-reproducing rules of normative racial and sexual identity—we must read this negativity as complicated by the ecstatic abandon that Helga repeatedly looks for in scenes that seem to redouble the stakes of being "queer, or even attractive, or bad, or brilliant" (another list with proverbial commas). Which is not to say that Helga's "queer sort of satisfaction" in these scenes is necessarily or always a positive one. Instead, the novel proliferates moments of disturbing, disruptive release from the vectors of white or black heteronormativity, scenes that look to reframe the terms of queer relationality from the socially sanctioned familial birthright to the anonymous ecstatic encounter, the potentially nonproductive labor of being beside oneself in proximity to others. *Quicksand*'s ecstatic sequences, in other words, signal the possibility of relations that live in but also exceed that list of attributes (gender, sexuality, race, class, *and* religion); relations that were, historically and in the form of the list, always already beside themselves.

The Elaborateness of Uninteresting Detail

First, a brief glance at another sort of mixedness: for all its modernism, *Quicksand* arrived at a moment and in a context where realism was still (or once again) a topic of critical and cultural debate. As the contentious reception of Claude McKay's *Home to Harlem* that same year would crystallize, responses to African American literature in the 1920s and '30s centered on questions of realism and idealism, or what Kenneth Warren has described as the "indexical expectations" of African American literature. As Warren explains, such expectations linked the literary progress of black authors to racial progress writ large, in the "belief that novels, poems, or plays constituted proxies for the state or the nature of the race as a whole."[38] Hence the representativeness of African American literature—its relation to the "nature of the race as a whole"—was a crucial point of contention, as debates over fiction's function as racial "propaganda" faced a broader cultural demand for "art" as literary verisimilitude.

The claim to verisimilitude, as African American authors understood keenly (and as we've seen Anna Julia Cooper describe) had for too long been co-opted by white spectatorial desire in search of the primitive "real," confining African American literature to a counteraesthetics of idealization. As Sterling Brown would write in February 1930, registering his frustration with black audiences that suffered black literature to maintain an indexical idealism, "One of the most chronic complaints concerns this matter of Representativeness. An author, to these sufferers, never intends to show a man who happens to be a Negro, but rather to make a blanket charge against the race. The syllogism follows: Mr. A. shows a Negro who steals; he means by this that all Negroes steal; all Negroes do not steal; Q.E.D. Mr. A. is a liar, and his book is another libel on the race."[39] Rejecting the dichotomy between art and propaganda, Brown would go on to suggest that while the impulse to idealism was a logical one, as African American authors worked to counter the sheer mass of racist representation past and present, the "time" for realism had arrived: "If we are coming of age," he wrote, "the truth should be our major concern." He continued, "Let the truth speak. There has never been a better persuader."[40]

The "floodtide" of 1928—and particularly the publication of *Home to Harlem*—became an important flash point for this debate over realism and representativeness, and for the "coming of age" of African American literature in the years following Alain Locke's 1925 anthology *The New Negro*. While W. E. B. Du Bois (in a joint review of *Quicksand* and *Home to Harlem*) famously noted that McKay's novel made him "feel distinctly like taking a bath" and Marcus Garvey deemed it "a damnable libel against the Negro," others lauded what they saw as its frank depiction of Harlem life.[41] James W. Ivy called the novel "frank to the verge of cruelty," praising it as "not a picture" but a "slice of Harlem Life"—realism so cuttingly real it left representation behind entirely, offering in its place a piece of Harlem in the flesh.[42] Those who condemned the sensationalism of *Home to Harlem* and Carl Van Vechten's *Nigger Heaven* (1926) frequently offered Larsen's *Quicksand* as a corrective. Du Bois, for example, praised the novel's evenhandedness, describing it as "not near nasty enough for New York columnists" and "too sincere for the South and middle West"—a description that registers the novel's own meditation on problems of place.[43] Noting the "propaganda motive" was "decidedly absent," Arthur Huff Fauset—who would go on to write the immensely influential *Black Gods of the Metropolis: Negro Cults of the Religious North* (1944)—declared the novel a step forward for Negro literature.[44]

Josef Sorett has pointed to the important ways in which such debates over black aesthetic and political progress were closely tied to narratives of secularization; as part of the aesthetic project of *The New Negro*, Locke and others constructed a new and prophetic "race-spirit" as a release from the bounds of religious orthodoxy, even as heterogeneous forms of Afro-Protestantism proliferated in Harlem and across the country.[45] Tracking the links between the New Negro movement's racial aesthetics and the production of a "spiritual grammar" for modern black pluralism, Sorett examines how New Negro aesthetics were delineated, mediated, and expanded by calls to the spirit, and by a complex and often ambivalent relationship to Afro-Protestantism. While writers like George Schuyler mocked black churches for their mimicry of white middle-class codes of respectability, Langston Hughes celebrated the performance vernaculars of the storefront church. In his 1926 essay "The Negro Artist and the Racial Mountain," Hughes embraced "the low-down folks, the so-called common element" as "the majority—may the Lord be praised!" and insisted on ecstasy as a wellspring of aesthetic possibility: "Their joy runs, bang! into ecstasy. Their religion soars to a shout. Work maybe a little today, rest a little tomorrow. Play awhile. Sing awhile. O, let's dance! These common people are not afraid of spirituals, as for a long time their more intellectual brethren were, and jazz is their child. They furnish a wealth of colorful, distinctive material for any artist because they still hold their own individuality in the face of American standardizations."[46] As Sorett argues, Hughes valorized the "folk" (and, particularly here, the Pentecostal "shout") as a spiritual and aesthetic resource for black art, over and against the possibility of its conforming to the demand for "primitive" or "authentic" blackness on the part of white audiences.[47] Despite the ways in which *Quicksand* navigates a similarly complex terrain, Larsen marks a curious absence in Sorett's study; appearing just three years after Hughes's essay (with decidedly less joy in its ecstasy), the novel complicates any spiritual "renaissance" by exploring how aesthetic and spiritual possibility remains delimited by the sexual logic of respectability and the reproductive demands of racial motherhood.

Perhaps because of its stark take on these demands, realism was a repetitive theme in *Quicksand*'s reception. In all, early reviewers read the novel as answering Brown's call for a less oppressively "representative" and thus more "truthful delineation."[48] The *New York Times*, for example, noted the novel's "lucid, unexaggerated manner" in contrast to the "exhibitionism" of *Nigger Heaven*, while a reviewer for the *Nation* suggested with qualified praise that Larsen's book was "an attempt to portray a real person in all her complexities, instead of being a complimentary or a spiteful version of an individual never really revealed."[49] As Larsen's biographer Thadious Davis notes, Eda Lou Walton's review in *Opportunity* magazine in July 1928 was among the most influential, and the one in which Larsen herself may have placed the most stock. Offering a tepid critique, Walton found particular fault with "the elaborateness of uninteresting detail" and "objective evidences of culture" that signaled the novel's middle-class aesthetic prerogatives and that linked its lengthy descriptions to the excessive detail of turn-of-the-century realism.[50]

It is worth lingering over that "elaborateness" insofar as it marks *Quicksand*'s complex interrogation of race, gender, and aesthetics. Indeed, the novel's emphasis on the pleasures of the detail—from its opening pages, rooted in Helga's "rare and intensely personal taste"—underscores what Naomi Schor has powerfully described as the detail's ideological and historical marginalization, its status as feminized, delegitimized, excessive, and dangerous. "The detail," Schor argues, "does not occupy a conceptual space beyond the laws of sexual difference: the detail is gendered and doubly gendered as feminine."[51] Within the long itinerary of the detail's subordination (as "ornamental" and "domestic") and recuperation in masculinist regimes of modernity (as, for example, in the Barthesian fragment), Schor points to the rise of realism—with its interrogation of *"the epistemological status of the detail"*—as a crucial nodal point, a site where the meaning of the detail is crucially at stake. As Schor signals, "realism is as much a discourse *on* the detail as a discourse *of* the detail,"[52] and here we might reposition Larsen's *elaborateness* as radical attentiveness to the aesthetic and material details of black female pleasure[53] in their powerful refusal to cohere into a representative whole. Such radical attentiveness, I argue, is not merely the mode of *Quicksand* but also its provocation; in this sense, I follow Alexandra Vazquez in insisting on "the reparative attention that details demand

and deserve."[54] Not merely an aesthetic category, the detail in Vazquez's study becomes an invitation to a different mode of reading (or listening), an attentiveness to the itinerant, the eccentric, and the elaborate that *Quicksand* demands as both aesthetics and politics.

Notwithstanding Walton's review, *Quicksand* secured Larsen's status as a major figure of the Harlem Renaissance. The novel satisfied critics on both sides of the art/propaganda debate, in large part because it dramatized the unrelenting tension between the aesthetic demand for realism—here, the representation of an idiosyncratic and thus conceivably "real person in all her complexities"—and the imperatives of solidarity and uplift embedded in "representativeness."[55] As Du Bois's bath indicates, the debate over representation and representativeness was never separate from the logic of sexual regulation embedded in constructions of racial difference. The white supremacist logic by which the "real" of black women's sexual desire was taken to be "representative" is one to which *Quicksand* is acutely attentive, as it probes both the possibilities and the dangers of representing ecstatic experience: experience that traverses the sexual and the spiritual, as well the individual and the collective in ways that demand our attention. As I'll argue below, ecstatic moments in *Quicksand* enable the novel to theorize these crossings, pointing up the singularity of the individual (queer, ecstatic, indeterminate) subject even as they embed the very possibility of that singularity in the queerness of collective existence.

In what follows, we will see this dynamic emerge repeatedly in the novel, most spectacularly in Helga's ecstatic conversion in a storefront church in Harlem. Read frequently as a breakdown in both Helga's and the novel's reasoning (rather than a realist engagement with the ambiguity of experience), critics have largely missed the ways in which this scene repeats and recirculates the novel's sustained interest in queer relationality and the ecstatic performances that facilitate it. Insisting on the imbrications of ecstatic feeling with performativity—as both a regulatory imperative and its unwieldy repetition—I'll read the ecstasy of Helga Crane as crucial to the novel's engagement with representing the "real" of social existence or the odd, intractable reality of being beside.

Stepping Out

Early in the pages of *Quicksand*, Helga Crane finds a queer moment of relational bliss. Having left her position as a teacher at Naxos—a Southern college resembling Tuskegee and Fisk—and traveled to Chicago, Helga wanders the streets, struggling to find both empathy and employment. Barred from the house of her white uncle by his new wife—who asks her to "please remember that my husband is not your uncle," policing the racialized bounds of affection and affiliation—Helga is soon afterward "accosted" by a white man in the street. Placing in dramatic juxtaposition the double bind of Helga's embodied position—her rejection from and vulnerability to the sexual logic of white patriarchy—these two moments leave Helga "numb," even as she recognizes herself (through the refracted gaze of her white relations) as "an obscene sore . . . at all costs to be hidden. She understood, even while she resented. It would have been easier if she had not."[56] As Mary Esteve has noted, the language of abscess and anesthesia in this passage insists on the traumatic impact of Helga's interactions and on the oddly numbing effect of severe psychic injury.[57] Yet shortly thereafter, the novel envisions an alternative to Helga's wounded understanding of family relations, and specifically to the reproductive logic of race that they both entail and police. Back in her room, contemplating her next move, she is overcome by a "desire to mingle":

> She stood intently looking down into the glimmering street, far below, swarming with people, merging into little eddies and disengaging themselves to pursue their own individual ways. A few minutes later she stood in the doorway, drawn by an uncontrollable desire to mingle with the crowd. The purple sky showed tremulous clouds piled up, drifting here and there with a sort of endless lack of purpose. Very like the myriad human beings pressing hurriedly on. Looking at these, Helga caught herself wondering who they were, what they did, and of what they thought. What was passing behind those dark molds of flesh. Did they really think at all? Yet, as she stepped out into the moving multi-colored crowd, there came to her a queer feeling of enthusiasm, as if she were tasting some agreeable, exotic food—sweetbreads, smothered with truffles

and mushrooms—perhaps. And, oddly enough, she felt, too, that she had come home. She, Helga Crane, who had no home.[58]

Rendered particularly strange insofar as it follows a sequence of "stinging" psychic assaults, this passage insists on the odd efficacies of pleasure against (or in and through) the violence of subjection. Merging and disengaging freely, opaque in the who/what details of existence, the crowd offers Helga a site of blissful incorporation: an alternate form of relation, a very different (if no less bodily) way of being on the street. Here Helga exchanges the biting pain of her earlier interactions in the street for the fleshy enthusiasm of eating exotic foods—the metaphors of "taste" and ingestion unsettling the rigidly demarcated space between in and out, self and other, as well as between the ostensibly disembodied work of aesthetic judgment and the bodily pleasure of savoring.[59] And while the emphasis on pleasure seems to (re)produce Helga as a singularly consuming subject, this passage also enables a strange sort of belonging, constituted in the very feeling of being collectively dispersed. Here is no simple communion: the queer relationality of this passage manifests grammatically, as homeless Helga—dis-located or ex-tended across the pronouns she/Helga Crane/who, a literally ecstatic syntax—finds an odd sort of home by merging with the "moving multi-colored crowd."

Transitioning into a chapter break, these lines produce a pause in Helga's defiant individuality, even as they shore up her "eccentricity," emphasizing the oddness of her "queer enthusiasm" in response to the acute experience of racism. In these terms, enthusiasm functions as an example of Helga's "disproportional" fits of feeling: emotional responses that refuse to line up with readerly expectations and that make the experience of reading the novel (as Ngai has observed) an oddly discomfiting one. Focusing on Helga's strange bouts of "irritation"—which diverge from the logic of adequate or proportionate feeling—Ngai argues that through this "affective opacity," the novel simultaneously resists the cultural demand for racialized subjects to be fully legible and the aesthetic demand for racially affiliated art to be transparently expressive.[60] Thus "irritation" characterizes the novel's resistance to the imperative of racial "representativeness" even as it disrupts the smooth aestheticization of racial otherness so central to American modernism.

Despite their seeming opposition, irritation and enthusiasm work similarly in this regard, insofar as they share an inappropriateness or inadequacy (or oddness) that confounds any effort to read the novel as simply an expression of racial solidarity. At least initially, Helga's "queer feeling of enthusiasm," a feeling explicitly predicated on the *lack* of identification ("Did they really think at all?"), seems to produce the same negative aesthetics that Ngai describes: it secures the "artform's potential to not-facilitate racial identification," as well as its potential to "not necessarily promote disidentification with positive or negative constructions of blackness."[61] But enthusiasm—if not, as we'll see, precisely a "good feeling"—also helps name the novel's equally persistent drive toward some alternative, more optimistic form of togetherness that might substitute for racially prescriptive modes of sympathy and affiliation. For the lack of enthusiasm is itself a problem in the novel, most explicitly at Naxos: "Enthusiasm, spontaneity, if not actually suppressed, were at least openly regretted as unladylike or ungentlemanly qualities. The place was smug and fat with self-satisfaction."[62] Overfed with the stultifying logic of the proper—of proportionate belonging and "knowing one's place"—Naxos stands in for the kind of representativeness that *Quicksand* treats as an engulfing negative. Displacing these ugly feelings in *Quicksand* are not the excesses of individual pleasure but the queer ecstasies of being-together, of stepping out, of commuting without exactly communing.[63]

The strange noncommunion of Helga's enthusiasm (delivered above in free indirect discourse) is not without its absorptive dangers: her decided attraction to the throng of "myriad human beings," her reduction of such beings to "dark molds of flesh," flirts with an exoticizing mode of spectatorship that the novel later engages in more direct terms. Aestheticizing and idealizing the crowd from her position above it, Helga projects an abstracted "swarm" where the narrative suggests instead an evening commute—the mark of a laboring class whose "pressing hurriedly on" conveys anything but "an endless lack of purpose." Nevertheless, as Helga goes down into the street, the effect is to commute the trauma of the familial cut into a less familiar, more transitory form of contact, briefly substituting a painful exposure for its pleasurable corollary. It may be worth noting here that "commute" etymologically yokes *togetherness* ("com") and *change* ("mutare"): in this novel of migration, the fugitive possibility of a collective change-in-motion is one to which Helga repeatedly returns.[64] In this sense, Helga Crane dramatizes what Nadia Ellis has described as "queered diasporic belonging," with her desire so often taking the form of "an urgent desire for an outside—an outside of the nation, an outside of traditional forms of genealogy and family relations, an outside of chronological and spatial limitations," a stepping out that is at once distinctly bodily and a striking release from the mold of flesh.[65] At home in the drift, here we see a vision of selfhood *as* extension or exposure—a movement into and through the world, whose reciprocal constitution of the subject is figured through taste, a moment of literal, pleasurable, visceral incorporation.[66]

A parallel moment of ecstatic transport unfolds when Helga trades the streets of Chicago for the thoroughfares of New York. Settling in Harlem, where the crowds are similarly mobile and myriad, Helga observes the procession: "Black figures, white figures, little forms, big forms, small groups, large groups, sauntered, or hurried by. It was gay, grotesque, and a little weird. Helga Crane felt singularly apart from it all."[67] If the feeling of being "singularly apart" is a defining one for Helga Crane—a distance that allows her (and, at least potentially, Larsen's readers) to aestheticize and consume racial difference—it is also a position that the novel repeatedly throws into question, as when Helga merges with the "gay, grotesque" movement, venturing out en masse to a cabaret. Descending into the club, "thinking that this was one of those places characterized by the righteous as a hell," Helga finds not an inferno but a singularly odd moment of plurality:

> They danced, ambling lazily to a crooning melody, or violently twisting their bodies, like whirling leaves, to a sudden streaming rhythm, or shaking themselves ecstatically to a thumping of unseen tomtoms. For a while, Helga was oblivious of the reek of flesh, smoke, and alcohol, oblivious of the oblivion of other gyrating pairs, oblivious of the color, the noise, and the grand distorted childishness of it all. She was drugged, lifted, sustained, by the extraordinary music, blown out, ripped out, beaten out, by the joyous, wild, murky orchestra. The essence of life seemed bodily motion. And when suddenly the music died, she dragged herself back to the present with a conscious effort; and a shameful certainty that not

only had she been in the jungle, but that she had enjoyed it, began to taunt her.[68]

Inaugurated by the third-person declarative ("They danced"), this scene presents ecstasy as more than a little weird: part of an anonymous "they," Helga is simultaneously surrounded and separate, sustained and shattered, as the feeling of being "singularly apart" transitions not into familiarity but into the redoubled oblivion of proximity—an oblivion the narrative bolsters by departing from the intimacy of free indirect discourse. Ecstasy—here as an adverb ("ecstatically"), as the quality of action—suggests this being-together without intimacy, or the proximity of many things at once: a departure from the straight time to which Helga is reluctantly returned at the end of the passage. "For a while," time is beside itself, both diegetically and (arguably) in the experience of reading this passage. If not explicitly "a request to stand out of time together," in Muñoz's terms, it nevertheless offers a departure from the linear unfolding of the plot, one that seems to compel our attention (and that has notably compelled much critical attention).

Importantly, the ecstatic temporality of this passage is not simply a break from the violence of the present—as the language of ripping and beating attests—but rather a linguistic "twisting" of that violence into something else. Like another ecstatic conversion scene to which we will soon turn, the cabaret sequence offers a climactic "outing" of the self, delimited only by the conscious drag of the present. Music is the medium of this outing or breach in decorum, the substance that Helga takes or is taken by (we're not sure which), as through it, the logic of the subject is made murky, mobile, or tripped out. Within and of the music, Helga, too, is beside herself, "blown out, ripped out, beaten out" by the orchestra; as the object of this passage's grammatical dislocation, "she" becomes more action than actor, less the subject of performance than its very material. Thus ecstasy does not so much expose the pent-up, feeling subject as it insists on the oddness of subjection itself: the overdetermined process of making sense or returning to one's senses, a process by which Helga is made to feel, at the end of the passage, a taunting sense of enjoyment and shameful certainty. Before these lines, it is not clear that we can read "ecstasy" as pleasure or "enjoyment"; less an affect than a movement or a style, ecstasy here is not about "promoting queer happiness," to use Sara Ahmed's terms.[69] Rather, in ecstasy, Helga's oblivion is also our own, for "where" we are—inside or "out" of her consciousness—remains utterly opaque. Tripping and tripling up, Larsen's repetitive verbs and adjectives ("drugged, lifted, sustained"; "blown out, ripped out, beaten out"; "joyous, wild, murky") denote nothing so much as words beside themselves, always only proximate to their object.[70]

As critics have noted, the cabaret dance offers a dramatic, even violent instance of self-loss, and to draw out this passage's emphasis on ecstatic relation is both to extend and to complicate a broader critical effort to account for the drive toward objectification—alternately a "death drive," a "fantasy of nonbeing," or an "ecstatic disappearance"—that seems to propel *Quicksand*'s narrative.[71] In their attention to both psychological and broader cultural forms of self-alienation, these readings provide a crucial base from which to rethink the novel's repeated, ambivalent approach to ecstasy: to the odd "outing" or exteriority that attends these moments of being (collectively) in motion. Critics have read this outing in very different terms: as alternately indicating sexual repression or expression, as dramatizing the plight of the liberal subject or problematizing that subject altogether. Thus while Ann duCille argues that Larsen's texts "depict openly sensual black female subjects," Claudia Tate suggests that *Quicksand* evinces a much less explicit "desire to recover and forget, express and silence a lost primary love."[72] Similarly, while Mary Esteve contends that Larsen's own status as author rescues a traditionally liberal subject "apart from racial or cultural identity," Barbara Johnson argues nearly the opposite, noting that *Quicksand* provides "a critique of the conception of the self as a locus of value."[73]

What enables such widely differing critical approaches to these ecstatic moments is how they seem to simultaneously shore up a kind of authenticity or essentialism—a primitive "jungle" of experience exposed (like Helga herself) to white desire—while signaling (in their emphasis on oblivion) the flight of any legible, centric, essential self. Ecstasy is thus quite literally a kind of crossing, or (for some critics) a crossing out—a negation of the overdetermined subject. Ngai describes these "subjective gaps or erasures" or "blank spots" as indicating the novel's resistance to racial transparency and compelled affiliation; similarly, Laura Doyle argues that such moments reproduce the tropes of essentialism only to "[reveal] that there is no there, there."⁷⁴ Building on these readings, I want to nevertheless suggest that such moments are not simply negations, for they point to and problematize togetherness (or plurality) in ways that exceed—without abandoning—the question of race (*and* gender, *and* sexuality, *and* class, *and* religion; as Butler reminds us, "the subject exceeds precisely that to which it is bound").⁷⁵ I'll continue to call such moments queer in the sense that they are, in Muñoz's terms, both "relational and antirelational"; drawing on Jean-Luc Nancy's articulation of being singular plural, Muñoz insists on the ways in which queerness marks a singularity (or eccentricity) that is "always relational to other singularities."⁷⁶ This quality of queerness is also, as we've seen, the mark of ecstasy: being beside the self is both an instance of extreme singularity and an acknowledgment of being in relation to others, a conception of being that is fundamentally (rather than incidentally) a being-with.

Ecstasy's queerness, then, emerges precisely in its odd relationality, its odd centrality. Not so much a good feeling or an emotion proper to Helga's interiority, ecstasy "outs" the subject while in fact expressing very little subjective content, refusing to reproduce feeling as a spectacle for public consumption. Risking the conflation of blackness with exteriority—where the "essence of life" might indeed be "bodily motion"—the cabaret dance produces (at least momentarily) a break in secularism's normative regulation of the boundaries between exterior/interior, privacy/publicity, and subject/object, and a different sense of what it might look like to be "sustained" *in* and *as* motion. Not simply a moment of private release from publicly authorized performances of race, gender, sexuality, and class, the cabaret scene instead presents the paradox of being both singular and plural, both eccentric subject and the object of collectivity: a "both" that is itself a movement between, "both" violent and pleasurable. We might also note that in place of the "proverbial commas," here, the comma marks the undelimited space *between* signifiers—it is both a (aural/visual) pause and a continuation, a syncopated musical rhythm that the passage references without fully denoting, a mark that parallels the body's own queer presence and absence. The comma, in other words, performs ecstasy's beside or between-ness while enacting its incalculable temporality ("for a while,").⁷⁷

As Shane Vogel cautions in his reading of Nancy and Muñoz, "We should resist here a naïve reading of queerness and ecstasy."⁷⁸ Part of what Muñoz's work provides, Vogel notes, is an account of the ecstatic "not as an experience or rupture of the self but as the very condition of the self, and this has implications not only for queerness but also for other modes of being such as brownness or blackness. The ecstatic 'stepping out' José describes, in other words, is not a stepping out of the self but the self as a stepping-out."[79] In *Quicksand*, ecstasy comes to name this constitutive "out-ness," in the cabaret and—to offer another example—in Helga's romantic interlude with Dr. Anderson, the newly married object of her sexual attraction or confusion. Recalling his sudden stolen, almost violent kiss in the back hallway of a Harlem party, Helga "lived over those brief seconds, thinking not so much of the man whose arms had held her as of the ecstasy which had flooded her. Even recollection brought a little onrush of emotion that made her sway a little."[80] While Helga's desire is explicitly sexual here, her focus is not on Dr. Anderson but on ecstasy itself; ecstasy's queerness is its capacity to flood or displace secularism's bounded and interiorized sexual subject, throwing it off balance, revealing its being-in-relation to others. In ecstasy, Helga slouches toward a being-with that both is and is not simply sexual.

Lost—or Saved

If Helga's ecstasy is not strictly sexual in these moments, it is also not distinctly religious; indeed, ecstasy as we've encountered it thus far in *Quicksand* bears little resemblance to what we might read as specifically "religious" experience. Furthermore, the novel as a whole is not particularly amenable to religious modes of thought; on the contrary, it offers an explicit critique of Christianity's collusion with white supremacy. Early in the novel, Helga recalls with "seething resentment" "one of the renowned white preachers of the state" who lectures to Naxos students on the merits of staying put:

> They had good sense and they had good taste. They knew enough to stay in their places and that, said the preacher, showed good taste. He spoke of his great admiration for the Negro race, no other race in so short a time had made so much progress, but he had urgently besought them to know when and where to stop. . . . And then he had spoken of contentment,

embellishing his words with scriptural quotations and pointing out to them that it was their duty to be satisfied in the estate to which they had been called, hewers of wood and drawers of water. And then he had prayed.[81]

Citing Joshua 9:21, which reaffirmed slavery as the curse of Canaan ("And the princes said unto them, Let them live; but let them be hewers of wood and drawers of water unto all the congregation; as the princes had promised them"), the preacher's sermon points to the logic of spiritual contentment that linked white racism to the post-Reconstruction gospel of black uplift through agricultural and industrial labor (a gospel that created and sustained institutions like Tuskegee). Here religious discourse reinforces the aesthetic propriety (or "good taste") of staying in one's place, an ideology of spiritual, political, and physical immobility that the novel repeatedly rejects. Like another kind of good taste—arbitrated by the upper-middle-class Harlem elites from whom Helga also flees—religious discourse at Naxos is a regulatory ideal, one that produces and manages the body's "proper" labor. It also produces blackness as a distinctly accelerated relationship to the nation's temporal unfolding ("no other race had made such progress in so little time"); here and elsewhere in the novel, white Christianity is invoked to manage and restrict black progress—staying in one's place becomes knowing when to stop with "time" itself.[82] In other words, *Quicksand* points to white Christianity as a particularly strident example of what Elizabeth Freeman calls "chrononormativity," or "the use of time to organize individual human bodies toward maximum productivity," a productivity itself determined by the bounds of the state.[83]

In this sense, *Quicksand* extends the critique of white Christianity that black feminists like Anna Julia Cooper and Frances E. W. Harper had offered a generation earlier. In *A Voice from the South*, for example, Cooper emphasized literature's capacity to "hold up the glass" to white Christianity in its regulation of racial, sexual, economic hierarchies. Praising Albion Tourgée's polemical realism, Cooper noted, "Not many could so determinedly have held up the glass of the real Christianity before those believers in a white Christ and these preachers of the gospel, 'Suffer the little *white* children to come unto me.' We all see the glaring inconsistency and feel the burning shame. We appreciate the incongruity and the indignity of having to stand forever hat in hand as beggars, or be shoved aside as intruders in a country whose resources have been opened up by the unrequited toil of our forefathers."[84] Realism, Cooper insisted, was in this context a corrective to the hegemonic force of an exclusionary gospel; here we see the aesthetic function of *Quicksand*'s "seething resentment" and the political function of Cooper's "burning shame" as crucial, conjoined, visceral responses to white Christianity's efforts to constrict black progress. And here, too, we see these responses directed toward the management of time itself, to being constrained in static timelessness or suspension ("having to stand forever hat in hand") against the historical imperative of the nation's debt to black labor. As both Cooper and Larsen recognized, such an enforcement of timelessness in the present was a function of white supremacist theology, a theology that also fundamentally relied on the regulation of middle-class motherhood and the arbitration of *whose* children might be (ultimately) saved. White Christianity, in other words, sacralizes the logic of property and kinship that Hortense Spillers has described, in which the symbolic currency of family is the location of a foundational maintenance of racial boundaries ("please remember that my husband is not your uncle").[85] Described in the opening pages of *Quicksand* as a distinct and recurrent "irritation," it seems worth treating this theology as the novel's provocation—the structuring logic from which it flees or migrates.

For many critics, the biting critique of white supremacist Christianity fully describes *Quicksand*'s engagement with religion; these same critics read Helga's turn or return to religion near the end of the novel—her unexpected and dramatic conversion in a storefront church in Harlem—as a capitulation to broader forces of sexual and psychic regulation. In this reading, the improvised religious meeting (with its own ecstatic tendencies) provides the cover for Helga's sexual expression, only to backfire when Helga marries the Reverend Pleasant Green and finds herself stuck in a disastrously prolific reproductive cycle in a tiny Alabama town: another sort of staying in place justified by the logic of sacrifice and delayed salvation.[86] While this reading is compelling—by the novel's conclusion Helga will bemoan the trap of "unfailing trust in 'de Lawd'"—it also reduces Helga's conversion to either sublimated sexual desire or mere delusion, insisting on a novelistic break in the otherwise realistic depiction of a modern, psychologically complex subject.[87] Esteve, for example, describes the conversion scene as "high burlesque," noting that if "up to now Larsen has been venturing primarily—though by no means exclusively—in a realist project, in the final episode all bets are off. Reader and writer have been abandoned to the cause of narratological causelessness."[88] In these terms, the novel does not simply describe but also mimics Helga's departure from reason, partaking of the ecstatic performance that it represents. Describing the scene as "high burlesque," Esteve diagnoses *Quicksand* with its own queer enthusiasm.

If indeed there is a kind of enthusiasm in this sequence, it is not a departure from the novel's realism, if only because—as I've signaled throughout—realism and reason are not coterminous. Furthermore, ecstasy's "narratological causelessness"—its association with the minor, the eccentric, the nonlinear or adjacent, and the repetitive—fully infuses the realist project as I've remapped it in the preceding chapters. As in these texts, ecstasy emerges in *Quicksand* not as a break with novelistic reason but as a continuation of the novel's broader critique of normative strictures. With a mixture of horror and attraction, *Quicksand* approaches religious ecstasy with the same level of detail and the same ambivalence embedded in those earlier texts; it also approaches the complex imbrications of sexuality and religion without reducing one to the other.[89] While Helga's initial entrance into the storefront church seems arbitrary—she is (once again) drifting, seeking shelter from the lashing rain—the ecstatic performance that she witnesses soon draws her critical attention:

> Men and women were swaying and clapping their hands, shouting and stamping their feet to the frankly irreverent melody of the song. Without warning the woman at her side threw off her hat, leaped to her feet, waved her long arms, and shouted shrilly: "Glory! Hallelujah!" And then, in wild, ecstatic fury jumped up and down before Helga clutching at the girl's coat, and screamed: "Come to Jesus, you pore los' sinner!" Alarmed for the fraction of a second, involuntarily Helga had shrunk from her grasp, wriggling out of the wet coat when she could not loosen the crazed creature's hold. At the sight of the bare arms and neck growing out of the clinging red dress, a shudder shook the swaying man at her right. On

the face of the dancing woman before her a disapproving frown gathered. She shrieked: "A scarlet 'oman. Come to Jesus, you pore los' Jezebel!"[90]

While this passage details the proximity between religious experience and sexual desire—they literally stand next to one another here, embodied by the man and woman to Helga's left and right—it does not collapse them. Spiritual practice unfolds to the rhythm of an irreverent melody while ecstatic experience enables a kind of spectacular, performative female embodiment, even as it looks to take in and regulate sexual expression. Drawing Helga's attention, ecstasy quite palpably takes hold of her here, a clutching or grasping that the novel does not merely caricature but presents in proliferating detail, with varying degrees of fascination and aversion. As in the cabaret scene, performance is the medium and the method of ecstasy, and religion is all the more powerful here for its being a performance:

> Helga Crane was amused, angry, disdainful, as she sat there, listening to the preacher praying for her soul. But though she was contemptuous, she was being too well entertained to leave. And it was, at least, warm and dry. So she stayed, listening to the fervent exhortation to God to save her and to the zealous shoutings and groanings of the congregation. Particularly she was interested in the writhings and weepings of the feminine portion, which seemed to predominate. Little by little the performance took on an almost Bacchic vehemence. Behind her, before her, beside her, frenzied women gesticulated, screamed, wept, and tottered to the praying of the preacher, which had gradually become a cadenced chant. When at last he ended, another took up the plea in the same moaning chant, and then another. It went on and on without pause with the persistence of some unconquerable faith exalted beyond time and reality.[91]

If the faith observed seems "beyond time and reality," Helga's observation, importantly, is not: contemptuous and entertained, she relates to the meeting with distinctly ironic distance. A few lines later, this distance turns almost anthropological: "She felt herself in the presence of a nameless people, observing rites of a remote obscure origin."[92] With its emphasis on physicality and ritual, this passage (again like the cabaret scene) seems at first to reproduce the (secular) logic of primitivism, exoticizing and eroticizing the storefront religious meeting as simply the next potential site for authentic black feeling. Yet Helga's interest—and her subsequent transformation from spectator to participant—disrupts this logic, privileging collective practice over "obscure origin" and pointing up the possibilities embedded in queer performance, notably in the women "behind her, before her, beside her." Fixated on the "almost Bacchic" performance, Helga observes a "feminine portion" whose religion enables (because it requires) the eccentric embodiment—at once "in" and "out" of body, physically liberated and spiritually compelled—which has been the crux of Helga's narrative. Queering the unconquerable distance between sexual desire and divine obligation, the storefront figures religious expression as a collective performance of being beside.

Thus without losing sight of the tremendous ambivalence attached to religiosity and religious discourse in *Quicksand*, we might nevertheless read this passage as disturbing the critical and cultural matrix by which the secular, apparently self-determining subject has become the privileged site of resistance to normative conceptions of race, gender, and sexuality. What emerges as a possibility in the ecstasy of the storefront church—and, eventually, in the unwilled ecstasy of Helga Crane—is what Michael Warner has described as a counterpublic: an improvisational collectivity that resists or retools the sensemaking mechanisms of a dominant public.[93] Made insensible—eccentric but also literally numb—by the trauma of the dominant and its demands on the sexualized subject, the storefront (itself a marginalized space in Harlem) proffers an alternate mode of sensemaking, one that demands a scandalously enthusiastic collective performance, an ecstatic public outing. Hence the burlesque or nonsense that Esteve and others have read in Helga's conversion: it is precisely ecstasy's "tumultuous derangement" of sense into which Helga is drawn as an alternative method of being and being-with.[94] Neither celebrating nor rejecting this alternative, *Quicksand* presents it in all its realism.

As did historical storefront churches in Harlem and other urban centers, the women behind, before, and beside Helga suggest a collectivity based less on denominational identity than on sheer proximity, a community born in movement. As Milton Sernett, Wallace Best, and others have argued, storefront churches—which emerged in Chicago,

New York, and other Northern cities in the first decades of the twentieth century as an effect of the Great Migration—enabled Southern migrants to quickly establish communities of worship and produced a sense of belonging to what Best describes as a broader "religious diaspora."[95] Eclectic in their theological and liturgical choices, these improvised and unaffiliated churches provided both spiritual uplift and a crucial material base from which to anchor black communities displaced by migration. With their exuberant worship styles—which marked these communities' loose ties to the Holiness and Pentecostal movements, as well as to Baptist and Methodist congregations in the rural South—these churches were the object of curiosity and contempt among more established religious institutions as well as among the (increasingly secular) black middle class. As Best notes, "Storefronts indicated that urban space—the streets themselves—would be contested space"; cropping up next to commercial buildings, clubs, and other secular institutions, the storefront and its charismatic services were eminently a phenomenon of urban juxtaposition.[96] Similarly, Merinda Simmons has argued that the Harlem storefront depicted in *Quicksand* borrows heavily from Afro-Caribbean practices of spiritual expression with its emphasis on "ecstatic movement and clamorous music . . . informed by African culture."[97] Drawing on Afro-Caribbean Vodou and other forms of religious expression that privileged female sexuality—and placing them in fluid proximity to urban revivalism in the US—the storefront suggests a space of "amalgamated religious identification[s]," an important site of collective self-determination.[98]

These historical juxtapositions unfold at both a narrative and a formal level in *Quicksand*. Thus from within the elaboration of anthropological detail, Larsen's language again takes on the quality of being beside itself: its rhythmic listing builds to a pitch that echoes and redoubles the "cadenced chant" it represents. Here we might further probe Butler's assertion that the list form ("gender, sexuality, race, class") and those "proverbial commas" suggest spheres that "we have not yet figured out how to think as relations we seek to mark."[99] Without losing sight of the force of this insight—which insists that static juxtaposition is inadequate to the dynamic interarticulation of these identities—we might note that Larsen's lists bear witness to the repetition with a difference that marks the subversive possibilities of the performative, as Butler has elsewhere described it.[100] In their ecstatic excess—the list produces two or three words where one might do, each repeating but also moderating the others (as in "gesticulated, screamed, wept")—Larsen's proverbial commas produce the linguistic break or pause where repetition signals something other than mere reification. In the spirit of Larsen's lists, sexual and religious ecstasies abut and repeat one another without being the same thing.[101] Producing words and bodies quite literally beside themselves, *Quicksand*'s ecstasy queers the list form itself, allowing us to revisit the deep strangeness of that elongated inventory (gender, sexuality, race, class, religion).

That strangeness—which is both linguistic and ritually embodied—emerges in Helga's performance: speaking in tongues marks her "coming out" or entry into the religious community. In its emphasis on the singular soul transformed in the context of exuberant collectivity, the narrative insists on the odd, even irritating quality of this convergence:

> For a single moment she remained there in silent stillness, because she was afraid she was going to be sick. And in that moment she was lost—or saved. The yelling figures about her pressed forward, closing her in on all sides. Maddened, she grasped at the railing, and with no previous intention began to yell like one insane, drowning every other clamor, while torrents of tears streamed down her face. She was unconscious of the words she uttered, or their meaning: "Oh God, mercy, mercy. Have mercy on me!" but she repeated them over and over.[102]

That Helga's conversion is decidedly unwilled and unpleasant (at least at first) marks an important distinction between this delirious sequence and the critical emphasis on expressive pleasure that would read Helga's ecstasy as displaced sexual desire. As the claustrophobia of this passage suggests, discourses of agency (and of sexual self-determination in particular) are inadequate to the task of describing charismatic performance, where God is the agent and glossolalia is by definition anything but the result of individual choice. In Michael Warner's words, "This, undoubtedly, is just why religion is so queer; it's not for fun that we play it."[103] As Warner argues in "Tongues Untied," his narrative of Pentecostal boyhood and queer secular academic adulthood, the analogy between queerness and ecstatic religion works not because they each depend on some innate, unchosen identity. On the contrary, ecstatic conversion—like "coming out" or even losing one's faith—seems to depend on the potential mutability of the self, its repeated rupture and reconfiguration, its ability to be born again and again and again.[104] Thus the (always uneasy) juxtaposition between queerness and charismatic performance works because each troubles the notion of individual agency, contests the space between individual experience and collective identity, and forges alternative forms of togetherness out of exclusion and disidentification.[105]

Again we can see how this quality of being beside unfolds at a formal level, as Larsen's rhythmic listing builds to a pitch that echoes and redoubles the "cadenced chant" it represents. In their ecstatic excess, Larsen's proverbial commas produce a "pregnant" pause or resting place, a rhythm in which repetition might signal something other than mere reification, queering the overdetermined space between sameness and difference. If there is a fantasy of birth without labor here, we can also see the women's writhing and weeping as a form of labor without birth, a labor of relationality that is neither biologically determined nor "chosen" in any straightforward sense. *Quicksand*'s queer enthusiasm unsettles the logic of choice embedded in the overlapping dualisms that structure Helga's narrative (lost or saved, white or black, straight or queer, national or cosmopolitan, moral or immoral). In the storefront, ecstasy functions not merely as a cancellation or disappearance of self but as an active working out of the strangeness of being beside oneself, being multiple, or being collective. To point again to the performative logic of punctuation, Helga Crane is "in that moment lost—or saved," another queerly pregnant pause wherein the dash enacts the refusal to name and determine a connective possibility that is nevertheless entertained or suspended in its spatial and temporal elongation.

The undecidability of this moment is crucial, and *Quicksand* signals the discomforts as much as the possibilities of this eccentric female-centered communion:

> From those about her came a thunder-clap of joy. Arms were stretched towards her with savage frenzy. The women dragged themselves upon their knees or crawled over the floor like reptiles, sobbing and pulling

their hair and tearing off their clothing. Those who succeeded in getting near to her leaned forward to encourage the unfortunate sister, dropping hot tears and beads of sweat upon her bare arms and neck.

The thing became real. A miraculous calm came upon her. Life seemed to expand, and to become very easy. . . . Gradually the room grew quiet and almost solemn, and to the kneeling girl time seemed to sink back into the mysterious grandeur and holiness of far-off simpler centuries.[106]

Helga's conversion occasions a strange proximity between joy and lamentation, rending grief and ecstatic overflow. Affect and effort are no longer figured as Helga's alone but are instead collectively embodied, as tears and sweat exceed individual boundaries, landing on the surface of another exposed skin. This physical proximity or being beside is, as the passage seems to imply, grotesque in multiple senses, registering an extravagance or exaggeration of feeling. And yet it is here that Larsen's prose seems at its most neutral—almost mere reportage—relaying the heights of ecstatic feeling from within the conventions of detached realist narration.

Indeed we might note how closely this scene parallels (without reproducing) William Dean Howells's account in *An Imperative Duty* of the black church to which Rhoda Aldgate drifts in what the novel's narrator describes as a waking "nightmare" of revealed blackness, finding herself amid "the tide of black worshippers."[107] Here we might recall the ways in which Howells's depiction relies on both grotesque sensory overload and an image of lost whiteness as lost bodily incorporation. Overwhelmed to faintness by the "musky exhalations" of the worshippers, Rhoda "beg[ins] to taste the odor"; she struggles to accept the "loss of her former [white] self, like that of the mutilated man who looks where his arm was, and cannot believe it gone."[108] As we've seen, in Howells's novel, ecstasy disaggregates whiteness even as it shores up an essentialist image of black religiosity; ecstasy, in these terms, marks a breakdown in the boundaries of self and sensation that must be quickly restored through Rhoda's marriage to Dr. Olney. Here, too, we might recall Anna Julia Cooper's critique of the leveling effect of religiosity in Howells's novel—its unthinking reification of blackness, another effect of realism's imbrication with technologies of racial reproduction: "Mr. Howells merely meant to press the button and give one picture from American life involving racial complications. The kodak does no more; it cannot preach sermons or solve problems."[109] Juxtaposed with what Cooper identified as Howells's striking insensibility—his failure to perceive the proper order of things—the stakes of *Quicksand*'s own scenes of realist ecstasy come into stark relief.

That both novels depict their mixed-race heroines as subjects of drift marks their relation to what Jennifer Fleissner has described as a key component of naturalist fiction: the depiction of oscillatory, rhythmic, rootless seeking as a serious critique of the historical terms of female intelligibility.[110] Indeed, Fleissner cites Larsen as an important extension of turn-of-the-century naturalism's "central concern: how to think a new kind of human subjectivity in which the tie to embodiment works not to subsume the individual but to produce her (or his) specificity and indeed—to use a Du Boisian term—*striving*."[111] Another way to frame this concern, as we've seen in my reading of *The Autobiography of an Ex-Colored Man*, might be through a reconceptualization of the flesh as a circuit, a site of collective excitation and being-in-motion. Here we might return to Alexander Weheliye's insistence on the flesh as a "force field," "a relational vestibule to alternate ways of being."[112] In his account of flesh as "vestibule"—a communicative entry point or antechamber—Weheliye's theorization echoes the spiritual and aesthetic possibilities of the Black Pentecostal storefront, its own reliance on the flesh as a performative vestibule or entry onto what we might call (following Ashon Crawley) something "otherwise."[113] As Crawley notes, the "otherwise" of Black Pentecostal aesthetics is a refusal of "western time's forward propulsion," and with it, the misrecognition of "otherwise possibilities already enacted, already here."[114] As I've suggested, that misrecognition has been enacted to a great extent in criticism of the novel, in its refusal to see the ecstatic as site for the potential (if never sustained) reordering of the secular terms of embodiment.

It is precisely such "otherwise possibilities" that Crawley unfolds in his reading of Helga's conversion scene as "the choreosonic play of black sociality."[115] While signaling that belief itself is not at stake in this passage, Crawley nevertheless points to the event that unfolds (not least in the stillness of language itself; in Crawley's terms, "Still, something happened").[116] Thus without losing sight of the hint of critique or parody embedded in Larsen's apparently neutral telling—the fact that it is difficult to read the narrator's tone as straight or mocking is itself telling, another juxtaposition—I want to take up Crawley's critical invitation in focusing instead on the conversion or transaction that they signify. That something transacts in and around Helga's unconscious utterance ("Have mercy on me!") is palpable, as the novel exchanges the logic of (conscious) individual agency for collective performance, for the ritualized transaction of being beside. Ecstasy is not proper to the individual: it happens within and between bodies, in the moving circuit of their relation, and hence its challenge to propriety and the proprietary subject. For a while, Helga finds release from the quicksands of secularism—with its rigid Manichaeisms—in the collectivity of the storefront church, as material vestibule, entry point, or refuge. For a while, time itself is launched backward into unspecified simpler, holier times: an expansive, ecstatic, queer temporality that (however temporary) resists the complex constrictions and immobility of the present.[117] For a while, for Helga, the thing becomes real. It will, by the end of the novel, become unreal; as *Quicksand* teaches us, the real is queer that way.

That what I've been calling "ecstatic moments" in *Quicksand* are precisely moments—queer episodes that seem to expand and/or condense time, disrupting linear narrative progression but also just as quickly slipping away—suggests their ambivalent status in the novel. For if Helga's ecstasy produces an alternate way of being a body in public, a stranger, potentially less restrictive form of sociality, it does not release her unequivocally from the asphyxiations of secularism. Rather, the nonendurance of ecstasy is a (realist) realization to which Helga repeatedly returns: "If she remembered that she had had something like this feeling before, she put the unwelcome memory from her with the thought: 'This time I know I'm right. This time it will last.'"[118] Later, after her marriage to the Reverend Pleasant Green, Helga figures satisfaction (notably) as having found a body: "Here, she had found, she was sure, the intangible thing for which, indefinitely, always she had craved. It had received embodiment."[119] The feeling doesn't last, in part because fixed and violent embodiment (as I've shown) is precisely what Helga Crane, in ecstasy, seeks to displace. It is, surely, the temporal or temporariness of ecstasy that has made it so difficult for critics to read ecstasy in *Quicksand* as anything other than bad faith. Yet spending a little time with bad faith, as *Quicksand* does—allowing for the ways in which it literally gives us pause or offers a break in the forward-lurching movement of Western modernity—may help us better recognize the imbrications of ecstasy with other queer temporalities, and the non-sense or alternative forms of sensemaking to which they give rise. Not the least because taking ecstasy seriously helps bring the dominant rhythms of the secular into relief.

If we might read the secular, at least in part, as a performative suturing of discordant temporalities—a way of stitching together heterogeneous understandings and experiences of time under the sign of modernity—*Quicksand* points to the pain of this suturing. As we've seen, there are important ways in which queer theory enables us to read the novel's critique of a secular world that demands linear progress in part through the sacralized, cyclical time of motherhood, even as it refuses (still) to recognize a future in which black children, too, might come unto the Lord.[120] Repeatedly in the novel, as Helga contemplates the irony of motherhood in America, she frames "giving birth" to black children as a "sin": "More black folk to suffer indignities. More dark bodies for mobs to lynch" and, later, "Why *do* Negroes have children? Surely it must be sinful."[121] In the context of American racial and sexual violence (in many cases) perfectly calibrated to white Christianity, the novel frames embodiment itself—and the giving body to others—as a "sin." Even so, Helga Crane's refusal of racial motherhood is not a refusal of the body as such but a refusal of its normative and instrumental temporality under the terms of secularism; for a while, ecstasy's queerness offers a way of being a body in motion without "receiving embodiment," or being the subject *of* a body, always subject to racial and sexual violence.

By the end of the novel, when Helga has been "used up" by the labor of bearing four children in quick succession, her "queer feeling of enthusiasm" has significantly diminished: "Her mind, swaying back to the protection that religion had afforded her, almost she wished that it had not failed her. An illusion. Yes. But better, far better, than this terrible reality. Religion had, after all, its uses. It blunted the perceptions. Robbed life of its crudest truths. Especially it had its uses for the poor—and the blacks."[122] Here we are returned to a familiar critique of religion as psychic and bodily regulation: even at its most pragmatic, belief blunts reality's hard edges, departs from the biting truth of poverty and systematic racial oppression. As Helga realizes—racked by the agonizing, repetitive time of childbearing—the delay embedded in the conviction of heavenly "recompense" constitutes one more version of staying put, the belief in the "white man's God" working in tandem with secular white racism.[123] Recognizing in her own critical realization the return of displeasure and dissatisfaction, Helga resists in terms that play up the ironic imbrications between spiritual contentment and bodily regulation: she determines that the suffocations of childbirth are "not to be borne. Again."[124] By the final pages of *Quicksand*, the fugitive spiritual possibility of rebirth has become a physical imperative. As Larsen's syntax indicates, this is a deathly bargain. Here we find the comma-heavy queerness of being beside (or being born, again) punctuated with a full stop: "It was so hard to think out a feasible way of retrieving all these agreeable, desired things. Just then. Later. When she got up. By and by. She must rest. Get strong. Sleep."[125] Circumscribing the Christian promise ("by and by") with a hard rest, the period enters us, ironically, into a gendered cyclical time from which there is (presumably) no relief ("Pie—by and by. That's the trouble.")[126] And if the novel closes, ominously, with another birth—a fifth delivery that (we imagine) will surely mean Helga's death—it nevertheless rejects the straight satisfaction of a definitive ending.

Now to Begin

They must be re-born again, and here is precisely the
difficulty.
—M. E. Strieby, "The Look Forward"

Early on, leaving Naxos on the train, Helga wonders, "Could she get a berth?"—and the rest of the novel seems to wring or ring out this lingering pun.[127] Born the daughter of a white Danish woman and a black American man, Helga is in fact born again and again in *Quicksand*: in Chicago, in New York, in Amsterdam, in the Harlem storefront, and finally in Alabama, where the promise and the trauma of rebirth are nearly the same thing. If the ecstasy of the storefront church enables physical abandon through spiritual compulsion, the community to which Helga is confined at the end of the novel demands the opposite, figuring maternity's physical compulsions as the way to spiritual freedom. *Quicksand* depicts religious expression as this "cross" or chiasmus, insisting on the proximity between repressive forms of spiritual administration—which have their own strict temporalities—and the "queer sort of satisfaction" emerging from moments of ecstatic abandon. The novel's "realism," I might argue, lives in this proximity: in the ongoing work of bearing and being born, of being with or beside ("They were all black together," Helga thinks of herself and her children).[128] Which might be another way of saying that the ecstatic, in *Quicksand* as in realism more broadly, is not a form of transcendence but rather an immanent otherwise: a way of imagining being singular and plural, not so much in the by and by as in the here and now, where "here" and "now" are also otherwise.

In an 1885 essay called "The Look Forward," Rev. M. E. Strieby (secretary of the American Missionary Association) rehearsed what we have seen as a familiar association of blackness with "natural" religiosity: "They are religious by nature. . . . They have been born again, 'coming through,' as they call it, after having had visions and dreams, in which they have been hung over hell and then wafted to Heaven, and yet with their vices untouched. To preach to them against stealing, lying and licentiousness is still unacceptable, for, as the old colored man said, 'it throws a coldness over the meetin.'"[129] The solution, as Strieby figured it, was to be "re-born again" (the solution was also, he suggested with all the weight of institutional authority, segregated churches). By 1929, *Quicksand* could ironically inhabit this imperative, offering an immanent critique of its directive to be "re-born again" while finding a queer, surreptitious, or fugitive sort of birth/berth within this structure of repetition. This particular achievement of the novel has gone largely unrecognized. Yet it makes possible, for example, a similar sense of queer possibility within the "born again" in James Baldwin's 1952 novel, *Go Tell It on the Mountain*; indeed we might point to Baldwin's novel as the queer child of Larsen's, insofar as it locates ecstasy as a form of fugitivity (and singularity) within and alongside the collective. In his reading of Baldwin's novel, Shane Vogel points to the ecstasy of John Grimes—the novel's queer protagonist—as a form of "cruising utopia," reading through Muñoz, Nancy, Baldwin, and (I would argue) Larsen to ecstasy as an understanding of the body itself as an "ex-tension":

"Through such movement—a spacing and an opening that is nothing other than the body—we are able to be other to ourselves and to be with others."[130] Ecstasy, being beside, is an immanent touching or communing—a general communicability that realism at once recognizes and tries to contain. In Larsen's and, later, Baldwin's cases, being "born again" is not a solution but a performative enactment (of singular existence, of collectivity). Which is why it remains, in both *Quicksand* and *Go Tell It on the Mountain*, unfinished—a kind of pregnant pause in an otherwise unrelenting motion: "Yet, as he moved among them, their hands touching, and tears falling, and the music rising—as though he moved down a great hall, full of splendid company—something began to knock in that listening, astonished, newborn, and fragile heart of his; something recalling the terrors of the night, which were not finished; his heart seemed to say; which, in this company, were now to begin."[131]

Coda

Behind, Before, Beside

Ecstasy abuts terror. If realism teaches us anything, it teaches us this. Rather than rehearsing fantasies of transcendence—of getting *beyond* histories of racial slavery, colonialism, genocide, and removal—ecstasy signals our being beside and within them. In ecstasy, bodies are transported, seized, possessed. From the "creeping strangeness" of Jim Conklin's gestures to Helga Crane's "involuntary" conversion, realism's performances of spiritual compulsion serve as striking testimony to the lingering question of black freedom after Reconstruction. Similarly, the realist reenactment of indigenous practices like the Ghost Dance bespeaks realism's effort to both check the power of contagious mass feeling and materialize the ghosts of colonial violence. Realism, in other words, is everywhere haunted by the frenzy it tries to contain or forget. Naturalizing racial and spiritual boundaries as part of its steadfast attention to the material world, realist practice nevertheless remains strikingly animated by ecstasy's occluded histories of violence. In this sense, realist ecstasy testifies to the temporal *besideness* of these histories, their haunting absence as well as their ongoing and often spectacular presence.

To approach realism with an eye for such hauntings is to encounter a set of practices deeply linked to the affective life of Jim Crow, in which proportions of blood and feeling were closely measured, and where the maintenance of racial boundaries was (and is) utterly interwoven with secularism's delineation of good and bad religion, immanence, and transcendence. Rather than a break from realism's secular imaginary, then, we must understand ecstasy as utterly central to it—and to the frenzied bodily semiotics of Jim Crow with which it was closely aligned. To be beside oneself under Jim Crow was to move with and against its violently proscribed repertoires of race, religion, gender, and sexuality. As we have seen, realism could and often did consolidate such repertoires. Here we might think back to Rhoda Aldgate, nearly suffocated by the excessive fleshiness and sensory turbulence of the black church in William Dean Howells's *An Imperative Duty*, a depiction almost certainly informed by popular accounts of black revivals as scenes of minstrel mimicry and sensory amalgamation. Yet realism could also bring the choreographies of post-Reconstruction secularism into striking relief. In this sense, we might think of James Weldon Johnson's anonymous ex-colored man, whose decision to pass signals a flight from the very real proximity between ecstasy and terror under Jim Crow, where race simultaneously determines and is determined by whether and how the boundaries of the individual body might be spiritually or materially transgressed.

While ecstasy names an out-of-body experience, in other words, it more often manifests the pleasures and dangers of being in a body, with and beside others. And if, as we have seen, the ecstatic body presents an unruly archive of past and present harms, it also becomes the site of a powerful "(counter)investment," where histories of possession and objectification might be performatively rescripted as ecstatic collectivity, a "tumultuous derangement" of the secular order of things.[1] In the post-Reconstruction era, that secular order—what W. E. B. Du Bois called a "new religion of whiteness"—constituted a form of separate but equal religious pluralism that reinforced the hegemony of white Protestantism and underwrote its colonial projects, constructing religious and racial difference in tandem while securing secular progress through the enforced obsolescence of "primitive" religions and peoples. Realist representations of ecstasy could and often did serve such projects, as the ostensible backwardness of embodied religion worked to reinforce the modernity of its observers. But in its troubling of the relationship between "body" and "experience," ecstasy could also assume a body whose *ex-stasis* exceeds realism's effort to fix the meaning of racialized flesh. Adjacent but not reducible to the logic of terror, ecstasy in such moments transmits a fundamental or ontological togetherness, a subterranean or surreal communicability at the very heart of the real.

Realism's fictions of autonomy, in other words, were always just that: fictions, haunted by what they never completely forget. So in the spirit of doubling back—a spirit this book has tried everywhere to catch or inhabit—consider once more the "frenzied women" that surround Helga Crane in the storefront church, in what *Quicksand* describes as a Bacchic performance: "Behind her, before her, beside her, frenzied women gesticulated, screamed, wept, and tottered to the praying of the preacher, which had gradually become a cadenced chant. When at last he ended, another took up the plea in the same moaning chant, and then another. It went on and on without pause with the persistence of some unconquerable faith exalted beyond time and reality."[2] In *Quicksand*, the potential for ecstatic self-loss is most often circumscribed by all the attending forms of loss written into the history of enforced embodiment. Read in such terms, the storefront, with its distinctly indecorous collectivity, might seem to offer only a temporary break from what the novel depicts as a suffocating regime of racial and sexual legibility. But read otherwise, the performance signals ecstatic abundance, as bodies and words beside themselves ("behind her, before her, beside her . . . gesticulated, screamed, wept, and tottered") exceed and trouble the singularity Helga seeks and from which she suffers. Together, the "frenzied women" enact a fundamental *besideness*, where what lies behind Helga is also what lies before her, as history and as future. Another, and then another, on and on: a collectivity-in-motion, in *ex-stasis*, defined less by static ties than by radical ongoingness, a persistent presence in and beyond the regime of the real.

ACKNOWLEDGMENTS

This book was written with and beside others. Its very existence is testimony to my inordinate good fortune in being surrounded by generous friends, family, colleagues, mentors, editors, and readers. What follows is a radically incomplete list of those who have buoyed me, kept me company in these pages, and sustained my faith in this book and its intellectual project.

My thanks first and foremost to my family, for teaching me everything I know about what it means to care deeply for others and to expand that circle of care at every turn. Paula Reckson—my dearest teacher and interlocutor—thank you for the profound gift of being with my babies while I was with this book. Like me, it quite simply would not be possible without you. Charlie Reckson, you resonate for me through everything; thank you for the many lessons in flying and falling. Samantha Reckson, thank you for the never-ending gifts of laughter and sibling camaraderie; I love you for everything you are. To Madeline, Charles, and David Leavitt, thank you for welcoming me into your family and for championing me and my work always. Judy Goldman, thank you for giving me my first glimpse of what it might look like to make a life in words.

I can trace the earliest inklings of this project back to my time as an undergraduate at NYU, where Elaine Freedgood, Cyrus Patell, and Ross Posnock first helped me recognize myself as a scholar. Their early belief in me and ongoing support of my work has meant everything. Bryan Waterman let me into a class I had no business taking and introduced me to Joseph Roach's *Cities of the Dead*, which transformed my sense of how history lives in and through the body. I will always be grateful for the formative and world-expanding conversations I had with George Schulman in a political theory reading group that continues to shape my thinking. In a very real sense, I learned how to read literature from Roger Deakins, whose memory I cherish and whose enthusiasm still suffuses any sense I have of prosody.

At Princeton I found a community that continues to sustain me. Daphne Brooks, Eduardo Cadava, and William Gleason saw and cultivated the best of this work, even in its earliest, most confused, and fledgling stages. They also modeled for me a life of scholarship rooted in a deeply ethical and loving commitment to one's students. I will never repay their patience and generosity, but I strive to reenact it daily in my own teaching. Diana Fuss and Alexandra Vazquez similarly provided me with models of radical brilliance combined with radical care—their beautiful and humane attention to the details continually inspires me. This project was in many ways born from conversations I was lucky to be part of in the faculty-graduate seminar at Princeton's Center for African American Studies (now the Department of African American Studies), the Center for the Study of Religion, and the Program in American Studies. I thank each of these programs for grants that supported my research, with particular thanks to Valerie Smith, Jenny Wiley Legath, and Hendrik Hartog. An Arthur P. Morgan Fellowship and a Charlotte Elizabeth Procter Fellowship also supported my graduate studies. I am grateful to Sarah Rivett and Gregory Jackson for convening a reading group on secularisms during my time at Princeton that shaped my early inquiry in the field. I learned and continue to learn a great deal from a truly fabulous group of religion scholars at Princeton who graciously welcomed me as an interloper. My thanks especially to R. Marie Griffith, Rachel Gross, Nicole Kirk, Rachel Lindsay, Emily Mace, Anthony Petro, Leigh Schmidt, and Judith Weisenfeld for patiently teaching me how to do religious studies. It has been one of my greatest joys to move through this profession alongside a fiercely brilliant cohort of graduate school friends and compatriots. My thanks to Adrienne Brown, Alicia Christoff, Michelle Coghlan, Nadia Ellis, Erin Forbes, Rachel Galvin, Briallen Hopper, Evan Kindley, Greg Londe, Anne Hirsch Moffitt, and Sonya Posmentier, without whom I would not have made it through.

A formative two years as a postdoctoral fellow at the University of Texas at Austin allowed me to imagine what I really wanted this book to be, and I remain exceptionally grateful for that gift of time. My thanks to Phillip Barrish, Chad Bennett, Brian Bremen, Mia Carter, Evan Carton, Elizabeth Cullingford, Ann Cvetkovitch, Brian Doherty, Neville Hoad, Martin Kevorkian, Julia H. Lee, Allen MacDuffie, Lisa Moore,

Gretchen Murphy, Wayne Rebhorn, Snehal Shingavi, and Jennifer Wilks for their immense generosity and collegiality. Special thanks to J. K. Barrett and Heather Houser, whose friendship and support at crucial moments enabled me to finish this book. During my time at UT, Wayne Lesser was a source of constant encouragement and exceptional kindness, and I miss him dearly. I was lucky to overlap in Austin with Gabrielle Calvocoressi and Angeline Shaka, who always inspire me. And I am so thankful that my Texas family now includes Lindsay Olinde, Joseph Kugler, Marie Kugler, and Cora Kugler, who make everything more joyful.

I have had the greatest fortune in landing amid a group of stunningly brilliant, kind, and supportive colleagues at Haverford College, who have mentored me in ways large and small. My thanks especially to Kimberly Benston, Frances Blase, Tom Devaney, Stephen Finley, Andrew Friedman, Linda Gerstein, Juli Grigsby, Christina Knight, Ken Koltun-Fromm, Laura McGrane, Maud McInerney, Jerry Miller, Rajeswari Mohan, Jaclyn Pryor, Deborah Roberts, Debora Sherman, Terry Snyder, Asali Solomon, Gustavus Stadler, Jill Stauffer, Christina Zwarg, David Watt, and Terrance Wiley. The Tri-Co Working Group in American Studies has been a crucial source of intellectual community; I am thankful to Lara Cohen, Travis Foster, Jennifer Harford-Vargas, Gina Patnaik, and Bethany Schneider for their part in these conversations, from which I have learned so much. More than anyone, Alison Cook-Sather helped me navigate the transition to teaching at a liberal arts college; I am thankful for her timely reminders that teaching is a never-ending process of becoming. Sarah Horowitz, Jeremiah Mercurio, and Semyon Khokhlov provided (and continue to provide) crucial support for my research and teaching. Grants from the Office of the Provost and the Hurford Humanities Center allowed me to complete my research at the National Anthropological Archives and to share this work at a number of conferences around the country. As this book was nearing completion, I had the privilege of serving as a Faculty Fellow in Visual Culture, Arts, and Media, where I was lucky to share space and ideas with Stephanie Bursese, Matthew Callinan, Courtney Carter, Noemí Fernández, Vicky Funari, John Muse, Kerry Nelson, Kent Watson, and James Weissinger. Conversations with students in my courses at Haverford have deeply informed this book, and I am especially thankful for the contributions of my research assistants, Emma Lumeij and Emily Chazen. Very special thanks to Katy Adair, Laura Been, Lou Charkoudian, Molly Farneth, and Erin Schoneveld, dazzling scholars and friends who have made parenting on the tenure track into a team sport. I feel very lucky to be part of the team.

It has been an immense privilege to get to share portions of this book with colleagues I admire deeply and who have helped me see its strengths and flaws more clearly. Among the friends I am always writing to and with, Erica Fretwell, Nicholas Gaskill, and Phillip Maciak are foremost. Thank you for being my ideal readers, for bringing out the best in this work, and for inspiring me toward ever more capacious models of scholarly generosity. Whether in person or on the page, being in your company is a tremendous joy. Tanaz Moghadam and Patrick Taurel, thank you for listening to me talk about this book for so many years, and for being such beautiful friends and humans. I am grateful to the Southern California Americanist Group for the intellectual community while in Los Angeles, and especially to Aaron DeRosa, Bert Emerson, Greta LaFleur, Sharon Oster, Stefanie Sobelle, and Kyla Wazana Tompkins. My thanks as well to the American Literature Working Group at Penn for offering me the chance to share my research on the Ghost Dance, with particular thanks to David Kazanjian, Keyana Parks, Evelyn Soto, and Mary Zaborskis. At various stages in the life of this project, my ideas have been nourished by conversations with Nancy Bentley, Carrie Tirado Bramen, Todd Carmody, Kristen Case, Peter Coviello, Ashon Crawley, Brad Evans, Tracy Fessenden, Kathi Kern, Jennifer Fleissner, Elizabeth Freeman, Michael Gillespie, Brian Hochman, John Kilgore, Laura Levitt, Kathryn Lofton, Molly McGarry, John Modern, Justine Murison, Emily Ogden, Sally Promey, Joan Richardson, Michael Robertson, Jess Row, Britt Rusert, Nick Salvato, Kyla Schuller, Donovan Schaefer, Kate Stanley, Pamela Thurschwell, Priscilla Wald, Alys Eve Weinbaum, and Autumn Womack. Fred Moten read this book at a crucial moment in its development, saw the best of what it might be, and offered me the gift of feedback that cuts through the messy details of execution and straight to the core of writerly hope and intention. To Fred and to my two anonymous readers at NYU Press, who each pressed me to refine the project in important ways, I am profoundly grateful.

It has been a joy to work with Eric Zinner and Dolma Ombadykow at NYU Press, and I am thankful for their steady guidance throughout. My thanks to Sam Martin for treating my manuscript with such care, and to Nicholas Carbonaro for his support and design expertise. Stephanie Batiste, Robin Bernstein, and Brian Herrera are truly a dream team of editors and have fostered this project in the most generous and rigorous ways possible. I am especially grateful to them for convening the "American Studies in Performance" seminar at the Radcliffe Institute for Advanced Study in 2017, where I had conversations that significantly shaped my revision process. My deepest thanks to Julius Fleming, Donatella Galella, Koritha Mitchell, and Rebecca Schneider, my fellow workshop participants who read this work with tremendous care and helped me see where to go next.

This book would not have been possible without the labor and assistance of archivists. I am grateful to Joe Struble at the George Eastman House for pointing me toward William Van der Weyde's retouched images, allowing me to consider the relationship between reenactment and photographic retouching. My thanks as well to Judith Gray at the American Folklife Center, to Gina Rappaport and Daisy Njoku at the National Anthropological Archives, and to Greg French of Greg French Early Photography. My humblest thanks to Max Bear and Fred Mosqueda, representatives of the Cheyenne and Arapaho, for permission to reprint James Mooney's photographs of the Ghost Dance and for trusting me to tell the truth about them.

Fellowships from the American Council of Learned Societies and the Huntington Library made it possible to complete significant portions of this book, for which I am inordinately grateful. Early versions of chapters 2 and 3 appeared as "A 'Reg'lar Jim Dandy': Archiving Ecstatic Performance in Stephen Crane," *Arizona Quarterly* 68, no. 1 (Spring 2012), and "Touching a Button," *American Literature* 88, no. 1 (March 2016). A small portion of chapter 3 also appeared as "William Vander Weyde, Leon F. Czolgosz, McKinley Assassin," Object Narrative, in *Conversations: An Online Journal of the Center for the Study of Material and Visual Cultures of Religion Journal* (2014). My thanks to Johns Hopkins University Press, Duke University Press, and the Center for the Study of Material and Visual Cultures of Religion at Yale University for their permission to reprint portions of these articles.

This book is for Ben Leavitt, my love and fellow traveler. Thank you for the beautiful details of our life together, for our magnificent daughters, and for making this work possible in every sense. It is also for Ada Evans Leavitt and Maxine Rainer Leavitt, who kept me company in utero during the writing of much of this book and who delayed its completion in the happiest ways possible. Being beside you is my greatest joy.

NOTES

INTRODUCTION: BEING BESIDE

1. As I signal later, I am borrowing here from Ann Pellegrini's important question, "What does secularism feel like?" Pellegrini, "Feeling Secular," 205.
2. Crane, *Monster*, 438.
3. Jacqueline Goldsby's work has been absolutely fundamental to this unraveling, as she charts the ways in which *The Monster* references but also abstracts the details of the 1892 lynching of Robert Lewis in Port Jervis, New York. See Goldsby, *Spectacular Secret*, 125–132.
4. Chesnutt, *Marrow of Tradition*, 80.
5. See Holland, *Raising the Dead*; Castronovo, *Necro Citizenship*.
6. I take inspiration here from Ashon Crawley's important articulation of the work of "otherwise possibilities": "Otherwise, as word—otherwise possibilities, as phrase—announces the fact of infinite alternatives to what is.... Otherwise possibilities exist alongside that which we can detect with our finite sensual capacities." Crawley, *Blackpentecostal Breath*, 2.
7. As film scholar Catherine Russell has argued, in ecstasy "the body becomes the signifier of that which has no referent," thus posing a significant challenge to the visual regimes of realism, with their reliance on (and production of) empirical data. Russell, "Ecstatic Ethnography," 286.
8. I draw here on Amy Kaplan's influential account of realism as "an enormous act of construction to organize, re-form, and control the social world." Kaplan, *Social Construction of American Realism*, 10.
9. See, for example, Gregory Jackson's account of realism as deeply indebted to the spiritual logic of (white) Protestant homiletics, which structure its epistemological and perceptual coordinates. As Jackson argues, realist homiletics "engage the material through experiential templates in an effort to illuminate the spiritual conditions of the real that reside beyond the empirical." Jackson, *Word and Its Witness*, 13.
10. Spillers, "Moving on Down the Line," 90.
11. The regime of secular-linear time I describe here is also a version of what Dana Luciano terms "chronobiopolitics," or "the sexual arrangement of the time of life," a technique of temporal and sexual population management. Luciano, *Arranging Grief*, 9.
12. Gordon, *Ghostly Matters*, xvi.

13. Modern, *Secularism in Antebellum America*, xxxiv.
14. Hartman, *Scenes of Subjection*, 115.
15. Ibid., 116.
16. I understand the opacity of the ecstatic in large part through Hartman's articulation of the significance—and subversive power—of the opacity of black performance under slavery. See Hartman, *Scenes of Subjection*, 36. I am grateful to Erica Fretwell for this connection.
17. Or similarly (with John Lardas Modern, riffing on Charles Taylor), "How does it feel to live within a secular age?" Pellegrini, "Feeling Secular," 205; Modern, *Secularism in Antebellum America*, 3.
18. See, for example, Asad, *Formations of the Secular*; Cady and Fessenden, *Religion, the Secular*; Coviello and Hickman, "Introduction"; Jakobsen and Pellegrini, *Secularisms*; Kahn and Lloyd, *Race and Secularism*; Mahmood, "Religious Reason"; Mahmood, *Politics of Piety*; Mahmood, *Religious Difference*; Pecora, *Secularization and Cultural Criticism*.
19. Pellegrini, "Feeling Secular," 210.
20. Jakobsen and Pellegrini, *Secularisms*, 12.
21. See, in particular, Fessenden, "Problem of the Postsecular"; Stein, "Angels in (Mexican) America."
22. McGarry, *Ghosts of Futures Past*, 5.
23. Modern, *Secularism in Antebellum America*, 6.
24. Taylor, *Secular Age*, 299–300; Modern, *Secularism in Antebellum America*, 6.
25. Modern, *Secularism in Antebellum America*, 12.
26. Williams, *Marxism and Literature*, 133–134.
27. Fanon, *Black Skin, White Masks*, 92.
28. In addition to those cited below, I am also drawing from Goldschmidt and McAlister, *Race, Nation*; Hickman, *Black Prometheus*; and Prentiss, *Religion and the Creation*.
29. Lloyd, "Introduction," 7.
30. Ibid., 7; Kahn, "Conclusion," 244.
31. Alexander, *Pedagogies of Crossing*, 296.
32. On the ways in which black success after emancipation was (and continues to be) met with reactionary violence, see Mitchell, *Living with Lynching*; Mitchell, "Identifying White Mediocrity."
33. Goldsby, *Spectacular Secret*, 102.
34. On the intersections between realism and an emergent discourse of pluralistic "cultures" across a range of turn-of-the-century disciplines, see Elliott, *Culture Concept*; Bramen, *Uses of Variety*.
35. Masuzawa, *Invention of World Religions*, 19.
36. Ibid., 20.
37. Smith, *Relating Religion*, 188.
38. See Wenger, *We Have a Religion*, 14–15.
39. Ibid., 20.

40. Jameson, *Antinomies*, 5.
41. See, for example, Barrish, *American Literary Realism*; Bentley, *Frantic Panoramas*; Glazener, *Reading for Realism*; Dawson, *Emotional Reinventions*; Kaplan, *Social Construction of American Realism*; Thrailkill, *Affecting Fictions*; Warren, *Black and White Strangers*. Kaplan, in particular, points to the ways in which "by containing the threat of social change, realistic narratives also register those desires which undermine the closure of that containment." Kaplan, *Social Construction of American Realism*, 10.
42. Glazener, *Reading for Realism*, 13 (emphasis mine).
43. James, *Varieties of Religious Experience*, 417.
44. Thrailkill, *Affecting Fictions*, 37.
45. Jameson, *Antinomies*, 65. On realism's move away from sympathetic identification and toward a broader effort to map and classify the diversity of human emotion, see Dawson, *Emotional Reinventions*.
46. Ibid., 155.
47. Ibid., 42.
48. I am indebted to Fred Moten for this point.
49. Taylor, *Archive and the Repertoire*, 26.
50. Roach, *Cities of the Dead*, 27.
51. Ibid., 2.
52. Taylor, *Archive and the Repertoire*, 143. In tracking performance beyond the status of the "live," Taylor revises Peggy Phelan's important claim that performance's ontology rests in its capacity to disappear. I explore this claim in further detail in chapters 2 and 3. See Phelan, *Unmarked*.
53. Taylor, *Archive and the Repertoire*, 143.
54. Brooks, *Bodies in Dissent*, 10. See Hartman, *Scenes of Subjection*.
55. Schechner, *Between Theater & Anthropology*, 35.
56. Gotman, *Choreomania*, 3.
57. Pellegrini, "Feeling Secular," 212.
58. Crawley, *Blackpentecostal Breath*, 2.
59. Stevenson, *Life Beside Itself*, 2.
60. Ibid.
61. Butler, *Precarious Life*, 24 (emphasis original).
62. Nancy, *Being Singular Plural*, 70.
63. Ibid., 71 (emphasis original).
64. Ibid.
65. Crawley, *Blackpentecostal Breath*, 20.
66. Spillers, "Moving on Down the Line," 98; Alexander, *Pedagogies of Crossing*, 328; Muñoz, *Cruising Utopia*, 185.
67. West, *Prophetic Fragments*, 161–162. As Albert Raboteau points out, in the antebellum period, the "egalitarian tendency[ies]" of evangelical revivalism could produce "occasions of mutual influence across racial boundaries whereby blacks converted whites and whites converted blacks in the heat of revival fervor,"

though such occasions did not themselves often convert the logic of spiritual equality into a sustained argument for white Southerners against the enslavement of fellow Christians. Raboteau, *Slave Religion*, 151.
68. Sedgwick, *Touching Feeling*, 13.
69. Ibid., 8.
70. Nyong'o, "Race, Reenactment," 89. See also Schneider, *Performing Remains*.
71. Muñoz, *Cruising Utopia*, 186.
72. Pecora, *Secularization and Cultural Criticism*, 22.
73. See, for example, Goldschmidt and McAlister, *Race, Nation*; Hickman, *Black Prometheus*; Kidd, *Forging of the Races*; Prentiss, *Religion and the Creation*; Sernett, *Bound for the Promised Land*; Sorett, *Spirit in the Dark*; Weisenfeld, *New World A-Coming*.
74. Stein, "Angels in (Mexican) America," 684.
75. Gordon, *Ghostly Matters*, 27.
76. I am drawing here on Shane Vogel's important articulation of the body as an "extension," to which I return in chapter 5: "Through such movement—a spacing and an opening that is nothing other than the body—we are able to be other to ourselves and to be with others." Vogel, "Touching Ecstasy," 54.

CHAPTER 1. RECONSTRUCTING SECULARISMS

1. Howells, *Imperative Duty*, 86. As Jeffory Clymer observes, "This is a particularly telling metaphor in the years when thousands of Civil War amputees were still daily visible," a metaphor in which "the 'mutilated' body also foreshadows how Rhoda's 'blackness' will be reified and narrativized in American culture as . . . an embodied disruption of the white norm." Clymer, "Race and the Protocol," 46. An important corollary to Howells's depiction of whiteness as a phantom limb is the post-Reconstruction depiction of a newly enfranchised black citizenry as "grafted" onto the national body; as Saidiya Hartman notes, "The description of black citizenship as a foreign appendage grafted onto the national body bespeaks the anxieties about amalgamation attendant to the enfranchisement of blacks." Hartman, *Scenes of Subjection*, 165.
2. James, *Principles of Psychology*, 210.
3. Ibid., 207.
4. Howells, *Imperative Duty*, 86–87.
5. Ibid., 67.
6. Ibid. In Harper's *Iola Leroy* (1892), for example, Dr. Latrobe asserts to Dr. Gresham his ability to detect such an occult "taint of blood": "There are tricks of blood which always betray them. My eyes are more practiced than yours. I can always tell them" (215). Readers are fully aware of the irony of this assertion, which is underlined in a subsequent chapter, "Dr. Latrobe's Mistake."
7. Howells also offers, in such moments, a distinctly privatized vision of how to deal with Jim Crow. See Birnbaum, "Racial Hysteria," 14.
8. Howells, *Imperative Duty*, 111.

9. Ibid., 115.
10. Ibid., 55.
11. As Michele Birnbaum has noted, this shift "mov[es] the mulatta from genre type to case study, from 'tragic' to 'hysterical figure,'" as female hysteria itself becomes a form of "racial dis-ease." Birnbaum, "Racial Hysteria," 8–9.
12. Howells, *Imperative Duty*, 121.
13. Du Bois, "Howells and Black Folk," 1147. On the relationship between Howellsian realism and Du Bois's account of double consciousness, see Wonham, "Howells, Du Bois," 136.
14. See, in particular, Asad, *Formations of the Secular*; Cady and Fessenden, *Religion, the Secular*; Coviello and Hickman, "Introduction"; Jacobsen and Pellegrini, *Secularisms*; Kahn and Lloyd, *Race and Secularism*; Mahmood, "Religious Reason"; Mahmood, *Politics of Piety*; Mahmood, *Religious Difference*; Pecora, *Secularization and Cultural Criticism*.
15. Lloyd, "Introduction," 7.
16. See Birnbaum, "Racial Hysteria," 8.
17. My thinking here is indebted to Todd Carmody's crucial excavation of the relationship between racial uplift and discourses of disability in the post-Reconstruction era. As Carmody demonstrates, an emergent legal and cultural discourse of handicap and rehabilitation was everywhere mapped onto the Progressive era's multiform projects of racial uplift, and "efforts to imagine African-American advance were shaped by the social, legal, and institutional developments that produced rehabilitation as both discourse and practice." Carmody, "In Spite of Handicaps," 58.
18. Modern, *Secularism in Antebellum America*, 21–22.
19. See Fessenden, *Culture and Redemption*; McGarry, *Ghosts of Futures Past*; Sorett, *Spirit in the Dark*.
20. Shulman, "White Supremacy and Black Insurgency," 37.
21. In describing race and religion as "co-constituting" categories, I follow Jared Hickman, who insists on the participial form "in order to highlight the historical fact that the category of 'religion,' no less than that of 'race,' was . . . an ongoing production of the metacosmic imagination sparked by global cultural encounter." Hickman, *Black Prometheus*, 50.
22. In making this argument, I am building on Frances Smith Foster's crucial account of the ways in which secularist literary history has largely misrecognized the contributions of Frances Ellen Watkins Harper and others who wrote predominantly for the Afro-Protestant press. As Foster notes, "Frances Harper's subordination of literature to serve a militant religion that she called Christianity did not obviate her concern for technique or talent. Rather it led her to seek out new ways in which the truths might be told and Christian soldiers might be enlisted." Foster, "Gender, Genre, and Vulgar Secularism," 55.
23. Wonham, "Howells, Du Bois," 138.
24. Ibid., 127.

25. Not least by Du Bois himself. On Du Bois as a sociologist of religion, see Zuckerman, *Du Bois on Religion*.
26. James, *Varieties of Religious Experience*, 156.
27. Howells, *Imperative Duty*, 89–90.
28. Ibid., 90.
29. Fretwell, *What We Feel*.
30. I borrow this sense of the choreosonic from Ashon Crawley, as the "interconnected concept of movement and sound" in black shout traditions. Crawley, *Blackpentecostal Breath*, 93.
31. Warren, *Black and White Strangers*, 66.
32. Ibid.
33. Crane, "Fears Realists Must Wait" (emphasis mine).
34. On questions of realism and emotional proportion in Howells, see Dawson, *Emotional Reinventions*, 39; Barton, "Howells's Rhetoric of Realism."
35. On Riis's discourse of contagion, see Wald, *Contagious*, 115–117. On Riis's Protestant vision, see Jackson, *Word and Its Witness*, 215–221, 249–276.
36. Hartman, *Scenes of Subjection*, 168.
37. Evans, *Burden of Black Religion*, 65.
38. Lincoln and Mamiya, *Black Church*, 54; Buel, *Mysteries and Miseries*, 498. On the growth of independent black denominations and religious organizations in this period, see Lincoln and Mamiya, *Black Church*; Higginbotham, *Righteous Discontent*; Sernett, *Bound for the Promised Land*; Best, *Passionately Human*; Weisenfeld, *New World A-Coming*.
39. Buel, *Mysteries and Miseries*, 507–509.
40. Ibid., 10.
41. Spillers, "Moving on Down the Line," 98.
42. Glaude's "structure of ambivalence" offers an important revision of Du Bois's "double life" and of the language of psychic pathology on which it drew. As Glaude notes, "I am more inclined to think about the ambiguities and ambivalences surrounding African American life in the United States in ways that extend beyond the psychic torment of black individuals." Glaude, *Exodus!*, 33.
43. Cooper, *Voice from the South*, 65.
44. Mary Helen Washington, for example, argues that Cooper is "never able to totally discard the ethics of true womanhood, and . . . does not imagine ordinary black working women as the basis for her feminist politics." Washington, introduction to *Voice from the South*, xlv–xlvi. Andreá N. Williams similarly notes that while Cooper argued for the importance of employment to women's progress, she also valorized professional status over physical labor, "implicitly arguing for the practicality of class distinctions over racial ones." Williams, *Dividing Lines*, 61, 166.
45. May, "Thinking from the Margins," 82.
46. Cooper, *Voice from the South*, 66–67.
47. Here I am drawing on Fred Moten's articulation of the "cut" in black radical performance, such that within Cooper's performative repetition of Church history

emerges a fugitive critique of racist religious institutions. See Moten, *In the Break*, 69.
48. Cooper, *Voice from the South*, 90.
49. Focusing on the dynamics of collective engagement and the intersubjective work of being "enthused," Cooper disperses Howells's fascination with and fetishization of black women's bodily difference, a dynamic that Ann duCille has described as "the invention of an other Otherness." DuCille, "Occult of True Black Womanhood," 592.
50. Cooper, *Voice from the South*, 193.
51. Ibid.
52. Ibid., 135.
53. Ibid., 137.
54. Eliot, *Adam Bede*, 180; Howells, "Editor's Study," 155.
55. Cooper, *Voice from the South*, 146–147.
56. Ibid., 147.
57. Ibid., 150.
58. Ibid., 160.
59. Warren, *Black and White Strangers*, 68.
60. Cooper, *Voice from the South*, 146–147 (emphasis original).
61. Ibid., 150.
62. Ibid., 116.
63. M. Giulia Fabi argues compellingly that reading the two novels alongside one another allows us to see them as part of a "process of reciprocal invention." See Fabi, "Reconstructing Literary Genealogies," 49.
64. Harper, *Iola Leroy*, 217.
65. Ibid., 218.
66. As Koritha Mitchell argues, Harper was adept at speaking to multiple constituencies at once, and used a range of techniques to "reach the broadest possible audience while maintaining a community-centered perspective." Mitchell, introduction to *Iola Leroy*, 49.
67. Harper, *Iola Leroy*, 218.
68. Ibid., 219.
69. Ibid., 93.
70. On the early modern application of this term to Muslims and Jews, and its transmogrification in early American debates over religious liberty, see Schlereth, *Age of Infidels*. As Frederick Douglass noted in an 1849 address to the American Anti-Slavery Society, "The cry of infidelity has long been raised against those who stand on the old platform and adhere to the Old Anti-Slavery Organization. While I was a member of the Methodist Episcopal Church, I had heard Garrison denounced as an infidel and I wanted to hear what his infidelity consisted in; and the moment I heard him pour out his soul in behalf of the downtrodden bondsman.... I wanted to know nothing further of his religious views." Douglass, "Too Much Religion," 188.

71. As Frances Smith Foster points out, Harper's radicalism has gone largely unrecognized in part because of her religious commitments, yet she belonged to "the same Christianity that produced Nat Turner and John Brown," each decried as enthusiasts in their time. Foster, "Gender, Genre, and Vulgar Secularism," 54.
72. Fretwell, *What We Feel*; Harper, *Iola Leroy*, 182.
73. Harper, *Iola Leroy*, 183.
74. Gates and West, *Future of the Race*, 81; Moten, *In the Break*, 198; Crawley, *Blackpentecostal Breath*, 38.
75. Harper, *Iola Leroy*, 184–185.
76. On the "(con)scripting of blackness," see Hartman, *Scenes of Subjection*, 168.
77. As Barbara Christian observes, Harper's "idealizing" of Iola Leroy served a vital purpose, helping to "refute the popular stereotype of the day that blacks were degenerates who could not advance either economically or culturally." In *Reconstructing Womanhood*, Hazel Carby argues that Harper goes well beyond this project of refutation, constructing a model of black female intellectual autonomy and deploying a dialogic structure that echoed her public lectures. Both Christian and Carby offer foundational frameworks through which to understand the project of black feminist "realism" as both an aesthetic and a political praxis. Christian, *Black Women Novelists*, 28; Carby, *Reconstructing Womanhood*, 85.
78. On the role of a "spiritual grammar" in the development of a New Negro aesthetic, see Sorett, *Spirit in the Dark*, 12–13, 20. See Blum, *W. E. B. Du Bois*; Blum and Young, *Souls of W. E. B. Du Bois*; Kahn, *Divine Discontent*.
79. Marable, *Black Leadership*, 60.
80. Zamir, "Du Bois, Leadership," 148.
81. Du Bois, *Souls*, 502.
82. Ibid.
83. On the longevity of Du Bois's interest in and attention to religious culture, see Marable, *Black Leadership*, 59–60.
84. Du Bois, *Souls*, 494.
85. See Du Bois, *Autobiography*, 120.
86. Gates and West, *Future of the Race*, 60.
87. Wolfenstein, *Gift of the Spirit*, 98; Zamir, "Du Bois, Leadership," 159.
88. James, "[Praise for *Souls*]," 227.
89. Gilroy, *Black Atlantic*, 129. Stephanie J. Shaw similarly emphasizes the "awe" in Du Bois's account of the awfulness of witnessing the revival, linking it to a Hegelian concept of the Absolute. See Shaw, *W. E. B. Du Bois*, 128.
90. Pinn, "Charting Du Bois's *Souls*," 80. Manning Marable similarly argues that "the shout was . . . a catharsis, the expression of transcendence, a cry of faith and hope, a physical and collective explosion that was necessary for a people trapped in the permanent vise of social anxiety and frustration." Marable, *Black Leadership*, 64.
91. Moten, *Stolen Life*, 32. Moten offers a powerful rereading of Du Bois's philosophy of blackness as preceding both the color line and the Kantian arrangement of

sense, asserting "black chant" as "an incantatory, ante-Kantian frenzy, a tumultuous derangement, wherein a terrible reality is lent to song and word in their interanimation." By naming the frenzy as a form of black genius, Moten intervenes in what scholars have largely identified as the coloniality of this trope. As William Hart notes, "The [secular] coloniality of power is the enabling condition for tropes such as fetishism, frenzy, and voodoo." Yet Hart also concedes that Du Bois's case is a complex one, deploying dominant discourse around black religious expressivity even as it might operate as an imminent revalorization of such modes of expression. Hart, "Secular Coloniality," 186.
92. Du Bois, *Souls*, 494.
93. Sundquist, *To Wake the Nations*, 512.
94. Du Bois, *Souls*, 504.
95. I am drawing here on Lauren Berlant's notion of the impasse as a kind of holding pattern in the face of untenable structures and genres of living; a combination of "wandering absorptive awareness" and "hypervigilance," and a form of being on the lookout for new and unarticulated possibilities of organizing (and disorganizing) existence. Berlant, *Cruel Optimism*, 4.
96. Du Bois, *Souls*, 505.
97. Psalm 23:4, King James Bible.
98. Du Bois, *Souls*, 504.
99. James, *Varieties of Religious Experience*, 126.
100. Du Bois, *Souls*, 529.
101. Ibid., 530.
102. Baker, *Long Black Song*, 102.
103. Sundquist, *To Wake the Nations*, 524–525.
104. Du Bois, *Souls*, 532.
105. Ibid., 535.
106. Ibid., 509. Susan Mizruchi argues forcefully that this scene marks the ritualistic exclusion of black Americans from a "universal grammar of suffering," marking the limits of a sentimental and nationalist discourse of mourning. Mizruchi, *Science of Sacrifice*, 269.
107. On the spectacle of lynching and its centrality to post-Reconstruction cultural representation, see Goldsby, *Spectacular Secret*. I treat the ritualistic aspects of lynching in more detail in chapters 2 and 4.
108. Zamir similarly notes the resonances between the ending of Du Bois's ode to Crummel and the final scene in "Of the Coming of John": "If the tragic end of 'Of the Coming of John' cuts short the visionary projections of the eulogy for Crummell, these projected trajectories are already threatened by the gothic omen of the death of 'the first-born' in the previous chapter." Zamir, "Du Bois, Leadership," 156. While Zamir suggests that each of these resonances suggest the limits of Du Bois's prophetic imaginary, I argue on the contrary that their very repetition across chapters demonstrates a commitment to a nonlinear but nevertheless prophetic understanding of history.

109. Du Bois, *Souls*, 513.
110. Ibid., 520.
111. It seems likely here that Du Bois references Elizabeth Stuart Phelps's hugely popular novel, *The Gates Ajar* (1868).
112. Benjamin, *Illuminations*, 258.
113. Du Bois, *Souls*, 364.
114. Edward Blum, for example, contends that "*Souls* entered the U.S. cultural landscape as a sacred text." Blum, *W. E. B. Du Bois*, 64.
115. Du Bois, "Souls of White Folk," 928.
116. Ibid., 923.
117. Hickman, *Black Prometheus*, 19.
118. I follow Anthony Pinn here, who suggests that approaching religion as an aesthetic practice and resource "allowed Du Bois to think in terms of the global arrangement of those of African descent and religion as a framework for addressing the consequences of the 'enlightenment project' worked out on and through their bodies." Pinn, "Charting Du Bois's *Souls*," 76.
119. It is important to distinguish between the centrality of race in the formation of secularism and the idea of race as a "secular" concept. As Vincent Lloyd points out, "Secularism names the regime that determines what does and does not count as appropriate religion for a particular sphere," a regime that has never been separate from the dynamics of racialization. Similarly, ideologies of "race" are fully managed and propelled by religious discourses and distinctions. Lloyd, "Introduction," 4.
120. Hickman, *Black Prometheus*, 49.
121. Spillers, "Moving on Down the Line," 90.
122. Attending to what unfolds between the lines, as Spillers notes, was and is a crucial methodology for an insurgent relation to white Christianity, "because it is between the lines of Scripture that the narratives of insurgence are delivered." Spillers, "Moving on Down the Line," 84.
123. Ibid., 85.
124. Edward Blum points out that historians have largely narrated the trajectory of Du Bois's religious conviction as a "predictable secularization tale—one that in some ways mirrors the supposed secularization of nineteenth- and twentieth-century America." Blum, *W. E. B. Du Bois*, 9.
125. Ibid., 63.
126. Du Bois, "Souls of White Folk," 927.
127. Ibid. In his 1915 essay "The White Christ," Du Bois made a similar point about white Christianity's involution with world war: "As to the widespread and costly murder that is being waged today by the children of the Prince of Peace, comment is quite unnecessary. It simply spells the failure of Christianity." Du Bois, "White Christ," 141.
128. Du Bois, "Souls of White Folk," 924.
129. Ibid., 937.

130. Douglass, "What to the Slave?," 380.
131. Nyong'o, "Race, Reenactment," 81, 94.
132. Du Bois, "Souls of White Folk," 938.
133. Lloyd, "Introduction," 7; Kahn, "Conclusion," 244.
134. Howells, "Modern American Mood," 84.
135. Notably, Howells's effort to carve out a space for authentic American patriotism parallels eighteenth-century attempts by philosophers and theologians to secure religious experience from the twin threats of enthusiasm and formalism. As Martin Jay has described, the "defense of authentic religious experience had to be waged on two fronts: against both the hollow 'formalism' of orthodox doctrine and the excessive 'enthusiasm' of delusional, false belief." Jay, *Songs of Experience*, 88. See also Taves, *Fits, Trances, and Visions*, 16–17.
136. As Amy Kaplan has argued, the formal balancing act of realism as Howells envisioned it "functioned as a strategy for containing social difference and controlling social conflict," working to "construct" an ordered version of America by imagining and containing the "otherness" that increasingly defined it. But as Kaplan also recognizes, such a "fantasy of total mastery," of perfect quiet, is precisely a fantasy—and a leaky one at that. Kaplan, *Social Construction*, 23, 62.
137. As Taves points out, in the late sixteenth and early seventeenth centuries, the charge of "enthusiasm" was directed toward the "Puritan emphasis on 'inward' or 'heart' religion," a theologically and politically motivated shift in attention from external structures of clerical authority to the self-authorizing force of individual experience—*experience* itself being defined in and through a rising tide of Protestant dissent. Taves, *Fits, Trances, and Visions*, 16.
138. Modern, *Secularism in Antebellum America*, 6. On secularism's surfacing of a racialized epidermis, see chapter 4.

CHAPTER 2. ARCHIVAL ENTHUSIASM
1. Crane, *Red Badge of Courage*, 59.
2. See, in particular, Fried, *Realism, Writing, Disfiguration*; Brown, *Material Unconscious*; Seltzer, *Bodies and Machines*.
3. I am indebted here to Michael Fried's important take on how Crane's works thematize the materiality of writing, as well as Mark Seltzer's insistence on the violence of that materiality. While Seltzer links this violence to a broader cultural logic of statistical personhood and social biomechanics, my reading works to embed this violence in a longer history of racialized representation and depersonalization. Fried, *Realism, Writing, Disfiguration*; Seltzer, *Bodies and Machines*, 111.
4. Brown, *Material Unconscious*, 138; Goldsby, *Spectacular Secret*.
5. I use the terms "archive" and "performance" with a strong sense of the ontological stickiness of each. *Red Badge* might even be said to dramatize this stickiness, for if, as Peggy Phelan argues, performance "becomes itself through disappearance," Crane's novel offers a similar paradox of becoming in which the young

soldier becomes himself only through (the possibility of) death. Yet *Red Badge* also mobilizes performance as a site of historical reproduction and transmission, testifying to what Fred Moten describes as a "conjunction of reproduction and disappearance" or what Diana Taylor has articulated as a necessary dialectic between the archive and the repertoire. My sense of "archive" draws from these accounts as well as from Jacques Derrida's effort in *Archive Fever* to disarticulate the archive from the authoritative project of memory: "The archive takes place at the place of originary and structural breakdown of the said memory." As I argue in this chapter, Jim's "jim-dandy" offers a strikingly compact iteration of the archive's originary forgetfulness, enacting both the violence of memory loss and the nearly constant reproduction of that violence. Phelan, *Unmarked*, 146; Moten, *In the Break*, 5; Taylor, *Archive and the Repertoire*; Derrida, *Archive Fever*, 11.

6. In one particularly pertinent example, Seltzer reads Henry's literal navel-gazing as symptomatic of a larger juxtaposition between natural and mechanical reproduction. Seltzer, *Bodies and Machines*, 113.

7. In her famous description of this semiotics, Hortense Spillers describes a "hieroglyphics of the flesh," in which a history of brutalization is masked by the cultural logic of skin color, the externalization of a violent New World script—writing on and in the flesh. That originary grammar, as Spillers contends, also marks a haunting repetition: "We might well ask if this phenomenon of marking and branding actually 'transfers' from one generation to another, finding its various *symbolic substitutions* in an efficacy of meanings that repeat the initiating moments?" Spillers, "Mama's Baby, Papa's Maybe," 67.

8. Here I follow Alexander Weheliye in his account of racialization as "a master code within the genre of the human represented by western Man" insofar as it "clearly distinguishes the good/life/full-human from the bad/death/not-quite-human." Weheliye, *Habeas Viscus*, 27.

9. Frederic, review of *Red Badge*. For a discussion of Frederic's review in relation to the novel's photographic apparatus, see Brown, *Material Unconscious*, 133.

10. Critics have had much to say about Crane's repetitions. Their most striking effect, as several have argued, is to confound linearity, substituting teleological narratives of secular-Protestant progress and heroic self-realization with the irony of recurrence. Max Cavitch, for example, highlights the radically depersonalizing force at the heart of Crane's lyric refrains: "Repetition solicits remembrance. But more than this, repetition is a figure of truth; it seeks to weary the clamor for persuasion with the self-evidence of iteration." As Cavitch suggests, Crane used repetition as a figure for despair—a nihilistic refusal of the very terms of sentimental personhood. Mary Esteve argues that Crane's repetitive description of figures like Jim Conklin—fallen, unfeeling, and subject to intense scrutiny—characterizes his "documentary anaesthetics," a narrative mode that resists the sense-making apparatuses of both literary realism and the liberal reform movements to which it was often linked. In contrast to Progressive Era realism's transformation and

consolidation of lived experience into narrative, Crane's sketches perform the opposite maneuver, "converting lived experience back into *sheer data*, back into pure anaesthetic experience" and thus (for Esteve) into a space of nonnarratable privacy. While Esteve's account of this resistance to the legibility of the subject is compelling, it ultimately recovers a notion of liberal personhood against which Crane's works everywhere attest. In this sense, my reading owes more to Jennifer Fleissner's account of Crane's obsessive repetitions, which mark the novel's investment in gendered selfhood as a compulsive labor not unlike the work of historical narration. Fleissner argues that the novel "enacts a project of attempted, necessarily failing, but continually repeated 'completeness' that is itself seen as defining of history and of 'becoming a man.'" Cavitch, "Stephen Crane's Refrain," 82; Esteve, *Aesthetics and Politics*, 103; Fleissner, *Women, Compulsion, Modernity*, 64.
11. Taylor, *Archive and the Repertoire*, 143.
12. Here I am indebted to Amy Kaplan's observation that "Crane is a master of forgetting" in his decontexualization of the war. While Kaplan argues that such forgetting allows Crane to press the Civil War into the service of 1890s US imperial militarization, I argue that the novel's forgetting is matched by an equally persistent, performative remembrance. Kaplan, "Nation, Region, and Empire," 266–284. See also Kaplan, "Spectacle of War."
13. Nyong'o, *Amalgamation Waltz*, 7.
14. Vogel, *Scene of the Harlem Cabaret*, 6.
15. *OED Online*, s.v. "jim-dandy, n. and adj."
16. Brown, *Material Unconscious*.
17. Cohen, *Studies in Slang, Part I*, 134. The song's immense popularity in the 1840s produced its own energetic metanarrative of origins. Writing in *Knickerbocker Magazine* in 1845, James Kennard Jr. included Dandy Jim among the figures he listed as "our truly original and American poets"—made profitable, Kennard noted, by the proxy performance of white minstrels like T. D. Rice. Eric Lott notes that by identifying the "black" idioms of the minstrel show as the only "truly national" poetry, Kennard's essay ends by ironically imagining national culture itself as black, while Lara Langer Cohen suggests that Kennard's essay treats minstrelsy unironically (despite or indeed because of its fraudulence) as the only "original" American poetry. Laurence Hutton's 1891 *Curiosities of the American Stage* credited Rice as the "veritable originator of the genus known to the stage as the 'dandy darky,' represented particularly in his creations of 'Dandy Jim of Caroline' and 'Spruce Pink.'" Lott, *Love & Theft*, 102–103; Cohen, *Fabrication of American Literature*, 82; Hutton, *Curiosities of the American Stage*, 119.
18. Robert Winans notes that "Dandy Jim from Caroline" has at least four different texts, while William Mahar prints at least eleven variations. Winans, "Early Minstrel Show Music," 149; Mahar, *Behind the Burnt Cork Mask*, 226–227.
19. Mahar, *Behind the Burnt Cork Mask*, 226. See Dickinson Family Library, Houghton Library, Harvard Library, Harvard University.
20. Miller, *Slaves to Fashion*, 99.

21. See Toll, *Blacking Up*, 69; Miller, *Slaves to Fashion*, 98–99.
22. Mahar, *Behind the Burnt Cork Mask*, 226.
23. Lott notes that the dandy figure "literally embodied the amalgamationist threat of abolitionism," while Daphne Brooks argues that the dandy's embodied threat to class boundaries was even more pressing in the wake of Reconstruction. Reconfigured by black performers such as George Walker, "the drag of dandyism," Brooks writes, became "both a threat and a catalyst toward the public adulation of the black body." Lott, *Love & Theft*, 134; Brooks, *Bodies in Dissent*, 260.
24. Hartman, *Scenes of Subjection*, 76.
25. Ibid., 76.
26. Songs circulating in advance of the 1844 election included "A Song, after the Manner of the Whigs, to the Tune of 'Dandy Jim of Caroline,'" *Mississippi Free Trader and Natchez Gazette*, August 3, 1844, issue 99, col. A; "Jimmy Polk of Tennessee," by J. Grenier, tune—"Dandy Jim of Caroline," *Raleigh Register, and North-Carolina Gazette*, August 13, 1844, issue 65, col. E; "Whig Melody," by F. J. Otterson, air—"Dandy Jim of Caroline," printed in the *Great Whig Procession of Artists and Tradesmen of New York City*, October 30, 1844. Songs in advance of the 1848 election included "Rough and Ready of the Rio Grande," "From the *Philadelphia True Sun*," tune—"Dandy Jim of Caroline" (in support of Zachary Taylor), *Raleigh Register, and North-Caroline Gazette*, July 26, 1848, issue 49, col. D; "Toe the Mark, 'Tis Taylor Can," tune—"Dandy Jim of Caroline," *Bangor Daily Whig & Courier*, October 31, 1848, issue 104, col. B; "The John Song," "Written for the Natick Free Soil Glee Club," *Emancipator and Free Soil Press*, November 1, 1848, issue 48, col. G; "Music for the Million," air—"Dandy Jim" (in support of Democrat Lewis Cass), *Vermont Patriot*, July 27, 1848, issue 31/135, col. B; "The Yankees' Cass Song," tune—"Dandy Jim," *Dover Gazette & Strafford Advisor*, November 4, 1848, issue 52, col. D.
27. The song appeared in the *North Star* on July 14, 1848.
28. Brooks, *Bodies in Dissent*, 1.
29. Paul Gilmore argues similarly that in his fiction as much as in his plays and lectures, Brown "turns the abolitionist platform into a minstrel stage and the minstrel stage into an abolitionist platform, thus revealing the logic of each." Gilmore, "De Genewine Artekil," 745.
30. McClendon, "Sounds of Sympathy," 91.
31. Dunbar, *In Old Plantation Days*, 142.
32. On Crane's debt to the racial stereotypes reproduced in nineteenth-century minstrelsy, see Robertson, *Stephen Crane, Journalism*.
33. Brown, "Reification, Reanimation," 182.
34. Ibid.
35. As Uri McMillan points out, performances of objecthood—or that raise the specter of objecthood—are particularly fraught in the historical context of chattel slavery and its reduction of human beings to commodities. See McMillan, *Embodied Avatars*, 8–10.

36. Bernstein, *Racial Innocence*, 80–81.
37. Crane, *Red Badge of Courage*, 55.
38. Richard Schechner notes the belated structure of performance itself: "Accidents conform to the basic performance pattern; even after the event is 'cleaned up' some 'writing' is left on the site: for example, bloodstains, knots of witnesses and the curious and so on. Only slowly does the event evaporate and the crowd disperse. I call such events 'eruptions.' An eruption is like a theatrical performance because it is *not* the accident itself that gathers and keeps an audience. They are held by a reconstruction or reenactment of the event." Schechner, "Towards a Poetics," 176–177. On performance as reenactment, see Roach, *Cities of the Dead*; Schneider, *Performing Remains*. On performance, trauma, and repetition, see Caruth, "Traumatic Awakenings," 89–108.
39. Crane, *Tales of War*, 83.
40. Crane, *Red Badge of Courage*, 13.
41. Addressing this violent form of socialization, Seltzer cites *Red Badge* as the literary exemplar of what he calls "wound culture": "the model of a sociality bound to pathology" where the wound functions as the symbolic nexus between individual and world. Seltzer, "Wound Culture," 9, 25.
42. As Mizruchi attests, the logic of sacrifice and surrogation was very much in the air that Crane breathed: the 1890s abounded in memorials to those sacrificed on the altar of national unity, and not long after the novel's appearance, William James would call for a "moral equivalent of war," a nonviolent expenditure of energy that might serve as surrogate for the "civilizing" militancy of American imperialism. Mizruchi, *Science of Sacrifice*.
43. Crane, *Red Badge of Courage*, 13. Mizruchi asserts, "For a novel whose reputed aim is to re-create the atmosphere of war, it's striking how much time is spent describing consumption." Mizruchi, *Science of Sacrifice*, 82.
44. Crane, *Red Badge of Courage*, 58.
45. In light of Jacqueline Goldsby's crucial reading of the dynamics of race and violence in Crane, it is impossible not to read Jim's death as resonant with the embedded logic of lynching in *The Monster*, a narrative which (as I discuss below) reproduces the Henry/Jim pairing as well as the dandy performance.
46. Roach, *Cities of the Dead*, 2. Roach's formulation also recalls Toni Morrison's famous account of the marginalized and repressed presence of African Americans in the canon of American literature: "We can agree, I think, that invisible things are not necessarily 'not-there.'" Morrison, "Unspeakable Things Unspoken," 11.
47. Crane, *Red Badge of Courage*, 57–58.
48. Ibid., 55.
49. Ibid., 57.
50. Ibid., 50.
51. Ibid., 57.
52. An August 17, 1847, item in the *North American*—entitled "The 'Bones' That the Negroes Use Are Not the Invention of 'Dandy Jim'"—signals the popular

use of castanets in Dandy Jim performances. In a dizzying archival gesture, the article cites the *Richmond Enquirer*'s citation of an old report "of the reception of Gen. Lafayette in Philadelphia, during his visit to this country, as the nation's guest in 1824." The article quotes the report:

> It is said, and we have it from one who, we believe was an eye-witness, that, after a review on Tuesday, a black man, tolerably well known to our citizens for his exhilirating [*sic*] faculty of whistling, pressed forward towards the General, and, after one or two efforts at mustering courage, Robert succeeded in saluting the General, and enquiring after his health. The General condescendingly returned the salute. After a moment's pause, "Perhaps," added Robert, "the General does not remember me?" "Were you in the army?" said the General. "I was a waiter to Gen. Mason, of the Virginia line," said the black. "Then," said the General, with a hearty shake of the hand, "I remember you; you was that roguish boy *that used to make castanets of the dry bones in the camp*, and disturb me in my marquee." ("The 'Bones'"; emphasis original)

If the article records a kind of minstrel diplomacy, it also registers the disruptive force of "Dandy Jim," and the extent to which its performers (and their predecessors) blurred the boundaries of race, class, and nation.

53. On performance as ritual, see Turner, *Ritual Process*; Schechner, *Between Theater & Anthropology*; Schechner, "Towards a Poetics."
54. As J. S. Bratton notes, questions of freedom and compulsion were always bound up in the performance and popularization of the hornpipe. Bratton, "Dancing the Hornpipe in Fetters," 66–68. The *OED* describes the hornpipe as "a dance of lively and vigorous character, usually performed by a single person, orig. to the accompaniment of the wind instrument" and lists its earliest appearance as 1485. The hornpipe appears to have had an early association with the stage: "From the 16th century onwards, hornpipes appeared in dance suites and incidental music for the stage by such composers as Anthony Holborne, Byrd, Purcell, Arne, and Handel. . . ." *OED Online*, s.v. "hornpipe, n.1."
55. Ngai, *Ugly Feelings*, 91.
56. Nancy Bentley notes how *Red Badge* participates in early film's "sliding and flickering movement," citing Joseph Conrad's retrospective notion that "Crane and [Conrad] must have been unconsciously penetrated by a prophetic sense of the technique and of the very spirit of the film-plays of which even the name was unknown to the world." Bentley, *Frantic Panoramas*, 296. See also Brown, *Material Unconscious*.
57. Frederic, "Stephen Crane's Triumph," 39; Norris, "Stephen Crane's Stories," 164.
58. *OED Online*, s.v. "imp, n.1." This image also, at least potentially, echoes widespread associations between the cross and the lynching tree; if Jim is a sacrificial figure in this sense, he is part of a turn-of-the-century imaginary of the lynching tree as a site of crucifixion. See Cone, *Cross and Lynching Tree*.

59. This reading both draws on and departs from Phelan's argument for the nonreproductive ontology of performance: "Performance's only life is in the present. Performance cannot be saved, recorded, documented, or otherwise participate in the circulation of representations of representations. . . . Performance's being, like the ontology of subjectivity proposed here, becomes itself through disappearance." *Red Badge* directly approaches the ontology that Phelan elaborates, particularly as it yokes performance and death; however, as I argue throughout, the novel also registers its own historicity precisely through the repetition of certain kinds of performance, demonstrating that disappearance and reproduction are symmetrical processes. Phelan, *Unmarked*, 146.
60. On the semantic history of "enthusiasm," see Tucker, *Enthusiasm*. On enthusiasm in literary and theoretical contexts, see Irlam, *Elations*; Mee, *Romanticism, Enthusiasm, and Regulation*; Clark, *Theory of Inspiration*. On enthusiasm in the American context, see Lovejoy, *Religious Enthusiasm*; Taves, *Fits, Trances, and Visions*; Kilgore, *Mania for Freedom*.
61. See Ruttenburg, *Democratic Personality*; Toscano, *Fanaticism*.
62. Ruttenburg, *Democratic Personality*, 23.
63. Ibid., 127.
64. Crucially, as Fessenden also notes, the gendering of religion is a multiform process, and (in the US context in particular) helps produce "religion's potential for *partnership* with the secular state in, among other projects, the management of race." Fessenden, "Afterword," 264. On enthusiasm and enchantment as techniques of management, see Ogden, "Beyond Radical Enchantment," 815–841.
65. Ruttenburg, *Democratic Personality*, 201.
66. On the history of racialization and the production of whiteness as property, see Harris, "Whiteness as Property," 1707–1791. Harris provides a useful framework for the hauntology of whiteness as property: "It is a ghost that has haunted the political and legal domains in which claims for justice have been inadequately addressed for way too long" (1791).
67. Ruttenburg, *Democratic Personality*, 287.
68. Kilgore, "Nat Turner," 1350.
69. See Kilgore, *Mania for Freedom*.
70. Critics have made much of this inheritance, noting Crane's embrace of the "popular amusements" that his father decried in an 1869 tract of that name. While most biographers concede religion's reverberative force in Crane, critics have more readily accepted a simple narrative of rejection. Thus R. W. Stallman notes that Crane's "writings are haunted by his religious background," while Christopher Benfey details the scandal surrounding Jonathan Townley Crane's rejection of the Holiness conception of a "second blessing," and Stephen's subsequent adaptation of this iconoclasm. Stallman, *Stephen Crane*, 5; Benfey, *Double Life*. Important exceptions in the criticism include Ralph Ellison's 1960 introduction to the novel (as I discuss in the final section of this chapter) and Delbanco, "American Stephen Crane," 49–76.

71. Benfey, *Double Life*, 29.
72. Crane, *Methodism and Its Methods*, 157. On black Holiness movements, see Sanders, *Saints in Exile*; on the Holiness movement in relation to fundamentalism, see Marsden, *Fundamentalism and American Culture*.
73. Crane, *Christian Duty*.
74. Crane, *Essay on Dancing*, 8.
75. See Smith, "Religion, Religions, Religious"; Masuzawa, *Invention of World Religions*.
76. Gotman, *Choreomania*, 6.
77. Kilham, "Sketches in Color," 305, cited in Evans, *Burden of Black Religion*, 70.
78. Kilham, "Sketches in Color," 308.
79. Esteve, *Aesthetics and Politics*.
80. "Negro Camp Meeting," 263.
81. "A Negro Camp Meeting in the South" offers a prime example of how "feminization and racialization . . . track a split between 'good' and 'bad' religion," to use Tracy Fessenden's formulation. Fessenden, "Afterword," 265.
82. Davenport, *Primitive Traits*, 50.
83. Hall, "Negro in Africa and America," 356.
84. Evans, *Burden of Black Religion*, 131.
85. Davenport, *Primitive Traits*, 42, 47.
86. Ibid., 56.
87. Ibid., 51.
88. See Bramen, *Uses of Variety*.
89. Crane, *Red Badge of Courage*, 31.
90. Crane, *Tales of Whilomville*, 56.
91. Ibid., 14.
92. Goldsby, *Spectacular Secret*, 114.
93. Cavitch, "Stephen Crane's Refrain," 44.
94. Crane, *Poems*, 20.
95. Crane, *Red Badge of Courage*, 59.
96. Here I follow Jean-Luc Nancy's conception of com-passion as "the contagion, the contact of being with one another in this turmoil. Compassion is not altruism, nor is it identification; it is the disturbance of violent relatedness." Nancy, *Being Singular Plural*, xiii.
97. Caruth, "Traumatic Awakenings," 90. On the history of repetition and reenactment in relation to trauma, see also Leys, *Trauma*, esp. 83–101.
98. Kristeva, *Powers of Horror*.
99. Ellison, *Shadow and Act*, 60.
100. Ibid., 67.
101. For an alternative reading of Ellison's essay, see Rowe, *Literary Culture*, 155.
102. As Ellison points out, Crane's interest in excess developed early, via a "youthful contact" with ecstatic religion —highly animated performances that blurred the

boundaries of subjectivity and spectatorship, transforming the body itself into a cipher. Ellison, *Shadow and Act*, 62.
103. Ibid., 67.
104. Here I'm drawing on Alex Woloch's insight, that the "strange significance of minor characters . . . resides largely in the way that the character disappears, and in the tension or relief that results from this vanishing." Woloch, *One vs. the Many*, 42.
105. Crane, *Red Badge of Courage*, 3.
106. See Pease, "Fear, Rage," 155–175; Rowe, *Literary Culture*; Kaplan, "Spectacle of War."

CHAPTER 3. THE GHOST DANCE AND REALISM'S TECHNO-SPIRITUAL FRONTIER

1. On Mooney's shadow as a visual signature, see Jacknis, "James Mooney," 186.
2. Apparently borrowed from Matilda Coxe Stevenson, first president of the American Women's Anthropological Society. See Fleming and Luskey, *North American Indians*, 143.
3. Mooney's papers are held at the Smithsonian's National Anthropological Archives; his images are included in the Bureau of American Ethnology Collection of Glass Negatives. As archival objects, Mooney's photographs remain tied to the institutional and colonial structures that produced them. See Hinsley, *Smithsonian and Native American*.
4. Throughout this chapter, my aim is not to produce knowledge about the Ghost Dance, as any such knowledge would help reify the very settler perspective that I attempt to historicize and unpack in these pages. Instead, I dwell on how realist practices borrowed, disavowed, and reproduced the Ghost Dance's embodied testimony to an ongoing, immeasurable proximity between the living and the dead.
5. As Mooney observed, the name of the dance varied across tribes: "In its original home among the Paiute it is called *Nänigükaw*, 'dance in a circle' (*nüka*, dance), to distinguish it from the other dances of the tribe. . . . By the Sioux, Arapaho, and most other prairie tribes it is called the 'spirit' or 'ghost' dance (Sioux, *Wanaghi wachipi*; Arapaho, *Thigû'nawat*), from the fact that everything connected with it related to the coming of the spirits of the dead from the spirit world, and by this name it has become known among the whites." Mooney, *Ghost-Dance*, 791. See also Hittman, *Wovoka*, 63. While many scholars have referred to the Ghost Dance as a "revitalization" movement, this description is a contested one. As Lee Irwin argues, prophetic movements such as the Ghost Dance were not simply efforts to revitalize Native cultures in the face of colonial decimation; they were also "an ongoing vitality, whose goals were based in Native patterns of practice and belief and whose expression was creative and syncretic." Irwin, *Coming Down*, 8.

6. Bentley and Elliott have each traced the relationship between late nineteenth-century literary realism and the rise of ethnography as a professional science, exploring how these forms align in their production of culture as a coherent and narratable set of practices. As Bentley argues, literary realism borrows the discourses of ethnography insofar as it produces and assimilates cultural otherness. See Bentley, *Ethnography of Manners*; Elliott, *Culture Concept*; Elliott, "Ethnography, Reform," 201–233. On the relationship between realism, naturalism, and the professionalization of the social sciences, see Mizruchi, *Science of Sacrifice*. On the celebration of cultural difference as a function of late nineteenth-century American exceptionalism, see Bramen, *Uses of Variety*.
7. On the "real" Indian, see Elliott, "Ethnography, Reform."
8. In other words, its temporality is utterly normative, and (in Fredric Jameson's terms) "absolutely committed to the density and solidity of what is." Jameson, *Antinomies*, 215.
9. On "imperialist nostalgia," see Rosaldo, *Culture and Truth*, cited in McGarry, *Ghosts of Futures Past*, 70.
10. Jameson, *Antinomies*, 31.
11. Schneider, *Performing Remains*, 30.
12. On the relationship between realist detail and the consciousness of the present, see Jameson, *Antinomies*.
13. Sources on the Ghost Dance are various and variously problematic, as many scholars have argued. This has to do in part with the influence of James Mooney's *The Ghost-Dance Religion and the Sioux Outbreak of 1890* (1896) on much of the scholarship that followed it. As Rani-Henrik Andersson notes, "It has become tradition to treat Mooney's study almost as a primary source on the Lakota ghost dance"—at the expense of Native voices and interpretations. Andersson, *Lakota Ghost Dance*, xii–xiii. Sam A. Maddra similarly notes the overreliance on Mooney, though he points out scholars (such as Michael Hittman and William S. E. Coleman) who have questioned the ideological coordinates of Mooney's report. Maddra, *Hostiles?*, 29. This chapter contributes to that ongoing project.
14. Mooney cites a message purportedly from Wovoka himself, delivered to Mooney by the Cheyenne delegate Black Short Nose: "After preliminary greetings, he stated that the Cheyenne and Arapaho were now convinced I would tell the truth about their religion, and as they loved their religion and were anxious to have the whites know that it was all good and contained nothing bad or hostile they would now give me the message which the messiah himself had given to them, that I might take it back to show Washington." Mooney, *Ghost-Dance*, 780–781.
15. Ibid., 772.
16. Ibid.
17. As Irwin notes, the dance's "messianic theme is vague because while non-Natives . . . tended to emphasize the cosmic drama of the Messiah as an evangelical Christian end-time scenario of final judgment, Native representations tended

to see it as a renewal and rebirth of the earth to its pristine beauty and abundance, the return of the many Native dead, and a recovery of a Native way of life." Irwin, *Coming Down*, 309.
18. See Barthes, *Camera Lucida*, 14–15, 31–32. Barthes's account of the relation between religion, photography, and death is also instructive: "For Death must be somewhere in a society; if it is no longer (or less intensely) in religion, it must be elsewhere; perhaps in this image which produces Death while trying to preserve life" (92). While Barthes suggests the photograph serves as an affective *replacement* for religion's management of life and death, I argue that the photograph serves as a site of spiritual exposure and possibility; in this sense, the photograph does not replace so much as it extends the technological realm of religious affects. As Jodi Byrd argues, this sense of was-ness is also a function of critical theory: "Although critical theory has focused much attention on the role of frontiers and Manifest Destiny in the creation and rise of U.S. empire, American Indians and other indigenous peoples have often been evoked in such theorizations as past tense presences." Byrd, *Transit*, xx.
19. Byrd, *Transit*, 37.
20. Ibid., xx.
21. Masuzawa, *Invention of World Religions*, 19–20. Tisa Wenger provides a useful gloss on the colonial history of "religion," which she describes as "a product of European cultural and colonial history that has no direct translation in Native American languages or other non-European tongues around the world." As Wenger argues, religion was also a strategic concept in the early twentieth century, applied to and occasionally adopted by indigenous communities as a means of making their communal customs legible within the normative Protestant-secular frameworks of religious freedom. Wenger, *We Have a Religion*, 5–6. On the coloniality of "religion" as a discursive marker, see Smith, "Religion, Religions, Religious."
22. In "teases," I borrow a term from Gerald Vizenor, who emphasizes the work of irony and humor in Native cultural practices, as it challenges (and indeed teases) the logic of savagery and civilization. Vizenor, *Fugitive Poses*, 23–47.
23. Indianness, as Byrd suggests, "becomes a site through which U.S. empire orients and replicates itself by transforming those to be colonized into 'Indians' through continual reiteration of pioneer logics." Byrd, *Transit*, xiii. On the reiterative performance of the frontier at the center of America's national imaginary, see Deloria, *Playing Indian*.
24. Taylor, *Archive and the Repertoire*, 143.
25. In a report for the *American Anthropologist*, First Lieutenant Nat P. Phister described the "Messiah craze" as "the creed to which the aboriginal inhabitants of our country have given such belief as to bring us to the verge of a great Indian war, after the Indian question had come to be regarded as practically settled." See Phister, "Indian Messiah," 105. US Army Brigadier General Marion Perry Maus concluded, "It is very probable that this craze is furthered by the more intelligent

and vindictive of the Indians ... and is probably furthered by designing white men who would reap the rewards of an Indian outbreak." Maus, "New Indian Messiah," 947. As Rev. M. N. Adams of the Good Will Mission, Sisseton Agency, Dakota, reported to the *Home Mission Monthly* in February 1891, "Our Indians have caught the craze of the so-called 'ghost dance,' which is in fact only the war dance, and in three different settlements on this reservation they are singing their war songs and dancing after the old style of the scalp dance, which means hostility to civilization, Christianity, and progress." "Words from Workers," 83. As L. G. Moses notes, "By the time Mooney reached the Cheyenne and Arapaho agency at Darlington, Indian Territory, Sioux ghost dancers and those other Sioux who had fled Pine Ridge in terror ... were camped within range of the field guns that ringed the agency compound." Moses, *Indian Man*, 53.
26. Mooney, *Ghost-Dance*, 783.
27. Ibid., 928.
28. Mooney, "Indian Ghost Dance."
29. Freud, *Totem and Taboo*, 3. On the impact of Morgan at the Bureau of Ethnology, see Elliott, *Culture Concept*. Taking up these lines, Jodi Byrd connects the projected temporality of vanishing to a photographic temporality. See Byrd, *Transit*, esp. xv, 37–38.
30. Wenger, *We Have a Religion*, 35.
31. Mooney, *Ghost-Dance*, 928.
32. Masuzawa helpfully describes the broader search for "the most primitive forms of religion, which were presumed to be equivalent, more or less, to those observable in the lives of contemporary savages, lives on the brink of disappearance." Masuzawa, *Invention of World Religions*, 12.
33. In so doing, Mooney's study offers a form of secular pluralism that a number of scholars have linked to the consolidation of white Protestantism hegemony in the US. See especially Jakobsen and Pellegrini, introduction to *Secularisms*; Fessenden, *Culture and Redemption*, esp. 3–6.
34. On secularism's production of "buffered" and "porous" subjects, see Taylor, *Secular Age*, 37–38.
35. Modern, *Secularism in Antebellum America*, 234.
36. Taylor, *Secular Age*, 27–44.
37. Elliott, "Ethnography, Reform," 216. Mooney's comparative approach is evident from the very first pages of his 1896 report, where his epigraphs juxtapose his own translation of an 1891 "Arapaho Ghost Song" with Bayard Taylor's 1879 poem "My Dead" and Edna Dean Proctor's 1893 poem "The Song of the Ancient People," all of which frame the text with a kind of cross-cultural catalog of mourning. As Kathleen Washburn argues, these epigraphs signal the mournful, sympathetic tenor of Mooney's report even as they plot Indians on a historical teleology of which Wounded Knee is the end. See Washburn, *Indigenous Modernity*, esp. 109n62.
38. Taylor, "'Contagious Emotions' and the Ghost Dance," 1059. As Taylor notes, "Able to resist the religious fevers 'common to all humanity,' ... Mooney's

epidemiological anthropology, with its penetrating gaze, sees through the myriad subjective symptoms of ecstatic belief to the objective truth of final causes" (1063).

39. Ibid., 1058. In my use of *biopolitical*, I draw on Lisa Stevenson's helpful gloss; for Stevenson, *biopolitics* is "a form of care and governance that is primarily concerned with the maintenance of life itself, and is directed at populations rather than individuals." Stevenson, *Life Beside Itself*, 3.
40. Raiford, *Imprisoned*, 12.
41. Fleming and Luskey, *North American Indians*, 143.
42. Mooney, *Ghost-Dance*, 654.
43. Jacknis, "James Mooney," 201.
44. Mooney, *Ghost-Dance*, 774.
45. Ibid., 775.
46. Ibid., 774.
47. Elliott, *Culture Concept*, 120.
48. Vizenor, *Survivance*, 13. See also Vizenor, *Fugitive Poses*.
49. As Hittman notes, each of Wovoka's additions likely held spiritual significance. Hittman, *Wovoka*, 111–113.
50. Jacknis describes Mooney's shadow as an "endearing flaw" while Fleming and Luskey note that Mooney "valued field photographs as historic documents but . . . did not have time to learn the techniques. His main means of communication was the written word. Yet his slightly out-of-focus photographs, with the shadow of his image, are haunting." Jacknis, "James Mooney," 186; Fleming and Luskey, *North American Indians*, 143.
51. On the "visionary perception" of the Ghost Dance, see Landrum, "Shape-Shifters, Ghosts," 260.
52. As Avery Gordon argues, haunting is both a function of our critical objects and a methodological imperative: "Following the ghosts is about making a contact that changes you and refashions the social relations in which you are located. It is about putting life back in where only a vague memory or a bare trace was visible to those who bothered to look." Gordon, *Ghostly Matters*, 22.
53. Mooney, *Ghost-Dance*, 922–923.
54. Like many of his contemporaries, Mooney aligned femininity with spiritual receptivity. As he noted of the Ghost Dance, "Young women are usually the first to be affected, then older women, and lastly men. Sometimes, however, a man proves as sensitive as the average woman." Mooney, *Ghost-Dance*, 923–924.
55. Ibid., 925.
56. Ibid., 923.
57. On realism as a mode of surveillance, see Seltzer, *Criminal Continuities*. More recently, scholars have moved beyond the idiom of surveillance to argue that realism internalizes distinctly Protestant modes of vision to visualize the relationship between spiritual and material realms. Gregory Jackson, for example, has described the "aesthetics of immediacy" in realism's production of spiritual

realities while Erica Fretwell has articulated realism's practice of "showing not-seeing," or the effort to materialize a felt but invisible presence. Jackson, *Word and Its Witness*; Fretwell, *What We Feel*.
58. Smith, "Spirit Photograph."
59. What James described as the "field" theory of consciousness resonates in fascinating ways with Mooney's fieldwork, which (as I argue throughout this chapter) produced and materialized a cross-temporal spiritual frontier as a function of realist narration. Similarly, James articulated the permeable "margin" between the material and the spiritual worlds as both a spatial and a temporal one. As James argued, the margin

> lies around us like a "magnetic field," inside of which our centre of energy turns like a compass-needle, as the present phase of consciousness alters into its successor. Our whole past store of memories floats beyond this margin, ready at a touch to come in; and the entire mass of residual powers, impulses, and knowledges that constitute our empirical self stretches continuously beyond it. So vaguely drawn are the outlines between what is actual and what is only potential at any moment of our conscious life, that it is always hard to say of certain mental elements whether we are conscious of them or not. (James, *Varieties*, 232)

60. McGarry, *Ghosts of Futures Past*, 66.
61. Smith, "Spirit Photograph."
62. As McGarry notes, spiritualism relied on the rhetoric of science in its production of spiritual evidence, while "an interest in Spiritualism ostensibly allowed some scientists to retain their professional identity as empirically based investigators while rejecting the stark materialism to which many of their colleagues subscribed. Rather than science vanquishing religion, as in the classic secularization narrative, here science and religion worked as mutually constitutive knowledges, together producing a materialist belief system to explain the immaterial world." McGarry, *Ghosts of Futures Past*, 129.
63. See Deloria, *Playing Indian*.
64. Sweezy, *Arapaho Way*, 63–64.
65. Such care, as Stevenson argues, is distinctly biopolitical, or pitched toward the organization and governance of populations rather than individuals. In this sense, such bureaucratic or institutional forms of care have manifested as distinctly indifferent to the communities they purportedly aim to protect. Stevenson, *Life Beside Itself*, 4.
66. Kicking Bear, "Kicking Bear's Speech," 310. While Mooney described Kicking Bear's speech as "perhaps the best statement of the Sioux version" of the Ghost Dance, Maddra points out that his source for the speech was an October 1890 report forwarded by James McLaughlin, the agent at Standing Rock, to the commissioner of Indian affairs. See Maddra, *Hostiles?*, 33.
67. Irwin, *Coming Down*, 8.

68. Gotman, *Choreomania*, 233.
69. Mooney, "Indian Ghost Dance."
70. In his introduction to *The Ghost-Dance Religion*, Mooney acknowledges "Mr Emile Berliner and the Berliner Gramophone Company, for recording, and Professors John Philip Sousa and F. W. V. Gaisberg, for arranging the Indian music." In the process of digitizing the records, archivists at the Library of Congress's Motion Picture, Broadcasting, and Recorded Sound Division noted that the "performance is probably by Mooney and not by authentic Native Americans. Bibliographic information lists performers as Charles and James Mooney, but no data has been found to verify the existence of Charles." Mooney, *Ghost-Dance*, 655. My efforts to obtain bibliographic information at the Recorded Sound Division and the American Folklife Center were unsuccessful, as the materials appear to have themselves vanished between departments.
71. Elliott, "Ethnography, Reform," 222–223.
72. Sterne, *Audible Past*, 221–222.
73. Ibid., 311.
74. Even when they acknowledged the impossibility of achieving a perfect transcription (as Mooney himself did), Philip Deloria notes that ethnographers still asserted the authority of their work, "claiming . . . not representational accuracy, but an accuracy that was essentialist." This ethnographic faith in turn enabled the early twentieth century's explosion of Indianist music (led by composers Charles Wakefield Cadman, Antonín Dvořák, Arthur Farwell, Natalie Curtis, and others), which sought to "[meld] ethnographic authenticity with privileged aesthetic vision." Deloria, *Indians in Unexpected Places*, 278, 197.
75. Pasler, "Sonic Anthropology," 8.
76. Deloria, *Indians in Unexpected Places*, 194–199.
77. As Stadler notes, the development of sound recording for commercial entertainment corresponded with a long-standing "white fascination with the sound of black voices and, in particular, with imagining black voices as in some senses excessively embodied and insufficiently linguistic—that is, as less or other than human." Stadler, "Never Heard Such a Thing," 98.
78. I take this use of the "artifactual" from Sterne, who notes that "the desire to artifactualize native cultures—themselves understood as acutely ephemeral—was a central motif in early writing about phonographic ethnography." Sterne, *Audible Past*, 318.
79. The Brilliant Quartette recorded a "camp meeting negro shout entitled Blind Tom" in 1894 for the Columbia Phonograph Company. Stadler notes that in the age of commercial sound recording, white fantasies of technological reproduction posited an "intimate link between blackness and phonographic recording," suggesting that the black voice was particularly suited to the "inhuman" voice of the phonograph. Stadler, "Never Heard Such a Thing," 98–99.
80. Sterne, *Audible Past*, 310.
81. Ibid., 310–311.

82. Mooney, *Ghost-Dance*, 953.
83. Ibid.
84. Sterne, *Audible Past*, 314.
85. Ibid., 289.
86. Bergland, *National Uncanny*, 4.
87. Byrd, *Transit*, 37.
88. Personal conversation with Judith Gray, reference specialist, American Folklife Center, February 19, 2015.
89. Fletcher wrote to Frederic Ward Putnam, director of the Peabody Museum of American Archeology and Ethnology, from her home in Washington on February 13, 1895: "I have bought a Graphophone, and already have taken important records. Monday night I had here 3 Otoe Indians and took down on the cylinders 22 songs, words and music and got at some very interesting material. It is my purpose when I have exploited the cylinders to file them in the museum for future reference." Fletcher's cylinders are archived at the American Folklife Center at the Library of Congress.
90. Mooney, "Indian Ghost Dance."
91. Pasler, "Sonic Anthropology," 10.
92. Schneider, *Performing Remains*, 139.
93. Byrd, *Transit*, 38.
94. Gordon, *Ghostly Matters*, 8.
95. Mooney, *Ghost-Dance*, 927.
96. Ibid., 869.
97. Ibid., 1059–1060.
98. Moses, *Indian Man*, 63.
99. Mooney, *Ghost-Dance*, 1060.
100. See Slotkin, *Gunfighter Nation*, 67–68.
101. See Maddra, *Hostiles?*, 4, 26.
102. Kasson, *Buffalo Bill*, 85, cited in Maddra, *Hostiles?*, 84.
103. As Maddra argues, "The Ghost Dance threatened assimilation on several fronts. First . . . it diverted the Indians' attention away from the assimilationists' agricultural and educational programs; second . . . it maintained a Lakota perspective on religious matters and reinforced the very communal ideas reformers were attempting to break down." Maddra, *Hostiles?*, 26.
104. Ibid., 131.
105. Ibid., 134.
106. Murphy, *People Have Never Stopped Dancing*, 76.
107. Anderson, *Snake Oil, Hucksters, and Hambones*, 66. See also McNamara, "Indian Medicine Show," 431–445.
108. As Joy Kasson notes, the visit to West Orange was most likely made on the strength of this financial connection between Cody and Edison. Kasson, *Buffalo Bill*, 255–263. On the details of the September 24, 1894, filming, see Sagala, *Buffalo Bill*; Musser, *Before the Nickelodeon*.

109. Musser, *Before the Nickelodeon*, 50.
110. Musser, *Edison Motion Pictures*, 125–126.
111. On the space of Edison's studio and its constraint on the dancers' movements, see Sagala, *Buffalo Bill*, 20.
112. Hearne, *Native Recognition*, 64.
113. Musser, *Before the Nickelodeon*, 64.
114. As Hearne argues, costuming in filmic representations of Native Americans could be as much about reinforcing racial schema as it could be about the cross-knit pleasures of racial performance and fluidity. See Hearne, *Native Recognition*, esp. 71–81.
115. I am drawing here on Catherine Russell's argument that possession rituals "[offer] a new regime of veracity to cinematic representation, an alternative realism that filmmakers have been drawn to for different ethnographic and aesthetic ends." Russell, "Ecstatic Ethnography," 279.
116. Sagala, *Buffalo Bill*, 20.
117. Byrd, *Transit*, xiii.
118. Doane, *Emergence of Cinematic Time*, 145, 163.
119. Ibid., 163.
120. As Kasson notes, Cody's film took on various titles in promotional materials and screening announcements, including *Indian War Pictures*, *Last Indian Battles*, *Indian Wars*, *Buffalo Bill's War Pictures*, and *Indian Wars Refought by United States Army*. Kasson, *Buffalo Bill*, 257.
121. Ibid.
122. Ibid., 260.
123. Sagala, *Buffalo Bill*, 87. Philip Deloria similarly observes that whether or not the story was circulated as a marketing ploy, it "captures perfectly the paradoxes of Indian people—and non-Indian audiences and filmmakers—caught in the curious mix of fiction, memory, realism, actuality, and expectation that came together at this precise moment." Deloria, *Indians in Unexpected Places*, 53.
124. On the existing record of the film, see Sagala, *Buffalo Bill*, 99; Kasson, *Buffalo Bill*, 262.
125. Schneider, *Performing Remains*, 27.
126. Ibid., 37.
127. As Nyong'o points out, there is no strict correspondence between reenactment (with its binding of multiple times) and critiques of chrononormativity: "The critique of linear time, that is to say, possesses limits of its own, and we cannot always valorize those who veer from the temporally straight and narrow, confidently equating linearity with chrononormativity." Nyong'o, "Race, Reenactment," 84.
128. Ibid., 87.
129. On Cody's effort to construct sets "in strict accordance with history," see Sagala, *Buffalo Bill*, 83.
130. Ibid., 90.

131. Mooney, *Ghost-Dance*, 796. On Lakota, Cheyenne, and other early delegates to Wovoka, see Andersson, *Lakota Ghost Dance*, 37–39.
132. Lear, *Radical Hope*, 151.
133. Ibid., 151.
134. Simpson, *Mohawk Interruptus*, 7.
135. Neihardt, *Black Elk Speaks*, 151 (emphasis mine).
136. I am drawing here on Mishuana Goeman's observation that "the 'real' of settler colonial society is built on the violent erasures of alternative modes of mapping and geographic understandings." Goeman, *Mark My Words*, 2.
137. Gotman, *Choreomania*, 250.
138. On the politics of recognition, see Coulthard, *Red Skin, White Masks*. Drawing on Frantz Fanon's crucial theorization of the maintenance of colonial power through the (re)production of "colonized subjects," Glen Sean Coulthard argues for a similar dynamic in settler-colonial states, where state recognition operates not as a source of liberal freedom but "rather as the field of power through which colonial relations are produced and maintained" (17).
139. Butler, *Undoing Gender*, 24.
140. As Rivkin argues, the construction of a singular "modernity" to which Indians did or did not belong is itself an extension of settler colonialism. See Rivkin, *Beyond Settler Time*, 8–9.
141. Byrd, *Transit*, 37.
142. Roach, *Cities of the Dead*, 209.
143. Gotman, *Choreomania*, 226 (original emphasis).
144. Butler, *Precarious Life*, 30.
145. Garland to Mooney, October 1900, James Mooney Papers, National Anthropological Archives.
146. See Underhill and Littlefield, introduction to *Hamlin Garland*, 21–40.
147. As Garland would later note, "My design was directly opposed to that of Remington, who carried to the study of these hunters all the contempt, all the conventional notions of a hard and rather prosaic illustrator. . . . His white hunters were all ragged, bearded, narrow between the eyes, and his red men stringy, gross of feature, and cruel." Newlin, *Hamlin Garland*, 360.
148. Garland, "Red Man's Present Needs," 177.
149. On the distinction between "progressive" and "traditional" Indians, see Lewis, "Reservation Leadership," 124–148.
150. Garland, "Rising Wolf—Ghost Dancer," 54.
151. Garland, "Silent Eaters," 219.
152. In his reading of the Ghost Dance as it appears in contemporary Native American literatures, Rivkin suggests that the Ghost Dance offers "less unbroken continuity than complex cross-temporal communications, impressions, and relations that exceed the unfolding of a timeline." In this sense, the Ghost Dance becomes an important site from which to imagine "Native futures not bound by the presumed givenness of settler national geographies and destinies." My reading

of non-Native reenactments of the dance suggests that it is precisely the ability to conjure cross-temporal relations that made the Ghost Dance so seductive to non-Native observers, even as that seduction was predicated on a settler-colonial timeline, in which the dance might erupt into the present precisely *because* it ostensibly belonged to the past. Rivkin, *Beyond Settler Time*, 131.
153. Garland, "Silent Eaters," 190.
154. Ibid., 224–225.
155. Hamlin Garland to James Mooney, October 1900, James Mooney Papers, National Anthropological Archives.
156. Garland, "Silent Eaters," 229.
157. Ibid.
158. Garland, "Red Man as Material," 182.
159. Ibid.
160. Garland, *Crumbling Idols*, 42.
161. Ibid., 54.

CHAPTER 4. TOUCHING A BUTTON

1. Howells, "Execution by Electricity," 23.
2. As I discuss later in this chapter, such long-distance feats included, by 1895, the illumination of the grounds of the Atlanta Exposition—the site of Booker T. Washington's famous "Atlanta Compromise" speech—from President Grover Cleveland's summer home in Buzzard's Bay, Massachusetts. See Jones, *Atlanta Exposition*. My argument here is drawn from Reckson, "Weyde, Czolgsoz, McKinley Assassin."
3. Howells, "Execution by Electricity," 23.
4. As Paul Gilmore notes, the nineteenth-century link between electrical technologies and the human body at once reinforced and troubled the idea of universal connectivity, "giv[ing] the lie to fantasies of complete identification." Gilmore, *Aesthetic Materialism*, 99.
5. On the contested social meanings of electricity and electrification in the US, see Nye, *Electrifying America*. On the Romantic embrace of electric technologies, and (in particular) Douglass's recognition that deracinated technologies functioned as both a promise and a threat, see Gilmore, *Aesthetic Materialism*.
6. Douglass invoked electricity with a full sense of the way in which its utopian promise of connectivity was often interarticulated with white supremacy. As Gilmore notes, "In the same way that spiritual electricity proposed that the electrical union of humankind was based in particular bodies while emphasizing that that union would only take place in a realm shorn of bodies altogether, the techno-utopian discourse around the telegraph and electricity offered the possibility of a harmonious human union through an abstract common personhood but tended to base that dream on the idea of all humanity being raised up to Euro-American standards." Gilmore, *Aesthetic Materialism*, 123.

7. In *The Gold Standard and the Logic of Naturalism*, Walter Benn Michaels links debates around push-button photography to the speculative logic of market capitalism. For Michaels, literary naturalism evinces this logic by depicting acts like touching a button (or rolling the dice) less as indeterminate than as overdetermined—which is to say, determined by the market. While Michaels describes such acts as embedded in the historical logic of capitalism, my effort is to demonstrate the disciplinary process of racialization that helps sustain (and cannot be separated from) this logic. Michaels, *Gold Standard*.
8. As Mark Essig notes, Edison reportedly snapped his fingers to indicate the instantaneous work of the closed circuit. Essig, *Edison*, 133.
9. Benjamin, *Illuminations*, 174–175.
10. Agamben, *Means without End*.
11. Berlant, *Cruel Optimism*, 198.
12. Or, more precisely, *as* the sign of modernity. As Alexander Weheliye has argued, the reproduction of black suffering functions not as an exception to the category of the human but as its constitutive principle. See Weheliye, *Habeas Viscus*, 322.
13. As Rachel Plotnick indicates, push buttons functioned in the first decades of the twentieth century as "symbolic mediators between users and electricity," sites where electricity's material force could be alternately demystified and abstracted. Plotnick, "At the Interface," 824.
14. Sontag, *On Photography*, 124.
15. On the relationship between the movement of electricity and the movement of affect in and across bodies, see Gilmore, *Aesthetic Materialism*; Bennett, *Vibrant Matter*. As Gilmore points out, in the nineteenth century, "metaphors of electrical effect and affect were more than just metaphors . . . aesthetic experience itself was often imagined to be . . . electrical itself." Gilmore, *Aesthetic Materialism*, 7. Conversely, it seems likely that the figurative use of button-pressing—to describe annoyance or excitation—would have emerged at precisely this moment of urban and domestic electrification. Certainly the sexual meaning of button-pressing was available by the time Lil Johnson recorded "Press My Buttons (Ring My Bell)" for Vocalion Records in 1936.
16. Weheliye, *Habeas Viscus*, 44–45.
17. Bernstein, *Racial Innocence*, 73.
18. I'm drawing here on several important articulations of the "interval" and its transformative potential. William Connolly, for example, describes the "fugitive interval of perception": the break or cut between sensory impression and its cultural organization. Connolly, "Materialities of Experience," 184. My account of the interval also draws heavily from Kara Keeling's description of the cyclical temporality of colonial violence and the interval through which the possibility of decolonization might be perceived. As Keeling argues, most often the interval is simply the endurance of colonialism's "infernal cycle," yet it also opens up or exposes the possibility of the unanticipated or unforeseeable alteration. Keeling, "In the Interval," 110.

19. Hart, "Secular Coloniality," 188.
20. Indeed, part of what realism seeks to name and contain in the ecstatic is precisely this entanglement, what philosopher Jean-Luc Nancy describes as a fundamental plurality of being, a being-with that is constitutive of being itself. See Nancy, *Being Singular Plural*.
21. Modern, *Secularism in Antebellum America*, 6.
22. On the self-as-circuit, see Hoffstader, *I Am Strange Loop*.
23. Modern, *Secularism in Antebellum America*, 6.
24. Essig, *Edison*, 251–260.
25. Howells, "State Manslaughter," 151.
26. Stieglitz, "Hand Camera," 215.
27. Bentley, *Frantic Panoramas*, 81.
28. Ibid., 91. On literary realism's alternately ambivalent and celebratory relationship to photography, see Burrows, *Familiar Strangeness*; Green-Lewis, *Framing the Victorians*; Novak, *Realism, Photography*; Trachtenberg, *Reading American Photographs*. On Howells's repeated use of the camera as a metaphor for realist writing, and on his invocation of photography as an embodied practice of instantaneity, see Clayton, "London Eyes," 374–394.
29. As Armstrong notes, "Death, at the heart of a technological apparatus within the body, becomes an invisible cipher and so is distanced from the public, whilst at the same time being made available to a wider audience via an information technology." Armstrong, *Modernism, Technology, and the Body*, 35.
30. Eduardo Cadava suggests that the temporal structure of the photograph—the constitutive withdrawal of its subject—is such that it "speaks to us of mortification": it is "a grave for the living dead." Cadava, *Words of Light*, 10–11. Resisting a constitutive link between photography and death, Schneider argues this connection may in fact be a function of modernist thinking about photography "rather than a condition of photography itself." Schneider, *Performing Remains*, 222n8.
31. Schneider, *Performing Remains*, 140; Barthes, *Camera Lucida*, 5.
32. Abel, "Skin, Flesh," 38–39.
33. On the constitutive disappearance of live performance, see Phelan, *Unmarked*, 146–166. As Schneider points out, this distinction has been largely predicated on how the archive itself determines what does and doesn't remain. On the problematic separation of archive and repertoire, see Taylor, *Archive and the Repertoire*, 18–23.
34. See Lesy, "William Van Der Weyde," 62–69; Clayton, "W. M. Van Der Weyde"; Reckson, "William Vander Weyde."
35. McGovern, "Vander Weyde's 'News-Photography,'" 682.
36. My thanks to Joe Struble of the George Eastman House for pointing me toward this possibility.
37. On the ritualization of electrocution, see Essig, *Edison*, 237; see also Moran, *Executioner's Current*, 88–91.

38. Wiegman, *American Anatomies*, 36; Fusco, "Racial Time, Marks, Metaphors," 16. Though addressing the production of gender rather than race, Rey Chow's delineation in modernism of "a logic of visuality that bifurcates 'subjects' and 'objects' into the incompatible positions of intellectuality and spectacularity" is also useful here. Chow, "Postmodern Automatons," 105.
39. My thanks to Nicholas Gaskill for this connection. Fanon, *Black Skin, White Masks*, 93. On Fanon's hailing and blackness as a form of surfacing, see Fleetwood, *Troubling Vision*, 21–28; Ahmed, *Cultural Politics*, 127. On photography's deictic gesture and the production of criminalized bodies, see Sekula, "Body and the Archive," 3–64.
40. On the dynamics of spectacle, spectatorship, and witness surrounding lynching photographs, see Goldsby, *Spectacular Secret*, 229–238; Apel and Smith, *Lynching Photographs*; Raiford, *Imprisoned*, 29–66, 209–221.
41. Here I am drawing on Robyn Wiegman's crucial distinction: "To mark the body is not the same as *being* a bodily mark." Wiegman, *American Anatomies*, 25.
42. Fleetwood, *Troubling Vision*, 6.
43. Barthes, *Camera Lucida*, 14.
44. On lynching as a function of modernity and of mass cultural production, see Goldsby, *Spectacular Secret*, 114–125, 169.
45. Martshukat, "Art of Killing by Electricity," 907.
46. Ibid., 910–911.
47. White, "Burning of Jim McIlherron," 16.
48. Johnson, "Changing Status of Negro Labor," 34.
49. Hicks, "Petition for Writ of Habeas Corpus," 201.
50. Stadler, "Never Heard Such a Thing," 102.
51. Thomas de la Peña, *Body Electric*, 113.
52. Essig, *Edison*, 280.
53. See Reckson, "William Vander Weyde."
54. See, for example, the centrality of the telegraph in Theodore Dreiser's 1901 story "Nigger Jeff," a fictionalized account of a lynching that Dreiser witnessed in 1893 while a reporter for the *St. Louis Republic*. Sent to report on a lynching, Dreiser's narrator finds himself implicated—via the seemingly benign electric message—in the violence of lynching's unimpeded communications of "justice." Just as the quick relay of (fabricated) information was central to the formation of the lynch mob, Dreiser's story insists on an unsettling parallel in the production and circulation of his own realist narrative, as the ambivalent reproduction of lynching becomes central to the realist project. Dreiser, "Nigger Jeff," 366–375. See Hopkins and Mulligan, "Lynching the Black Male Body," 229–247.
55. Seltzer, *Bodies and Machines*, 11.
56. As Fred Moten argues, "An image from which one turns is immediately caught in the production of its memorialized, re-membered reproduction." Moten, *In the Break*, 200.
57. Young, *Embodying Black Experience*, 27, 58.

58. On the necromantics of citizenship as it reinforces racial subjection, see Castronovo, *Necro Citizenship*.
59. Manning, *Minor Gesture*, 2.
60. Cadava, *Words of Light*, 11–12.
61. My thanks to Joe Struble of the George Eastman House for suggesting this possibility.
62. Smith, "Photographer's Touch," 328.
63. I'm drawing here on Robin Bernstein's description of an effigy as something that "bears and brings forth collectively remembered, meaningful gestures and thus surrogates for that which a community has lost." Bernstein, *Racial Innocence*, 23.
64. On "temporal drag" as an alternative practice of "archiving culture's throwaway objects," see Freeman, *Time Binds*, xxiii. We might also think here of Leigh Raiford's notion of critical black memory, in which photography serves not as static record of past violence but as a still-generative site through which to rebuild forms of community in the present. See Raiford, *Imprisoned*.
65. Schneider, *Performing Remains*, 30.
66. Doane, *Emergence of Cinematic Time*, 162–163.
67. In contrast, Edison's January 4, 1903, film *Electrocuting an Elephant*—which documents the live execution of a circus elephant named Topsy—collapses human and animal death, linking the speed of film to the lethal work of electricity. Invoking the popular minstrel character to position the black/animal body as simultaneously childlike and threatening, the film works to punish this threat. My thanks to Gustavus Stadler for this connection.
68. Rauchway, *Murdering McKinley*, 53. My argument here is drawn from Reckson, "Weyde, Czolgsoz, McKinley Assassin."
69. Bhabha, *Location of Culture*, 364. Bhabha cites from Walter Benjamin's *Understanding Brecht* (1973).
70. Thomas de la Peña, *Body Electric*, 105.
71. Bennett, *Vibrant Matter*, 28.
72. Johnson, *Autobiography*, 106.
73. Ibid., 107.
74. Sorett, *Spirit in the Dark*, 8.
75. Ibid., 24.
76. Bennett, *Vibrant Matter*, 27; Sorett, *Spirit in the Dark*, 10.
77. Johnson's works continuously return to the figure of John Brown, who appears in the preface to *The Book of American Negro Spirituals* (1925), in the preface to *God's Trombones* (1927), and once more in *Along This Way* (1933).
78. Johnson, *Autobiography*, 29.
79. Richard Dyer, for example, notes the association of "shine" and blackness as a function of the "racial character of [photographic] technologies," which privileged white skin in the development of film stock and lighting techniques. Dyer, *White*, 83. I'm grateful to Erica Fretwell for this observation.

80. Such a gesture might be usefully situated at the intersection of "incorporating" and "inscribing" practices as Paul Connerton has described them; see Connerton, *How Societies Remember*, 74. Touching a button is at once a "mnemonics of the body" and a practice of marking or inscribing racial identity. On gesture as a practice of inscription, see Noland, *Agency and Embodiment*.
81. Johnson, *Along This Way*, 506.
82. Baker, *Modernism and the Harlem Renaissance*, 16.
83. Edwards, *Charisma and Fictions*, 16.
84. Ibid., 9.
85. Ibid., 16.
86. Washington, *Up from Slavery*, 140–141.
87. Contemporary accounts of this electric spectacle appeared (for example) in the *New York Times*, the *Austin Daily Statesman*, the Boston *Daily Advertiser*, and the *Raleigh News and Observer*. "President Will Press"; "Atlanta Exposition"; "Press the Button"; "Touched the Button." See also Jones, *Atlanta Exposition*, 57. On the racial politics of the Atlanta Exposition, see Perdue, *Race and the Atlanta Exposition*.
88. Washington, *Up from Slavery*, 240.
89. As Robert Stepto points out, Washington repeatedly substitutes public reportage for private history; documents like Creelman's "allow Washington to authenticate certain events and his successful participation in them, without recourse to personal or subjective (and hence questionable) commentary." Stepto, *From Behind the Veil*, 42.
90. Washington, *Up from Slavery*, 249.
91. Johnson, *God's Trombones*, 837.
92. Johnson, *Along This Way*, 504.
93. Ibid., 506.
94. See Biers, *Virtual Modernism*. Mark Goble argues similarly that the narrator of *The Autobiography* takes on a phonographic quality himself, figuring the unstable relationship between race and the reproduction of sound. See Goble, *Beautiful Circuits*, 195.
95. Le Bon, *Crowd*, 100–101.
96. Durkheim, *Elementary Forms of Religious Life*, 158.
97. DuBois, *Darkwater*, 103.
98. Spillers, "Moving on Down the Line," 254.
99. Edwards, "Seemingly Eclipsed Window of Form," 592.
100. Ibid.
101. My thanks to Phil Barrish for this observation.
102. Johnson, *Along This Way*, 158.
103. Ibid., 161.
104. Ibid., 505.
105. Johnson, *Autobiography*, 113; Benston, *Performing Blackness*, 274.
106. Johnson, *Autobiography*, 110.

107. Ibid., 113.
108. Goldsby, *Spectacular Secret*, 200–201 (emphasis mine).
109. Johnson, *Autobiography*, 113.
110. Ahmed, *Cultural Politics*, 26–27.
111. Johnson, *Autobiography*, 113.
112. Dreiser, *Picture and a Criticism of Life*, 153.
113. Ibid.
114. James Weldon Johnson and Grace Nail Johnson Papers, box 67, folder 298, Beinecke Library.
115. Johnson, *Along This Way*, 482.
116. Ibid.
117. Ahmed, *Promise of Happiness*, 223.
118. Johnson, *Along This Way*, 315.
119. Ibid., 317.
120. That Johnson figured his own narrative in the terms of melodrama registers his close attention to the genres of black suffering. As Saidiya Hartman has argued, nineteenth-century melodrama mobilized the suffering body as a site of ethical legibility while reifying blackness as a form of abjection. See Hartman, *Scenes of Subjection*.
121. Goldsby, *Spectacular Secret*, 165–166 (emphasis mine).
122. Ibid., 205.
123. Bennett, *Enchantment*, 154.
124. Johnson, *Autobiography*, 5 (emphasis mine).
125. Noland, *Agency and Embodiment*, 8.
126. Agamben, *Means without End*, 57.
127. Berlant, "Contact."
128. Schuyler, *Black No More*, 16; Ellison, *Invisible Man*, 7.
129. Moten, *In the Break*, 1.

CHAPTER 5. BORN, AGAIN
1. Larsen, *Quicksand and Passing*, 8. This edition is hereafter cited as *Quicksand*.
2. Ibid.
3. Locke, "1928," 353.
4. Glazener, *Reading for Realism*, 3.
5. Ngai, *Ugly Feelings*.
6. Butler, *Bodies That Matter*, 123.
7. In pointing to what exceeds the list of attributes (gender, sexuality, race, class, and religion) in subject formation, I am drawing on Butler's articulation of the subject in and of power: "If the subject is neither fully determined by power nor fully determining of power (but significantly and partially both), the subject exceeds the logic of noncontradiction, is an excrescence of logic, as it were." Butler, *Psychic Life*, 17.
8. Laura Doyle notes that the Hughes epigraph initiates a logic of crossing that operates both formally and thematically in *Quicksand*, from the anagrammatic

"Naxos" (a hybrid representation of Tuskegee and Fisk as highly "saxon"-ized institutions), to Helga's transatlantic journeys, to the novel's larger approach to "modernity's racial criss-crossings." Doyle, *Freedom's Empire*, 401. Deborah McDowell was the first to point out the "Naxos"/ "Saxon" anagram in her 1986 introduction to the novel. McDowell, "Introduction," xvii. On the complexities of Hughes's religious thought, see Best, *Langston's Salvation*.

9. Taves, *Religious Experience*, 16.
10. Janet Jakobsen and Ann Pellegrini argue as much in their introduction to *Secularisms*—a volume that insists on the plurality and particularity of secularism as "a formation that develops *in relation to* religion." Jakobsen and Pellegrini, introduction, to *Secularisms*, 12.
11. Merinda Simmons's reading of the relationship between religious experience in *Quicksand* and Zora Neale Hurston's anthropological study of Afro-Caribbean Vodou, *Tell My Horse*, serves as an important exception. Against the critical tendency to read spirituality and maternity as combined forces of repression and disempowerment in *Quicksand*, Simmons argues that the specific physicality of religious expression in the novel helps unsettle a Western dichotomy between body and spirit in ways that link it to religious practices within the African diaspora. Simmons, "Slain in the Spirit," 93–110.
12. Pellegrini, "Testimonial Sexuality," 94.
13. Sedgwick, *Tendencies*, 8–9.
14. Peterson, "Forward," xi–xii. This is certainly not the only sense in which "queerness" has been applied critically to Larsen's texts. *Passing*, for example, has long been read as a novel of both racial and sexual passing, with Deborah McDowell arguing that the novel gestures to (without fully allowing) a lesbian relationship between its two main female characters, and Judith Butler indicating that the psychoanalytic vectors of the novel might help us map the methods "by which sexual difference is articulated and assumed." McDowell, *"Changing Same"*; Butler, "Passing, Queering," 267. As I will discuss later, "queerness" in *Quicksand* helps name the overlaps of religious, racial, and sexual feeling in the novel, as well as the convergences of subjective experience and social belonging. I am drawing throughout on Siobhan Somerville's crucial work on intertwined discourses of racial and sexual difference at the turn of the century and, more broadly, her insistence that queer reading move away from a "singular focus on sexuality to one equally alert to the resonances of racialization." Somerville, *Queering the Color Line*, 6.
15. *Quicksand* bears all the characteristics of the migration narrative as Farah Griffin has outlined it; the novel is "marked by an exploration of urbanism, an explication of sophisticated modern power, and . . . a return South." Especially helpful is Griffin's emphasis on the status of the "stranger" in the migration narrative: a largely anonymous, urban figure "whose membership within a group involves being at once outside and within its boundaries," a dis-location that *Quicksand* continually probes. Griffin, *"Who Set You Flowin'?,"* 3–4, 7.

16. Sedgwick, *Touching Feeling*, 8.
17. As Tracy Fessenden points out, postsecular criticism often positions the "postsecular" not simply as a release from the naïve historical account of secularization but from the complexities of religion and religious practice itself. In this sense, it retains the "lingering impress of the secularization narrative." Fessenden, "Problem of the Postsecular," 157. Jordan Stein notes that this is also a problem of historiographic method: "To write the history of secularism is to write the history of a descriptive misrecognition of actual processes of change. . . . The history of secularism is the history of a story we told, not of a thing that happened." Stein, "Angels in (Mexican) America," 684.
18. Lloyd, "Introduction," 6.
19. Ibid., 5.
20. Fessenden, "Afterword," 261, 263.
21. Mahmood, "Sexuality and Secularism," 50.
22. Ibid., 51.
23. I'm grateful to Phillip Maciak for this observation.
24. Stein, "Angels in (Mexican) America," 684.
25. Muñoz, *Cruising Utopia*, 186.
26. Ibid., 187.
27. Ibid.
28. On the temporality and optimism of contact, see Berlant, "Contact."
29. I am drawing here on Shane Vogel's reading of Muñoz, an essay I address later in this chapter. Vogel, "Touching Ecstasy," 47–57. I am also drawing on Nadia Ellis's important account of queer diasporic longing as it "produces a productive tension between attachment and a drive toward intense and idiosyncratic individuation (unencumbered by location, heritage, or even, indeed, by materiality)." Ellis, *Territories*, 6.
30. Ann duCille, for example, reads Larsen alongside Jessie Fauset, arguing that "Fauset's and Larsen's forays into the forbidden realm of female sexual desire appear progressive, counterconventional, and perhaps the most courageous, if tentative, literary efforts to explore sexual politics from a female perspective since Kate Chopin published *The Awakening* in 1899." DuCille, *Coupling*, 86. Deborah McDowell allows for much less sexual progressiveness in *Quicksand*; nevertheless, she argues that the novel presents the dilemma of "how to express female sexual desire, and especially lesbian desire, without becoming an icon of racist projection." McDowell, *"Changing Same,"* 97.
31. Carby, *Reconstructing Womanhood*, 169.
32. Johnson, "Quicksands of the Self," 169.
33. In describing the work of the comma, I am drawing on Jennifer DeVere Brody's attention to the performativity of punctuation, its "performative excess and bodily play." Brody, *Punctuation*, 9.
34. Nancy, *Inoperative Community*, 37.
35. Davis, *Nella Larsen*, 243.

36. See Jakobsen and Pellegrini, *Love the Sin*, 76–77.
37. Edelman, *No Future*.
38. For Warren, this "indexical" quality was a defining feature of African American literary production during the Jim Crow era—an era that for Warren historically delimits what we might call "African American literature." I draw from Warren's characterization here without conceding his broader point that this literature is a formation proper to the historical past. Warren, *What Was African American Literature?*, 13.
39. Brown, "Our Literary Audience," 42.
40. Ibid., 43.
41. Du Bois, "Two Novels," 359; Garvey, "*Home to Harlem*," 358.
42. Ivy, "*Home to Harlem*," 356–357.
43. Du Bois, "Two Novels," 360.
44. Davis, *Nella Larsen*, 279.
45. Sorett, *Spirit in the Dark*, 33.
46. Hughes, "Negro Artist," 56.
47. Sorett, *Spirit in the Dark*, 39.
48. Brown, "Our Literary Audience," 43.
49. "A Mulatto Girl," 16–17; Parsons, "Three Novels," 540.
50. Davis, *Nella Larsen*, 280. On the links between *Quicksand* and late nineteenth-century realism in the Jamesian mode, and especially with James's *Portrait of a Lady*, see Lay, "Parallels," 475–486.
51. Schor, *Reading in Detail*, xlii.
52. Ibid., 180 (emphasis original).
53. By "pleasure" here I mean a historical variation on the sexual topos that Hortense Spillers marks as central to regimes of enslavement. As Spillers notes, "Under these arrangements [of captivity] the customary lexis of sexuality, including 'reproduction,' 'motherhood,' 'pleasure,' and 'desire' are thrown into unrelieved crisis." Spillers, *Black, White, and in Color*, 221.
54. Vazquez, *Listening in Detail*, 28.
55. Ngai makes a similar claim in arguing that *Quicksand* dramatizes "the tension between two aesthetic positions at the heart of literary modernism: the claim to a racially distinctive aesthetic . . . and the aestheticization of racial difference itself." Ngai, *Ugly Feelings*, 177.
56. Larsen, *Quicksand*, 29. As Claudia Tate has pointed out, such scenes elucidate the refractive quality of subjection more broadly, as "the gaze of the racist other determines Helga's bodily ego and constitutes her subjectivity." Tate, *Psychoanalysis*, 120.
57. Esteve, *Aesthetics and Politics*, 166.
58. Larsen, *Quicksand*, 30.
59. In her essay "Eating the Other," bell hooks describes the dynamic by which black cultural forms provide the material of pleasure or authenticity for a consuming white majority. Extending this argument, Kyla Wazana Tompkins has elaborated

the relationship between eating and subjection, noting that "eating and food culture are nexuses through which the white relationship to otherness is often negotiated." In presenting Helga as both (potentially) devoured and devouring, *Quicksand* points to this model of consuming the other even as it registers racialized consumption as a broader, multidirectional process. hooks, *Black Looks*; Tompkins, "Everything 'Cept Eat Us," 207. See also Tompkins, *Racial Indigestion*.
60. Ngai, *Ugly Feelings*, 175.
61. Ibid., 200.
62. Larsen, *Quicksand*, 4.
63. I am drawing here on Jean-Luc Nancy's articulation of "communication," or what he describes as "the ecstasy of the sharing: 'communicating' by not 'communing.' These 'places of communication' are no longer places of fusion, even though in them one *passes* from one to the other; they are defined and exposed by their dislocation." Nancy, *Inoperative Community*, 25.
64. Griffin has argued for the importance of reading *Quicksand* as a migration narrative whose heroine "attempts to escape the confinement of American cities and the racial provincialism of the Harlem black bourgeoisie by escaping first to Europe and finally to the American South." As Griffin notes, neither provides a sustainable alternative. Griffin, *"Who Set You Flowin'?,"* 155.
65. Ellis, *Territories*, 3–4.
66. See Vogel, "Touching Ecstasy," 50.
67. Larsen, *Quicksand*, 58.
68. Ibid., 59.
69. Ahmed, *Promise of Happiness*, 106.
70. We might productively compare this scene to Zora Neale Hurston's description of the New World Cabaret in "How It Feels to Be Colored Me," published the same year as *Quicksand*. Deploying tropes of primitivism to underline the whiteness of her companion who remains "untouched" by the music, Hurston does not so much reveal the racialized subject as she calls attention to the "veneer" and painted surface of racialization itself. Hurston, "How It Feels," 828.
71. On the "death drive" in *Quicksand*, see Fleissner, *Women, Compulsion, Modernity*, esp. 265–272; Tate, *Psychoanalysis*, 131–147. On the "fantasy of nonbeing," see Brown, *Glamour in Six Dimensions*, 131. On Helga's "ecstatic disappearance," see Johnson, "Quicksands of the Self," 258. In their effort to account for both deliberate and compulsory forms of self-alienation, all these readings might be said to emerge from and grapple with Hazel Carby's claim that *Quicksand* "is the first text by a black woman to be a conscious narrative of a woman embedded within capitalist social relations." Carby, *Reconstructing Womanhood*, 170.
72. DuCille, *Coupling*, 87; Tate, *Psychoanalysis*, 125.
73. Esteve, *Aesthetics and Politics*, 171; Johnson, "Quicksands of the Self," 262.
74. Doyle, *Freedom's Empire*, 401.
75. Butler, *Psychic Life*, 17.
76. Muñoz, *Cruising Utopia*, 11.

77. As I noted previously, my reading of the performative work of the comma owes much to Brody's account of punctuation as it "stages an intervention between utterance and transcription, speech and writing, activism/activity and apathy, body and gesture." Brody, *Punctuation*, 9.
78. Vogel, "Touching Ecstasy," 48.
79. Ibid.
80. Larsen, *Quicksand*, 105.
81. Ibid., 3.
82. More recently, Koritha Mitchell has termed this response to black achievement as "know-your-place aggression . . . the flexible, dynamic array of forces that answer the achievements of marginalized groups such that their success brings aggression as much as praise." See Mitchell, "Identifying White Mediocrity," 253.
83. Freeman, *Time Binds*, 3.
84. Cooper, *Voice from the South*, 192–193.
85. Dana Luciano notes the ideological force of (white) motherhood as temporal structure, "emblematizing at once the cyclical rhythms of nature and a repository of the timeless truth of affection that stabilizes the race's travel toward the future." As Luciano suggests, drawing from Spillers, the position of motherhood was "reserved for those whose offspring counted as subjects with recognized futures." Luciano, *Arranging Grief*, 59; Spillers, "Mama's Baby, Papa's Maybe."
86. Tate, for example, argues that Helga "can transfer desire—here characterized as disgust—to socially sanctioned sexual desire only by marrying Green." Tate, *Psychoanalysis*, 137. Similarly, Griffin notes that in this sequence, "sexual ecstasy becomes conflated with Helga's own sense of religious ecstasy. When her sexual activity leads to the misery of childbirth, she immediately begins to reject religion." Griffin, *"Who Set You Flowin'?,"* 159. In less categorical terms, McDowell observes that Larsen "dramatizes the fine line between sexual and religious ecstasy, often said to be characteristic of fundamentalist religious sects." McDowell, *"Changing Same,"* 85.
87. Larsen, *Quicksand*, 134.
88. Esteve, *Aesthetics and Politics*, 168.
89. Here I am guided by both Molly McGarry and Ann Pellegrini, who each cite Michael Warner's important line "You can reduce religion to sex only if you don't especially believe in either one." Warner, "Tongues Untied," 229.
90. Larsen, *Quicksand*, 112.
91. Ibid., 113.
92. Ibid.
93. See Warner, *Publics and Counterpublics*. While focusing on secular institutions, Michael C. Dawson also points to the importance of the black church as "an essential part of the Black subaltern counterpublic"—one that has notably resisted the privatization of religion against the force of a dominant white Protestant secularism. Dawson, "Black Counterpublic?," 206.
94. Moten, *Stolen Life*, 32.

95. See Sernett, *Bound for the Promised Land*, 160–162; Best, *Passionately Human*, 61. See also Weisenfeld, *New World A-Coming*.
96. Best, *Passionately Human*, 51.
97. Simmons, "Slain in the Spirit," 102.
98. Ibid., 96.
99. Butler, "Passing, Queering," 267.
100. See Butler, *Gender Trouble*; Butler, *Bodies That Matter*; Butler, *Psychic Life of Power*. My reading benefits here from Amy Hollywood's crucial elaboration of the uses of "ritual" in Butler's notion of performativity, where "ritual remains an untheorized ballast for the force of language." As Hollywood argues, the mistake of "reducing ritual to language . . . runs parallel to the error made by those ritual theorists who claim ritual is meaningless"; both fail to recognize the way that "social realities are constituted by ritual action." Hollywood, "Performativity," 101, 108.
101. As Molly McGarry as argued, religion "is more (and other) than sublimated, displaced sexuality. . . . Conjoining a history of sexuality to a history of religion demands resistance both to casting spirituality as false consciousness and to reviving it in an implicit apologia that fails to acknowledge its place in the history of the bodily regulation of queer subjects." McGarry, "Quick, the Dead," 251–252.
102. Larsen, *Quicksand*, 113–114.
103. Warner, "Tongues Untied," 229.
104. As Warner and others have pointed out, it is partly through the Protestant logic of conversion—the idea of shedding a former self, of coming out or becoming something else—that the religious and the secular have come to resemble one another over time, even to bear a familial relation. See Warner, "Tongues Untied," 231.
105. See Muñoz, *Disidentifications*.
106. Larsen, *Quicksand*, 114.
107. Howells, *Imperative Duty*, 111.
108. Ibid., 114.
109. Cooper, *Voice from the South*, 201–202.
110. Fleissner, *Women, Compulsion, Modernity*, 197.
111. Ibid., 273.
112. Weheliye, *Habeas Viscus*, 44–45.
113. Crawley, *Blackpentecostal Breath*, 1–8.
114. Ibid., 34.
115. Ibid., 267.
116. Ibid., 266.
117. As Crawley suggests, "Perhaps refuge is only ever temporal, something that is carried and enacted rather than a place and a time." Ibid.
118. Larsen, *Quicksand*, 118.
119. Ibid., 120.
120. See Luciano, *Arranging Grief*.

121. Larsen, *Quicksand*, 75, 104.
122. Ibid., 133.
123. Ibid.
124. Ibid., 134.
125. Ibid., 135.
126. Ibid., 134.
127. Ibid., 15.
128. Ibid., 135.
129. Strieby, "Look Forward," 357. On the racial politics of the American Missionary Association, see Richardson, *Christian Reconstruction*; Weisenfeld, "Who Is Sufficient?," 493–507.
130. Vogel, "Touching Ecstasy," 54.
131. Baldwin, *Go Tell It on the Mountain*, 209.

CODA: BEHIND, BEFORE, BESIDE

1. Hartman, *Scenes of Subjection*, 75; Moten, *Stolen Life*, 32.
2. Larsen, *Quicksand*, 113.

BIBLIOGRAPHY

Abel, Elizabeth. "Skin, Flesh, and the Affective Wrinkles of Civil Rights Photography." *Qui Parle* 20, no. 2 (2012): 35–69.
Agamben, Giorgio. *Means without End: Notes on Politics*. Translated by Vincenzo Binetti and Cesare Casarino. Minneapolis: University of Minnesota Press, 2000.
Ahmed, Sara. *The Cultural Politics of Emotion*. New York: Routledge, 2004.
———. *The Promise of Happiness*. Durham, NC: Duke University Press, 2010.
Alexander, M. Jacqui. *Pedagogies of Crossing: Meditations on Feminism, Sexual Politics, Memory, and the Sacred*. Durham, NC: Duke University Press, 2005.
Anderson, Ann. *Snake Oil, Hucksters, and Hambones: The American Medicine Show*. Jefferson, NC: McFarland, 2000.
Andersson, Rani-Henrik. *The Lakota Ghost Dance of 1890*. Lincoln: University of Nebraska Press, 2008.
Apel, Dora, and Shawn Michelle Smith. *Lynching Photographs*. Los Angeles: University of California Press, 2008.
Armstrong, Tim. *Modernism, Technology, and the Body: A Cultural Study*. Cambridge: Cambridge University Press, 1998.
Asad, Talal. *Formations of the Secular: Christianity, Islam, Modernity*. Stanford, CA: Stanford University Press, 2003.
"The Atlanta Exposition: President Cleveland Pressed the Button and the Machinery of the Fair Was Put in Motion." *Austin Daily Statesman*, September 19, 1895. ProQuest Historical Newspapers. Accessed June 14, 2010. http://ezproxy.lib.utexas.edu/login?url=search-proquest-com.ezproxy.lib.utexas.edu/docview/1621277844?accountid=7118.
Baker, Houston A., Jr. *Long Black Song: Essays in Black American Literature and Culture*. Charlottesville: University of Virginia Press, 1972.
———. *Modernism and the Harlem Renaissance*. Chicago: University of Chicago Press, 1987.
Baldwin, James. *Go Tell It on the Mountain*. New York: Dell, 1952.
Barrish, Philip. *American Literary Realism, Critical Theory, and Intellectual Prestige, 1880–1995*. Cambridge: Cambridge University Press, 2001.
Barthes, Roland. *Camera Lucida: Reflections on Photography*. Translated by Richard Howard. New York: Hill and Wang, 1982.
Barton, J. C. "Howells's Rhetoric of Realism: The Economy of Pain(t) and Social Complicity in *The Rise of Silas Lapham* and *The Minister's Charge*." *Studies in American Fiction* 29, no. 2 (Autumn 2001): 159–187.

Benfey, Christopher. *The Double Life of Stephen Crane: A Biography*. New York: Knopf, 1992.

Benjamin, Walter. *Illuminations: Essays and Reflections*. Translated by Harry Zohn. New York: Schocken, 1939.

———. *Understanding Brecht*. London: N. L. B., 1973.

Bennett, Jane. *The Enchantment of Modern Life: Attachments, Crossings, and Ethics*. Princeton, NJ: Princeton University Press, 2001.

———. *Vibrant Matter: A Political Ecology of Things*. Durham, NC: Duke University Press, 2010.

Benston, Kimberly. *Performing Blackness: Enactments of African American Modernism*. New York: Routledge, 2000.

Bentley, Nancy. *The Ethnography of Manners: Hawthorne, James, Wharton*. Cambridge: Cambridge University Press, 1995.

———. *Frantic Panoramas: American Literature and Mass Culture, 1870–1920*. Philadelphia: University of Pennsylvania Press, 2009.

Bergland, Renée L. *The National Uncanny: Indian Ghosts and American Subjects*. Hanover, NH: Dartmouth College Press, 2000.

Berlant, Lauren. "Contact." *Supervalent Thought*. Accessed May 18, 2011. http://supervalentthought.com/2011/04/14/contact/.

———. *Cruel Optimism*. Durham, NC: Duke University Press, 2011.

Bernstein, Robin. *Racial Innocence: Performing American Childhood from Slavery to Civil Rights*. New York: New York University Press, 2012.

Best, Wallace. *Langston's Salvation: American Religion and the Bard of Harlem*. New York: New York University Press, 2017.

———. *Passionately Human, No Less Divine: Religion and Culture in Black Chicago, 1915–1952*. Princeton, NJ: Princeton University Press, 2005.

Bhabha, Homi. *The Location of Culture*. New York: Routledge, 1994.

Biers, Katherine. *Virtual Modernism: Writing and Technology in the Victorian Era*. Minneapolis: University of Minnesota Press, 2015.

Birnbaum, Michele. "Racial Hysteria: Female Pathology and Race Politics in Frances Harper's *Iola Leroy* and W. D. Howells's *An Imperative Duty*." *African American Review* 33, no. 1 (Spring 1999): 7–23.

Blum, Edward J. *W. E. B. Du Bois: American Prophet*. Philadelphia: University of Pennsylvania Press, 2007.

Blum, Edward J., and Jason R. Young. *The Souls of W. E. B. Du Bois: New Essays and Reflections*. Macon, GA: Mercer University Press, 2009.

"The 'Bones' That the Negroes Use Are Not the Invention of 'Dandy Jim.'" *North American* August 17, 1846, issue 2298, col C. *Nineteenth-Century U.S. Newspapers*. Accessed July 10, 2009. www.infotrac.galegroups.com.

Bramen, Carrie Tirado. *The Uses of Variety: Modern Americanism and the Quest for National Distinctiveness*. Cambridge, MA: Harvard University Press, 2001.

Bratton, J. S. "Dancing the Hornpipe in Fetters." *Folk Music Journal* 6, no. 1 (1990): 66–68.

Brody, Jennifer DeVere. *Punctuation: Art, Politics, and Play*. Durham, NC: Duke University Press, 2008.
Brooks, Daphne. *Bodies in Dissent: Spectacular Performances of Race and Freedom, 1850–1910*. Durham, NC: Duke University Press, 2005.
Brown, Bill. *The Material Unconscious: American Amusement, Stephen Crane, and the Economies of Play*. Cambridge, MA: Harvard University Press, 1996.
———. "Reification, Reanimation, and the American Uncanny." *Critical Inquiry* 32, no. 2 (Winter 2006): 175–207.
Brown, Judith. *Glamour in Six Dimensions: Modernism and the Radiance of Form*. Ithaca, NY: Cornell University Press, 2009.
Brown, Sterling. "Our Literary Audience." *Opportunity* 8, no. 2 (February 1930): 42–46, 61.
Buel, James W. *Mysteries and Miseries of America's Great Cities; Embracing New York, Washington City, San Francisco, and New Orleans*. St. Louis: Historical, 1883.
Burrows, Stuart. *A Familiar Strangeness: American Fiction and the Language of Photography, 1839–1945*. Athens: University of Georgia Press, 2010.
Butler, Judith. *Bodies That Matter: On the Discursive Limits of "Sex."* Abingdon-on-Thames, UK: Taylor & Francis, 2015.
———. *Gender Trouble: Feminism and the Subversion of Identity*. New York: Routledge, 2015.
———. "Passing, Queering: Nella Larsen's Psychoanalytic Challenge." In *Bodies that Matter: On the Discursive Limits of "Sex,"* 122–138. London: Routledge Classics, 1993.
———. *Precarious Life: The Powers of Mourning and Violence*. New York: Verso, 2006.
———. *The Psychic Life of Power: Theories in Subjection*. Stanford, CA: Stanford University Press, 2006.
———. *Undoing Gender*. New York: Routledge, 2009.
Byrd, Jodi. *The Transit of Empire: Indigenous Critiques of Colonialism*. Minneapolis: University of Minnesota Press, 2011.
Cadava, Eduardo. *Words of Light: Theses on the Photography of History*. Princeton, NJ: Princeton University Press, 1997.
Cady, Linell E., and Tracy Fessenden, eds. *Religion, the Secular, and the Politics of Sexual Difference*. New York: Columbia University Press, 2013.
Carby, Hazel. *Reconstructing Womanhood: The Emergence of the Afro-American Woman Novelist*. New York: Oxford University Press, 1987.
Carmody, Todd. "In Spite of Handicaps: The Disability History of Racial Uplift." *American Literary History* 27, no. 1 (Spring 2015): 56–78.
Caruth, Cathy. "Traumatic Awakenings." In *Performance and Performativity*, edited by Andrew Parker and Eve Kosofsky Sedgwick, 89–108. New York: Routledge, 1995.
Castronovo, Russ. *Necro Citizenship: Death, Eroticism, and the Public Sphere*. Durham, NC: Duke University Press, 2001.
Cavitch, Max. "Stephen Crane's Refrain." In *American Literature's Aesthetic Dimensions*, edited by Cindy Weinstein and Christopher Looby, 73–90. New York: Columbia University Press, 2012.

Chesnutt, Charles. *The Marrow of Tradition* (1901). Edited by Eric Sundquist. New York: Penguin, 1993.
Chow, Rey. "Postmodern Automatons." In *Feminists Theorize the Political*, edited by Judith Butler and Joan W. Scott, 101–120. New York: Routledge, 1992.
Christian, Barbara. *Black Women Novelists: The Development of a Tradition, 1892–1976*. Westport, CT: Greenwood Press, 1980.
Clark, Timothy. *The Theory of Inspiration: Composition as a Crisis of Subjectivity in Romantic and Post-Romantic Writing*. Manchester, UK: Manchester University Press, 1997.
Clayton, Owen. "London Eyes: William Dean Howells and the Shift to Instant Photography." *Nineteenth Century Literature* 65, no. 3 (December 2010): 374–394.
Clayton, Sachiko. "W. M. Van Der Weyde" (2008). New York Public Library Blog. Accessed July 23, 2013. www.nypl.org.
Clymer, Jeffory A. "Race and the Protocol of American Citizenship in William Dean Howells' *An Imperative Duty*." *American Literary Realism* 30, no. 3 (Spring 1998): 31–52.
Cohen, Gerald. *Studies in Slang, Part I*. Frankfurt: Verlag Peter Lang, 1999.
Cohen, Lara Langer. *The Fabrication of American Literature: Fraudulence and Antebellum Print Culture*. Philadelphia: University of Pennsylvania Press, 2011.
Cone, James H. *The Cross and the Lynching Tree*. Maryknoll, NY: Orbis, 2011.
Connerton, Paul. *How Societies Remember*. Cambridge: Cambridge University Press, 1989.
Connolly, William. "Materialities of Experience." In *New Materialisms: Ontology, Agency, and Politics*, edited by Diana Coole and Samantha Frost, 178–200. Durham, NC: Duke University Press, 2010.
Cooper, Anna J. *A Voice from the South: By a Black Woman of the South*. Chapel Hill: University of North Carolina Press, 2017.
Coulthard, Glen Sean. *Red Skin, White Masks: Rejecting the Colonial Politics of Recognition*. Minneapolis: University of Minnesota Press, 2014.
Coviello, Peter, and Jared Hickman. "Introduction: After the Postsecular." *American Literature* 86, no. 4 (2014): 645–654.
Crane, Jonathan Townley. *Christian Duty in Regard to American Slavery: A Sermon Preached in the Trinity Methodist Episcopal Church, Jersey City, on Sabbath Morning, December 11, 1859*. Jersey City, NJ: R. B. Kashow, 1860.
——— . *An Essay on Dancing*. New York: Nelson and Philips, 1849.
——— . *Methodism and Its Methods*. New York: Nelson and Philips, 1876.
Crane, Stephen. "Fears Realists Must Wait: An Interesting Talk with William Dean Howells." *New York Times*, October 28, 1894, 20. ProQuest Historical Newspapers. Accessed January 16, 2006. http://ezproxy.haverford.edu/login?url=search-proquest-com.ezproxy.haverford.edu/docview/95113318?accountid=11321.
——— . *The Monster* (1898). In *Stephen Crane: Prose and Poetry*, edited by J. C. Levenson, 389–448. New York: Library of America, 1996.
——— . *The Poems of Stephen Crane: A Critical Edition*. New York: Cooper Square, 1976.

———. *The Red Badge of Courage: An Episode of the American Civil War* (1895). Edited by Fredson Bowers. Charlottesville: University of Virginia Press, 1969.
———. *Tales, Sketches, and Reports.* Edited by Fredson Bowers. Charlottesville: University of Virginia Press, 1969.
———. *Tales of War* (1900). Charlottesville: University of Virginia Press, 1970.
———. *Tales of Whilomville* (1899–1900). Charlottesville: University of Virginia Press, 1969.
Crawley, Ashon T. *Blackpentecostal Breath: The Aesthetics of Possibility.* New York: Fordham University Press, 2017.
Davenport, Frederick Morgan. *Primitive Traits in Religious Revivals: A Study in Mental and Social Evolution* (1905). New York: Macmillan, 1917.
Davis, Thadious. *Nella Larsen, Novelist of the Harlem Renaissance: A Woman's Life Unveiled.* Baton Rouge: Louisiana State University Press, 1996.
Dawson, Melanie V. *Emotional Reinventions: Realist-Era Representations beyond Sympathy.* Ann Arbor: University of Michigan Press, 2015.
Dawson, Michael C. "A Black Counterpublic? Economic Earthquakes, Racial Agenda(s), and Black Politics." *Public Culture* 7, no. 1 (Fall 1994): 195–223.
Delbanco, Andrew. "The American Stephen Crane: The Context of *The Red Badge of Courage*." In *New Essays on "The Red Badge of Courage,"* edited by Lee Mitchell, 49–76. Cambridge: Cambridge University Press, 1986.
Deloria, Philip J. *Indians in Unexpected Places.* Lawrence: University Press of Kansas, 2004.
———. *Playing Indian.* New Haven, CT: Yale University Press, 1998.
Derrida, Jacques. *Archive Fever: A Freudian Impression.* Translated by Eric Prenowitz. Chicago: University of Chicago Press, 1996.
Doane, Mary Ann. *The Emergence of Cinematic Time: Modernity, Contingency, the Archive* Cambridge, MA: Harvard University Press, 2002.
Douglass, Frederick. "Too Much Religion, Too Little Humanity: An Address Delivered in New York, New York, on 9 May 1849." In *The Frederick Douglass Papers: Speeches, Debates, and Interviews*, vol. 2, *1847–1854*, edited by John W. Blassingame and John R. McKivigan, 176–193. New Haven, CT: Yale University Press, 1991.
———. "What to the Slave Is the Fourth of July? An Address Delivered in Rochester, New York, on 5 July 1852." In *The Frederick Douglass Papers: Speeches, Debates, and Interviews*, vol. 2, *1847–1854*, edited by John W. Blassingame and John R. McKivigan, 359–388. New Haven, CT: Yale University Press, 1991.
Doyle, Laura. *Freedom's Empire: Race and the Rise of the Novel in Atlantic Modernity, 1640–1940.* Durham, NC: Duke University Press, 2008.
Dreiser, Theodore. "Nigger Jeff." *Ainslee's* 8, no. 4 (November 1901): 366–375.
———. *A Picture and a Criticism of Life: New Letters.* Vol. 1, edited by Donald Pizer. Chicago: University of Chicago Press, 2008.
Du Bois, W. E. B. *The Autobiography of W. E. B. Du Bois.* New York: International Publishers, 1968.
———. "The Browsing Reader: Two Novels." *Crisis* (June 1928). Reprinted in *Voices of a Black Nation: Political Journalism in the Harlem Renaissance*, edited by Theodore G. Vincent, 359–360. San Francisco: Ramparts Press, 1973.

———. *Darkwater: Voices from within the Veil*. New York: Harcourt, Brace, and Howe, 1920.

———. "Howells and Black Folk" (1913). In *W. E. B. Du Bois: Writings*, 1147–1148. New York: Library of America, 1996.

———. *The Souls of Black Folk* (1903). In *W. E. B. Du Bois: Writings*, 357–547. New York: Library of America, 1996.

———. "The Souls of White Folk" (1920). In *W. E. B. Du Bois: Writings*, 923–938. New York: Library of America, 1996.

———. "The White Christ" (1915). In *Du Bois on Religion*, edited by Phil Zuckerman, 141–142. Walnut Creek, CA: AltaMira Press, 2000.

duCille, Ann. *The Coupling Convention: Sex, Text, and Tradition in Black Women's Fiction*. New York: Oxford University Press, 1993.

———. "The Occult of True Black Womanhood: Critical Demeanor and Black Feminist Studies." *Signs* 19, no. 3 (Spring 1994): 591–629.

Dunbar, Paul Laurence. *In Old Plantation Days*. New York: Dodd, Mead, 1903.

Durkheim, Émile. *The Elementary Forms of Religious Life* (1912). Translated by Carol Cosman. New York: Oxford University Press, 2001.

Dyer, Richard. *White*. London: Routledge, 1997.

Edelman, Lee. *No Future: Queer Theory and the Death Drive*. Durham, NC: Duke University Press, 2004.

Edwards, Brent. "The Seemingly Eclipsed Window of Form: James Weldon Johnson's Prefaces." In *The Jazz Cadence of American Culture*, edited by Robert G. O'Meally, 580–601. New York: Columbia University Press, 1998.

Edwards, Erica R. *Charisma and the Fictions of Black Leadership*. Minneapolis: University of Minnesota Press, 2012.

Eliot, George. *Adam Bede* (1859). New York: Penguin Classics, 1980.

Elliott, Michael. *The Culture Concept: Writing and Difference in the Age of Realism*. Minneapolis: University of Minnesota Press, 2002.

———. "Ethnography, Reform, and the Problem of the Real: James Mooney's Ghost-Dance Religion." *American Quarterly* 50, no. 2 (June 1998): 201–233.

Ellis, Nadia. *Territories of the Soul: Queered Belonging in the Black Diaspora*. Durham, NC: Duke University Press, 2015.

Ellison, Ralph. *Invisible Man* (1952). New York: Vintage International, 1995.

———. *Shadow and Act*. New York: Random House, 1964.

Essig, Mark. *Edison and the Electric Chair: A Story of Light and Death*. New York: Walker, 2005.

Esteve, Mary. *The Aesthetics and Politics of the Crowd in American Literature*. Cambridge: Cambridge University Press, 2007.

Evans, Curtis J. *The Burden of Black Religion*. New York: Oxford University Press, 2008.

Eytinge, Sol, Jr. "A Negro Camp Meeting in the South." *Harper's Weekly* 16 (August 10, 1872): 620.

Fabi, M. Giulia. "Reconstructing Literary Genealogies: Frances E. W. Harper's and William Deans Howells's Race Novels." In *Soft Canons: American Women Writers and Masculine Tradition*, edited by Karen L. Kilcup, 48–66. Iowa City: University of Iowa Press, 1999.

Fanon, Frantz. *Black Skin, White Masks*. Translated by Richard Philcox. New York: Grove Press, 1953.

Fessenden, Tracy. "Afterword: Critical Intersections: Race, Secularism, Gender." In *Race and Secularism in America*, edited by Vincent Lloyd and Jonathon Kahn, 257–270. New York: Columbia University Press, 2016.

———. *Culture and Redemption: Religion, the Secular, and American Literature*. Princeton, NJ: Princeton University Press, 2007.

———. "The Problem of the Postsecular." *American Literary History* 26, no. 1 (January 2014): 154–167.

Fleetwood, Nicole. *Troubling Vision: Performance, Visuality, and Blackness*. Chicago: University of Chicago Press, 2011.

Fleissner, Jennifer L. *Women, Compulsion, Modernity: The Moment of American Naturalism*. Chicago: University of Chicago Press, 2004.

Fleming, Paula Richardson, and Judith Luskey. *The North American Indians in Early Photographs*. New York: Harper and Row, 1986.

Foster, Frances Smith. "Gender, Genre, and Vulgar Secularism: The Case of Frances Ellen Watkins Harper and the AME Press." In *Recovered Writers / Recovered Texts: Race, Class, and Gender in Black Women's Literature*, edited by Dolan Hubbard, 46–59. Knoxville: University of Tennessee Press, 1997.

Frederic, Harold. Review of *The Red Badge of Courage*, by Stephen Crane. *New York Times*, January 26, 1896, 22. Reprinted in *Stephen Crane: The Critical Heritage*, edited by Richard M. Weatherford, 119. London: Routledge, 1973.

———. "Stephen Crane's Triumph" (1896). In *Critical Essays on Stephen Crane's "The Red Badge of Courage,"* edited by Donald Pizer, 35–41. Boston: G. K. Hall, 1990.

Freeman, Elizabeth. *Time Binds: Queer Temporalities, Queer Histories*. Durham, NC: Duke University Press, 2011.

Fretwell, Erica. *What We Feel*. Forthcoming manuscript.

Freud, Sigmund. *Totem and Taboo* (1913). Translated by James Strachey. New York: W. W. Norton, 1990.

Fried, Michael. *Realism, Writing, Disfiguration: On Thomas Eakins and Stephen Crane*. Chicago: University of Chicago Press, 1987.

Fusco, Coco. "Racial Time, Racial Marks, Racial Metaphors." In *Only Skin Deep: Changing Visions of the American Self*, edited by Coco Fusco and Brian Wallis, 13–50. New York: Henry N. Abrams, 2003.

Garland, Hamlin, *Crumbling Idols*. Chicago: Stone and Kimball, 1894.

———. "The Red Man as Material" (1903). In *Hamlin Garland's Observations on the American Indian, 1895–1905*, edited by Lonnie E. Underhill and Daniel F. Littlefield Jr., 179–182. Tucson: University of Arizona Press, 1976.

———. "The Red Man's Present Needs" (1902). In *Hamlin Garland's Observations on the American Indian, 1895–1905*, edited by Lonnie E. Underhill and Daniel F. Littlefield Jr., 165–177. Tucson: University of Arizona Press, 1976.

———. "Rising Wolf—Ghost Dancer" (1899). In *The Book of the American Indian*, edited by Keith Newlin, 51–66. Lincoln: University of Nebraska Press, 2005.

———. "The Silent Eaters" (1900). In *The Book of the American Indian*, edited by Keith Newlin, 159–270. Lincoln: University of Nebraska Press, 2005.

Garvey, Marcus. "*Home to Harlem*: An Insult to the Race." *Negro World*, September 29, 1928. Reprinted in *Voices of a Black Nation: Political Journalism in the Harlem Renaissance*, edited by Theodore G. Vincent, 357–358. San Francisco: Ramparts Press, 1973.

Gates, Henry Louis, Jr., and Cornel West. *The Future of the Race*. New York: Vintage, 1996.

Gilmore, Paul. *Aesthetic Materialism: Electricity and American Romanticism*. Stanford, CA: Stanford University Press, 2009.

———. "'De Genewine Artekil': William Wells Brown, Blackface Minstrelsy, and Abolitionism." *American Literature* 69, no. 4 (December 1997): 743–780.

Gilroy, Paul. *The Black Atlantic: Modernity and Double-Consciousness*. Cambridge, MA: Harvard University Press, 1993.

Glaude, Eddie S. *Exodus! Religion, Race, and Nation in Early Nineteenth-Century Black America*. Chicago: University of Chicago Press, 2000.

Glazener, Nancy. *Reading for Realism: The History of a U.S. Literary Institution, 1850–1910*. Durham, NC: Duke University Press, 2012.

Goble, Mark. *Beautiful Circuits: Modernism and the Mediated Life*. New York: Columbia University Press, 2010.

Goeman, Mishuana. *Mark My Words: Native Women Mapping Our Nations*. Minneapolis: University of Minnesota Press, 2013.

Goldsby, Jacqueline. *A Spectacular Secret: Lynching in American Life and Literature*. Chicago: University of Chicago Press, 2006.

Goldschmidt, Henry, and Elizabeth McAlister, eds. *Race, Nation, and Religion in the Americas*. Oxford: Oxford University Press, 2004.

Gordon, Avery. *Ghostly Matters: Haunting and the Sociological Imagination*. Minneapolis: University of Minnesota Press, 2011.

Gotman, Kélina. *Choreomania: Dance and Disorder*. New York: Oxford University Press, 2018.

Green-Lewis, Jennifer. *Framing the Victorians: Photography and the Culture of Realism*. Ithaca, NY: Cornell University Press, 1996.

Griffin, Farah. *"Who Set You Flowin'?": The African American Migration Narrative*. New York: Oxford University Press, 1995.

Hall, G. Stanley. "The Negro in Africa and America." *Pedagogical Seminary* 12, no. 3 (1905): 350–368.

Harper, Frances E. W. *Iola Leroy; or, Shadows Uplifted* (1892). Edited by Koritha Mitchell. New York: Broadview Editions, 2018.

Harris, Cheryl I. "Whiteness as Property." *Harvard Law Review* 106, no. 8 (June 1993): 1707–1791.

Hart, William D. "Secular Coloniality." In *Race and Secularism in America*, edited by Vincent W. Lloyd and Jonathon Kahn, 178–206. New York: Columbia University Press, 2016.
Hartman, Saidiya V. *Scenes of Subjection: Terror, Slavery, and Self-making in Nineteenth-Century America*. New York: Oxford University Press, 2010.
Hearne, Joanna. *Native Recognition: Indigenous Cinema and the Western*. Albany: SUNY Press, 2012.
Hickman, Jared. *Black Prometheus: Race and Radicalism in the Age of Atlantic Slavery*. Oxford: Oxford University Press, 2017.
Hicks, Frank. "Petition for Writ of Habeas Corpus (May 2, 1921)." In *Lynching in America: A History in Documents*, edited by Christopher Waldrep, 200–202. New York: New York University Press, 2006.
Higginbotham, Evelyn Brooks. *Righteous Discontent: The Women's Movement in the Black Baptist Church, 1880–1920*. Cambridge, MA: Harvard University Press, 1994.
Hinsley, Curtis M. *The Smithsonian and the Native American: Making a Moral Anthropology in Victorian America*. Washington, DC: Smithsonian Institution Press, 1994.
Hittman, Michael. *Wovoka and the Ghost Dance*. Edited by Don Lynch. Lincoln: University of Nebraska Press, 1997.
Hofstader, Douglas. *I Am Strange Loop*. New York: Basic, 2007.
Holland, Sharon Patricia. *Raising the Dead: Readings of Death and (Black) Subjectivity*. Durham, NC: Duke University Press, 2000.
Hollywood, Amy. "Performativity, Citationality, Ritualization." *History of Religions* 42, no. 2 (November 2002): 93–115.
hooks, bell. *Black Looks: Race and Representation*. Cambridge, MA: South End Press, 1992.
Hopkins, Patricia D., and Roark Mulligan. "Lynching the Black Male Body in Theodore Dreiser's 'Nigger Jeff': Did He 'Get It All In'?" *American Literary Realism* 45, no. 3 (Spring 2013): 229–247.
"hornpipe, n.1." In *OED Online*. Oxford University Press, March 2017. Accessed April 4, 2017. www.oed.com/.
Howells, William Dean. "Editor's Study." *Harper's* 76 (1887): 153–155.
———. "Execution by Electricity." *Harper's Weekly* 1, no. 14 (1888): 23.
———. *An Imperative Duty* (1891). Edited by Paul R. Petrie. New York: Broadview Editions, 2010.
———. "The Modern American Mood" (1897). In *The American 1890s: A Cultural Reader*, edited by Susan Harris Smith and Melanie Dawson, 77–86. Durham, NC: Duke University Press, 2000.
———. "State Manslaughter" (1904). In *Voices against Death: American Opposition to Capital Punishment, 1787–1975*, edited by Philip English Mackey, 150–155. New York: B. Franklin, 1976.
Hughes, Langston. "The Negro Artist and the Racial Mountain" (1926). In *Within the Circle: An Anthology of African American Literary Criticism from the Harlem*

Renaissance to the Present, edited by Angelyn Mitchell, 55–59. Durham, NC: Duke University Press, 1994.

Hurston, Zora Neale. "How It Feels to Be Colored Me" (1928). In *Zora Neale Hurston: Folklore, Memoirs, and Other Writings*, edited by Cheryl Wall, 826–829. New York: Library of America, 1995.

Hutton, Lawrence. *Curiosities of the American Stage*. New York: Harper & Brothers, 1891.

"imp, n.1." In *OED Online*. Oxford University Press, March 2017. Accessed April 4, 2017. www.oed.com/.

Irlam, Shaun. *Elations: The Poetics of Enthusiasm in Eighteenth-Century Britain*. Stanford, CA: Stanford University Press, 1999.

Irwin, Lee. *Coming Down from Above: Prophecy, Resistance, and Renewal in Native American Religions*. Norman: University of Oklahoma Press, 2008.

Ivy, James W. "*Home to Harlem*: A Slice of Life." *Messenger*, May–June 1928. Reprinted in *Voices of a Black Nation: Political Journalism in the Harlem Renaissance*, edited by Theodore G. Vincent, 356–357. San Francisco: Ramparts Press, 1973.

Jacknis, Ira. "James Mooney as Ethnographic Photographer." *Visual Anthropology* 3, nos. 2–3 (1990): 179–212.

Jackson, Gregory. *The Word and Its Witness: The Spiritualization of American Realism*. Chicago: University of Chicago Press, 2009.

Jakobsen, Janet R., and Ann Pellegrini, eds. *Secularisms*. Durham, NC: Duke University Press, 2008.

———, eds. *Love the Sin: Sexual Regulation and the Limits of Religious Tolerance*. New York: New York University Press, 2003.

James, William. "[Praise for *Souls*]" (1903). In *The Souls of Black Folk*, edited by Henry Louis Gates Jr. and Terri Hume Oliver, 227. New York: W. W. Norton, 1999.

———. *The Principles of Psychology*. New York: Henry Holt, 1890.

———. *The Varieties of Religious Experience: A Study in Human Nature*. London: Longmans, Green, 1902.

Jameson, Fredric. *The Antinomies of Realism*. London: Verso, 2013.

Jay, Martin. *Songs of Experience: Modern American and European Variations on a Universal Theme*. Berkeley: University of California Press, 2005.

"jim-dandy, n. and adj." In *OED Online*. Oxford University Press, March 2017. Accessed April 4, 2017. www.oed.com/.

Johnson, Barbara. "The Quicksands of the Self: Nella Larsen and Heinz Kohut." In *Female Subjects in Black and White: Race, Psychoanalysis, Feminism*, edited by Elizabeth Abel, Barbara Christian, and Helene Moglen, 252–265. Berkeley: University of California Press, 1997.

Johnson, James Weldon. *Along This Way* (1933). In *Writings*, edited by William L. Andrews, 131–604. New York: Library of America, 2004.

———. *The Autobiography of an Ex-colored Man* (1912). In *Writings*, edited by William L. Andrews, 3–127. New York: Library of America, 2004.

———. "The Changing Status of Negro Labor." In *Selected Writings of James Weldon Johnson, Volume II: Social, Political, and Literary Essays*, edited by Sondra Kathryn Wilson, 30–35. New York: Oxford University Press, 1995.

———. "Circumstantial Evidence; or, The Ordeals of Adele." James Weldon Johnson and Grace Nail Johnson Papers, box 67, folder 298. Beinecke Library.

———. *God's Trombones: Seven Negro Sermons in Verse* (1927). In *Writings*, edited by William L. Andrews, 834–867. New York: Library of America, 2004.

Jones, Sharon Foster. *The Atlanta Exposition*. Charleston, SC: Arcadia, 2010.

Kahn, Jonathon S. "Conclusion: James Baldwin and a Theology of Justice in a Secular Age." In *Race and Secularism in America*, edited by Jonathon S. Kahn and Vincent W. Lloyd, 239–255. New York: Columbia University Press, 2016.

———. *Divine Discontent: The Religious Imagination of W. E. B. Du Bois*. Oxford: Oxford University Press, 2011.

Kahn, Jonathon S., and Vincent W. Lloyd, eds. *Race and Secularism in America*. New York: Columbia University Press, 2016.

Kaplan, Amy. "Nation, Region, and Empire." In *The Columbia History of the American Novel*, edited by Emory Elliott, 266–284. New York: Columbia University Press, 1991.

———. *The Social Construction of American Realism*. Chicago: University of Chicago Press, 1988.

———. "The Spectacle of War in Crane's Revision of History." In *New Essays on "The Red Badge of Courage,"* edited by Lee Mitchell, 77–108. Cambridge: Cambridge University Press, 1986.

Kasson, Joy S. *Buffalo Bill's Wild West: Celebrity, Memory, and Popular History*. New York: Hill and Wang, 2000.

Keeling, Kara. "'In the Interval': Frantz Fanon and the 'Problems' of Visual Representation." *Qui Parle* 13, no. 2 (Spring/Summer 2003): 91–117.

Kicking Bear. "Kicking Bear's Speech, October 9, 1890." In Rani-Henrick Andersson, *The Lakota Ghost Dance of 1890*, 309–311. Lincoln: University of Nebraska Press, 2008.

Kidd, Colin. *The Forging of Races: Race and Scripture in the Protestant Atlantic World, 1600–2000*. New York: Cambridge University Press, 2006.

Kilgore, John Mac. *Mania for Freedom: American Literatures of Enthusiasm from the Revolution to the Civil War*. Chapel Hill: University of North Carolina Press, 2017.

———. "Nat Turner and the Work of Enthusiasm." *PMLA* 130, no. 5 (October 2015): 1347–1362.

Kilham, Elizabeth. "Sketches in Color." *Putnam's Monthly*, March 1870, 305.

Kristeva, Julia. *Powers of Horror: An Essay on Abjection*. Translated by Leon S. Roudiez. New York: Columbia University Press, 1982.

Landrum, Cynthia. "Shape-Shifters, Ghosts, and Residual Power: An Examination of Northern Plains Spiritual Beliefs, Location, Objects, and Spiritual Colonialism." In *Phantom Past, Indigenous Present: Native Ghosts in North American Culture and*

History, edited by Colleen E. Boyd and Coll Thrush, 255–279. Lincoln: University of Nebraska Press, 2011.

Larsen, Nella. *Quicksand and Passing*. Edited by Deborah E. McDowell. New Brunswick, NJ: Rutgers University Press, 2005.

Lay, Mary M. "Parallels: Henry James's *The Portrait of a Lady* and Nella Larsen's *Quicksand*." *CLA Journal* 20, no. 4 (1977): 475–486.

Lear, Jonathan. *Radical Hope: Ethics in the Face of Cultural Devastation*. Cambridge, MA: Harvard University Press, 2008.

Le Bon, Gustave. *The Crowd: A Study of the Popular Mind*. New York: Macmillan, 1896.

Lesy, Michael. "William Van Der Weyde and the American Morality Play." *Aperture* no. 194 (2009): 62–69.

Lewis, David Rich. "Reservation Leadership and the Progressive-Traditional Dichotomy: William Wash and the Northern Utes, 1865–1928." *Ethnohistory* 38, no. 2 (1991): 124–148.

Leys, Ruth. *Trauma: A Genealogy*. Chicago: Chicago University Press, 2000.

Lincoln, C. Eric, and Lawrence H. Mamiya. *The Black Church in the African American Experience*. Durham, NC: Duke University Press, 1990.

Lloyd, Vincent W. "Introduction: Managing Race, Managing Religion." In *Race and Secularism in America*, edited by Jonathon S. Kahn and Vincent W. Lloyd, 1–23. New York: Columbia University Press, 2016.

Locke, Alain. "1928: A Retrospective Review." In *Voices of a Black Nation: Political Journalism in the Harlem Renaissance*, edited by Theodore G. Vincent, 353–356. San Francisco: Ramparts Press, 1973.

Lott, Eric. *Love & Theft: Blackface Minstrelsy & the American Working Class*. New York: Oxford University Press, 2013.

Lovejoy, David S. *Religious Enthusiasm in the New World*. Cambridge, MA: Harvard University Press, 2014.

Luciano, Dana. *Arranging Grief: Sacred Time and the Body in Nineteenth-Century America*. New York: New York University Press, 2007.

Maddra, Sam A. *Hostiles? The Lakota Ghost Dance and Buffalo Bill's Wild West*. Norman: University of Oklahoma Press, 2006.

Mahar, William J. *Behind the Burnt Cork Mask: Early Blackface Minstrelsy and Antebellum American Popular Culture*. Urbana: University of Illinois Press, 1999.

Mahmood, Saba. *Politics of Piety: The Islamic Revival and the Feminist Subject*. Princeton, NJ: Princeton University Press, 2005.

———. *Religious Difference in a Secular Age: A Minority Report*. Princeton, NJ: Princeton University Press, 2015.

———. "Religious Reason and Secular Affect: An Incommensurable Divide?" *Critical Inquiry* 35, no. 4 (Summer 2009): 836–862.

———. "Sexuality and Secularism." In *Religion, the Secular, and the Politics of Sexual Difference*, edited by Linell E. Cady and Tracy Fessenden, 47–58. New York: Columbia University Press, 2013.

Manning, Erin. *The Minor Gesture*. Durham, NC: Duke University Press, 2016.

Manning, Marable. *Black Leadership*. New York: Columbia University Press, 1998.
Marsden, George M. *Fundamentalism and American Culture*. New York: Oxford University Press, 2008.
Martshukat, Jürgen. "'The Art of Killing by Electricity': The Sublime and the Electric Chair." *Journal of American History* 89, no. 3 (2002): 907.
Masuzawa, Tomoko. *The Invention of World Religions; or, How European Universalism Was Preserved in the Language of Pluralism*. Chicago: University of Chicago Press, 2005.
Maus, Marion P. "The New Indian Messiah." *Harper's Weekly* 34 (December 6, 1890): 947.
May, Vivian M. "Thinking from the Margins, Acting from the Intersections: Anna Julia Cooper's *A Voice from the South*." *Hypatia* 19, no. 3 (Spring 2004): 74–91.
McClendon, Aaron. "Sounds of Sympathy: William Wells Brown's *Anti-Slavery Harp*, Abolition, and the Culture of Early and Antebellum American Song." *African American Review* 47, no. 1 (Spring 2014): 83–100.
McDowell, Deborah E. *"The Changing Same": Black Women's Literature, Criticism, and Theory*. Bloomington: Indiana University Press, 1995.
———. Introduction to *Quicksand and Passing*, ix–xxxi. New Brunswick, NJ: Rutgers University Press, 1986.
McGarry, Molly. *Ghosts of Futures Past: Spiritualism and the Cultural Politics of Nineteenth-Century America*. Berkeley: University of California Press, 2008.
———. "The Quick, the Dead, and the Yet Unborn: Untimely Sexualities and Secular Hauntings." In *Secularisms*, edited by Janet R. Jakobsen and Ann Pellegrini, 247–282. Durham, NC: Duke University Press, 2008.
McGovern, Chauncy Montgomery. "Vander Weyde's 'News-Photography.'" *Broadway Magazine* 2, no. 9 (1898): 682.
McMillan, Uri. *Embodied Avatars: Genealogies of Black Feminist Art and Performance*. New York: New York University Press, 2015.
McNamara, Brooks. "The Indian Medicine Show." *Educational Theater Journal* 23, no. 4 (December 1971): 431–445.
Mee, Jon. *Romanticism, Enthusiasm, and Regulation: Poetics and the Policing of Culture in the Romantic Period*. Oxford: Oxford University Press, 2012.
Michaels, Walter Benn. *The Gold Standard and the Logic of Naturalism*. Berkeley: University of California Press, 1987.
Miller, Monica. *Slaves to Fashion: Black Dandyism and the Styling of Black Diasporic Identity*. Durham, NC: Duke University Press, 2009.
Mitchell, Koritha. "Identifying White Mediocrity and Know-Your-Place Aggression: A Form of Self-Care." *African American Review* 51, no. 4 (Winter 2018): 253–262.
———. Introduction to *Iola Leroy*, by Frances E. W. Harper, 13–50. New York: Broadview Editions, 2018.
———. *Living with Lynching: African American Lynching Plays, Performance, and Citizenship, 1890–1930*. Champaign: University of Illinois Press, 2011.
Mizruchi, Susan. *The Science of Sacrifice: American Literature and Modern Social Theory* Princeton, NJ: Princeton University Press, 1998.

Modern, John Lardas. *Secularism in Antebellum America: With Reference to Ghosts, Protestant Subcultures, Machines, and Their Metaphors: Featuring Discussions of Mass Media, Moby-Dick, Spirituality, Phrenology, Anthropology, Sing Sing State Penitentiary, and Sex with the New Motive Power.* Chicago: University of Chicago Press, 2011.

Mooney, James. *The Ghost-Dance Religion and the Sioux Outbreak of 1890* (1896). Lincoln: University of Nebraska Press, 1991.

———. "The Indian Ghost Dance." James Mooney Papers. National Anthropological Archives, Smithsonian Institute. January 18, 1910.

Moran, Richard. *Executioner's Current: Thomas Edison, George Westinghouse, and the Electric Chair.* New York: Alfred A. Knopf, 2002.

Morrison, Toni. "Unspeakable Things Unspoken: The Afro-American Presence in American Literature." *Michigan Quarterly Review* 28, no. 1 (Winter 1989): 1–34.

Moses, L. G. *The Indian Man: A Biography of James Mooney.* Lincoln: University of Nebraska Press, 2002.

Moten, Fred. *In the Break: The Aesthetics of Black Radical Tradition.* Minneapolis: University of Minnesota Press, 2003.

———. *Stolen Life (Consent Not to Be a Single Being).* Durham, NC: Duke University Press, 2018.

"A Mulatto Girl." *New York Times*, April 8, 1928, 16–17.

Muñoz, José Esteban. *Cruising Utopia: The Then and There of Queer Futurity.* New York: New York University Press, 2009.

———. *Disidentifications: Queers of Color and the Performance of Politics.* Minneapolis: University of Minnesota Press, 1999.

Murphy, Jacqueline Shea. *The People Have Never Stopped Dancing: Native American Modern Dance Histories.* Minneapolis: University of Minnesota Press, 2007.

Musser, Charles. *Before the Nickelodeon: Edwin S. Porter and the Edison Manufacturing Company.* Berkeley: University of California Press, 1991.

———. *Edison Motion Pictures, 1890–1900: An Annotated Filmography.* Washington, DC: Smithsonian Institution Press, 1997.

Nancy, Jean-Luc. *Being Singular Plural.* Stanford, CA: Stanford University Press, 2009.

———. *The Inoperative Community.* Minneapolis: University of Minnesota Press, 2006.

"A Negro Camp Meeting in the South." *Harper's Weekly* 16 (August 10, 1872): 620.

Neihardt, John G. *Black Elk Speaks: Being the Life Story of a Holy Man of the Ogalala Sioux.* New York: William Morrow, 1932.

Newlin, Keith. *Hamlin Garland: A Life.* Lincoln: University of Nebraska Press, 2008.

Ngai, Sianne. *Ugly Feelings.* Cambridge, MA: Harvard University Press, 2005.

Noland, Carrie. *Agency and Embodiment: Performing Gestures/Producing Culture.* Cambridge, MA: Harvard University Press, 2009.

Norris, Frank. "Stephen Crane's Stories of Life in the Slums: Maggie and George's Mother." In *The Literary Criticism of Frank Norris*, edited by Donald Pizer, 164–165. Austin: University of Texas Press, 1964.

Novak, Daniel A. *Realism, Photography, and Nineteenth-Century Fiction.* New York: Cambridge University Press, 2008.

Nye, David E. *Electrifying America: Social Meanings of a New Technology.* Cambridge, MA: MIT Press, 1992.

Nyong'o, Tavia. *The Amalgamation Waltz: Race, Performance, and the Ruses of Memory.* Minneapolis: University of Minnesota Press, 2009.

———. "Race, Reenactment, and the 'Natural-Born Citizen.'" In *Unsettled States: Nineteenth-Century American Literary Studies*, edited by Dana Luciano and Ivy Wilson, 76–102. New York: New York University Press, 2014.

Ogden, Emily. "Beyond Radical Enchantment: Mesmerizing Laborers in the Americas." *Critical Inquiry* 42, no. 4 (Summer 2016): 815–841.

Parsons, Alice Beal. "Three Novels." *Nation*, May 9, 1928, 540.

Pasler, Jean. "Sonic Anthropology in 1900: The Challenge of Transcribing Non-Western Music and Language." *Twentieth-Century Music* 11, no. 1 (March 2014): 7–36.

Pease, Donald. "Fear, Rage, and the Mistrials of Representation in *The Red Badge of Courage*." In *American Realism: New Essays*, edited by Eric J. Sundquist, 155–175. Baltimore: Johns Hopkins University Press, 1982.

Pecora, Vincent P. *Secularization and Cultural Criticism: Religion, Nation, & Modernity.* Chicago: University of Chicago Press, 2006.

Pellegrini, Ann. "Feeling Secular." *Women & Performance: A Journal of Feminist Theory* 19, no. 2 (July 2009): 205–218.

———. "Testimonial Sexuality; or, Queer Structures of Religious Feeling: Notes toward an Investigation." *Journal of Dramatic Theory and Criticism* 20, no. 1 (2005): 93–102.

Perdue, Theda. *Race and the Atlanta Cotton States Exposition of 1895.* Athens: University of Georgia Press, 2010.

Peterson, Carla. "Forward: Eccentric Bodies." In *Recovering the Black Female Body: Self-representations by African American Women*, edited by Michael Bennett and Vanessa D. Dickerson, ix–xvi. New Brunswick, NJ: Rutgers University Press, 2000.

Phelan, Peggy. *Unmarked: The Politics of Performance.* New York: Routledge, 2017.

Phister, Nat. P. "The Indian Messiah." *American Anthropologist* 4, no. 2 (April 1891): 105–108.

Pinn, Anthony B. "Charting Du Bois's *Souls*: Thoughts on 'Veiled' Bodies and the Study of Black Religion." In *The Souls of Black Folk: New Essays and Reflections*, edited by Edward J. Blum and Jason R. Young, 69–84. Macon, GA: Mercer University Press, 2009.

Plotnick, Rachel. "At the Interface: the Case of the Electric Push Button, 1880–1923." *Technology and Culture* 53, no. 4 (2012): 815–845.

Prentiss, Craig R., ed. *Religion and the Creation of Race and Ethnicity: An Introduction.* New York: New York University Press, 2003.

"The President Will Press the Button: He Will in This Way Start the Machinery at Atlanta." *New York Times*, August 7, 1895. *ProQuest Historical Newspapers*. Accessed June 20, 2019. http://ezprozy.haverford.edu/login?url=search-proquest-com.proxy.haverford.edu/docview/95248640?accountid=11321.

"Press the Button: Pres. Cleveland to Set Atlanta's Exposition in Motion." *Boston Daily Advertiser*, August 7, 1895. *Nineteenth-Century U.S. Newspapers*. Accessed June 14,

2010. http://find.galegroup.com.ezproxy.lib.utexas.edu/ncnp/infomark.do?&source =gale&prodId=NCNP&userGroupName=txshracd2598&tabID=T003&docPage =article&searchType=AdvancedSearchForm&docId=GT3006974180&type= multipage&contentSet=LTO&version=1.0.

Raboteau, Albert J. *Slave Religion: The 'Invisible Institution' in the Antebellum South.* Oxford: Oxford University Press, 1978.

Raiford, Leigh, *Imprisoned in a Luminous Glare: Photography and the African American Freedom Struggle.* Chapel Hill: University of North Carolina Press, 2011.

Rauchway, Eric. *Murdering McKinley: The Making of Theodore Roosevelt's America.* New York: Hill and Wang, 2004.

Reckson, Lindsay. "William Vander Weyde, Leon F. Czolgosz, McKinley Assassin." Object Narrative. In *Conversations: An Online Journal of the Center for the Study of Material and Visual Cultures of Religion* (2014). http://mavcor.yale.edu/.

Richardson, Joe M. *Christian Reconstruction: The American Missionary Association and Southern Blacks, 1861–1890.* Tuscaloosa: University of Alabama Press, 1986.

Riis, Jacob A. *How the Other Half Lives: Studies among the Tenements of New York* (1890). New York: Penguin Classics, 1997.

Rivkin, Mark. *Beyond Settler Time: Temporal Sovereignty and Indigenous Self-Determination.* Durham, NC: Duke University Press, 2017.

Roach, Joseph. *Cities of the Dead: Circum-Atlantic Performance.* New York: Columbia University Press, 1996.

Robertson, Michael. *Stephen Crane, Journalism, and the Making of Modern American Literature.* New York: Columbia University Press, 1997.

Rosaldo, Renato. *Culture and Truth: The Remaking of Social Analysis.* Boston: Beacon Press, 1989.

Rowe, John Carlos. *Literary Culture and U.S. Imperialism: From the Revolution to World War I.* New York: Oxford University Press, 2000.

Russell, Catherine. "Ecstatic Ethnography: Maya Deren and the Filming of Possession Rituals." In *Rites of Realism: Essays on Corporeal Cinema*, edited by Ivone Margulies, 270–293. Durham, NC: Duke University Press, 2003.

Ruttenburg, Nancy. *Democratic Personality: Popular Voice and the Trial of American Authorship.* Stanford, CA: Stanford University Press, 1998.

Sagala, Sandra K. *Buffalo Bill on the Silver Screen: The Films of William F. Cody.* Norman: University of Oklahoma Press, 2013.

Sanders, Cheryl J. *Saints in Exile: The Holiness-Pentecostal Experience in African American Religion and Culture.* New York: Oxford University Press, 1996.

Schechner, Richard. *Between Theater & Anthropology.* Philadelphia: University of Pennsylvania Press, 2011.

———. "Towards a Poetics of Performance." In *Performance Theory*, 153–186. New York: Routledge, 2003.

Schlereth, Eric R. *An Age of Infidels: The Politics of Religious Controversy in the Early United States.* Philadelphia: University of Pennsylvania Press, 2013.

Schneider, Rebecca. *Performing Remains: Art and War in Times of Theatrical Reenactment*. London: Routledge, 2011.

Schor, Naomi. *Reading in Detail: Aesthetics and the Feminine*. New York: Routledge, 2006.

Schuyler, George S. *Black No More: Being an Account of the Strange and Wonderful Workings of Science in the Land of the Free, A.D. 1933–1940* (1931). New York: Modern Library, 1999.

Sedgwick, Eve Kosofsky. *Tendencies*. Durham, NC: Duke University Press, 1993.

———. *Touching Feeling: Affect, Pedagogy, Performativity*. Durham, NC: Duke University Press, 2006.

Sekula, Allen. "The Body and the Archive." *October* 39 (1986): 3–64.

Seltzer, Mark. *Bodies and Machines*. New York: Routledge, 1992.

———. *Criminal Continuities: Henry James and the Art of Power*. Dissertation. Berkeley: University of California Press, 1982.

———. "Wound Culture: Trauma in the Pathological Public Sphere." *October* 80 (Spring 1997): 3–26.

Sernett, Milton C. *Bound for the Promised Land: African American Religion and the Great Migration*. Durham, NC: Duke University Press, 1997.

Shaw, Stephanie J. *W. E. B. Du Bois and "The Souls of Black Folk."* Chapel Hill: University of North Carolina Press, 2013.

Shulman, George. "White Supremacy and Black Insurgency as Political Theology." In *Race and Secularism in America*, edited by Jonathon S. Kahn and Vincent W. Lloyd, 23–42. New York: Columbia University Press, 2016.

Simmons, Merinda. "Slain in the Spirit: Sexuality and Afro-Caribbean Religious Expression in Nella Larsen's *Quicksand*." In *The African Diaspora and the Study of Religion*, edited by Theodore Louis Trost, 93–110. New York: Palgrave Macmillan, 2007.

Simpson, Audra. *Mohawk Interruptus: Political Life across the Borders of Settler States*. Durham, NC: Duke University Press, 2014.

Slotkin, Richard. *Gunfighter Nation: The Myth of the Frontier in Twentieth-Century America*. Norman: University of Oklahoma Press, 1998.

Smith, Jonathan Z. "Religion, Religions, Religious." In *Relating Religion: Essays in the Study of Religion*, 179–196. Chicago: University of Chicago Press, 2004.

Smith, Shawn Michelle. "The Photographer's Touch." In *Pictures and Progress: Early Photography and the Making of African American Identity*, edited by Maurice O. Wallace and Shawn Michelle Smith, 321–328. Durham, NC: Duke University Press, 2012.

———. "A Spirit Photograph." Mirrorofrace.org. Accessed June 19, 2015. http://mirrorofrace.org/a-spirit-photograph/.

Somerville, Siobhan. *Queering the Color Line: Race and the Invention of Homosexuality in American Culture*. Durham, NC: Duke University Press, 2000.

Sontag, Susan. *On Photography*. New York: Picador, 1973.

Sorett, Josef. *Spirit in the Dark: A Religious History of Racial Aesthetics*. New York: Oxford University Press, 2016.

Spillers, Hortense J. *Black, White, and in Color: Essays on American Literature and Culture*. Chicago: University of Chicago Press, 2003.

———. "Mama's Baby, Papa's Maybe: An American Grammar Book." *Diacritics* 17, no. 2 (Summer 1987): 64–81.

———. "Moving on Down the Line: Variations on the African-American Sermon." In *Black, White, and in Color: Essays on American Literature and Culture*, 251–276. Chicago: University of Chicago Press, 2003.

Stadler, Gustavus. "Never Heard Such a Thing: Lynching and Phonographic Modernity." *Social Text* 28, no. 1 (2010): 87–105.

Stallman, R. W. *Stephen Crane: A Biography*. New York: G. Braziller, 1968.

Stein, Jordan Alexander. "Angels in (Mexican) America." *American Literature* 86, no. 4 (2014): 683–711.

Stepto, Robert. *From Behind the Veil: A Study of Afro-American Narrative*. Champaign: University of Illinois Press, 1979.

Sterne, Jonathan. *The Audible Past: Cultural Origins of Sound Production*. Durham, NC: Duke University Press, 2003.

Stevenson, Lisa. *Life Beside Itself: Imagining Care in the Canadian Arctic*. Oakland: University of California Press, 2014.

Stieglitz, Alfred. "The Hand Camera—Its Present Importance" (1897). In *Photography in Print: Writings from 1816 to the Present*, edited by Vicki Goldberg, 214–217. Albuquerque: University of New Mexico Press, 1988.

Strieby, M. E. "The Look Forward." *American Missionary* 39, no. 12 (December 1885): 352–358.

Sundquist, Eric J. *To Wake the Nations: Race in the Making of American Literature*. Cambridge, MA: Harvard University Press, 1998.

Sweezy, Carl. *The Arapaho Way: A Memoir of an Indian Boyhood*. New York: Clarkson N. Potter, 1966.

Tate, Claudia. *Psychoanalysis and Black Novels: Desire and the Protocols of Race*. New York: Oxford University Press, 1998.

Taves, Ann. *Fits, Trances, and Visions: Experiencing Religion and Explaining Experience from Wesley to James*. Princeton, NJ: Princeton University Press, 1999.

———. *Religious Experience Reconsidered: A Building-Block Approach to the Study of Religion and Other Special Things*. Princeton, NJ: Princeton University Press, 2009.

Taylor, Charles. *A Secular Age*. Cambridge, MA: Harvard University Press, 2007.

Taylor, Diana. *The Archive and the Repertoire: Performing Cultural Memory in the Americas*. Durham, NC: Duke University Press, 2007.

Taylor, Matthew. "'Contagious Emotions' and the Ghost Dance: James Mooney's Science, Black Elk's Fever." *ELH* 81, no. 3 (Fall 2014): 1055–1082.

Thomas de la Peña, Carolyn. *The Body Electric: How Strange Machines Built America*. New York: New York University Press, 2003.

Thrailkill, Jane F. *Affecting Fictions: Mind, Body, and Emotion in American Literary Realism.* Cambridge, MA: Harvard University Press, 2007.

Toll, Robert. *Blacking Up: The Minstrel Show in Nineteenth-Century America.* New York: Oxford University Press, 1977.

Tompkins, Kyla Wazana. "'Everything 'Cept Eat Us': The Antebellum Black Body Portrayed as Edible Body." *Callaloo* 30, no. 1 (Winter 2007): 201–224.

———. *Racial Indigestion: Eating Bodies in the 19th Century.* New York: New York University Press, 2012.

Toscano, Alberto. *Fanaticism: On the Uses of an Idea.* London: Verso, 2017.

"Touched the Button: Atlanta Exposition Opened Yesterday by President Cleveland." *News and Observer,* September 19, 1895. *Nineteenth-Century U.S. Newspapers.* Accessed June 14, 2010.

Trachtenberg, Alan. *Reading American Photographs: Images as History from Mathew Brady to Walker Evans.* New York: Hill and Wang, 1989.

Tucker, Susie I. *Enthusiasm: A Study in Semantic Change.* Cambridge: Cambridge University Press, 1972.

Turner, Victor. *The Ritual Process: Structure and Anti-structure.* Chicago: Aldine, 1969.

Underhill, Lonnie E., and Daniel F. Littlefield Jr. Introduction to *Hamlin Garland's Observations on the American Indian, 1895–1905,* 21–40. Tucson: University of Arizona Press, 1976.

Vazquez, Alexandra T. *Listening in Detail: Performances of Cuban Music.* Durham, NC: Duke University Press, 2013.

Vincent, Theodore G., ed. *Voices of a Black Nation: Political Journalism in the Harlem Renaissance.* San Francisco: Ramparts Press, 1973.

Vizenor, Gerald. *Fugitive Poses: Native American Scenes of Absence and Presence.* Lincoln: University of Nebraska Press, 2000.

———. *Survivance: Narratives of Native Presence.* Lincoln: University of Nebraska Press, 2008.

Vogel, Shane. *The Scene of the Harlem Cabaret: Race, Sexuality, Performance.* Chicago: University of Chicago Press, 2009.

———. "Touching Ecstasy: Muñozian Theory and the Extension of the Soul." *Social Text* 32, no. 4 (2014): 47–57.

Wald, Priscilla. *Contagious: Cultures, Carriers, and the Outbreak Narrative.* Durham, NC: Duke University Press, 2008.

Warner, Michael. *Publics and Counterpublics.* New York: Zone, 2014.

———. "Tongues Untied: Memoirs of a Pentecostal Boyhood." In *Curiouser: On the Queerness of Children,* edited by Steven Bruhm and Natasha Hurley, 215–224. Minneapolis: University of Minnesota Press, 2004.

Warren, Kenneth W. *Black and White Strangers: Race and American Literary Realism.* Chicago: University of Chicago Press, 1995.

———. *What Was African American Literature? The W. E. B. Du Bois Lectures.* Cambridge, MA: Harvard University Press, 2012.

Washburn, Kathleen. *Indigenous Modernity and the Making of Americans, 1890–1935*. Los Angeles: University of California Press, 2008.
Washington, Booker T. *Up from Slavery* (1901). Edited by William L. Andrews. New York: Oxford University Press, 1995.
Washington, Mary Helen. Introduction to *A Voice from the South*, xxvii–lvi. Oxford: Oxford University Press, 1988.
Weheliye, Alexander G. *Habeas Viscus: Racializing Assemblages, Biopolitics, and Black Feminist Theories of the Human*. Durham, NC: Duke University Press, 2014.
Weisenfeld, Judith. *New World A-Coming: Black Religion and Racial Identity during the Great Migration*. New York: New York University Press, 2017.
———. "'Who Is Sufficient for These Things?': Sara G. Stanley and the American Missionary Association, 1864–1868." *Church History* 60, no. 4 (December 1991): 493–507.
Wenger, Tisa. *We Have a Religion: The 1920s Pueblo Indian Dance Controversy and American Religious Freedom*. Chapel Hill: University of North Carolina Press, 2009.
West, Cornel. *Prophetic Fragments*. Grand Rapids, MI: William B. Eerdmans, 1988.
White, Walter F. "The Burning of Jim McIlherron: An N.A.A.C.P. Investigation." *Crisis* 16, no. 1 (1918): 16–20.
Wiegman, Robyn. *American Anatomies: Theorizing Race and Gender*. Durham, NC: Duke University Press, 1995.
Williams, Andreá N. *Dividing Lines: Class Anxiety and Postbellum Black Fiction*. Ann Arbor: University of Michigan Press, 2013.
Williams, Raymond. *Marxism and Literature*. Oxford: Oxford University Press, 1977.
Winans, Robert B. "Early Minstrel Show Music, 1843–1852." In *Inside the Minstrel Mask: Readings in Nineteenth-Century Blackface Minstrelsy*, edited by Annemarie Bean, James V. Hatch, and Brooks McNamara, 141–162. Hanover, NH: Wesleyan University Press, 1996.
Wolfenstein, Eugene Victor. *A Gift of the Spirit: Reading "The Souls of Black Folk."* Ithaca, NY: Cornell University Press, 2007.
Woloch, Alex. *The One vs. the Many: Minor Characters and the Space of the Protagonist in the Novel*. Princeton, NJ: Princeton University Press, 2009.
Wonham, Henry B. "Howells, Du Bois, and the Effect of 'Common-Sense': Race, Realism, and Nervousness in *An Imperative Duty*." In *Criticism and the Color Line: Desegregating American Literary Studies*, edited by Henry B. Wonham, 126–139. New Brunswick, NJ: Rutgers University Press, 1996.
"Words from Workers." *Home Mission Monthly* 5, no. 4 (February 1891): 84–86.
Young, Harvey. *Embodying Black Experience: Stillness, Critical Memory, and the Black Body*. Ann Arbor: University of Michigan Press, 2010.
Zamir, Shamoon. "'The Sorrow Songs'/'Song of Myself': Du Bois, the Crisis of Leadership, and Prophetic Imagination." In *The Black Columbiad: Defining Moments in African American Literature and Culture*, edited by Werner Sollars and Maria Diedrich, 145–166. Cambridge, MA: Harvard University Press, 1994.
Zuckerman, Phil, ed. *Du Bois on Religion*. Walnut Creek, CA: AltaMira Press, 2000.

INDEX

Page numbers in *italics* refer to figures.

Abel, Elizabeth, 9, 167
abolitionism, 76–78, 256n23, 256n29
actualities, 144. *See also* film
affect: as comportment, 49, 66; and disembodiment, 11, 245n45; and ecstatic embodiment, 12; and electricity, 24, 160–161, 272n15; and enthusiasm, 87; and gesture, 72; and Jim Crow, 5, 12, 14, 21, 55, 57, 59, 65–66, 234; as movement, 214–216; and realism, 10–11; as realist data, 11, 17–18; as religious comportment, 49; as religious excess, 35; and secularism, 6, 12, 20, 30, 55; and temporality, 11, 187; and terror, 182–183
African American literature, 206–207, 210–211, 212, 216. *See also* literature
African Methodist Episcopal Church, 32, 36, 175, 249n70
Afro-Protestantism: Frances E. W. Harper on, 219, 247n22, 249n66, 250n71; New Negro movement on, 184, 208; secularism and, 30. *See also* black Christianity
Agamben, Giorgio, 158, 196
Ahmed, Sara, 192, 194, 216
Alexander, M. Jacqui, 8, 17
Along This Way (Johnson), 185, 188, 190, 193–194
Ancient Society (Morgan), 115–116, 264n29
Andersson, Rani-Henrik, 262n13

Anglo-Protestantism, 8–9, 44; constructed as true religion, 7, 29, 35, 39, 47–48, 64–65, 282n93; secularism, 30, 33, 38; violence of, 38. *See also* white Christianity
Anthony, Susan B., 41
archives, 13, 196; of "Dandy Jim" performances, 69; enthusiasm and, 102; ethnography and, 129; hauntology and, 14; of minstrelsy, 75; of performance, 14, 70, 253n5; *Red Badge* grappling with, 22–23; of regular events, 68; silences and, 14
artifactualization, 133, 146, 267n78
assimilation: of Native Americans, 111–112, 117, 121, 129, 140, 143, 150–153, 262n6, 268n103
Atlanta Exposition of 1895, 186, 271n2
Autobiography of an Ex-Colored Man, The (Johnson), 24, 149, 160–162, 181–187, 235

Baker, Houston, 56, 185
Baldwin, James, 201–202, 232–233
baptism, 56, 58
Baptists, 17, 39, 224
Barthes, Roland, 81–82, 176, 209; on photographs, 111, 164, 167, 172–174, 263n18
Benjamin, Walter, 59, 158
Bentley, Nancy, 109, 165–166, 258n56, 262n6
Berlant, Lauren, 159, 196, 251n95, 279n28

305

Berliner, Emile, 131, 133, *134*, 136–138, 141, 156, 267n70
besideness, 48, 59; vs. beyond, 17, 204; black Christianity and collective, 223–224, 282n93; Butler on, 15–17, 149; ecstasy as, 15–16, 18, 149, 233, 236; Howells and, 32; Larsen and, 224–227, 231, 233; Muñoz on, 19–20; *Quicksand* and, 200–201, 278n15; racialization and, 17, 172; realism and, 17–18; realist ecstasy as, 12, 20; Sedgwick on, 18–19, 201; singularity and, 217
biopolitics, 117, 265n39. *See also* chronobiopolitics
black Christianity: affective comportment of, 49; affective force of, 38; Afro-Protestantism as, 30, 51, 184, 208, 247n22; black feminist scholars on, 39; "black pneuma" and, 48; charismatic services of, 224; collective besideness in, 223–224, 282n93; constructed as excessive, 30; constructed as primitivism, 36, 45; constructed as radical alterity, 32–34, 37; double consciousness and, 32; Du Bois on, 250n83, 250n91, 252n124; ecstasy in, 223–224; electric conversion and, 183–185, 188–192, 195–197, 275n77, 277n120; fanaticism and, 37, 92; as frenzy, 22, 50, 52–54, 56, 61, 94, *94*, 190–191, 226; Howells on, 21–22, 38, 48–49, 52, 227, 235; independent denominations in, 36–37, 248n28; jouissance and, 11, 203; lynching and, 191–192; modernization and, 35; politics of respectability and, 185–186; in post-Reconstruction era, 36, 92; *Quicksand* and, 210; ring shout and, 190–191; secularism and, 47, 282n93; on white Christianity and true religion, 7, 29, 35, 39, 47–48, 64–65, 282n93
black feminist thought: on archive gaps, 14; on black Christianity, 39; Cooper and, 22, 206, 219–220, 227–228, 248n44, 248n47, 249n49; on fanaticism, 39–41, 44, 50; on white feminists, 42
bodily movement: affect as ecstasy and, 12; affect without, 11, 245n45; archives and, 13, 70; communicability of, 71–72, 87, 96, 99; of Native Americans, 122, 149; objectification of, 22, 218, 235; *Quicksand* and, 214–216; reenactment of, 12, 70
Book of the American Indian, The (Garland), *108, 151*
Brown, Bill, 69, 72
Brown, John, 90, 250n71
Brown, Sterling, 207
Brown, William Wells, 76–78
Buel, James W., 36–37
Bureau of American Ethnology, 103, 110–111, 114–115, 118, 131
Butler, Judith, 15–17, 149, 199, 205–206, 217, 224–225, 277n7, 278n14
button-pressing technology, 163, 276n80; affect of, 158, 272n13; for electric chair, 157–158, 165, 271n2, 271n4; for electricity, 186–187, 276n87; as gesture, 23, 161–162, 179; as performance, 161; photography and, 158, 272n8; power seized in, 196; race and, 158–159, 272n7; repetition and, 161, 169, 196; temporality of, 162, 167–168, 175
Byrd, Jodi, 111, 144, 263n18, 263n23, 264n29

Carby, Hazel, 204, 250n77, 281n71
charisma: black Christianity and, 224; black political power and, 185; electrifying speech and, 183–185, 188–192, 195–197, 275n77, 277n120; Johnson authoring, 186–187; of preacher J. Brown, 183–185, 275n77; religion and queerness with, 225–226

Chesnutt, Charles W., 2, 4, 10
choreography, 113–114, 116, 124, 156, 166–167, 169
choreomania, 91. *See also* Gotman, Kélina
Christianity: African Methodist Episcopal Church in, 32, 36, 175, 249n70; Afro-Protestantism in, 30, 51, 184, 208, 219, 247n22, 249n66, 250n71; Anglo-Protestantism in, 7–9, 29–30, 33, 35, 38–39, 40, 47–48, 64–65; Baptists in, 17, 39, 224; Congregationalists, 39; Du Bois on, 39, 60–65, 235, 252n127; Episcopal church in, 39–41, 44, 58; as "good" delineation, 8; Methodists in, 39, 90, 99, 224; Pentecostalism in, 24, 203, 208, 224, 225–226, 228, 248n30; secularism connections with, 5–6; "separate but equal" and, 8; Southern revivalism and, 40, 52; Spillers on, 4, 17, 61–63, 189–190, 220, 252n122; US moral matrix as, 37
Christian secularism, 6
chronobiopolitics, 220, 243n11, 282n85
chrononormativity, 219–220, 269n127
Cody, William F., 269n129; Ghost Dance photos and films by, 108, 139–141, 145–147, 268n108, 269n120; *Indian War Pictures*, 145–146, 148, 269n120, 269nn123–124; Wounded Knee realist restaging by, 145–146, 148, 269n120, 269n123
colonialism, 148, 261n3; Fanon on, 270n138; frenzy viewed by, 162, 250n91; Ghost Dance and, 114–115, 263n25, 270n152; Ghost Dance performers and, 270n152; as ghosting, 130–131; Native Americans and, 127, 149, 270n140, 270n152; power of, 270n138; reenactments and, 23, 112, 150; religion in, 9; temporality and violence in, 272n18; whiteness and, 61
communicability: body, feelings and fantasy of, 71–72, 87, 96, 99; ecstasy and contagious, 12, 149, 233, 235; of enthusiasm, 2–3, 12–13, 99; gestures of, 98–99; of public enthusiasm, 67; realism containing, 233; of religious feeling, 35–36, 70, 99, 117
compassion, 100, 260n96
Congregationalists, 39
Connolly, William, 272n18
contact: electricity and performance of, 182, 196–197; ethnographic, 117–118; and skin, 7, 159–160, 163, 176, 182, 185, 195; social, 204, 213, 260n96, 265n52; temporality and, 204
conversion, 161–164, 175; charismatic speaking and, 183–185, 188–192, 195–197, 275n77, 277n120; lynching and, 189, 192
Cooper, Anna Julia: black feminist texts of, 22, 206, 219–220, 227–228, 248n44, 248n47, 249n49; class politics of, 40, 248n44; *A Voice from the South*, 22, 30–31, 37–47, 49–50
Crane, Jonathan Townley, 90, 259n70
Crane, Stephen, 100–102; on "Dandy Jim," 75, 78–79; family of, 90–91, 99, 259n70, 260n72; *The Monster* by, 1–3, 69, 97–99, 243n3, 257n45; *The Red Badge of Courage* by, 22–23, 68–102, 253n5, 255n12, 257n43, 258n56; repetitions of, 68, 71, 75–76, 78–79, 86, 98, 100, 102, 254n10
Crawley, Ashon, 16, 48, 228–229, 243n6, 248n30
Crowd, The (Le Bon), 189
Crummell, Alexander, 58
cultural memory, 1, 13, 15, 53, 70, 75, 130; gesture and, 161
cultures, 3; ethnography salvaging, 111, 129, 132, 137, 264n37, 267n78; lynching as modern, 174, 274n44; realism and, 10, 15, 244n34; of white consuming black culture, 212, 280n59
Czolgosz, Leon, 177–180, *180*

dance: condemnation of, 91; death in, 129; enthusiasm linked with, 91; hornpipe as, 83, 85–87, 258n54; of Native Americans, 122; *Quicksand* and cabaret, 215–218, 222, 281n70; *Quicksand* on ecstatic, 214–216; religion and, 91, 208. *See also* Ghost Dance

"Dandy Jim of Caroline": abolitionism and minstrelsy of, 76–77, 256n23, 256n29; archive of, 69; S. Crane on, 75, 78–79; "jim-dandy" and Jim Crow roots of, 72, 256n23; minstrel figure as, 22, 69, 84, 87, 96, 257n52; minstrelsy and, 255nn17–18; performances of, 73, 74; sexuality and, 73; songs to, 72, 76, 256n26

data, 11, 17–18, 119, 243n7, 254n10, 267n70

Davenport, Frederick Morgan, 95–96

death: archives and, 69; choreography of, 166–167, 169; in dance, 129; Edison on executions as, 158, 160, 168, 177–178, 272n8, 275n67; Ghost Dancers and ghosts of, 123–124; of "jim-dandy," 82–84; objectification of corpses and, 167; realism and, 85–86; reenactment of, 169; as ritual, 81, 83–84, 169, *171*, *172*, *173*, *177*, 257n52, 273n37; technology for, 166, 273n29. *See also* electrical execution

detail: as historical, 79–81, 147, 243n3, 268n108; photography and, 46, 131; realist aesthetics and, 106–107, 131, 155, 206–210, 222, 224, 262n7, 262n12

Doane, Mary Ann, 144, 178

double consciousness: as black prophetic vision, 32; Du Bois on, 32, 38, 52–54, 247n13; hysteria and, 26–28, 31, 55, 247n11; religious rebirth and, 31, 38, 51–52, 247n13

Douglass, Frederick, 64, 76, 158, 249n70, 271nn5–6

Du Bois, W. E. B., 4, 29, 189, 195, 228, 248n25, 250n91; on black Christianity, 250n83, 250n91, 252n124; on Christianity, white supremacy, and global imperialism, 39, 60–65, 235, 252n127; on double consciousness, 32, 38, 52–54, 247n13; on ecstatic frenzy, 18, 22, 50, 52–54, 56, 60–61; "Of the Coming of John," 22, 30–31, 38, 55–59, 251n108; *The Souls of Black Folk*, 22, 38–39, 51–53, 59; "The Souls of White Folk," 39, 50, 59–65

Dunbar, Paul Laurence, 78

Durkheim, Émile, 42, 189

ecstasy. *See specific subjects*

Edison, Thomas, 269n111; on electricity and executions, 158, 160, 168, 177–178, 272n8, 275n67; Ghost Dance and, 108, 141, 143–145, 268n108

Edwards, Brent, 190

Edwards, Erica, 185–186

electrical execution: death and, 173, 193, 274n41; as instantaneous, 160; speed of modernity and, 175, 274n54; technology for, 166, 273n29; violence and, 23–24, 159–160

electric chair: button-pressing and, 157–158, 165, 271n2, 271n4; Howells on, 23, 157–158, 164–169; instantaneous death and, 160; as legal lynching, 174, 192–193; modernity and, 159, 164, 272n12; photography and, 23–24, 165–166; racial terror and, 23–24, 159–160, 172, *172*, 175; racial violence scripted in, 160; ritual and, 169, *171*, *172*, *173*, *177*, 273n37; temporality and, 193; Van der Weyde and photography of, 23, 160–162, 168–182, *170*, *171*, *172*, *173*, *177*, *178*, 197, 271n2, 275n68

electricity: affect and, 41–42, 56, 160–161, 164, 182, 192, 272n15;

African Methodist Episcopal Church warning on, 175; American connectivity through, 157–158, 271n5; *Autobiography* and affect of, 24; button-pressing and, 186–187, 276n87; ecstatic possibility of, 23–24; Edison on, 158, 160, 168, 177–178, 272n8, 275n67; Jim Crow and influence of, 184; Johnson on speech in, 188–192, 195–197, 277n120; life figured and disfigured in, 182; modernity channeling, 160, 272n13; performance and, 161; as performance of contact, 182, 196–197; racial terror and, 24, 161, 174–175, 181; self and circuit of, 182–183; as sublime, 174; as white racial superiority, 174–175

electric theology, 182

Ellison, Ralph, 101–102, 197, 259n70, 260n102

embodiment: as ecstatic, 3, 162–163; of electrified feelings, 192; of racial minstrelsy, 70; of religion, 70, 91, 96, 163; and spiritual possession, 67, 223

enthusiasm, 97, 253n137; black feminist scholars on, 39–41, 44, 50; black genius and, 46; as collective feeling, 41–42, 56, 164, 182; communicability and, 12–13, 99; and cross-class organization, 44; and dance, 91; and experience, 87; as "false" religion, 48; fanaticism and, 87–89; and literary character, 102; and minstrelsy, 66; modernity and, 66; Pentecostalism worship style and, 24, 203, 208, 224, 225–226, 248n30; politics and, 89–90; possession and, 88–89; privacy and, 67; as queer, 211–212, 221; *Quicksand* and, 211–213; racialization and religion with, 91–92; ring shout and, 190–191

Episcopal church, 39–41, 44, 58

epistemological comportment, 7

ethnography: archives and, 129; as contact, 117–118; Ghost Dance and, 23, 109; indigeneity and, 23, 107, 109, 111–112, 127, 130–138, 141, 149–150; as local color, 12, 53, 92–96, 94; primitivism in, 222–223, 281n70; racial and religious difference produced by, 109, 137; realism and, 23, 109, 116–117, 123–124, 262n6; recordings and, 132, 135, 267n74, 268n89; of religion, 31, 109; and salvage, 111, 129, 132, 137, 264n37, 267n78; and uncertainty, 15; and whiteness, 103–108, 261n2; Wounded Knee in, 23, 264n37

ex-static, 18–20, 54, 100, 164, 201

fanaticism: black Christianity and, 37, 92; enthusiasm and, 87–89; mortification and, 40–41; uses of, 39–50; and whiteness, 4, 50

Fanon, Frantz, 7, 172, 270n138, 274n39

Fessenden, Tracy, 30, 88–89, 202, 259n64, 260n81, 279n17

film, 85–86, 141–147, 177–178, 243n7, 258n56

Fredric, Harold, 85

Freeman, Elizabeth, 219, 275n64

frenzy: besideness and ecstatic, 18; black church and, 22, 50, 52–54, 56, 61, 94, 94, 190–191, 226; double consciousness and, 26–28, 31, 55, 247n11; Du Bois on black church and, 18, 22, 50, 52–54, 56, 60–61; as imperial-colonial construction, 54, 162, 250n91; Johnson on black church and, 190–191; realism and, 233–234

Freud, Sigmund, 115, 133, 148

Fried, Michael, 69, 253n3

"fugitive intervals," 162, 176, 181–182, 195, 272n18. *See also* Connolly, William; Keeling, Kara

Garland, Hamlin, 150–155, 270n147
gesture, 185, 276n80; Agamben on, 158, 196; button-pressing as, 23, 161–162, 179; Hartman on, 75; as itinerant archive, 196; of lynching, 98–99; of photography, 167, 273n33; of religious ecstasy, 2–3, 5, 95, 244n16; and stillness, 158–159, 166–167, 171, *172*, 175–179, 182
Ghost Dance, 265n51; choreography and, 116, 124; Cody and media of, 108, 139–141, 145–147, 268n108, 269n120; colonialism and, 114–115, 263n25; and cultural decimation, 148, 150, 270n136; as ecstatic religion, 115; Edison and, 108, 141, 143–145, 268n108; ethnography and, 23, 109; Garland on, 150–155; and hypnosis, 123–125, *125*, *126*; Mooney on, 103–156, *120*, *123*, *125*, *126*, *130*, 261n1, 261n4, 262nn13–14, 263n25, 264n33, 264nn37–38, 265n50, 265n54, 266n66, 267n70; Mooney performances and recordings of, 131–132, 136–137; naming of, 103, 135, 261n5, 262n17; photography of, 117–119, 265n50; prophecy and performance of, 23, 110–111, 141, *142*, 143–144, 262n13, 262n17, 269n114; realism and, 149–150, 154; reenactment of, 23; repetition and, 138, 146–147; ritual of, 106–107, 110, 115, 140, 144, 151; temporality of, 133, 135, 152–153, 262n8; vitality and uncertainty of, 130; white Christianity and, 116, 153–154; after Wounded Knee, 109–110, 112, 137–139
Ghost Dance Religion and the Sioux Outbreak of 1890, The (Mooney), 114–117, 124
Gilroy, Paul, 50, 53–54
Glazener, Nancy, 10, 198–199
Goldsby, Jacqueline, 8, 69, 81, 98, 191–192, 195, 243n3, 251n107, 257n45
Gordon, Avery, 4, 13, 138, 265n52
Go Tell It on the Mountain (Baldwin), 201–202, 232–233
Gotman, Kélina, 14, 91, 130, 148

Hall, G. Stanley, 94, *94*
Harlem Renaissance, 24. *See also* New Negro movement
Harper, Frances Ellen Watkins, 247n22, 249n66, 250n71; *Iola Leroy*, 22, 27, 30–31, 35–38, 47–50, 219, 246n6
Hartman, Saidiya, 5, 14, 36, 75, 246n1, 277n120
haunting: Ellison on, 101–102, 260n102; and frenzy, 233–234; and Ghost Dance, 138; Gordon on, 4, 13, 138, 265n52; Pellegrini on, 15; performance and, 14–15; of post-Reconstruction era, 20; realism and, 17, 67; *Red Badge* and performance as, 71; of religion, 4–5; and secularism, 4–5, 163; and US colonialism, 111
hauntology: of performance, 13, 113; realism as, 4; of realist archive, 14; of white supremacy, 2, 259n66
Holiness movement, 90–91, 224, 259n70
Home to Harlem (McKay), 206–207
hornpipe, 85–87, 258n54
Howells, William Dean, 32, 253nn135–136; on black church, 21–22, 38, 48–49, 52, 227, 235; on electric chair, 23, 157–158, 164–169; *An Imperative Duty*, 22, 26–31, 34–37, 43–49, 52, 64–66, 92, 227, 235, 246n1; realism and, 34–35, 43, 45, 248n34
Hughes, Langston, 199, 208, 277n8
hypnosis, 123–125, *125*, *126*
hysteria, 26–27, 35

Imperative Duty, An (Howells), 22, 26–31, 34–37, 43–49, 52, 64–66, 92, 235, 246n1; *Iola Leroy* compared with, 35, 37–38, 46, 249n63; *Quicksand* compared with, 227–228

imperialism, 4, 144, 250n91, 262n9; Du Bois on global, 39, 60–65, 235, 252n127; of US, 162, 257n42; white Christianity, supremacy and, 39, 60–61, 63–64

Indian War Pictures (Cody), 145–146, 148, 269n120, 269nn123–124

indigeneity, 23, 111, 121, 140, 149–150

Iola Leroy; or, Shadows Uplifted (Harper), 22, 27, 30–31, 47–50, 219, 246n6; *An Imperative Duty* compared with, 35, 37–38, 46, 249n63

Jackson, Gregory, 243n9, 248n35, 265n57
James, Henry, 53
James, William, 11, 26, 31, 53, 257n42, 266n59
Jameson, Fredric, 10–11, 109, 262n8
Janet, Pierre, 26
Jim Crow secularism, 1–4, 7, 9, 50, 184; and affective, 5, 12, 14, 21, 55, 57, 59, 65–66, 234; Hartman on, 5, 14, 36, 246n1, 277n120
"jim-dandy," 68–73, 76–79, 87, 100–101, 253n5, 255n17; death of, 82–84; "Dandy Jim" Jim Crow roots and, 72, 256n23
Johnson, James Weldon, 174, 193; *Along This Way*, 194; *The Autobiography of an Ex-Colored Man*, 24, 149, 155–156, 160–162, 181–187, 235; on electrifying speech, 188–192, 195–197, 277n120
jouissance, 11, 203

Kahn, Jonathon S., 7–8, 64
Kaplan, Amy, 243n8, 245n41, 253n136, 255n12
Keeling, Kara, 272n18

Kicking Bear, 113–114, 118, 129, 139, 153, 266n66
Kristeva, Julia, 100

Larsen, Nella, 220–221, 224–227, 231–233, 279n30, 282n86; *Quicksand* by, 19, 24, 162, 197–216, 278n14
Le Bon, Gustave, 42, 189
literature, 3, 166, 228, 262n6, 272n7, 273n28; African American, 206–207, 210–211, 212, 216; characters in, 46, 102, 249n63, 261n104
liveness, 13, 85, 110, 127, 157, 161, 167
Lloyd, Vincent W., 7–8, 29, 64, 202, 252n119
local color, 12, 53, 92–96, 94
L'Ouverture, Toussaint, 185
Luciano, Dana, 220, 243n11, 282n85
lynching, 24, 57; *Along This Way* on, 194; Du Bois on, 38, 58, 195; and electric chair, 174, 192–193; gestures of, 98–99; Goldsby on, 69, 81, 98, 191–192, 195, 243n3, 257n45; and modernity, 159, 174–175, 274n44, 275n54; and parallels to religious experience, 191–192; photography and, 172, 274n40; ritual of, 8, 51, 58; temporality of, 193

Mahmood, Saba, 202
Manning, Erin, 176
Marrow of Tradition, The (Chesnutt), 2
Masuzawa, Tomoko, 9–10, 112, 263n21, 264n32
McGarry, Molly, 6, 30, 127, 266n62, 282n89, 283n101
McKay, Claude, 206–207
Methodists, 39, 224; African Methodist Episcopal Church as, 32, 36, 175, 249n70; S. Crane and family as, 90–91, 99, 259n70, 260n72
Middle Passage, 17, 58

migration narratives, 214, 278n15, 281n64
Miller, Monica, 73
minstrelsy, 86; archive of, 75; W. Brown using, 76–78; Dandy Jim and, 255nn17–18; "Dandy Jim of Caroline" and, 22, 69, 84, 87, 96, 257n52; ecstasy as, 13; embodiment and, 70; enthusiasm and, 66; gender and, 93–94. *See also* "jim-dandy"
Mitchell, Koritha, 241, 249n66, 282n82
Modern, John Lardas, 6–7, 29, 116, 244n17
modernity: black religion and, 35; electric chair and, 159, 164, 272n12; electricity channeled in, 160, 272n13; enthusiasm and, 66; feminized religion and, 202; haunting in, 5; imperialism and, 4, 65; lynching and, 159, 174–175, 274n44, 275n54; Native Americans and, 115–116; photography and, 159, 272n12; white supremacist terror and, 50, 54, 60–61, 64
Monster, The (S. Crane), 1–3, 69, 97–99, 243n3, 257n45
Mooney, James: archives and papers of, 103, 261n3; Ghost Dance and, 103–156, *120*, *123*, *125*, *126*, *130*, 261n1, 261n4, 262nn13–14, 263n25, 264n33, 264nn37–38, 265n50, 265n54, 266n66, 267n70; Ghost Dance performances and recordings by, 131–132, 136–137; realist reenactment by, 137–138; shadow in photography and, *120*, 122, *123*, 125, *125*, *126*, *130*, 265n52
Morgan, Lewis Henry, 115–116, 264n29
Moten, Fred, 48, 54, 181, 197, 250n91, 274n56; on black radical performance, 248n47, 253n5
Muñoz, José Esteban, 17, 19–20, 203–205, 215, 217–218, 232, 279n29
Mysteries and Miseries of America's Great Cities (Buel), 36–37

NAACP, 174, 195
nationalism, 66
Native Americans: artifactualization of, 133, 146, 267n78; assimilation of, 111–112, 117, 121, 129, 140, 143, 150–153, 262n6, 268n103; audio recording and, 132–133; bodily movement of, 122, 149; Byrd on, 111, 144, 263n18, 263n23, 264n29; colonialism and, 127, 149, 270n140, 270n152; dance of, 122; and disappearance, 111–113, 116; Garland on, 150–155, 270n147, 270n149; haunting by, 111; humor and survivance, 112, 263n22; indigeneity and, 23, 111, 121, 140, 149–150; modernity and, 115–116; objectification of, 112–113; performances demanded of, 107; removal as ghosting of, 135; survivance and, 121, 140, 148–150; US imperialism and, 139, 144
Native cosmologies, 110, 117, 122, 127, 141
naturalism: in literature, 228, 262n6, 272n7
neurasthenia, 28
New Negro, The, anthology (Locke), 207, 208
New Negro movement, 8, 184, 208. *See also* Harlem Renaissance
Ngai, Sianne, 85, 198–199, 212–213, 216, 280n55
Norris, Frank, 85–86
Nyong'o, Tavia, 19, 64, 71, 146–147, 269n127

objectification: of African Americans, 78–79; of corpses, 167; of moving bodies, 22, 218, 235; of Native Americans, 112–113; photography and, 159, 171–172, 274n38; slavery and performances of, 1, 256n35
"Of the Coming of John" (Du Bois), 22, 30–31, 38, 55–59, 251n108

Parliament of World Religions, 8–9
Pellegrini, Ann: on haunting, 15; on secularism, 5–6, 200, 243n1, 264n33, 278n10, 282n89
Pentecostalism, 24, 203, 208, 224, 225–226, 228, 248n30
performance: archive of, 14, 70, 253n5; button-pressing as, 161; of "Dandy Jim of Caroline," 73, *74*; ecstasy as, 2–3, 17; electricity and, 161; of Ghost Dance, 141, *142*, 143–144, 269n114; Ghost Dance and realist, 131–132; Ghost Dance prophecy and, 23, 110–111, 262n13, 262n17; hauntology of, 13, 14–15, 113; history of violence and, 87; Larsen on ecstatic, 221, 225–227, 232; Mooney and Ghost Dance, 131–132, 136–137; Moten and, 248n47, 253n5; objectification and, 256n35; punctuation as, 226, 279n33, 282n77; realism as, 11; *Red Badge* and, 71; religious ecstasy and, 2–3; repetition and, 14, 48, 86, 210, 224, 248n47, 257n38, 259n59; as ritual, 258n53, 283n100; Roach on, 13, 82; Schneider on, 19, 110, 257n38, 273n33; Taylor on, 13, 71, 113, 245n49. *See also* bodily movement
performative historiography, 71
Peterson, Carla, 200–201, 278n14
phonograph, 132, 188, 267n77, 276n94
photographic realism, 43–44, 46, 117–119, 166, 265n50, 273n28
photography, 254n9; Barthes on, 111, 164, 167, 172–174, 263n18; button-pressing and, 158, 272n8; Cody and Ghost Dance, 108, 139–141, 145–147, 268n108, 269n120; for detail, 46, 131; electric chair and, 23–24, 165–166; ethnography and, 103, *104*, *105*, *106*, *107*, *108*, 261n2; gesture of, 167, 273n33; of Ghost Dance, 23, 107–108, 117–119, 265n50; ghosting and, 122, *123*, 125, 265n52; lynching and, 172, 274n40; modernity and, 159, 272n12; objectification and, 103, 159; racialization and, 118–119, 171–172, 265n50, 274n38; realist writing and, 166, 273n28; of ritual, 121; Schneider on, 167, 171, 177, 273n30; spirit photograph and, 124–125, *128*, 129; temporality of, 264n29; Van der Weyde on, 23, 160–162, 168–182, *170*, *171*, *172*, *173*, *177*, *178*, *197*, 271n2, 275n68; whiteness and, 275n79
Pinn, Anthony, 53–54, 252n118
Plessy v. Ferguson, 8
politics, 21–22, 89–90, 185–186
possession: as enfleshment, 67; enthusiasm and, 88–89; realism and dis-, 17, 42–43; realism and entangled being as, 163, 273n20; threat of, 95
possessive individualism (and possessed individualism), 81
post-Reconstruction era: black freedom during, 5; and black religion, 36, 92; disability in, 29, 247n17; politics of respectability in, 185–186; racialized citizenship and, 65–66; racial terror of, 81; secularism and, 29–30; violence of, 8, 12, 30, 75, 98, 244n32
Pratt, Richard H., 111
preaching, 183–185, 275n77
primitivism, 36, 45, 222–223, 281n70
Principles of Psychology, The (James), 26
profanation, 15–16, 39, 64
prophecy, 23, 32, 110–111, 262n13, 262n17
punctuation: comma and lists, 199, 205, 224–226; comma influence in, 201, 205–206, 217, 231, 279n33, 282n77; in performance, 226, 279n33, 282n77; repetition of, 225–226, 254n7, 254n10

queerness: black female embodiment and, 200, 222; charisma and, 225–226; ecstasy and, 15, 24, 203–204, 225–226; ecstatic temporality and, 19, 203–205, 215, 217, 229, 283n117; enthusiasm as, 211–212, 221; Larsen and, 278n14, 279n30, 282n86; Muñoz and, 19–20, 203, 217–218, 232, 279n29; *Quicksand* and, 24, 198–199; rebirth and, 203, 231

Quicksand (Larsen), 19, 24, 162, 197–216, 278n14; besideness and, 200–201, 278n15; black Christianity and, 210; conversion in, 225–227, 283n101, 283n104; death drive in, 216; ecstatic dance and bodily movement in, 214–216; *An Imperative Duty* compared with, 227–228; irritation in, 198–200; as migration narrative, 214, 278n15, 281n64; queer enthusiasm in, 211–212; queerness disturbing in, 198–199; realism and, 198, 208–210, 221; religion and, 229–230; religious experience in, 218, 229–230; sexuality and, 218

race: biopolitical constructions of, 32, 37–38, 44, 46, 234, 246n6; button-pressing and, 158–159, 272n7; electric chair and, 160; embodiment and, 32, 37–38, 44, 46, 234, 246n6; "epidermal racial schema," 7, 172; ethnography and, 109, 123–124, *124*, 137; music and sign of, 132, 267n77; phonograph and, 188, 276n94; photography and, 118–119, 171–172, 265n50, 274n38; primitivism and, 222–223, 281n70; proportionality, 32, 37–38, 44, 46, 234, 246n6; racism, 1–3, 8, 30, 73, 247n21; religion and, 71, 122–123, *123*; secularism and, 5–6

Race and Secularism in America (Lloyd and Kahn), 7–8

racialization, 21; affect and, 28, 247n11; and enthusiastic religion, 91–92; and hysteria, 26–28; post-Reconstruction citizenship as, 65–66; secularism and, 29, 37–38

Raiford, Leigh, 117, 275n64

realism, 243n7, 245n45, 269n115; and aesthetics of proportion, 34–35, 38, 44–45, 66, 213, 248n34; affect and, 10–11; African American literature and verisimilitude in, 206; Barthes on details of, 81–82; and besideness, 17–18; boundaries reinforced and redrawn by, 30; choreographed, 113–114; choreography of ecstasy and, 156; communicability contained by, 233; cultural memory and, 15; death and, 85–86; dispossession and, 17, 42–43; economic and cultural stratification in, 10; entangled being and, 163, 273n20; ethnography and, 23, 109, 116–117, 262n6; frenzy and, 233–234; Ghost Dance and, 149–150, 154; Harlem Renaissance and, 24; as hauntology, 4, 17, 67; Howells and, 34–35, 43, 45, 248n34; Jim Crow and, 14; as performative enactment, 11; photography and, 43–44, 46, 166, 273n28; and race, 71, 122–123, *123*; racialized desire in, 3; racial terror confronted by, 25; realist detail in, 106–107, 262n7; religion and, 122–123, *123*, 230–231; religious ecstasy and, 2–3, 5, 244n16; as repertoire, 12–14; repetition and, 12–13; temporality of, 11–12, 18; white supremacist frame of, 39; Wounded Knee and, 23, 264n37

realist. *See specific subjects*

rebirth, 58, 162, 205; double consciousness and, 31, 38, 51–52, 247n13; queerness and, 203, 231; racial politics and, 232, 284n129

Reconstruction. *See* post-Reconstruction era

recordings: "actuality" films and, 177–178; ethnography and, 132, 135, 267n74,

268n89; of Ghost Dance, 23, 107–108, 131–132; Mooney and Ghost Dance, 131–132, 136–137; and race, 132–133, 267n77, 267n79; temporality of, 133, *134*, 135, 144, *178*

Red Badge of Courage, The (S. Crane), 68–102, 257n43, 257n45, 258n56; archives in, 22–23; consumption in, 81, 257n43; repetition in, 68, 71, 75–76, 78–79, 86, 98, 100, 102, 254n10

reenactment, 107; colonialism and, 23, 112, 150; of enslavement and liberation, 59, 62; of Ghost Dance, 23; by Mooney, 137–138; realist representation in, 25; temporality of realist, 25, 109, 149, 177; temporal uncertainty in, 146; terror reproduced with, 194; trauma in repetition and, 100, 260n97

reform movements, 35, 38, 46–47, 92, 109, 164; realist aesthetics and, 41–43

regionalism: race and, 73, 96; Southern camp meetings as, 12, 53, 92–96, *94*; Southern life and, 39, 42, 224; Southern revivalism as, 40, 52

religion, 21; dance and, 91, 208; as defined by Anglo-Protestantism, 7, 29, 35, 39, 47–48, 64–65, 282n93; Du Bois and sociology of, 248n25; embodiment and, 70, 91, 96, 163, 229–230; ethnography of, 31, 109; Fessenden on, 88–89, 202, 259n64, 260n81; Ghost Dance and, 115; global modernity and, 4–5, 202; Pentecostalism and, 24, 203, 208, 224, 225–226, 248n30; power and, 199, 205–206, 224–225, 277n7, 278n11; *Quicksand* and, 199, 205–206, 224–225, 229–230, 277n7, 278n11; racialization and, 30, 59–60, 64, 235, 247n21; religious experience as, 225–227, 283n101, 283n104; secularism of, 1–2, 5–6, 8, 29, 34, 163, 234; sexuality and, 220–222, 282n89

religious experience: affect and excess of, 35; as "collective catharsis," 41–42, 56, 164, 182; communicability of, 35–36, 70, 99, 117; contagion and, 35–36; conversion scene as, 225–227, 283n101, 283n104; dance and, 208; fanaticism and, 39–50; gestures of, 98–99; Methodism and, 99; queerness and, 24, 225–226; *Quicksand* and, 218, 229–230; racialization of, 91–92; rebirth and, 226, 231–233; sexuality and, 220–222, 282n89; slavery exorcised in, 53

repertoire, 5, 12–15, 161, 234

repetition: button-pressing and, 161, 169, 196; contact bound by, 182; S. Crane and, 68, 71, 75–76, 78–79, 86, 98, 100, 102, 254n10; detail and historical, 79–81, 147, 243n3, 268n108; Ghost Dance and, 138, 146–147; of literary characters, 102, 261n104; of performance, 14, 48, 86, 210, 224, 248n47, 257n38, 259n59; of post-Reconstruction violence, 8, 12, 30, 75, 244n32; of punctuation, 225–226, 254n7, 254n10; realist history and, 79; realist practices demanding, 106–107; *Red Badge* using, 68, 71, 75–76, 78–79, 86, 98, 100, 102; revelation built with, 194; revival language using, 191, 195; of trauma, 79, 100, 195, 231, 257n38, 260n97

retouching, 78, 164, 176, *177*

revivalism: race and, 17, 245n67; storefront churches and, 223–224. *See also* Second Great Awakening

Riis, Jacob, 35–36, 248n35

ritual: death as, 81, 83–84, 169, *171*, *172*, *173*, *177*, 257n52, 273n37; electric chair death with, 169, *171*, *172*, *173*, *177*, 273n37; of Episcopal church, 39–40; of Ghost Dance, 106–107, 110, 115, 140, 144, 151; of lynching, 8, 51, 58; performance as, 258n53, 283n100; photography of, 121; possession in, 2–3; secularism and, 1–2, 8

Roach, Joseph, 13, 82, 150
Russell, Catherine, 243n7, 269n115
Ruttenburg, Nancy, 87–89

Schneider, Rebecca: on performance, 19, 110, 257n38, 273n33; on photographs, 167, 171, 177, 273n30
Schor, Naomi, 200
Schuyler, George, 197, 208
Second Great Awakening, 77, 87–89
secularism, 59, 264n34; as affect, 6, 12, 20, 30, 55; and Afro-Protestantism, 30, 35, 47, 282n93; and Anglo-Protestantism, 30, 33, 38; black personhood adjudicated by, 7; constructions of black Christianity, 35; as epistemological comportment, 7; Fessenden on, 30, 279n17; haunting and violence of, 4–5, 163; modernity and, 230; Modern on, 6–7; Pellegrini on, 5–6, 200, 243n1, 244n17, 264n33, 278n10, 282n89; politics of, 21–22; post-Reconstruction era and, 29–30; progress and, 59; racialization and, 7, 29, 37–38, 172; as regulatory regime, 5–6; religion and, 1–2, 5–6, 8, 29, 35, 163, 234; sexuality and, 6; as "structure of feeling," 7, 14; whiteness and, 7–8, 49, 64; as white supremacy, 7–8, 38, 49, 62. *See also* imperialism; Jim Crow secularism
Sedgwick, Eve Kosofsky, 18–19, 200–201
Seltzer, Mark, 175, 253n3, 254n6, 257n41
sexuality: Fessenden on, 88–89, 202, 259n64, 260n81; jouissance and, 11, 203; *Quicksand* and, 218; religious conversion and, 220–222, 282n89; and religious difference, 8; secularism and, 6; Spillers on, 280n53
"Silent Eaters, The" (Garland), 151–154
Sitting Bull, 123, 127, *128*, 150–151
slavery, 1, 51, 53–55, 59, 62, 256n35
Smith, Jonathan Z., 9–10
Sorett, Josef, 30, 50, 184, 208

Souls of Black Folk, The (Du Bois), 22, 38–39, 51–53, 59
"Souls of White Folk, The" (Du Bois), 39, 50, 59–65
Southern revivalism, 40, 52
Spanish-American War, 65
Spillers, Hortense, 38, 254n7, 280n53, 282n85; on Christianity, 4, 17, 61–63, 189–190, 220, 252n122
spirit photography, 124–125, *128*, 129
spiritualism, 5–6, 266n62
Stein, Jordan, 21, 202, 279n17
Sterne, Jonathan, 132–133, 135, 267n78
Stevenson, Lisa, 15, 19, 129, 265n39, 266n65
stillness, 158–159, 166–167, 171, *172*, 175–179, 182
"structure of feeling," 7, 14, 53. *See also* Williams, Raymond
sublime, 53, 174
Sundquist, Eric, 56
survivance, 121, 140, 148–150; as resistance, 121, 265n49. *See also* Vizenor, Gerald

Taves, Ann, 67, 87, 199, 253n137
Taylor, Diana, 13, 71, 113, 245n52, 253n5
temperance movement, 46–47
temporality: of affect, 11, 187; of button-pressing, 162, 167–168, 175; of colonial violence, 272n18; of electric chair, 193; of Ghost Dance, 133, 135, 152–153, 262n8; of lynch mob, 193; of modernity, 193; Native Americans and, 111–113, 115–116; of photography, 264n29; queerness and utopian, 15, 19, 203–205, 215, 217, 229, 283n117; of realism, 11–12, 18; of realist reenactments, 25, 109, 146, 149, 177; of recording, 133, *134*, 135, 144, 178
"terrible real," 195. *See also* lynching
terror: affective circuit and, 182–183; ecstasy and proximity to, 195, 234; electric chair and, 23–24, 159–160, 172, *172*, 175; electricity and, 24, 161, 174–175, 181; modernity and, 50, 54,

60–61; post-Reconstruction era and, 81; realism and, 25; slavery and, 53; of white supremacy, 54
Thrailkill, Jane, 11
trauma: as historical, 20, 23, 48, 71, 213; of Middle Passage, 17, 48; of post-Reconstruction era, 98; in reenactment and repetition, 100; repetition of, 79, 195, 231, 257n38, 260n97
Turner, Nat, 89–90

Van der Weyde, William: photography of electric chair and, 23, 160–162, 168–182, 197, 241; photos by, *170, 171, 172, 173, 177, 178, 180*
vanishing: of minor characters, 261n104; of Native Americans, 23, 107, 109, 111–113, 116, 127, 130–138, 141, 149–150, 267n70
Varieties of Religious Experience, The (James), 31, 266n59
verisimilitude, 44, 149, 156, 206
violence: of Anglo-Protestantism, 38; electric chair and, 23–24, 159–160; Ellison on, 197; fanaticism and, 4, 50; history of performance and, 87; post-Reconstruction era and, 8, 12, 30, 75, 244n32; and racial technologies, 197; *Red Badge* and, 70, 257n45; reenactment and, 23, 150
visuality, 9, 85, 103, 121, 143, 160, 166, 172–173; and Jim Crow racialization, 115, 172–173, 179, 182, 274n38
Vizenor, Gerald, 121, 263n22
Vogel, Shane, 72, 217–218, 232, 246n76, 279n29
Voice from the South, A (Cooper), 22, 30–31, 37–47, 49–50

Warner, Michael, 223, 225, 282n89, 283n104
Warren, Kenneth, 34, 44, 206, 280n38
Washington, Booker T., 186–187, 271n2, 276n89

Weheliye, Alexander, 161, 181, 228, 254n8, 272n12
Wenger, Tisa, 9, 115, 263n21
West, Cornel, 17, 48, 52
white Christianity: Anglo-Protestantism and, 7–9, 29–30, 33, 35, 38–39, 44, 47–48, 64–65; and chrononormativity, 219–220, 269n127; Ghost Dance and, 116, 153–154; imperialism and, 39, 60–61, 63–64; Jackson on realism and, 3–4, 243n9, 265n57; and Jim Crow, 46–47; lynching and, 83, 86–88, 258n58; and secularism, 7, 29, 35, 39, 47–48, 64–65, 282n93; and white supremacy, 218–220, 235
whiteness, 246n1; and colonial conquest, 61; as consumption and expenditure, 81, 257n42; fanaticism of, 4, 50; and ghosting, 130–131; hauntology of, 259n66; photography and, 275n79; post-Reconstruction citizenship and, 65–66; *Quicksand* and, 211–212; secularism as, 7–8, 49, 64
white supremacy, 156; Chesnutt on, 10; Du Bois on, 39, 60–65, 235, 252n127; electricity as, 174–175; as haunted, 2; *An Imperative Duty* and, 29; imperialism of, 39, 60–61, 63–64; Larsen and, 220; modernity and, 50, 60–61, 64; realism framed by, 39; Scripture and, 64; secularism as, 7–8, 38, 49, 62; Spillers on, 38, 220, 282n85; terror of, 54; and white Christianity, 218–220, 235
Williams, Raymond, 7
world religions, 8–9, 61–62. *See also* Parliament of World Religions
Wounded Knee: Ghost Dance after, 109–110, 112, 137–139; massacre at, 103, 109–111, 133, 140–141, 143–145; realist ethnography of, 23, 264n37; restaging of, 145–146, 148, 269n120, 269nn123–124
Wovoka, 103, 110–111, 119–122, *120*, 129, 139, 147–148, 262n14, 265n49

ABOUT THE AUTHOR

Lindsay V. Reckson is assistant professor of English at Haverford College.